Aude Mahy (ed.)

Advertising Food in Europe

A Comparative Law Analysis

Aude Mahy (ed.)

Advertising Food in Europe

A Comparative Law Analysis

THE LEGAL PUBLISHER
lexxion
BERLIN
BRUSSELS

A catalogue record for this book is available from the German National Library, detailed bibliographical data can be found on the internet at http://dnb.d-nb.de.

ISBN: Print 978-3-86965-249-8
E-Book 978-3-86965-250-4

www.lexxion.eu

Cover: Tozman Satz & Grafik, Berlin
Typeset: Michael Bellenbaum

Preface & Acknowledgments

This volume finds its origin in a comparative law seminar, devoted to the regulation of food advertising in the EU and neighbouring countries, which was held in December 2013 in Brussels. It builds upon some of the authors'/speakers' preparatory work and the various discussions that took place on this occasion. I would like to thank my colleagues at Loyens & Loeff for bearing with me throughout the whole editorial process of this edited collection, especially Yves Van Couter, Filip Pauwels and Inge Marcellis as well as every contributor for accepting to share his expertise with us.

Brussels, June 2014 *Aude Mahy*

Contents

PART I

INTRODUCTION

CHAPTER 1
Setting the Scene

Aude Mahy

I. Introduction

While food law is mainly regulated at the European level and despite the fact that free movement of goods is one of the most essential pillars of the European Union, technical obstacles to the free movement of food products are still widespread. They occur when national authorities lay down specific and local requirements to be met by a given product, regardless of the fact that this product comes from another Member State where it is lawfully produced or marketed. Such national requirements may, amongst other things, relate to the designation, form, size, weight, composition, presentation, labelling or packaging of a product.

Such obstacles can considerably hamper food business operators in their commercial strategy. It is therefore of primary importance to anticipate such difficulties by examining how the free movement of goods is actually implemented by the Member States and to what extent they are allowed to adopt specific national measures.

This introductory chapter will set the framework of the relevant rules applicable at the European level with respect to food advertising in order to facilitate the understanding of the national chapters.

We will start with an explanation on how the European system allows national authorities to have specific requirements, first from a general point of view (see title I: Free movement of goods: Cross-links between EU and national laws) and secondly, when applied to the issue of labelling and advertising foodstuffs (see title II: Free movement of food: advertising & labelling issues). A third point will briefly discuss the various European legislations prohibiting misleading (food) advertising and the methodology used to assess whether a consumer could be misled (see title III: Misleading advertising: A European definition – a national perception). We shall bring this introductory chapter to a close with an overview of Member States' obligations and powers with respect to the enforcement of Food Law (see title IV: Enforcement of Food Law).

II. The Free Movement of Goods: Cross-Links between the EU and National Laws

1. Introduction

To measure how free movement of goods should be implemented by Member States, one must first determine whether the matter in question is already harmonised at the European level. This allows us in turn to assess the extent to which national authorities may adopt or retain national requirements.

2. Harmonised matters

Harmonised matters are those for which standard requirements are set at the European level. Such standards can for instance relate to the technical specifications of a given product or its conditions of sale.

The harmonisation may be partial (e.g. food advertising) or comprehensive (e.g. European Directive relating to cocoa chocolate products[1]). It may be embedded in a *Regulation,* which is directly applicable in the Member States, or in a *Directive,* which lays down common (standard, minimum or maximum) requirements. The latter will require national implementations in order to be enforceable vis-à-vis operators.

The principle applicable to harmonised rules is quite straightforward: when a matter is harmonised, the nature or provisions of the harmonising legisla-

1 Directive 2000/36/EC of the European Parliament and of the Council of 23 June 2000 relating to cocoa and chocolate products intended for human consumption

tion will determine whether and in which manner Member States may adopt national rules that deviate from and/or complement European requirements.

Any (possible) obstacle to trade concerning a matter or product covered by harmonising legislation is thus to be analysed in the light of the provisions of such legislation. In this regard, it is worth noting that a national measure that does not comply with the limits set by the European act will be held illegal and inapplicable, *regardless of the fact that the relevant products are imported or domestic.*

3. Non-harmonised matters

a. Principle of free movement of goods

In the absence of harmonisation, national measures are to be analysed in the light of the principle of free movement of goods as laid down by the Treaty on the Functioning of the European Union ('TFEU').[2]

This principle states that Member States may not adopt any quantitative restriction on the import of goods coming from another Member State or any measure having equivalent effect.

The terms *'measures of equivalent effect'* have been defined by the Court of Justice of the European Union (CJEU) as covering *'all trading rules enacted by Member States which are capable of hindering, directly or indirectly, actually or potentially, intra-Community trade'*.[3]

For example, a measure will be regarded as an obstacle to trade if it is of such a nature as to render the marketing of the relevant products more difficult or more expensive. This could be the case if the marketing is excluded from certain channels of distribution or requires additional costs relating to the necessity to package the products in question in special packs that comply with the requirements in force on the market of their destination.

2 TFEU, Art. 34 & 36 (ex. Art. 28 & 30 TEC).

3 For the first time in the 'Dassonville' case (Case 8/74 *Dassonville*, ECR, 1974, 837).

A measure may be regarded as an obstacle to the free movement of goods even if the national measure does not make a distinction between domestic and imported products.[4]

b. Justifications for technical obstacles to trade

According to the TFEU, however, a national measure representing a technical obstacle to trade may be admissible if it is duly justified on one of the following grounds:

1) the public morality, public policy or public security;
2) the protection of health and life of humans, animals or plants;
3) the protection of national treasures possessing artistic, historic or archaeological value; or
4) the protection of industrial and commercial property.

This list of admissible grounds has been interpreted extensively by the CJEU, which has laid down the concept of '*imperative requirements*'. Under this definition of imperative requirements, the application of a national measure may be justified on one of the aforementioned grounds but also by other requirements regarded as mandatory such as consumer protection.[5]

In any case, when it is duly justified by an imperative requirement, the obstacle to trade must be proportionate to the aim to be achieved. This means that if a Member State has a choice between various measures to attain the same objective, it must choose the means which restricts free trade the least.[6]

4 Case 261/81 *Rau v De Smedt*, ECR 1982, 3961.

5 Case 120/78 *Cassis de Dijon, ECR, 1979, 649;* Case 261/81 *Rau v De Smedt*, ECR, 1982, 3961; Case 178/84 *Commission v Germany*, ECR, 1987, 1227, Case C-241/89 *SARRP*, ECR, 1990, I-04695, paragraph 31.

6 Case 261/81 *Rau v De Smedt*, ECR 1982, 3961, Case C-241/89 *SARRP*, ECR, 1990, I-04695, paragraph 31; Joined Cases C-34/95 to C36/95 *De Agostini and TV-Shop* [1997] ECR I-3843, paragraph 45; see also Case C-239/02 *Douwe Eghberts*, ECR, 2002, I-7037, paragraph 51.

c. Mutual recognition principle

The CJEU has developed the principle of mutual recognition, which ensures the free movement of goods of products that do not fall under the scope of European harmonised legislation.[7] This principle is now embedded in EU Regulation (EC) No 764/2008, which lays down procedures relating to the application of certain national technical rules to products lawfully marketed in another Member State.[8]

According to that principle, a Member State may not prohibit on its territory the sale of products that are lawfully marketed or manufactured in another Member State, even if those products were manufactured in accordance with technical rules different from those to which domestic products are subject.

The only exceptions to this principle are restrictions that are justified on one of the imperative grounds, subject to compliance with the proportionality principle explained above.

The burden of proof falls on the Member State of destination; it is therefore up to the national authority to demonstrate that the national technical rule imposed to imported products[9] is duly justified by an imperative ground and that the measure adopted is the one that restricts free trade the least.

d. Effect of a technical rule that illegally hampers free movement of goods

A national measure infringing the principle of free movement of goods will not be applicable to imported products but will remain in force for domestic products. This is the opposite of what occurs in the non-harmonised area where national rules exceeding the limits set out under an harmonised legislation are held illegal as regards both imported and domestic products.

7 Case 120/78 *Cassis de Dijon*, ECR, 1979, 649; Case C-110/05 *Commission* v *Italy*, ECR, 2009, I-519, paragraph 34.

8 Regulation (EC) No 764/2008 of the European Parliament and of the Council of 9 July 2008 laying down procedures relating to the application of certain national technical rules to products lawfully marketed in another Member State and repealing Decision No 3052/95/ EC (*OJ*, 13.08.2008, L 218/21).

9 'Imported products' means products imported from another Member State.

II. Free Movement of Food: Advertising and Labelling Issues

1. Introduction

In the European Union, the cornerstone legislation on food labelling and advertising is – until December 2014 – Directive No. 2000/13 (the 'Labelling Directive').[10] This Directive concerns the labelling of food intended to consumers and certain aspects relating to the presentation and advertising thereof.[11]

The Labelling Directive/FIC Regulation is general and applies horizontally (one refers to 'horizontal rules' when they apply to all foodstuffs in general and to 'vertical rules' when they only concern particular foodstuffs). Rules of a specific nature that apply vertically are laid down in specific European or national regulations dealing with those products.[12]

According to the Labelling Directive/FIC Regulation, Member States may maintain or adopt rules in addition to those it lays down. The extent of the powers left to the national authorities nevertheless depends on whether the relevant national requirement relates to food labelling & presentation or to food advertising[13]:

- *If the rule impacts the labelling & presentation of foodstuffs*
  The limits of the powers retained by the Member States are set by the Labelling Directive/FIC Regulation itself, which exhaustively lists the grounds on which non-harmonised national provisions prohibiting trade

10 Directive 2000/13/EC of the European Parliament and of the Council of 20 March 2000 on the approximation of the laws of the Member States relating to the labelling, presentation and advertising of foodstuffs (OJ 2000 L 109, p. 29), as lastly amended by Regulation (EC) No 596/2009.

11 Art. 1(1) of Directive No 2000/13.

12 Directive 2000/13, *op. cit.*, recital No 5.

13 Directive 2000/13/EC, *op. cit.*, Art. 18. Regulation 1169/2011, see footnote n° 14, art. 38. See also: Case C-239/02 *Douwe Eghberts*, ECR, 2002, I-7037; see also Case C-241/89 *SARRP*, ECR, 1990, I-04695, paragraphs 14&15 which came to the same conclusion, even if the decision is based on Directive 79/112, which was replaced by Directive 2000/13.

in foodstuffs may be justified (see *infra* 2.2.). The FIC Regulation adds that any discrimination as regards food from other Member States is prohibited.[14]

- *If the rule impacts the advertising of foodstuffs*
  The Directive does not specify the conditions under which a Member State may adopt non-harmonised provisions. Consequently, compliance of a related national measure is to be assessed in the light of the provisions of the TFEU on the free movement of goods (see *infra* 2.3.).

The Labelling Directive is now replaced by European Regulation No. 1169/2011 on the provision of food information to consumers ('FIC Regulation'),[15] which will be applicable as from 13 December 2014. The Regulation will be directly applicable in all Member States. The FIC Regulation specifies in a slightly different manner the bounds within which a Member State may adopt national rules in terms of food labelling or advertising, but the essence remains the same.[16]

---

14 Regulation 1169/2011, *op. cit.*, Act 38(1).

15 Regulation (EU) No 1169/2011 of the European Parliament and of the Council of 25 October 2011 on the provision of food information to consumers, amending regulations (EC) No 1924/2006 and (EC) No 1925/2006 of the European parliament and of the council, and repealing commission directive 87/250/EEC, Council Directive 90/496/EEC, Commission Directive 1999/10/EC, Directive 2000/13/EC of the European Parliament and of the Council, Commission Directives 2002/67/EC and 2008/5/EC and Commission Regulation (EC) No 608/2004.

16 The relevant provisions under the FIC Regulation are articles 38 and 39 which respectively state as follows:
'1. As regards the matters specifically harmonised by this Regulation, Member States may not adopt nor maintain national measures unless authorised by Union law. Those national measures shall not give rise to obstacles to free movement of goods, **[NEW]** *including discrimination as regards foods from other Member States. 2. Without prejudice to Article 39, Member States may adopt national measures concerning matters not specifically harmonised by this Regulation provided that they do not prohibit, impede or restrict the free movement of goods that are in conformity with this Regulation'* (Art. 38).
And
'In addition to the mandatory particulars referred to in Article 9(1) and in Article 10, Member States may, in accordance with the procedure laid down in Article 45, adopt measures requiring additional mandatory particulars for specific types or categories of foods, justified on grounds of at least one of the following: (a) the protection of public health; (b) the protection of consumers **[NEW]**; *(c) the prevention of fraud; (d) the protection of industrial and commercial property rights, indications of provenance, registered designations of origin and the prevention of unfair competition'* (Art. 39).

2. Food labelling and presentation

a. Central methodological premise

As indicated above (2.1.), the conditions under which a Member State may depart from the requirements laid down by the Labelling Directive/FIC Regulation for adopting non-harmonised labelling or presentation rules (e.g. form of the food) have to be analysed in light of the terms of the Directive/FIC Regulation.

Basically, if a product complies with the Labelling Directive/FIC Regulation in terms of labelling and presentation requirements, its trade may not be forbidden by a Member State applying non-harmonised national rules.[17]

By way of an exception, such non-harmonised national rules could still be admissible if they are justified on one of the following grounds:

i. the protection of public health;

ii. the prevention of fraud ; or

iii. the protection of industrial and commercial property rights, indications of provenance, registered designations of origin and prevention of unfair competition.

As a consequence, if a Member State adopts a non-harmonised measure concerning food labelling or presentation and if this measure is not justified on one of the 3 aforementioned grounds, it will be illegal and not applicable.

The aforementioned bounds set by the Labelling Directive/FIC Regulation also apply to specific cases where the Directive/Regulation expressly allows Member States to adopt or retain non-harmonised rules. This is for instance the case for:

- the mandatory indication on labels of the country of origin or place of provenance of foods[18];

17 It should be noted that, in addition to the rules set up by the Directive 2000/13/Regulation 1169/2011, various vertical harmonising legislations are adopted at the European level.

18 Directive 2000/13, *op. cit.*, Art. 3(2); Regulation 1169/2011, *op. cit.*, Art. 39(2).

- additional mandatory indications that must be placed on the label of certain foodstuffs (and not to foodstuffs in general)[19];
- specific rules regarding food information concerning non-prepackaged foods (Member States *must* however ensure that the consumer still receives sufficient information).[20]

It is worth noting that, if the limits laid down by the Labelling Directive/FIC Regulation are exceeded, the national measure will be illegal as regards both imported foodstuffs and domestic foodstuffs.

b. Specific assessment: The issue of the product name

Besides these general principles, the Labelling Directive/FIC Regulation provides for a specific methodology to be adopted when it comes to determining the name under which a food may be sold.

Labels of pre-packaged foodstuffs must mention the name under which the product is sold. This name is the one provided for at the European level either through a Directive or a Regulation and may not be substituted by a trade mark, brand name or a fantasy name.[21]

The question of the name may however become more demanding for products whose names are not defined by any European act. In such circumstances, identifying the name of the product requires to follow a specific methodology which is composed of one principle and two exceptions:

i. The principle

Where no definition is provided by EU law, the food business operator has the choice between marketing its product under the name legally used in

19 Directive 2000/13, *op. cit.*, Art.4(2); Regulation 1169/2011, *op. cit.*, Art. 39(1).

20 Directive 2000/13, *op. cit.*, Art. 14; Regulation 1169/2011, *op. cit.*, Art. 44(2).

21 Directive 2000/13, *op cit.*, Art. 3(1)(1), 5(1) and 5(2); Regulation 1169/2011, Art. 17.

the Member State of production or under the name used in the Member State in which the product is sold to the final consumer or to mass caterers.[22]

ii. The exceptions

In two circumstances, where the product is sold to the final consumer or to mass caterers under the name legally used in the Member State of production, the Member Sate of marketing may adopt measures impeding the product's marketing[23]:

(a) Additional labelling requirements

In case the consumer of the country of marketing could be misled as to the true nature of the foodstuff and its distinction from other foodstuffs, additional descriptive information in proximity to the sales name may be required.[24]

(b) Prohibition to use the name legally used in the country of production

Such prohibition may be imposed in exceptional cases, where the two following conditions are met:

- the name designating the food is so different, *as regards its composition or manufacture*, from the foodstuff known under that name in the country of marketing, that it cannot be considered as belonging to the same category of goods; and

22 A name legally used means the legal name of the product (for which a legal definition is provided for by the laws, regulations or administrative decisions of the relevant Member State) or, in absence thereof, the customary name, or a description of the foodstuff, and if necessary of its use, which is clear enough to let the purchaser know its true nature and distinguish it from other products with which it might be confused.

23 Please note that this only applies to the product 'imported' from another Member State at the exclusion of the food products imported from third countries (and subject to the application of bilateral treaties between the EU and EFTA countries).

24 See in this regard: Case C-448/98 *Guimont* [2000] ECR I-10663 concerning the French legislation reserving the designation Emmenthal to a certain category of cheese with rind; Case 261/81 *Rau* v *De Smedt* [1982] ECR 3961 concerning the Belgian requirement that margarine be sold in cubes.

- an additional descriptive information is not sufficient to ensure correct information for consumers.[25]

In this context, determining what characterises a product is therefore of primary importance. *De facto*, the Member State of marketing will only be allowed to hamper the use of the name legally used in the Member State of production in case such a name refers to a product which has other characteristics for the consumer of the Member State of marketing.

3. Food advertising

The Labelling Directive/FIC Regulation does not specify the conditions under which Member States may adopt national non-harmonised provisions on food advertising; their legality must thus be assessed in the light of the rules laid down by the TFEU (see *supra* 1.3.).[26]

In this regard, the question frequently raised is whether a national provision on food advertising could constitute a quantitative restriction on imports of goods.

In this respect the *concrete impact* on the market[27] access must be taken into consideration. With respect to food advertising, the CJEU held that the fact that an operator is compelled to discontinue an advertising scheme

25 See in this regards CJEU, Case 298/87, 14 July 1988 *Smanor*, ECR, 1988, 4489 which ruled on a preliminary question concerning the prohibition of the use of the name 'deep-frozen yogurt' and the follow-up interpretative communication issued by the European Commission (1991) with respect to the vinegar, yogurt and caviar (Commission interpretative communication of 15 October 1991 on the names under which foodstuffs are sold [OJ, 91/C270/02]).

26 This is confirmed by Article 38(2) of the FIC Regulation which states that : «*Without prejudice to Article 39, Member States may adopt national measures concerning matters not specifically harmonised by this Regulation provided that they do not prohibit, impede or restrict the free movement of goods that are in conformity with this Regulation* »

27 Joined Cases C-267/91 and C-268/91 Keck and Mithouard [1993] ECR I-6097, paragraph 17 *'for national provisions restricting or prohibiting certain selling arrangements not to be caught by Article 28 EC, they must not be such as to prevent access to the market by products from another Member State or to impede access any more than it impedes access by domestic products'* – see paragraph 17); See also Case C-239/02 *Douwe Eghberts*, ECR I-7037, § 51.

which he considers to be particularly effective *may* constitute an obstacle to imports.[28]

Therefore, where a (non-harmonised) national measure relates to the advertising of food products, its validity will depend on the origin of the relevant product:

- *for domestic products*, the measure will be applicable (from a free movement of goods point of view) because the Labelling Directive/FIC Regulation does not impose the conditions under which a Member State may adopt additional rules on Food advertising);
- *for imported products* (coming from another Member State/EEA Member), the advertising rule will be applicable only if it does not constitute an obstacle to importation (as interpreted by the CJEU) or if such obstacle is duly justified by an imperative ground as defined by the TFEU and the related CJEU case-law (see supra 1.3.).

28 Case C-241/89 *SARRP*, ECR, 1990, I-04695, § 29.

III. Misleading Advertising: A European Definition – A National Perception

1. Overview of the applicable texts at the European level

a. Introduction

The ban on misleading advertisement is a well-established prohibition laid down in numerous European legislations. Information that is misleading towards consumers will also be regarded as unfair vis-à-vis the competitors.

As far as foodstuffs are concerned, no less than 6 different texts – general or food-related – may potentially apply.[29] They are summarised below.

b. General law prohibitions

Under general law, the Unfair Commercial Practices Directive[30] constitutes the main body of EU legislation regulating misleading advertising and other unfair practices in business-to-consumer transactions. It applies in all sectors.

It aims at ensuring that consumers are not misled or exposed to aggressive marketing and that any claim made by traders in the EU is clear, accurate and substantiated, thus enabling consumers to make informed and meaningful choices.

Under the Unfair Commercial Practices Directive, the concept of *'misleading commercial practice'* is broadly defined. This ranges from false information to misleading omissions and also includes deceptive practices even if the

29 See in this regard the interesting article of S. Leible, 'Consumer Information beyond Food Law', *EFFL*, Lexxion, 2010/6, p. 316.

30 Directive 2005/29/EC of the European Parliament and of the Council of 11 May 2005 concerning unfair business-to-consumer commercial practices in the internal market and amending Council Directive 84/450/EEC, Directives 97/7/EC, 98/27/EC and 2002/65/EC of the European Parliament and of the Council and Regulation (EC) No 2006/2004 of the European Parliament and of the Council.

information is factually correct.[31] Still, to be regarded as misleading for the consumer, the practice in question must cause or be likely to cause the average consumer to take a *transactional decision*, i.e. buying the good that he would not have bought otherwise.

In parallel, the Directive on Misleading and Comparative Advertising[32] provides rules concerning the business-to-business relationship. The purpose of this Directive is to protect traders against misleading advertising

---

31 According to Directive 2005/29, *op.cit.*, Art. 6 and 7, a commercial practice is misleading when:

(1) it contains false information and is therefore untruthful *or if*

(2) in any way, including overall presentation, deceives or is likely to deceive the average consumer, even if the information is factually correct, in relation to:

- the existence or nature of the product;
- the main characteristics of the product, such as its availability, benefits, risks, execution, composition, accessories, after-sale customer assistance and complaint handling, method and date of manufacture or provision, delivery, fitness for purpose, usage, quantity, specification, geographical or commercial origin or the results to be expected from its use, or the results and material features of tests or checks carried out on the product;
- the extent of the trader's commitments, the motives for the commercial practice and the nature of the sales process, any statement or symbol in relation to direct or indirect sponsorship or approval of the trader or the product;
- the price or the manner in which the price is calculated, or the existence of a specific price advantage;
- the need for a service, part, replacement or repair;
- the nature, attributes and rights of the trader or his agent, such as his identity and assets, his qualifications, status, approval, affiliation or connection and ownership of industrial, commercial or intellectual property rights or his awards and distinctions;
- the consumer's rights or the risks he may face.

(2) the marketing of a product, including comparative advertising, creates confusion with any products, trademarks, trade names or other distinguishing marks of a competitor;

(2) the trader does not comply with commitments contained in codes of conduct by which the trader is bound, where the trader indicates in a commercial practice that he is bound by the code.

(2) the trader omits material information that the average consumer needs (or provides it in an unclear, unintelligible, ambiguous or untimely manner), according to the context, to take an informed transactional decision.

32 Directive 2006/114/EC of the European Parliament and of the Council of 12 December 2006 concerning misleading and comparative advertising (OJ L, 376, 27.12.2006, p. 21). The Directive also applies to products covered by the agricultural sphere (see Recital 12).

and the unfair consequences thereof and lays down the conditions under which comparative advertising is permitted.[33]

Misleading advertising is regarded as a behaviour that injures or is likely to injure a competitor and is therefore considered as an unfair practice towards competitors.

It is worth noting that the prohibitions set out under this Directive are a minimum requirement, such that the Member States are allowed to apply stricter rules, thus ensuring extensive protection, with regard to misleading advertising for traders and competitors.[34]

c. Specific food law rules

To quote the European Commission, the Unfair Commercial Practices Directive '*works as a safety net which fills the gaps which are not regulated by other EU sector-specific rules*'.[35] This Directive accordingly applies only insofar as there are no specific Union law provisions regulating specific aspects of unfair commercial practices, such as information requirements and rules on the way information is to be presented to the consumer.[36]

The Directive consequently complements the rules applying to specific sectors (such as the food sector), which will prevail in case of conflicts.

When it comes to the rules applicable to the food sector, the ban on misleading food information is covered by the so-called General Food Law Act. The prohibition is probably as broad as it could be, as it prohibits any misleading of the consumer through *the labelling, advertising and presentation of*

33 See Art. 1. According to Directive 2006/114/EC, *op.cit.*, Art. 2 (b), 'misleading advertising' means '*any advertising which in any way, including its presentation, deceives or is likely to deceive the persons to whom it is addressed or whom it reaches and which, by reason of its deceptive nature, is likely to affect their economic behaviour or which, for those reasons, injures or is likely to injure a competitor*'.

34 Directive 2006/114/EC, *op.cit.*, Art. 8.

35 Communication of 14 March 2013 from the Commission to the European Parliament, the Council and the European Economic and Social Committee on the application of the Unfair Commercial Practices Directive, COM(2013)138 final.

36 Directive 2005/29/EC, op.cit. Recital 10.

foodstuffs, including their shape, appearance or packaging, the packaging materials used, the manner in which they are arranged and the setting in which they are displayed, and the information which is made available about them through whatever medium.[37]

This general prohibition is nevertheless detailed in the Labelling Directive/FIC Regulation, which states that any food labelling, advertising, presentation of a foodstuff[38] or any related method used:

- must not be such as it *could* mislead the purchaser to a material degree, particularly[39]:

    (a) as to the characteristics of the food and, in particular, as to its nature, identity, properties, composition, quantity, durability, country of origin or place of provenance, method of manufacture or production;

    (b) by attributing to the food effects or properties which it does not possess;

    (c) by suggesting that the food possesses special characteristics when in fact all similar foods possess such characteristics, in particular by specifically emphasising the presence or absence of certain ingredients and/or nutrients;

    (d) [**new insertion by the FIC Regulation**] by suggesting, by means of the appearance, the description or pictorial representations, the presence of a particular food or an ingredient, while in reality a component naturally present or an ingredient normally used in that food has been substituted with a different component or a different ingredient.

37 Regulation (EC) No 178/2002 of the European Parliament and of the Council of 28 January 2002 laying down the general principles and requirements of food law, establishing the European Food Safety Authority and laying down procedures in matters of food safety (OJ L 31, 1.2.2002, p. 1–24), Art. 16.

38 In particular its shape, appearance or packaging, the packaging materials used, the way in which the food is arranged and the setting in which it is displayed.

39 Directive 2000/13, *op. cit.*, Art. 2(1) and (3); Regulation 1169/2011, *op. cit.*, Art. 7.

- **[New insertion by the FIC Regulation:]** must be accurate, clear and easy to understand for the consumer.
- must not attribute to any foodstuff the property of preventing, treating or curing a human disease, or refer to such properties (subject to Community provisions applicable to natural mineral waters and foodstuffs for particular nutritional uses).

In addition to these general food-related regulations[40], more specific food law provisions are laid down by other legislations with respect to misleading advertising, amongst which (i) the Regulation on the Nutrition & Health Claims made on food, (ii) the Regulation on the Protection of Geographical indication of origin for agricultural products and foodstuffs and (iii) the Regulation on organic products.

i. Nutrition & health claims

According to the Nutrition & Health Claims Regulation[41], a nutrition or health claim must not be false, ambiguous or misleading, even if its use is authorised under the scope of said Regulation.

ii. Products with a geographical indication of origin and traditional specialities

The European Regulation on food quality schemes[42] protects foodstuffs that have a registered Protected Designation of Origin (PDO), Protected Geographical Indication (PGI) and products that are recognised as Traditional Specialities Guaranteed (TSG).

40 See in particular Regulation 1924/2006, *op.cit.*, Recital 3, Regulation No 1151/2012, *op.cit.*, Recital (8) and Art. 3, which stress the complementary nature of their provisions with respect to the Labelling Directive.

41 Regulation (EC) No 1924/2006 of the European Parliament and of the Council of 20 December 2006 on nutrition and health claims made on foods (OJ L 12, 18.01.2007, p. 3), Art. 3(2)(a).

42 Regulation (EU) No 1151/2012 of the European Parliament and of the Council of 21 November 2012 on quality schemes for agricultural products and foodstuffs(OJ L 343, 14.12.2012, p. 1), Art. 13 & 24.

Therefore, PDO and PGI indications are protected against:

(a) any direct or indirect commercial use of a registered name in respect of products not covered by the registration;

(b) any misuse, imitation or evocation, even if the true origin of the products or services is indicated or if the protected name is translated or accompanied by an expression such as *'style'*, *'type'*, *'method'*, *'as produced in'*, *'imitation'* or similar, including when those products are used as an ingredient;

(c) any other false or misleading indication as to the provenance, origin, nature or essential qualities of the product that is used on the inner or outer packaging, advertising material or documents relating to the product concerned, and the packing of the product in a container liable to convey a false impression as to its origin;

(d) any other practice liable to mislead the consumer as to the true origin of the product.

TSGs are protected against any misuse, imitation or evocation, or against any other practice liable to mislead the consumer. Furthermore, Member States have to ensure that sales descriptions used at national level do not give rise to confusion with names that are registered.

iii. Regulation on organic products

The European Regulation concerning organic products[43] prohibits the use of the terms *'organic'*, *'eco'*, *'bio'*, their derivatives or diminutives, alone or combined, for a product that does not satisfy the requirements set out under this Regulation. This prohibition applies in all languages used in the European Union.

The prohibition applies to labelling, advertising and commercial documents.

43 Council Regulation (EC) No 834/2007 of 28 June 2007 on organic production and labelling of organic products and repealing Regulation (EEC) No 2092/91 (OJ L 189, 20.7.2007, p. 1), Art. 23.

In any case, these terms may not be used for a product for which it has to be indicated in the labelling or advertising that it contains GMOs, consists of GMOs or is produced from GMOs according to EU provisions.

Furthermore, any terms, including terms used in trademarks, or practices used in labelling or advertising liable to mislead the consumer or user by suggesting that a product or its ingredients satisfy the requirements set out under this Regulation shall not be used.

2. The concept of consumer: A European definition, a national understanding

As explained above (1(3)b), consumer protection is one of the imperative grounds allowing a Member State to hinder the free movement of goods, on the condition that the national measure is proportionate to the aim to be achieved, meaning that between various measures to attain the same objective, the chosen one is the least restrictive on free trade.

Hence, ensuring that the consumer is not misled by advertising or labelling is part of the level of consumer protection that Member States must ensure.

In this regard, although the Court of Justice considers that the person deserving protection under the term 'consumer' is '*reasonably well-informed, reasonably observant and circumspect*'[44], the identification of such consumer pertains to the national interpretation.

Basically, the interpretation of whether and how a consumer could be misled will differ between Member States depending on the legal traditions of

44 CJEU, 6 July 1995, Case Mars, C-470/93, *ECR 1995 Page I-01923*, § 24; CJEU, 16 July 1998, Case C-210/96 ('Marketing standards for eggs'), ECR, *1998 Page I-04657*, §§ 29 to 37. See also the critical analysis of Mr A. Meisterernst further to the adoption of the FIC Regulation: A. Meisterernst, 'A New Benchmark for Misleading Advertising', EFFL, Lexxion, 2/2013, p. 91.

that Member State.[45] This is precisely the difficult point for the food business operators, because it may lead to significant differences in application.

In practice, the national court will analyse on a case-by-case basis whether an advertisement or label is misleading by referring to the group of consumers who are exposed to the labelling or advertising and who may or may not be misled in the actual situation.

In this regard, the CJEU has held that the courts may instruct a survey on the actual expectations of the consumer if they still have doubts as to the extent to which the statement at issue might mislead the consumer.[46]

As a consequence, although the ban on misleading advertising is uniformly imposed at the European level, no standard pan-European guidelines could be laid down in order to be directly and uniformly implemented in every Member State.[47]

IV. Enforcement of Food Law

Enforcement of food law is left to the national authorities. Member States thus have the duty of laying down rules and ensuring effective controls at all stages of the food chain on measures and penalties applicable to in-

45 See in particular, Judgment of the Court (Fifth Chamber) of 16 January 1992, Case C-373/90. *Criminal proceedings against X* (*ECR.*, 1992 Page I-00131) : *'It is for the national court, however, to ascertain in the circumstances of the particular case and bearing in mind the consumers to which the advertising is addressed, whether the latter could be misleading* (...)'; and CJEU, 16 July 1998, Case C-210/96 ('Marketing standards for eggs'), *op.cit.*

46 CJEU, 16 July 1998, Case C-210/96 ('Marketing standards for eggs'), *op.cit.*

47 See for an analysis of the power limits of the authority control of the country of manufacturing & labelling : K. Lilholt Nilsson, 'Misleading ? To Whom ?', *EFFL*, 1/2012, p. 22.

fringements of food and feed law. They must apply effective, proportionate and dissuasive penalties.[48]

As a result, national peculiarities are also to be found at the enforcement stage.

V. Conclusion

To bring a close to this introductory chapter, we may observe that a large part of the food-related requirements are set at the European level and that Member States are further limited in their possibility to hamper the promotion and trade of foodstuffs that are legally manufactured or marketed in another Member State. This undoubtedly facilitate the free movement of food products.

However, national peculiarities are still widespread as consumer protection, fair competition between traders and the safeguard of public health are grounds allowing Member States to impose national measures to any food product marketed in their territory.

Finally, the question of enforcement of food law is totally left at the Member States discretion. In this regard, they have as general guidance to apply '*effective, proportionate and dissuasive penalties*'.

The following national chapters aim to shed some light on all these national peculiarities which may hamper the free movement of goods with respect to food advertising.

48 Regulation No 178/2002, *op. cit.*, Art. 17(2): *'Member States shall enforce food law, and monitor and verify that the relevant requirements of food law are fulfilled by food and feed business operators at all stages of production, processing and distribution. (…) Member States shall also lay down the rules on measures and penalties applicable to infringements of food and feed law. The measures and penalties provided for shall be effective, proportionate and dissuasive'*; See also Regulation (EC) No 882/2004 of 29 April 2004 on official controls performed to ensure the verification of compliance with feed and food law, animal health and animal welfare rules (OJ L 165, 30.4.2004, p. 1), Art. 54 & 55; Directive 2005/29, *op.cit.* Art. 11 to 13.

CHAPTER 2
Structure of the Comparative Analysis: Shedding some Light on the Questions Raised

Aude Mahy

I. Possible Bans on Food Advertising

1. Is there any general national legislation or code of conduct regulating the promotion of foodstuffs?

As the subject-matter of food advertising is only partially regulated by Union law, Member States are allowed to adopt national provisions in relation thereto, provided that the aspects covered by these provisions are not already harmonised at the European level and that the provisions do not impede the free movement of goods.

This section of national chapters aims at identifying whether the relevant jurisdictions have laid down any horizontal legislation[1] with respect to food advertising and how these restrictions are applied by the courts.

The national chapters will also point out the existence of any main national self-disciplinary codes put in place by the industry and how they are interpreted by the self-regulatory bodies, as these codes may have a considerable impact on operators' behaviour.

2. Is there any specific national restriction or prohibition (mandatory legislation and code of conduct)?

Aside from the general food rules, the legislative national arsenal may contain specific advertising restrictions.

1 *i.e.* legislation concerning all foodstuffs and not certain foodstuffs in particular.

These restrictions either relate to certain products in particular (e.g. alcoholic beverages, energy drinks) or aim at protecting a specific sections of the population (such as children, pregnant women, persons who are hospitalised).

Specific restrictions on the promotion of foodstuffs are to some extent regulated at the European level. They are essentially contained within legislation on specific channels of communication, namely audiovisual communications.[2] For the rest, Member States may adopt legislation of their own choosing. It is therefore of primary importance for food business operators to be aware of the possible restrictions they may face when promoting their products internationally.

To date, the principles established by Union law are as follows:

a. With respect to certain foodstuffs

When it comes to advertising restrictions concerning certain foodstuffs in particular, the main (even the sole) product category whose promotion is clearly restricted is that of **alcoholic beverages**.

In this regard, television advertising and teleshopping for alcoholic beverages must *at least*[3] comply with the following criteria:

(a) it may not be aimed specifically at minors or, in particular, depict minors consuming these beverages;

(b) it shall not link the consumption of alcohol to enhanced physical performance or to driving;

(c) it shall not create the impression that the consumption of alcohol contributes towards social or sexual success;

2 Directive 2010/13/EU of 10 March 2010 on the coordination of certain provisions laid down by law, regulation or administrative action in Member States concerning the provision of audiovisual media services (Audiovisual Media Services Directive), Art. 9(1)(e) and 22.

3 The Audiovisual Media Services Directive states that Member States remain free to impose more detailed or stricter rules provided that such rules are in compliance with Union law [Art 4(1)].

(d) it shall not claim that alcohol has therapeutic qualities or that it is a stimulant, a sedative or a means of resolving personal conflicts;

(e) it shall not encourage immoderate consumption of alcohol or present abstinence or moderation in a negative light;

(f) it shall not place emphasis on high alcoholic content as being a positive quality of the beverages.

Moreover, under the Audiovisual Media Services Directive, Member States are requested to encourage co- and/or self-regulatory regimes at national level with respect to, amongst others, the advertisement of alcohol in audio-visual communication.[4]

b. With respect to a specific section of the population

As far as the protection of a specific section of the population is concerned, **children** are at the centre of attention.

Firstly, with respect to alcohol:

- As indicated above, an audiovisual communication may not be aimed specifically at minors or, in particular, depict minors consuming these beverages;
- Further to a 2001 recommendation of the EU[5], the Member States are encouraged to establish effective mechanisms, in cooperation with the producers and the retailers of alcoholic beverages and relevant non-governmental organisations, in the fields of promotion, marketing and retailing notably to ensure that:
  - producers do not produce alcoholic beverages specifically targeted at children and adolescents;

4 Audiovisual Media Services Directive, *op cit.*, Art 4(7).

5 Council Recommendation 2001/458/EC of 5 June 2001 on the drinking of alcohol by young people, in particular children and adolescents [Official Journal L 161 of 16.06.2001].

  - alcoholic beverages are not designed or promoted to appeal to children and adolescents. Particular attention should be paid to the use of styles (motifs, colours, etc.) associated with "youth culture", the images used, the promotion of ideas associated with alcohol consumption (implications of social success, sexual or athletic prowess, featuring of children in drink promotion campaigns and sponsoring of alcoholic drinks (sponsoring of sporting or musical events, sport merchandising, etc.)

Moreover, restricting the promotion of 'unhealthy food' is also one of the main objectives of the authorities:

- Member States and the European Commission are required to encourage media service providers to develop codes of conduct regarding inappropriate audio-visual commercial communication, accompanying or included in children's programmes, of foods and beverages containing nutrients and substances with a nutritional or physiological effect, in particular those such as fat, trans-fatty acids, salt/sodium and sugars, excessive intakes of which in the overall diet are not recommended.[6]
- The EU Pledge was born in this context.[7] The EU pledge is an agreement entered into by its members (which are major players in the manufacture of snacks and foodstuffs intended to children) to change food and beverage advertising in the European Union to children under the age of twelve. In short, the member of the pledge commit:
  - not to advertise food and beverage products to children under the age of twelve on TV, print and internet, except for products which fulfil specific nutritional criteria based on accepted scientific evidence and/or applicable national and international dietary guidelines.
  - not to communicate on products in primary schools, except where specifically requested by, or agreed with, the school administration for educational purposes.

6 Audiovisual Media Services Directive, *op cit.*, Art. 9(1)(e).

7 http://www.eu-pledge.eu/

II. Misleading Advertising

1. What are the national rules on misleading advertising with respect to foodstuffs?

The ban on misleading advertisement is a well-established prohibition laid down in numerous European legislations. Information that is misleading towards consumers will also be regarded as unfair vis-à-vis competitors.

As far as foodstuffs are concerned, no less than six different texts – general or food-related – may potentially apply.

Furthermore, the Directive on Misleading and Comparative Advertising[8] laid down a series of rules that constitute a minimum requirement, such that Member States are allowed to apply stricter rules.

Under this section, national chapters will examine the rules laid down by the national jurisdictions in further detail – unless they constitute a mere implementation of European legislation.[9]

2. What are the national landmark cases regarding misleading advertising for foodstuffs?

Ensuring that the consumer is not misled by advertising or labelling is part of the level of consumer protection that Member States must ensure.

In this regard, the notion of 'consumer' has been defined by the CJEU as a person who is 'reasonably well-informed, reasonably observant and

8 Directive 2006/114/EC of the European Parliament and of the Council of 12 December 2006 concerning misleading and comparative advertising (OJ L, 376, 27.12.2006, p. 21). The Directive also applies to products covered by the agricultural sphere (see Recital 12).

9 For further detail on the rules laid down at the European level: see Chapter 1.1. ('Advertising food in Europe: setting the scene'), section 3(1) : *'Overview of the applicable texts at the European level'.*

circumspect'.[10] However, assessing whether and how such consumer could be misled will differ between Member States, depending on the legal traditions of that Member State.[11]

This may lead to significant differences in application: in practice, the national court will examine on a case-by-case basis whether an advertisement or label is misleading by reference to the group of consumers who are exposed to the labelling or advertising and who may or may not be misled in the actual situation.

Under this section, the national chapters will shed some light on how the courts deal with the fluid concept of a 'consumer that could be misled'. They will review the landmark cases as they apply to food products.

III. Mandatory Labelling: Name of the Product

Are there any national definitions of a foodstuff that could hamper the marketing of an imported food product?

Vertical national legislation which is not harmonised at the European level is still a widespread phenomenon, in particular regarding the naming of food products.

Such national acts have the potential to impede the free movement of goods, especially when the food business operator has to use a different name for its product depending on the national peculiarities applicable in the country of marketing.

---

10 CJEU, 6 July 1995, Case Mars, C-470/93, *ECR 1995 Page I-01923*, § 24; CJEU, 16 July 1998, Case C-210/96 ('Marketing standards for eggs'), ECR, *1998 Page I-04657*, §§ 29 to 37. See also the critical analysis of A. Meisterernst further to the adoption of the FIC Regulation: A. Meisterernst, 'A New Benchmark for Misleading Advertising', EFFL, Lexxion, 2/2013, p. 91.

11 See in particular CJEU, 16 January 1992, Case C-373/90. *Criminal proceedings against X* (*ECR.*, 1992 Page I-00131) : *'It is for the national court, however, to ascertain in the circumstances of the particular case and bearing in mind the consumers to which the advertising is addressed, whether the latter could be misleading* (...)'; and CJEU, 16 July 1998, Case C-210/96 ('Marketing standards for eggs'), *op.cit.*

This is particularly true when a product is imported from a non-EU country.[12]

This possible obstacle to trade is largely avoided thanks to the rules established by European legislation providing for a specific methodology in determining the name under which a food may be sold .[13]

However, products bearing a name legally used in the EU country of production or in the EU country where it is first placed on the market are not immune to difficulties. A food business operator could for instance faces obstacles to trade if the consumer of the country of marketing might be misled as to the true nature of the foodstuff based upon the name used in the country of production.

In such circumstances, the Member State of marketing may adopt measures impeding the product's marketing. These measures may be either the requirement of additional labelling (additional descriptive information in proximity to the sales name) or, more rarely, the prohibition to use the name legally used in the country of production.[14]

This section of national chapters aims at identifying the vertical national non-harmonised legislation with respect to the name of food products where they may potentially hamper the free movement of goods.

12 Subject to the application of bilateral treaties such as treaties between the EU and EFTA countries.

13 Directive 2000/13 of the European Parliament and of the Council of 20 March 2000 on the approximation of the laws of the Member States relating to the labelling, presentation an advertising of foodstuffs (OJ 2000 L 109, p. 29), as lastly amended by Regulation (EC) N° 596/2009. Art. 3(1)(1), 5(1) and 5(2); Regulation (EU) N° 1169/2011 of the European Parliament and of the Council of 25 October 2011 on the provision of food information to consumers, amending regulations (EC) N° 1924/2006 and (EC) N° 1925/2006 of the European Parliament and of the Council, and repealing commission directive 87/250/EEC, Council Directive 90/496/EEC, Commission Directive 1999/10/EC, Directive 2000/13/EC of the European Parliament and of the Council, Commission Directives 2002/67/EC and 2008/5/EC and Commission Regulation (EC) N° 608/2004, Art. 17, (applicable as from 13 December 2014).

14 For further detail, reference is made to Chapter 1.1. (section 2(2)(b): '*Specific assessment: the issue of the product name*').

IV. Voluntary Labelling

1. "Clean labels": Are there any national definitions or requirements with respect to claims such as 'natural', 'pure', 'home-made', 'additive-free'?

Nowadays, consumers demand for quality and traditional products has become the centre of attention of food business operators: the promotion of food products stresses more and more their natural and healthy character.

Hence, aside from the nutrition & health claims, which are already highly regulated at the European level, food business operators are riding on the wave of 'clean labelling'. Their food products are then *'additive-free'*, *'100 % natural'*, *'pure'* or *'home-made'*.

The use of these terms is however only partially harmonised by Union law. In addition, the rules are scattered among various bits of legislation, making an assessment of compliance even more difficult.

The EU has laid down requirements for the use of the term '**natural**' with respect to:

- *natural flavouring*: Natural flavouring substances correspond to substances that are naturally present and have been identified in nature, i.e. flavouring substances obtained by appropriate physical, enzymatic or microbiological processes from material of vegetable, animal or microbiological origin either in the raw state or after processing for human consumption by one or more of the traditional food preparation processes;[15]
- *nutrition claims*: the terms 'naturally' or 'natural' may only be used as a prefix to a nutrition claim where the related food naturally meets the condition(s) laid down in by the EU Nutrition and Health Claims

15 Regulation (EC) No 1334/2008 of the European Parliament and of the Council of 16 December 2008 on flavourings and certain food ingredients with flavouring properties for use in and on foods and amending Regulation (EC) No 1601/91 of the Council, Regulations (EC) No 2232/96 and (EC) No 110/2008 and Directive 2000/13/EC., Art. Art. 3(2)(c) and 16.

Regulation[16] (hereafter EU Claims Regulation) for the use of these claims, e.g. 'naturally rich in fibre' (without the food being fortified with fibre).

Furthermore, the term '**mountain product**' may only be used to describe agricultural foodstuffs in respect of which both the raw materials and the feedstuffs for farm animals come essentially from mountain areas and, in the case of processed products, the processing also takes place in mountain areas.[17]

Finally, '**traditional specialities guaranteed**' (TSG) are protected against any misuse, imitation or evocation, or against any other practice liable to mislead the consumer.[18]

No further horizontal harmonisation exists. Therefore, any further general legislation with respect to 'clean labelling' is to be found within the national jurisdictions, bearing always in mind the principle of the free movement of goods on the one hand and the protection of the consumer on the other hand.

Under this section and from this perspective, the national chapters will review the (possible) existing legislation as well as the relevant case-law.

---

16 Regulation (EC) No 1924/2006 of the European Parliament and of the Council of 20 December 2006 on nutrition and health claims made on foods.

17 Regulation (EU) No 1151/2012 of 21 November 2012 of the European Parliament and of the Council on quality schemes for agricultural products and foodstuffs, Art. 31. It is worth noting that by 4 January 2014, the Commission has to present a report to the European Parliament and to the Council on the case for a new term, 'product of island farming' (Regulation 1151/2012, Art. 32).

18 Regulation (EU) No 1151/2012 of the European Parliament and of the Council of 21 November 2012 on quality schemes for agricultural products and foodstuffs(OJ L 343, 14.12.2012, p. 1), Art. 24.

2. Nutrition & health claims

For Non-EU countries:

What are the laws and regulations, including case-law, regulating the use of nutrition or health claims regarding foodstuffs?

This section will examine the issue for non-EU countries, namely Norway and Switzerland.

It aims at providing the reader with a short summary of the legal framework applicable to the use of nutrition and health claims made on food in the relevant jurisdiction and any possible link with the EU Claims Regulation.

For EU countries:

Within the list of health claims authorised pursuant to Regulation 1924/2006, are there any related substances which are prohibited or considered as a medicinal substance within the analysed jurisdiction?

The use of nutrition and health claims is highly regulated within the European Union. In particular, European law provides that a health claim may only be made on foods if it has been expressly authorised by a Regulation issued by the Commission. In this regard, a list of permitted health claims made on foods, other than those referring to the reduction of disease risk and to children's development and health, has been quite recently established and is applicable since 13 December 2012.[19]

It is however worth noting that the fact that a substance or product is included in the list of permitted health claims does not constitute an authorisation for the marketing of that substance. A decision on whether the substance can be used in foodstuffs and a classification of a certain

19 Commission Regulation (EU) No 432/2012 of 16 May 2012 establishing a list of permitted health claims made on foods, other than those referring to the reduction of disease risk and to children's development and health as amended from time to time.

product as a foodstuff or a medicinal product remain governed by specific (national) legislations.[20]

This section of the relevant national chapters aims at identifying whether, among the substances or products in relation to which a health relationship has been recognised by the European Commission and included as such in the list of permitted health claims made on foods, certain substances are prohibited or regarded as a medicinal substance within the relevant jurisdiction.

a. Are there any national laws and regulations permitting food business operators to make reference to recommendations or endorsements by national associations, medical, nutrition or dietetic professionals, and health-related charities?

When using nutrition or health claims for the promotion of their products, food business operators frequently wish to refer to recommendations or endorsements made by medical, nutrition or dietetic professionals.

The use of such references is however still regulated at the national level.[21]

This leads the operators that are willing to design an international promotional campaign to assess whether the reference to doctors or nutritionists is allowed within each jurisdiction for which the advertising is intended.

Moreover, according to the EU Claims Regulation, a health claim shall not be allowed if it makes reference to recommendations of individual doctors or health professionals and other associations which are not allowed by the national law in which the claim is made.[22]

20 See in particular: Commission Regulation (EU) No 432/2012, *op. cit.*, recital 17.

21 Regulation (EC) No 1924/2006 of the European Parliament and of the Council of 20 December 2006 on nutrition and health claims made on foods, Art. 11.

22 Regulation (EC) No 1924/2006 of the European Parliament and of the Council of 20 December 2006 on nutrition and health claims made on foods, Art. 12.

b. Is the use of nutrition or health claims on non-prepackaged food further regulated at the national level?

As far as nutrition and health claims are concerned, non-prepackaged foodstuffs (including fresh products such as fruit, vegetables or bread) benefit from certain exceptions with respect to the obligations laid down by the EU Claims Regulation.[23]

These products, when bearing a nutrition or health claim, do not have to provide nutritional information to the consumer, nor state the importance of a varied and balanced diet and a healthy lifestyle and the quantity of the food and pattern of consumption required to obtain the claimed beneficial effect.

However, the EU Claims Regulation expressly grants national authorities the possibility to adopt national provisions in this regard, at least as long as no further measures are adopted at the European level.

This section of national chapters aims at identifying whether such national measures have been adopted and, if so, how they are applied.

c. Is a notification procedure required prior to/for marketing foodstuffs bearing nutritional or health claims?

In order to facilitate efficient monitoring, the EU Claims Regulation expressly enables Member States to require a prior notification of the labels of products bearing a nutrition or a health claim by the manufacturer or the person placing these product on the market.[24]

The establishing of a procedure for the prior notification by the manufacturer or person placing on the market to the competent national authority constitutes a possibility, not an obligation, for Member States.

The aim of this section is to determine, within the national chapters, whether the relevant jurisdictions have put this kind of procedure in place and how food business operators have to deal with this.

---

23 Regulation 1924/2006, *op cit.*, Art. 1(2)al.2

24 Regulation (EC) No 1924/2006, op cit., Art. 26.

In addition, it is worth noting that a similar possibility has been granted to Member States with respect to food supplements[25] and fortified food (food with added vitamins and minerals).[26] As these kind of foodstuffs always bear at least a nutrition claim, the national chapters will also review whether a mandatory national prior notification has been established for these products in particular.

V. Enforcement of Food Law and Self Regulating Bodies

If there is one topic which is only regulated at the local level, it is the enforcement of food law

According to all relevant food law acts, it is up to Member States to lay down measures and penalties applicable to infringements and to ensure effective controls at all stages of the food chain.

25 Directive 2002/46/EC of the European Parliament and of the Council of 10 June 2002 on the approximation of the laws of the Member States relating to food supplements, Art. 10.

26 Regulation (EC) No 1925/2006 of the European Parliament and of the Council of 20 December 2006 on the addition of vitamins and minerals and of certain other substances to foods, Art. 15.

These penalties must be *'effective, proportionate and dissuasive'*[27]; it is obvious that these criteria may give rise to significant differences in practice.

Under this section, national chapters will examine the actions and proceedings that food business operators may face in case of non-compliance with the labelling or advertising requirements. Such actions and proceedings could be initiated by public authorities (e.g., criminal sanction/fine, administrative penalties, seizures or removal of the products, etc.), competitors (e.g. cease-and-desist proceedings, indemnification procedure) or by consumers/ (consumer) associations.

Procedures that could be initiated in the context of self-regulatory bodies in relation to food advertising will also be reviewed, including an analysis of the (binding) effect of their decisions.

27 Regulation (EC) No 178/2002 of the European Parliament and of the Council of 28 January 2002 laying down the general principles and requirements of food law, establishing the European Food Safety Authority and laying down procedures in matters of food safety (OJ L 31, 1.2.2002, p. 1–24), Art. 17(2): *'Member States shall enforce food law, and monitor and verify that the relevant requirements of food law are fulfilled by food and feed business operators at all stages of production, processing and distribution. (…) Member States shall also lay down the rules on measures and penalties applicable to infringements of food and feed law. The measures and penalties provided for shall be effective, proportionate and dissuasive'*; See also Regulation (EC) No 882/2004 of 29 April 2004 on official controls performed to ensure the verification of compliance with feed and food law, animal health and animal welfare rules (OJ L 165, 30.4.2004, p. 1), Art. 54 & 55; Directive 2005/29/EC of the European Parliament and of the Council of 11 May 2005 concerning unfair business-to-consumer commercial practices in the internal market and amending Council Directive 84/450/EEC, Directives 97/7/EC, 98/27/EC and 2002/65/EC of the European Parliament and of the Council and Regulation (EC) No 2006/2004 of the European Parliament and of the Council, Art. 11 to 13.

PART II

NATIONAL CHAPTERS

AT

CHAPTER 3
Austria

Andreas Natterer and Eva-Maria Kostenzer

I. Possible Bans on Food Advertising

1. Is there any general national legislation or code of conduct regulating the promotion of foodstuffs?

Austrian food law in general is mainly influenced by European legislation. There is no horizontal national legislation that comprehensively regulates the promotion of foodstuffs. As a basic rule, advertising for foodstuffs is allowed as long as it is not misleading.[1] Furthermore, it is prohibited to refer to the prevention, treatment or curing of human diseases.[2] This rule does not apply to claims about the dietetic effect of dietary foods or to reduction of disease risk claims that are authorised according to Regulation 1924/2006.[3]

Apart from those mandatory horizontal rules on food advertising the Austrian Food Codex (ÖLMB)[4] contains various vertical standards for specific products but also some general annotations to the basic rules of sec. 5 LMSVG. Accordingly, food advertising includes every statement made when placing a foodstuff on the market that has objectively ascertainable and verifiable content. The statement can be made expressly or by omission, e.g. by maintaining silence.[5] The ÖLMB is not a binding legal act but is considered to be an objectified expert opinion, especially with regard to

1 Sec. 5, para. 2 of the Austrian Act on Food Safety and Consumer Protection (Lebensmittelsicherheits- und Verbraucherschutzgesetz, LMSVG).

2 Sec. 5, para. 3 LMSVG.

3 Regulation 1924/2006 of the European Parliament and the Council on nutrition and health claims made on foods, OJ 2006 L 404/9.

4 At <http://www.lebensmittelbuch.at/> (last accessed on 17 February 2014).

5 Chapter A3.8.2 ÖLMB.

consumer expectation and common business practice.[6] As the national authorities regularly prosecute any non-compliance with the ÖLMB its rules should not be disregarded.

2. Is there any specific national restriction or prohibition (mandatory legislation and code of conduct)?

a. With respect to certain foodstuffs: Alcoholic beverages

Due to the generally accepted potential addictive effect of the consumption of alcoholic beverages, there are several restrictions on their promotion, which will be illustrated in the following.

Advertising for alcoholic beverages is regulated by a dual system of national mandatory regulations and self-regulations.[7]

On the public television and radio, advertising for alcoholic beverages must not address minors or depict minors drinking alcoholic beverages. It is also prohibited to link the consumption of alcohol to enhanced physical performance, driving, the support of social or sexual success or any therapeutic, stimulating, calming or conflict resolving effect. Furthermore, abstinence or a moderate consumption of alcohol must not be depicted in a negative way. The alcohol strength of a drink shall not be pointed out as a positive attribute.[8] On private radio broadcasting advertising for spirits is prohibited.[9]

6 Natterer, *Lebensmittelrecht* (2008), at para. 128 with further references.

7 Mandatory restrictions can be found in sec. 13, para. 5 Austrian Broadcasting Corporation Act (ORF-G; the ORF-G deals with the public Austrian Broadcasting Corporation Österreichischer Rundfunk (= ORF) only), sec. 35 Audio-visual Media Services Act (AMD-G; the AMD-G covers inter alia privately owned TV-stations), and sec. 19 Private Radio Broadcasting Act (PrR-G); with the AMD-G and the PrR-G Art. 15 of Council Directive 89/552/EEC on the coordination of certain provisions laid down by Law, Regulation or Administrative Action in Member States concerning the pursuit of television broadcasting activities, OJ 1989 L 298/23, repealed by the Audiovisual Media Services Directive 2010/13/EU, OJ 2010 L 95/1, was implemented. See also the European Convention on Transfrontier Television which entered into force in Austria in 1998.

8 See sec. 13, para. 5 ORF-G; sec. 35 AMD-G contains restrictions similar to those of the ORF-G.

9 Sec. 19 PrR-G.

In addition to these mandatory regulations the general terms and conditions for commercial advertising on public broadcasting services prohibit commercial advertising for spirits and only allow commercial advertising for alcoholic mixed drinks after prime time (7:25 p.m.).

Besides the rules for broadcasting services the Austrian advertising and marketing communication industry drew up diverse self-regulating standards for responsible advertising. With regard to the promotion of alcoholic beverages, the industry devised the Ethic Code for the Austrian advertising industry[10] and the Communication Codex of the Austrian Breweries Association.[11] These self-regulating standards basically repeat the principles of the mandatory regulations. Furthermore, advertising of beer shall not depict beer consumption in dangerous situations or link beer consumption to operating machines, violent behaviour or to pregnancy.

b. With respect to certain sections of the population: Minors

Advertising to minors who are under 18 years old underlies various restrictions with regard to the medium used as well as the content. Basically, advertising which directly calls upon children under 14 years[12] to buy the advertised product or to persuade their parents or other adults to do so is considered an aggressive and, therefore, unfair commercial practice.[13] While direct statements such as "buy this product" or "get this product now" are prohibited, indirect advertising slogans which depict a product as especially appealing (e.g. "wouldn't it be nice to have this product?") are allowed.[14]

---

10 At <http://werberat.at/layout/ETHIK_KODEX_6_2012.pdf> (last accessed on 17 February 2014).

11 At <http://portal.wko.at/wk/format_detail.wk?angid=1&stid=591570&dstid=335> (last accessed on 17 February 2014).

12 Whether also minors between 14 and 18 years are "children" in the sense of annex no. 28 Unfair Competition Act (UWG) is still disputed; see OGH, September 18, 2012, docket no. 4 Ob 110/12y – *Stickersammelbuch*.

13 Sec. 1, para. 3 in conjunction with sec. 1a and annex no. 28 Unfair Competition Act (UWG).

14 OGH, July 9, 2013, docket no. 4 Ob 95/13v – *video games and others*.

This general rule is specified and amended with regard to advertising on broadcasting services. On public broadcasting services, advertising towards children under 14 years is not allowed immediately before and after children's programmes.[15] For public broadcasting services and all private TV broadcasting services commercial communication on alcoholic beverages to minors is prohibited.[16] Moreover, advertising must not lead to physical or psychic damage of minors. Therefore, it is prohibited to directly call on minors to buy or rent products or services, while making use of their credulity and lack of experience. It is also not allowed to invite minors to ask their parents or third persons to buy the advertised product or service. Advertising must not take advantage of the confidence minors have in their parents, teachers or other persons. Furthermore, it is not allowed to show minors in dangerous situations without justifiable reason.[17]

In addition, the Ethic Code for the Austrian advertising industry establishes some additional rules with regard to advertising to children under 12 years and teenagers. For example, advertising to children must be indicated as such in order to obviate any confusion with a part of the programme. Advertising for products like tobacco, alcohol, medicinal products, dietary supplements or slimming preparations shall not be directed to children and teenagers.

With regard to foodstuffs or drinks that contain nutrients or substances with nutritional or physiological effects and should therefore not be consumed excessively, in particular fat, trans fatty acids, salt/sodium and sugar, each broadcasting service provider must issue guidelines for advertising those products in the course of children's programmes.[18] In order to fulfil this duty, the ORF[19] and the Organization of Private Broadcasting Transmitters issued the Code of Conduct for audio-visual commercial communication

15 Sec. 14, para. 2 ORF-G.

16 Sec. 13, para. 5 no. 1 ORF-G; sec. 35 no. 1 AMD-G.

17 Sec. 13, para. 6 ORF-G; sec. 36, paras. 1 and 2 AMD-G.

18 Sec. 13, para. 8 ORF-G; sec. 36, para. 3 AMD-G.

19 See *supra* note 7.

in children's programmes.[20] According to this code advertising for these foodstuffs in the course of programmes addressed to children under 12 years shall, amongst other things, not promote the excessive consumption of these products or counteract a healthy and balanced diet. Advertising should also not suggest that an inactive lifestyle is better than physical exercise or that the consumption of these foodstuffs enhances performance in school or promotes social success or popularity amongst peers.

Finally, advertising in schools, which was liberalized in 1997, underlies certain restrictions. According to sec. 46, para. 3 of the School Teaching Act (SchUG) advertising in school or in the course of school events for purposes not related to school matters will only be allowed if it does not interfere with the fulfilment of the functions of school in Austria. The director of the school has to decide whether advertising or sponsoring is allowed in each individual case. In doing so, the director must consider the guidelines of the Federal Ministry for Education. Accordingly, advertising for tobacco and alcohol is forbidden.

II. Misleading Advertising

1. What are the national rules on misleading advertising with respect to foodstuffs?

Misleading advertising with respect to foodstuffs is regulated by sec. 5, para. 2 LMSVG.[21] Identical provisions have always been part of Austrian food law but can be considered as the (anticipated) implementation of Art. 2, para. 1 Directive 2000/13/EC.

The Austrian provision prohibits placing products on the market or to advertise them with claims that could be misleading. Misleading claims are, in particular, (1) statements that could be deceptive regarding the charac-

20 At <http://portal.wko.at/wk/format_detail.wk?angid=1&stid=714979&dstid=335> (last accessed on 17 February 2014).

21 See *supra* note 1.

teristics of the foodstuff, such as its nature, identity, properties, composition, quantity, durability, origin or provenance, method of manufacture or production; (2) statements about effects or properties of the foodstuff which it does not possess; and (3) statements which suggest that the foodstuff possesses special characteristics when in fact all similar foodstuffs possess such characteristics.

According to sec. 5, para. 4 LMSVG the prohibition in para. 2 shall also apply to the presentation of foodstuffs.

The assessment whether advertising might be misleading can be based on the Austrian case law on sec. 2 Unfair Competition Act (UWG), which regulates misleading commercial practices.[22] The Austrian Supreme Court (OGH) considers advertising as misleading if the addressee's conception of its meaning deviates from the real circumstances.[23] As a consequence, even information which is actually true can be misleading.[24] With regard to the conception the level of attention of the average informed and reasonably circumspect consumer is relevant.[25] The OGH principally adopted the consumer model established by the European Court of Justice[26] but additionally pointed out that the level of attention depends on the respective situation, in particular the importance of the advertised goods for the consumer. For example, the consumer will pay less attention if he buys everyday commodities of low value.[27]

22 Andreas Natterer, *Lebensmittelrecht, supra* note 6, at para. 51.

23 OGH, September 25, 2001, docket no. 4 Ob 144/01 g – *St. Barbara Brot.*

24 Blass et al. (Eds.), *Kommentar zum Lebensmittelrecht*, 3rd edition (2013), LMSVG sec. 5, at para. 10.

25 Ibid.; Axel Anderl/Clemens Appl in Wiebe/Kodek (eds.), *UWG,* 2nd ed. 2012, sec. 2, at para. 68.

26 Case C-470/93, Mars GmbH [1995] ECR I-1923, para. 24; Case C-303/97, Sektkellerei G.C. Kessler GmbH und Co. [1999] ECR I-513, para. 36; Case C-220/98, Estée Lauder Cosmetics [2000] ECR I-117, para. 27.

27 OGH, October 24, 2000, docket no. 4 Ob 196/00 b – *Spielzeugbausteine.*

With regard to food labelling the responsible consumer is expected to consider the packaging of or the advertising for the product as a whole.[28] However, the responsible and circumspect consumer cannot be regarded as a food expert. For example, "Kombucha" has to be completely fermented tea according to the general opinion of food experts. Therefore, the OGH decided that the name "Kombucha-tea-drink" for a drink which was not completely fermented could mislead consumers, although the product's ingredients were completely listed on the product because even if the circumspect consumer does read the list of ingredients he will not necessarily know what the composition of the product actually should be according to the name under which the product is sold.[29]

2. What are the national landmark cases regarding misleading advertising for foodstuffs?

One of the national landmark cases with regard to misleading advertising for foodstuffs concerned a product named "forest berry fruit bar" ("Waldbeeren Fruchtschnitte").[30] In this case the OGH had to examine a question often discussed in European food law, namely the (alleged) divergence between consumer expectations due to catch-up pictures of fruit on the packaging and the actual nature of these food products.

The front of the packaging of the fruit bar shows many forest berries. The back of the packaging contains, inter alia, the list of ingredients. According to this list, the product contains (in this order) apple powder, oligofructose syrup, raisins, dried apricot bits, dried apple bits, aronia juice concentrate, multiple fruit juice concentrate 2.6 % (in variable proportion: raspberry, blackberry, blueberry and forest berry). For the production of 2.6 % multi-fruit concentrate for 40 g fruit bar, 10 g forest berries are used. The forest berries are pressed to juice without any further additives, and this juice is

---

28 See Natterer, *Lebensmittelrecht, supra* note 6, at para. 51; see also Case C-51/94, European Commission v Germany [1995] I-3599, para. 34.

29 OGH, March 22, 2001, docket no. 4 Ob 287/00 k, ÖBl 2002/5 – *Kombucha-Teegetränk*.

30 OGH, February 15, 2011, docket no. 4 Ob 228/10 y – *Waldbeeren Fruchtschnitte*.

dehydrated to produce the concentrate. If you broke the red-brown bar in two, you could smell a light scent of forest berries.

The plaintiff sought injunctive relief against the defendant because in his view the presentation of the product, and especially the packaging, gives the false impression that the bar contains in particular forest berries when actually the product is mainly made of other fruits such as dried apples and only a small fraction of multiple-fruit juice concentrate of forest berries. In light of the packaging, the consumer has no reason to read the list of ingredients in small print, which is why this list of ingredients does not negate the misleading nature.

The OGH stated that the composition of a product is one of the essential characteristics that, in case of incorrect details or other misleading aspects, may constitute a misleading business practice. The information provided about the composition includes more than the details on the composition of the relevant goods, such as the list of ingredients. The name of a product also gives rise to expectations among the targeted public, e.g. in respect of material characteristics or the composition and the resulting quality.[31]

Furthermore, the OGH clarified that the individual parts of the label, especially when placed to catch the consumer's attention, might influence the – legally relevant – overall impression so that an adequate rectifying note should be added to avoid a potentially misleading nature.[32] Even if the OGH did not clearly state so, a complete and correct list of ingredients may be insufficient to rectify a consumer deception caused by pictures of fruits.[33]

According to the OGH in the case at hand, the empowered consumer neither expects a product named "forest berry fruit bar" to be made from whole fruits nor – in proportion to the other fruit ingredients – to be mainly made from forest berries. In fact, the consumer's expectation is primarily characterised by the assumption that a "forest berry fruit bar" is made

31 Ibid.

32 Ibid.; see also OGH November 15, 1976, docket no. 4 Ob 379/76 – *Kürbis-Salatöl* = ÖBl 1997/37.

33 See for Germany OLG Cologne, January 18, 2008, docket no. 6 U 144/07, para. 27 – *Fruit2day*; LG Hamburg, April 23, 2009, docket no. 312 O 722/08, para. 38 – *Fruit Smoothie*; see also VwGH, September 20, 2012, docket no. 2011/10/0128 – *Analogkäse*.

from real forest berries (and not merely flavouring) and also tastes of such fruit. However, the actual quantitative relation between the basic blend of the fruit bar and the amount of the fruit for which it is named only plays a minor role in consumer expectations and thus also with respect to the purchase decision of the consumer. As far as the "forest berry fruit bar" is concerned, the amount of forest berries processed to berry concentrate which is then added to the fruit bar is in any case sufficiently high to meet consumer expectations in respect of the fruit content. As a consequence, the packaging does not create false consumer expectations about the product.[34]

The judgment clearly shows that a generally binding rule is impossible but that the evaluation shall be made on a case-by-case basis. Since the consumers' perceptions might be different in respect to different food products, it cannot be otherwise. In case of tea-like beverages, such as the so-called "fruit teas", pursuant to the Austrian Food Codex (ÖLMB) which is considered to be a codified opinion of consumer expectations, pictures of fruits are expressly allowed, even if the product contains only flavours. In the case at hand, the OGH did not see any typical consumer expectation related to the product. Therefore, the well-informed consumer is supposed to refer to the list of ingredients to inform himself about the composition of the product. However, the OGH clearly indicated that his judgment would have been different if the fruit bar did not contain a considerable quantity of forest fruits, even in the form of a multiple-juice concentrate, but only flavours. In any case, the consumer expects to smell and taste that forest berries have been used in this product.

34 OGH, February 15, 2011, docket no. 4 Ob 228/10 y – *Waldbeeren Fruchtschnitte*.

III. Mandatory Labelling: Name of the Product

Are there any national definitions of a foodstuff that could hamper the marketing of an imported food product?

Mandatory legal definitions for the following products do not exist in Austria, but the Austrian Food Codex (ÖLMB) determines certain specifications.[35]

1. Energy drinks

Energy drinks may only be labelled as such if they contain at least 250 mg caffeine per 1000 ml and 11 g carbohydrates respectively 44 kcal per 100 ml. It is allowed to add vitamins, mineral nutrients, taurine (reference value 400 mg/100 ml), glucuronolactone (240 mg/100 ml) and inositol (20 mg/100 ml). Drinks with less carbohydrates or a lower energy value may not be labelled as energy drinks.[36]

2. Sport drinks

Drinks and beverage powder with mineral nutrients are defined as foodstuff that can compensate for a loss of water and mineral nutrients caused by sweating. Such a product can be labelled as iso-, hypo- or hypertonic if the drink has a certain osmolality. In general, drinks with mineral nutrients contain sodium, potassium, calcium and magnesium. In order to inform the consumer, the added amount or the content of the mineral nutrients and their name will be declared on the packaging (mg/100 ml). Names such as “mineral-salt-drink”, “mineral-nutrients-drink”, “multi-mineral-drink” and similar names may be used.[37]

---

35 See *supra* note 4.

36 Chapter B26.3 of the ÖLMB; see also VwGH, July 4, 2005, docket no. 2003/10/0030 – *Energicum Brausegranulat.*

37 Chapter B26.2 ÖLMB.

AT

3. Yogurt

Yogurt is made of milk with a fat content of less than 10 % using certain yogurt cultures. Depending on the yogurt cultures, yogurt can also be indicated as "mild" yogurt. Furthermore, yogurt can be semi-solid or stirred. The smell and taste are sour, slightly acerbic and have a typical yogurt aroma. For the production of cream yogurt cream with 10 % fat or more is used. If milk from animals other than cows is used, it has to be indicated in the name of the product.

Fruit yogurts additionally contain fruits, fruit preparations or concentrates, sugars and sweeteners, cereals or spices. The fruit content must be at least 7 % fresh fruit. It is allowed to add water and label the product as "yogurt-drink" if the milk content is at least 51 %.[38]

4. Cheese

Cheese is a fresh or matured product made of cheese milk, whey or fermented milk curd.[39] Milk cream, whey cream or buttermilk can be added to cheese milk. Fat and proteins that were not extracted from milk may not be added. Furthermore, certain rennet, salt, herbs and spices, bacteria, yeast and fungi cultures that are non-hazardous to health, water and flavouring foodstuffs can be added during the cheese production process.

The ÖLMB classifies cheese into categories according to the water content in the fat-free cheese mass and the fat content in the dry matter. In addition, specific characteristics for the most common cheese types such as "Emmentaler", "Bergkäse (Mountain cheese)" or "Alpenkäse (Alp-cheese)" are determined.[40]

38 Chapters B32.5.1.3 and B32.6 ÖLMB.

39 With regard to the labelling of so-called "analogue cheese" see VwGH, September 20, 2012, docket no. 2011/10/0128 – *Analogkäse*.

40 For further details, see chapter B32.3 ÖLMB.

5. Bread

As Austria is a country with a long tradition of bread and bakery products various bread-types exist. According to chapter B18 ÖLMB bread is mostly made with leaven or yeast dough. Further ingredients such as salt, spices, starch, dairy products, sugars, citric acid, tartaric acid and others may be added.

With regard to the flour types bread is differentiated between "rye bread", "wheat bread", "brown bread" and "others". As far as the preparation is concerned, ÖLMB determines numerous bread-types and their method of preparation, e.g. "cottage and farmhouse bread", "wholemeal bread", "crisp-bread" and so on.

Bakery products that have been deep-frozen may be sold without any corresponding indication. Prebaked products may be labelled as "fresh" if they get fully baked before their consumption. This is not allowed for bakery products that were baked, frozen and directly sold after thawing.

IV. Voluntary Labelling

1. "Clean labels": Are there any national definitions or requirements with respect to claims such as 'natural', 'pure', 'home-made', 'additive-free'?

a. 'Natural'

According to Austrian case law claims referring to the naturalness or environmental compatibility very likely influence the consumer's purchase decision, which is why the industry must strictly assess the possibility of deceiving the consumer.[41] As a consequence, a product that was chemically

41 See OGH, April 17, 2013, docket no. 4 Ob 44/13 v – *natürliches Keimlingsmehl,* with further references.

treated or contains a chemically treated ingredient, e.g. in order to extend its durability, shall not be labelled as "natural".[42]

b. 'Pure'

In order to label a foodstuff with the term "pure", a similar high standard as for "natural" has to be met. Such terms may only be used if they are definitely true and do not mislead the consumer.[43] In a case before the OGH a salad dressing made of yogurt and herbs with no preservatives contained modified starch in order to obtain a certain consistency. Because modified starch is a chemically treated ingredient, the product may not be labelled as "pure". The indication of modified starch in the list of ingredients does not eliminate the misleading character of the labelling.[44]

c. 'Home-made'/'grand-mother recipe'

It is misleading to advertise products with artisan terms if the products actually are factory-made. For example, the labelling "Something good from the grange" for products of a well-known industrial company that produces canned food implies that the producer has a relation to a big farm with controlled suppliers of premium agricultural products, that the products are especially fresh and that they were manufactured in a special non-industrial way.[45] Therefore, the respective labelling has been considered to be misleading.

d. 'Additive-free'

Claims such as "additive-free", "without genetically modified organisms" or "free from preservatives" can be used as long as they are true and the use

---

42 OGH, March 25, 1986, docket no. 4 Ob 316/86 – *bottichfrisches Sauerkraut.*

43 OGH, October 20, 1998, docket no. 4 Ob 268/98 k – *Stockerauer Salaterdäpfel.*

44 OGH, November 29, 2005, docket no. 4 Ob 200/05 y – *naturreines Salat Dressing.*

45 OGH, February 9, 1988, docket no. 4 Ob 414/87 – *Gutes vom Gutshof*; see Lothar Wiltschek, *UWG, 7th ed. (2003)*, sec. 2, at para. 459.

of the additives is allowed according to the law. On the contrary, if the use of additives for the foodstuff is forbidden anyway, a corresponding claim suggests that the foodstuff possesses special characteristics when in fact all similar foodstuffs possess such characteristics. According to sec. 5, para. 2, no. 3 LMSVG such advertising based on self-evident product information is misleading. However, in case that the legal basis is clearly indicated, the claim is not misleading anymore and therefore allowed.[46]

e. 'Fresh'

"Fresh" does not at any rate mean that the product was produced immediately before consumption. The term can also signify that the advertised foodstuff has the same characteristics as a freshly produced foodstuff, e.g. the taste and smell of milk with extended shelf life compared to fresh milk.[47] However, it is essential that the consumer is able to understand what is meant by "fresh" in the concrete case.

2. Nutrition & health claims

a. Within the list of health claims authorised pursuant to Regulation 1924/2006, are there any related substances which are prohibited or considered as a medicinal substance within the analysed jurisdiction?

Within the list of health claims authorised pursuant to Regulation 1924/2006 there are no related substances that are expressly prohibited or solely considered as medicinal substances within the Austrian jurisdiction. The only uncertainty concerns melatonin, a substance that has always been considered as a medicinal product. Although the EFSA opinions on melatonin have been published various proceedings are still pending. On the other

46 E.g. "additive-free* – *according to the Regulation on food additives"; see Andreas Natterer and Eva-Maria Kostenzer, *Irreführende Werbung mit Selbstverständlichkeiten im Lebensmittelrecht*, ecolex (2013), pp. 353 et sqq.

47 OGH August 20, 2002, docket no. 4 Ob 173/02 y – *Länger frische Vollmilch.*

hand, the customs authorities consider melatonin in any dosage as a medicinal product.

b. Are there any laws and regulations permitting food business operators to make reference to recommendations or endorsements by national associations, medical nutrition or dietetic professionals and health-related charities?

According to Article 12, lit. c) Regulation 1924/2006, health claims which make reference to recommendations of individual doctors or health professionals and other associations not referred to in Article 11 shall not be allowed. Article 11 determines that in the absence of specific Community rules concerning recommendations of or endorsements by national associations of medical, nutrition or dietetic professionals and health-related charities, relevant national rules may apply in compliance with the provisions of the Treaty. As there is no corresponding prohibition in the Austrian food law, such recommendations or endorsements are allowed.[48]

With regard to recommendations by individual health professionals the Higher Administrative Court (VwGH) recently decided that also dieticians are health professionals in the sense of Article 12, lit. c) Regulation 1924/2006. Therefore, the health-related recommendation in the case at hand of a single dietician was not compliant with Regulation 1924/2006.[49]

c. Is the use of nutrition or health claims on non-prepackaged food further regulated at the national level?

No rules with regard to Article 1, para. 2, subpara. 2 Regulation 1924/2006 have been adopted on the national level.

48 See Blass et al. (Eds.), *Kommentar zum Lebensmittelrecht, supra* note 28, EG-Claims VO, Art. 11, at para. 2.

49 VwGH, May 28, 2013, docket no. 2012/10/0105 – *Diätologin.*

d. Is a notification procedure required prior to/for marketing foodstuffs bearing nutritional or health claims?

National notification procedures required prior to or for marketing of foodstuffs bearing nutritional or health claims do not exist, not even for fortified food or food supplements.

V. Enforcement of Food Law and Self Regulating Bodies

1. Which actions may one risk in case of non-compliance with the labelling or advertising requirements

a. Public authorities

In case a foodstuff does not fulfil the Austrian labelling or advertising requirements, several sanctions may follow, depending on the kind of violation.

First of all, a system of official controls is maintained. In case the national authority becomes aware of any non-compliance with food regulations, it can impose measures in order to remedy the non-conformance or minimise risks. Such measures are inter alia restriction or prohibition of placing the product on the market, closing of a business, withdrawal of the product from the market, (public) information to the customers and consumers, adaption of the labelling and the immediate duty to report on the implementation of the imposed measures. In case the food business operator does not fulfil the measures or if the products are injurious to health the authorities can confiscate the products. Furthermore, the public has to be informed if the authority has a reasonable suspicion that the products could endanger the health of a major population group.[50]

50 Sec. 39, 41 and 42 LMSVG; for further details, see Natterer, *Lebensmittelrecht*, *supra* note 6, at paras. 102 et seqq.

Apart from these measures, the food business operator also risks criminal sanctions. In case a foodstuff is placed on the market that is injurious to health the competent authority is the respective district court. The responsible person may face a prison sentence up to one year or a financial penalty of up to 360 daily rates. The height of the daily rates has to be determined in each individual case according to the economic capacity of the responsible person and may vary between EUR 2,– and EUR 500,–.[51]

For all other infringements of food law, including labelling or advertising requirements, the competent administrative authority has to initiate an administrative criminal law proceeding. According to sec. 90 LMSVG someone who places foodstuffs on the market or advertises them with misleading particulars or in a misleading manner may be sentenced with a penalty up to EUR 50.000,–, or up to EUR 100.000,– in case of recurrence. Sec. 90, para. 3 LMSVG refers to diverse national food regulations as well as legislative acts of the European Union listed in the annex and equally penalises violations of these acts with up to EUR 50.000,– respectively ERU 100.000,–. Also, non-compliance with imposed measures according to sec. 39 LMSVG can be sentenced with these amounts. Sec. 90, para. 7 LMSVG determines that the authority has to set an act of prosecution within one year after the infringement; otherwise, the prosecution is statute-barred.

As far as infringements by broadcasters are concerned the Austrian Communications Authority (KommAustria) is competent as a panel authority with the powers of a court. Amongst various duties, KommAustria is also responsible for monitoring compliance with Austrian advertising regulations in broadcasts of the Austrian Broadcasting Corporation (ORF) and private broadcasters. In case of a suspected legal violation, the broadcaster in question is given an opportunity to submit a comment. If this response is not sufficiently substantiated to dispel the suspicion of a legal violation KommAustria reports the case to the Federal Communications Senate (BKS) or initiates a procedure in order to investigate the suspected violation. Decisions on violations of fundamental importance are made public.

51 In case of death of a human being or a danger to life and limb of a larger number of persons the prison sentence may rise to three years. For further details, see sec. 81 et seqq. LMSVG.

b. Competitors and consumer associations

In case of misleading or aggressive commercial practices competitors and certain Consumer Protection Associations are entitled to file an action for injunction pursuant to sec. 14 UWG. If they succeed, the consequences for the losing party can be far-reaching. Apart from the obligation to terminate the unfair commercial practice, the procedural costs of the opposing party have to be refunded. Furthermore, the opposing party can obtain an interim order that obliges the losing party to immediately withdraw the product from the market. In case of certain violations the court can decide that the decision has to be published at the losing party's cost.[52] According to sec. 16 UWG also compensation for loss of profit can be claimed. However, damage claims play a minor role compared to injunctive relief due to requirements of proof and the need for prompt remedial action.[53]

2. Are there any national self-regulating bodies with respect to advertising for foodstuffs?

Members of the Austrian advertising and marketing communication industry elected the Austrian Advertising Council as the self-control body of the industry. Every person is entitled to lodge a complaint at the Austrian Advertising Council against advertising efforts.[54] In addition, the Council can open a procedure on its own accord. The Council is competent for all advertising efforts published in Austria from companies which have their registered seat or any subsidiary located in Austria. The Council decides whether the advertising in question complies with the Ethic Code for the Austrian advertising industry. In case the complaint is not unfounded, the Council asks the advertiser to respond to the complaint. Subsequently, the Council will decide if any action is necessary, in particular that the advertiser has to be more sensitive in the future or that the campaign should be

52 See sec. 24, 25 UWG

53 Georg E. Kodek/Petra Leupold in Wiebe/Kodek, *UWG, supra* note *25,* sec. 16, at para. 1.

54 See Code of Procedure of the Austrian Advertising Council at <http://werberat.at/verfahrensordnung.aspx> (last accessed on 17 February 2014).

stopped immediately. The decision is not binding but will be published on the homepage of the Council.[55] Furthermore, it can be published in other media.

55 At <http://werberat.at/verfahrenliste.aspx> (last accessed on 17 February 2014).

CHAPTER 4
Belgium

Aude Mahy and Filip Pauwels

I. Possible Bans on Food Advertising

1. Is there any national legislation (or national codes of conduct) on the advertising of foodstuffs?

In Belgium the advertising of foodstuffs is regulated by legislation as well as by the food industry itself, via codes of conducts.

a. Legislation

The Belgian Act of 24 January 1977[1], amongst other things, forms the basis for the protection of consumers' health when it comes to foodstuffs. Based on this Act and in the interest of consumer protection, a Royal Decree was adopted on 17 April 1980 setting out the rules for the advertising of foodstuffs (hereinafter 'R.D. on Food Advertising').[2]

Together with the general legislation on market practices and consumer protection[3], these rules form the basic framework of the national rules applicable to the advertising of foodstuffs.[4]

1 Act of 24 January 1977 concerning the protection of the health of consumers with respect to foodstuffs and other products, *Official Belgian Gazette* 8 April 1977.

2 Royal Decree of 17 April 1980 concerning the Advertising of Foodstuff, *Official Belgian Gazette* 6 May 1980.

3 Act of 6 April 2010 concerning market practices and consumer protection, *Official Belgian Gazette* 12 April 2010 which is the implementation of the following EU Directives: 85/577/EEC, 93/13/EEC, 97/7/EC, 2005/29/EC and 2006/114/EC.

4 The Royal Decree of 13 September 1999 on the Labelling of Prepackaged Foodstuffs may also have a certain impact.

Before a decision of the Court of Justice of the European Union ('CJEU'), some of the rules of the R.D. on Food Advertising had the effect of illegally fettering the free movement of foodstuffs, according to the CJEU (see the introductory chapter 1).[5]

As a result of this decision, the R.D. on Food Advertising was amended in 2012, and now states that the provisions of this R.D. are not applicable to foodstuffs that have been legally manufactured and/or marketed in other EU Member States, in Turkey or in countries that have signed the Agreement on the European Economic Area.

However, the relevant requirements continue to apply to domestic products and products imported from third-countries (except EEA and Turkey).[6]

This being said, the rules on the advertising of foodstuffs set out by this Royal Decree can be divided into two categories. The first category prohibits the use of specific elements such as words, images, references, etc. while the second category concerns the perception that is created by the advertising. In addition to the advertising of foodstuffs, both categories of prohibitions also apply to labelling.[7]

i. Under the first category, no promotional material for foodstuffs may:

(1) Use the words 'ill' ('sick', ...), 'illness' ('sickness', 'disease', ...), the name of any illness or refer to the symptoms of any illness or of people who are ill.[8] Such use can, however, be allowed for claims authorised under the EU Claims Regulation. No.1924/2006 on nutrition and health claims made on food ('EU Claims Regulation').

5 CJEU, 15 July 2004, *C-239/02, (*Douwe Egberts NV) § 53–56.

6 CJEU, 15 July 2004, *C-239/02, (*Douwe Egberts NV) § 57.

7 R.D. on Food Advertising, *op cit,* Art. 6.

8 R.D. on Food Advertising, *op cit.*, Art. 2, 1°.

(2) Use or represent people, clothing or devices that evoke the medical, paramedical or pharmaceutical professions.[9]

Being confident about the qualities of their food products, food business operators may be tempted to have a credible health care professional endorse their ads/commercials to encourage consumers to believe the statements made about the relevant product. As a result, they tend to forget about this prohibition or try to circumvent it. The latter was the case in a television ad for milk products in which a man appeared wearing white professional clothing with a name tag that read 'foodstuffs expert'.[10] In the ad, the 'foodstuffs expert' explained to children the importance of Vitamin D. The ad violated this prohibition, and the advertiser was requested to remove it. In its defence, the advertiser argued that under Belgian law a 'foodstuffs expert' is, unlike a dietician, not considered a paramedical profession. Disregarding this, the Jury for Ethical Advertising Practices ("JEP"[11]) concluded that the representation of the man in white professional clothing evoked a paramedical profession to the target audience, which is prohibited.

(3) References to medical recommendations, certificates or approvals that contain claims that are not authorised under the EU Claims Regulation.[12]

(4) References to a Minister or government bodies competent for health care, except upon their explicit approval.[13]

9 R.D. on Food Advertising, art. 2, 5°.

10 Jury for Ethical Advertising Practices ("JEP") decision of 7 October 2005 (Danone), www.jep.be; see also JEP decision of 19 August 2008 (Campina), www.jep.be, this decision concerns an infomercial which featured a dietician and foodstuffs expert and advanced claims about the need for daily doses of calcium and the use of milk products.

11 Jury for Ethical Advertising Practices – See *infra* chapter V.2 for more information about this non-judicial but self-disciplinary body of the advertising industry.

12 R.D. on Food Advertising, art. 2, 7°.

13 R.D. on Food Advertising, art. 2, 8°.

ii. The second category of prohibitions

As indicated, the second kind of rules laid down by the R.D. on Food Advertising concerns the perception that is created with the advertisement:

(1) Statements, indications, names, references, images or signs that are or could be misleading as to the nature, the identity, the capacity, the composition, the method of production/preparation, the condition, the storage, the characters, the origin, the provenance or the use of the foodstuffs or of the raw materials and ingredients..[14]

(2) References that incite or exploit emotions of fear or anger.[15] The criteria for assessing this are subjective and, in practice, are seldom crystal clear. An ad can incite emotions of fear in one person because of his/her past, age, culture, etc. but does not necessarily create the same emotions for someone else.

    In one ad for fruit nectar it was stated that *"One in two Belgians has calcium deficiency"* and that 1 glass of nectar is equal to 1 glass of milk. The President of the Commercial Court of Brussels held that such a statement constitutes an infringement of the prohibition as it exploits the emotions of parents who might be anxious about calcium deficiency in their children.[16]

    Another example of the ambit of this prohibition was an advertisement for eggs. The ad displayed a picture of a box of eggs that looked particularly unhygienic and unappetising. The slogan stated: *"You will never fear eggs again"* and stressed the eggs' well-balanced proportion of Omega-3/Omega-6 marketed by the advertiser. As this ad clearly exploited emotions of fear, an organisation that assists consumers' associations (OIVO/CRIOC) filed a complaint.[17]

---

14 R.D. on Food Advertising, art. 2, 9°.

15 R.D. on Food Advertising, art. 2, 6°.

16 President of the Commercial Court of Brussels, 30 March 1992, *Jaarboek Handelspraktijken 1992*, 115. It should be noted that this decision was rendered before the entry into force of the EU Claims Regulation according to which the claim would also have been prohibited because of non-compliant comparative nutrition claim.

17 Article of 28 February 2009 on http://www.oivo.be/NL/doc/dcdc/all/document-4216.html

(3) Claims involving objective and measurable elements with respect to the composition of the product that cannot be justified.[18]

(4) Mentioning the fact that vitamins and provitamins have been added if they have only been added for technologic and organoleptic[19] purposes (e.g. Vitamin C that would have been added for antioxidant purpose).

(5) The other prohibitions implement the provisions set out in Directive 2000/13/EC ('Labelling Directive'), which are now embedded in Regulation No. 1169/2001 on the provision of food information to consumers ('FIC Regulation').[20] One of these prohibitions is that one cannot suggest that a foodstuff has special properties when, in fact, all similar foodstuffs have essentially the same properties. Another prohibition is that one cannot attribute curative properties or refer to the prevention, treatment or cure for any human disease, or refer to such properties.[21]

It is worth noting that the rules of this horizontal[22] Royal Decree on Food Advertising are applicable without prejudice to any other Belgian (i.e. the Belgian Act on Market Practices and Consumer Protection[23]) and European legal provisions (i.e. the EU Claims Regulation).

This means, for example, that when claiming nutritional or health properties, the EU Claims Regulation will automatically prevail. However, if such a claim is (still) on hold by the European Commission, the claim will be allowed to the extent that it complies with the general principles of the EU Claims Regulation *and* with the rules of this R.D. on Food Advertising. As a consequence, no claim may attribute to any foodstuff the property of

---

18 R.D. on Food Advertising, art. 4, 1°.

19 Meaning to be perceived by a sense organ such as taste, smell, etc.

20 Directive 2000/13/EC of the European Parliament and of the Council of 20 March 2000 on the approximation of the laws of the Member States relating to the labelling, presentation and advertising of foodstuffs, Art. 2 and Regulation (EU) No. 1169/2011 of 25 October 2011 on the provision of food information to consumers, Art. 7. For further detail on the FIC Regulation, please see introductory chapter 1.1. of this book.

21 R.D. on Food Advertising, arts. 4.2. & 4.5.

22 Applicable to all foodstuffs.

23 Act of 6 April 2010 concerning market practices and consumer protection, *op cit.*

prevention, treatment or cure for a human disease, or refer to such properties (see *supra* § 4(b)). In this respect it should be noted that Belgium has published an indicative (which is thus non-binding) list of what is *not* regarded as attributing such characteristics.[24]

For example, if the European Commission puts on hold the claim *"Helps your body's natural defences"* in respect to substance X, the person who places the product on the market will appreciate that the aforementioned list indicates that such claim is not regarded as attributing to substance X the property of preventing, treating or curing a human disease, or refer to such properties.

As the rules of this R.D. on Food Advertising do not apply to foodstuffs that have been legally manufactured and/or brought into the market in another EU Member State, in Turkey or in countries that have signed the Agreement on the European Economic Area, these rules do not apply to claims which are 'on hold' for such foodstuffs.

Aside from the above, one should always bear in mind the channel of communication that is used for the advertisement of foodstuffs. Certain channels of communication may be subject to specific legislation. Moreover, depending on where the ad takes place, different legislation may apply. Television broadcasting in Belgium is, for example, regulated at the level of the Belgian Communities[25], which means that if a business operator wishes to promote a foodstuff during a commercial break on a Flemish television channel, it should first check whether its commercial complies with the Flemish Decree

24 http://health.belgium.be/internet2Prd/groups/public/@public/@dg4/@foodsafety/documents/ie2law/839652.pdf

25 The Kingdom of Belgium is a federal state divided into three regions (Brussels-Capital, Flanders and Wallonia) and into three linguistic communities (French, Dutch and German – the three official languages). The competences of these regions and communities complement those of the federal state. Although Belgian legislation comprises both federal legislation (laws and royal decrees) and legislation enacted by the communities (decrees) and regions (ordinances), the judiciary is exclusively organised at the federal level.

on radio and television broadcasting.[26] In addition to numerous provisions concerning advertising in general, these decrees also contain restrictions with respect to certain categories of foodstuffs and to the advertising of foodstuffs targeted at children and younger audiences.

b. Codes of conduct

The Belgian food industry has taken initiatives to self-regulate the advertising of foodstuffs.[27] One of the more successful initiatives is the Code on the Advertising of Foodstuffs[28], which is an important inter-professional code of conduct and was created by the Belgian Federation of the Food Industry[29] and the Union of Belgian Advertisers.[30] These self-disciplinary rules, inspired by the ICC Code, entered into force on 1 May 2005 and apply to all the members of these associations irrespective of the channels of communication used for the advertising of their foodstuffs and of the Belgian region where the foodstuffs are promoted.

For the enforcement of this Code, a self-disciplinary body named the "*Jury for Ethical Advertising Practices*" (hereinafter the 'JEP') was appointed.[31]

The restrictions set out in this Code can be classified into 4 categories: nutrition and health claims, misleading advertising, advertising aimed at children and 'healthy lifestyle' claims. The latter kind of restrictions implies that:

(1) the advertising of foodstuffs may not encourage or condone excessive consumption;

---

26 Flemish Decree of 27 March 2009 on radio and television broadcasting, *Belgian Official Gazette*, 30 April 2009. The similar decrees for the other Belgian communities are the following: the Coordinated Decree of 26 March 2009 on the audio visual services (of the French-speaking community) and the Decree of 27 June 2005 on the audio visual media services and film screenings (of the German-speaking community).

27 See for example *supra* I.2.1(b) and I.3.1.2(b).

28 This Code can be consulted via http://www.jep.be/media/pdf/sectoriele_code/FEVIA_nl.pdf

29 FEVIA – www.fevia.be

30 UBA – www.ubabelgium.be

31 See *infra* V.2 for more information on the enforcement of this Code.

(2) the size of the portions shown in the advertising must be appropriate to the situation which is advanced; and

(3) the advertising may not suggest a diet that is unbalanced or unhealthy or detract from the importance of a healthy and active life.

2. Is the advertising of certain (categories of) foodstuffs restricted or prohibited by any national mandatory and/or soft law (e.g. code of conduct, case law)?

In Belgium there are a number of categories of foodstuffs (alcoholic beverages, sugary sweets, lemonades, etc.) to which specific rules apply in addition to the general rules on the advertising of foodstuffs set out under chapter 2.

a. Alcoholic beverages

For a country with such an established beer tradition and far more beer varieties than there are days in a year, it is not surprising that the advertising of alcoholic beverages is strictly regulated in order to avoid overconsumption. As the consumption of alcoholic beverages is age-restricted,[32] the advertising of alcoholic beverages towards minors is prohibited. However, the advertising of alcoholic beverages in general is also subject to various restrictions that are not only set out in legislation but also applied by the food industry itself through a code of conduct.

i. Legislation

As explained above, advertising on radio and television is regulated at the Belgian Community level. Except for the aforementioned prohibition on advertising alcoholic beverages to minors, to date only the Flemish

32 It is prohibited to sell, serve or offer alcoholic beverages (of more than 0,5 % vol.) to people younger than 16 years. With respect to spirits, it is prohibited to sell, serve or offer them to people younger than 18 years.

Community[33] has implemented the restrictions on the advertising of alcoholic beverages, as set out in the Audiovisual Media Services Directive.[34]

One may not, therefore, give the impression on any Flemish radio or television channels that the consumption of alcoholic beverages has any positive effects on physic performance, the ability to drive a motor vehicle[35], or contributes to sexual or social success.[36]

The latter was at issue in an advertisement showing a man, preparing an alcoholic drink of a certain brand, looking across the street at the people drinking at a party at another terrace and attracting the attention of one of the women. The ad then showed the woman and the other people crossing the street and walking up to him followed by him offering her the relevant drink and gesturing to the two men at the other party that she and the others had just left.[37]

At first instance, the JEP considered this ad to violate the aforementioned restriction because, in its view, it is clear that by offering the alcoholic drink the protagonist attracts people to his party hereby increasing his social status and success compared to the organisers of the other party. However, on appeal, the JEP overruled the first instance decision concluding that in the ad there is no change in social status or success of the protagonist. Both parties are similar (alcoholic beverages are served at both). The ad was based upon the idea that the people moved from one party to the other because

33 Flemish Decree of 27 March 2009 on radio and television broadcasting, *Belgian Official Gazette* 30 April 2009.

34 Directive 2010/13/EU of the European Parliament and of the Council of 10 March 2010 on the coordination of certain provisions laid down by law, regulation or administrative action in Member States concerning the provision of audiovisual media services (Audiovisual Media Services Directive).

35 These prohibitions are further interpreted under the Code on the Advertising of Alcoholic Beverages (see *infra* I.2.1(b)) which states that the creation of a link between the consumption of alcoholic beverages, on the one hand, and conducting a motor vehicle or good performances at work, on the other hand, is only authorised if the message is to warn people about the risks related to the consumption of such beverages.

36 Audiovisual Media Services Directive, *op cit.*, Art. 22 and Flemish Decree of 27 March 2009 on radio and television broadcasting, *Belgian Official Gazette* 30 April 2009, Art. 68.

37 JEP decision of 4 July 2013 (Bacardi Martini).

a certain brand of alcohol was served at the other party and not because there were no alcoholic beverages served at the first. As a result, the ad was not considered to violate the aforementioned restriction.

Furthermore, under the Flemish Decree, ads may not suggest that the product has therapeutic properties or a stimulating, relaxing or de-stressing effect. In addition, the advertising may not use minors (under the age of 18), encourage excessive consumption or seek to place temperance or non-excessive consumption in a poor light, nor emphasise their product's high alcohol content as a positive characteristic.

ii. Code of conduct

The most practical and complete set of rules on the advertising of alcoholic beverages was created by the alcoholic beverages industry in collaboration with consumer organisations. The first Code of conduct on the advertising of alcoholic beverages was created in 2005.[38] Since 25 April 2013, a new version of this Code has come into force, which was signed by the Belgian Brewers, the Belgian Federation for Wine and Distilled alcoholic beverages, the federations for hotels, restaurants and bars, Comeos[39], the Council for Advertising[40], consumer organisations and the Minister of Health.[41]

As with the Code on the Advertising of Foodstuffs it is the JEP[42] that is entrusted with the enforcement of the Code on the advertising of alcoholic beverages. One of the differences, however, between the scope of application of the two codes is that for alcoholic beverages, the code applies not only to food business operators, but also to many media and publicity agencies through their membership in the Council of Advertising. This means that

38 The 'Arnoldus Covenant'.

39 Association that represents Belgian trade and services.

40 The Council for Advertising is an inter-professional association composed and financed by advertisers, publicity agencies and various media. More than 80 % of the advertising on the Belgian market is created or distributed/diffused by its members. (http://www.conseildelapublicite.be)

41 This Code can be consulted via http://www.jep.be/media/Alcoholconvenant%20NL%20 2013.pdf

42 See *infra* V.2 for more information on the JEP.

even if the food business operator is not a member of any of the aforementioned associations, the media or publicity agency that is a member of this Code still has to abide by this Code when promoting the products of this food business operator.

This Code is practical since it covers not only all channels of communication but also includes the general rules on the advertising of foodstuffs and applies them to alcoholic beverages.[43] The restrictions as set out by the Flemish Decree on radio and television are also covered by this Code and thus apply to all channels of communication and cover the whole Belgian territory.

Aside from the restrictions and prohibition explained above and reiterated in this Code, it contains a number of additional restrictions and prohibitions:

- *As regards the location that appears in the ad,* it is forbidden to promote alcoholic beverages in social or health care institutions and work premises, except for their catering facilities. In catering facilities or shops, the alcoholic beverages must be physically separated from the non-alcoholic beverages. Outside, however, on the public road, it is forbidden to give alcoholic beverages free of charge or to offer them for sale at a symbolic price. There was recently such an infringement at a cross-country event in Bruges where the runners were offered (500 metres before the finish line) a small free glass of beer (just for tasting).[44]
- *As for content,* an advertisement may not give the impression that the consumption of an alcoholic beverage will help to solve, reduce or cope with physical, psychological or social problems or a state of anxiety, or that it will improve psychological and physical (including sporting) performances. Further, no ad may denigrate other beverages or suggest that an alcoholic beverage is a necessity to live happily or to create a festive atmosphere. In practice, the word 'necessity' is an important element in this last prohibition. In a commercial for a brand of beer,

43 For example, the prohibition of promoting excessive consumption is also covered in this Code. An infringement of this prohibition was the case in an advertisement for a brand of beer where the idea of the marketing campaign was that if you could quickly collect 24 crowns of the relevant beer (within a limited time), then you would receive one free ticket to go to the movies (JEP decision, 30 November 2009 (Carlsberg)).

44 JEP decision of 22 May 2013 (Brouwerij De Halve Maan).

images were shown of a party with some people holding a beer of the relevant brand, of an airplane taking off and of DJ Axwell. The text and voice over of this commercial stated: "*X presents – Where's the party – by X – That calls for a X*" and "*Get spotted and join us to fly off to the party of your life...*". In this commercial, alcohol consumption was clearly linked to the festive atmosphere but, according to the JEP, the ad did not suggest that it was a necessity for partying.[45]

- *With respect to the target audience,* not only may the ad not be directed towards children, it may not target pregnant women either. An instance of the latter occurred in a radio spot featuring a telephone conversation between two brewers of Brewery X and a pregnant woman. The latter asked the men whether drinking their brand beer could cause her any harm, even though she was pregnant with twins. The brewers responded jokingly that there was no risk except that of getting a beer belly.[46]
- *Concerning the media used,* the Code contains an appendix setting out specific rules according to the type of communication channel used and alcoholic beverage advertised. For example, depending on the type of alcoholic beverage, the promotion has to include an educational slogan such as: "*Taste our know-how wisely*" or "*Beer brewed carefully, to be consumed with care*". The positioning of such slogans as well as their font, size, colour, timing, etc. depends on the communication channel used and is detailed in Appendix B to the Code. It is of note that most

45 JEP decision of 4 July 2013 (Carlsberg).

46 JEP decision of 27 May 2003 (Interbrew).

complaints that the JEP receive about alcoholic beverages concern the absence of the required educational slogan.[47]

b. Sugary sweets (candy)

As previously explained, advertising on radio and television is regulated at the Belgian Community level. Only the Flemish Decree on radio and television[48] requires ads for sugary sweets on television to conspicuously display one of the following logos[49]:

47 JEP decisions: 7 July 2010 (AB Inbev), 21 December 2006 (Fourcroy), 21 November 2007 (Fourcroy), 8 January 2007 (Gazet van Antwerpen), 13 December 2011 (Havana Distribution), 8 December 2010 (Hubo), 5 August 2002 (Interbrew), 9 December 2012 (Coolcoups); 12 December 2005 (Delhaize), 5 December 2006 (Delhaize); 22 November 2011 (Diageo); 18 March 2004 (Duvel Moortgat); 22 April 2009 (Ets. P. Bruggeman); 22 June 2012 (Brouwerij Haacht); 27 September 2006 (Brouwerij Alken Maes); 4 October 2004 (Bockor Brouwerij); 2 April 2008 (Carlsberg); 4 June 2008 (Carlsberg); 18 December 2006 (Moët Hennesy); 1 September 2011 (Brouwerij Alken Maes); 16 October 2010 (J. Portugal Ramos Vinhos S.A.); 4 May 2008 (Jet Import); 11 October 2006 (La Libre); 20 December 2006 (La Libre); 20 June 2006 (La Libre); 15 February 2006 (Laurent Perrier); 21 December 2006 (Laurent Perrier); 15 December 2010 (Lejay Lagoute); 24 October 2008 (Maxxium); 24 March 2013 (Pernod Ricard Belgium); 5 January 2007 (Recto Recto); 8 April 2011 (Saipm); 2 November 2011 (Stad Antwerpen); 20 December 2006 (Vins de Bordeaux); 4 July 2013 (Bacardi Martini).

48 Flemish Decree of 27 March 2009 on radio and television broadcasting, *Official Belgian Gazette* 30 April 2009, Art. 69.

49 Such logo has to be clearly visible throughout the whole relevant commercial in a proportion of 1/10 of the height of the frame used for the commercial.

c. Butter, butter products, margarine and low fat margarine

In stores where margarine, low fat margarine or cooking fat are offered for sale together with butter or butter products[50], the latter two must be clearly separated from other edible fats to avoid any confusion.[51]

Except in the list of ingredients, it is prohibited to make any reference to egg yolk, whey or whey powder in the advertising of margarine or low fat margarine.[52]

To further avoid the risk of confusion, no illustrations or pictures of animals, people, tools or devices that evoke the production process or the marketing of butter or butter products[53] may be used to advertise other fats such as margarine.[54]

d. Lemonade

When advertising lemonades, it is prohibited to use images representing fruits unless the lemonade contains a minimum 10 % of fruit juice.[55]

This prohibition, however, does not apply to lemonades that have been legally manufactured and/or put on the market in other EU Member States, in

50 Meaning butter extract, ghee, water free milk fat and butter of low fat milk – see Royal Decree of 6 May 1988 regarding butter and butter products, *Official Belgian Gazette* 3 June 1988 Art. 7.

51 Royal Decree of 2 October 1980 concerning the production and marketing of margarine and dietary fats, *Official Belgian Gazette,* 14 October 1980, Art. 6.

52 Royal Decree of 2 October 1980 concerning the production and marketing of margarine and dietary, *op cit.*, Art. 5 § 2.

53 Meaning butter extract, ghee, water free milk fat and butter of low fat milk – see Royal Decree of 6 May 1988 regarding butter and butter products, *Official Belgian Gazette* 3 June 1988, Art. 6.

54 Royal Decree of 6 May 1988 regarding butter and butter products, *Official Belgian Gazette,* 3 June 1988, Art. 6.

55 Royal Decree of 4 October 1995 concerning lemonades, *Official Belgian Gazette* 30 December 1995, Art. 3 § 5.

Turkey or in countries that have co-signed the Agreement on the European Economic Area.[56]

Another restriction prohibits the mention, in the advertising of lemonade, of the fact that natural mineral water or spring water has been used unless the following cumulative conditions are met:[57]

(1) The natural mineral water or spring water must comply with the applicable requirements;

(2) The water that is used in the production process must exclusively be one kind of natural mineral water or spring water;

(3) The name of the spring must be indicated on the labelling and advertising of the product;

(4) The product must be produced at the place where the spring is exploited; and

(5) Any reference to the special properties of the natural mineral water or the spring water is prohibited.

Contrary to the restriction mentioned in section 1, this prohibition remains applicable even for lemonades that have been legally manufactured and/or put on the market in other EU Member States, in Turkey or in countries that have co-signed the Agreement on the European Economic Area.[58]

---

56 Royal Decree of 4 October 1995 concerning lemonades, *op cit*, Art. 1 § 2.

57 Royal Decree of 4 October 1995 concerning lemonades, *op cit*, Art. 3 § 6.

58 Royal Decree of 4 October 1995 concerning lemonades, *op cit*, Art. 1 § 2.

3. Is the advertising of (certain) foodstuffs towards a specific section of the population restricted or prohibited by any national mandatory and/or soft law (e.g. code of conduct, case law)?

In the interest of the health of certain sections of the population requiring special care because of their age or situation, the advertising of foodstuffs targeting such persons is restricted and, for some foodstuffs, even prohibited. In Belgium the vast majority of these restrictions and prohibitions are designed to protect minors and, to a lesser extent, pregnant women, the elderly and the sick.

a. Minors

In addition to general rules on advertising of foodstuffs aimed at minors, there are, in Belgium, specific rules on advertising alcoholic beverages towards minors.

i. Advertising of foodstuffs directed towards minors in general

(a) Legislation

Although the Royal Decree on Food Advertising sets out the rules on the advertising of foodstuffs in general, it does not contain any restriction or prohibition that is specifically designed to protect the interests of minors.

The decrees on the audio-visual media of the various communities in Belgium, however, do contain such rules such as, for example, measures regarding product placement, sponsoring and the content of adverts.[59] These rules, however, also apply to the advertising of non-food products.

59 Flemish Decree of 27 March 2009 on radio and television broadcasting, *Official Belgian Gazette* 30 April 2009, Decree on the audio visual media services and film screenings, *Official Belgian Gazette* 6 September 2005 (of the German-speaking community) and the Coordinated Decree of 26 March 2009 on the audio visual services (of the French-speaking community) and the Coordinated Decree of 26 March 2009 on the audio visual services (of the French-speaking community).

Regarding ads for foodstuffs in general, only the Flemish Decree on radio and television broadcasting states that no audiovisual commercial communication on radio or television directed towards children and young persons may encourage excessive consumption or commend foods and beverages that contain elements such as fats, trans fats, salt and sugars, of which excessive consumption is not recommended.[60]

(b) Code of Conduct

The Code on the Advertising of Foodstuffs[61] contains various restrictions on the advertising of foodstuffs in general to minors, which apply to all those who adhere to the Code irrespective of the channel of communication used and the community where the advertising takes place. This Code does make a distinction between advertising aimed at children and advertising directed towards children and young persons.

With respect to,the advertising of foodstuffs directed at children (the age limit is, however, not specified):

- Food business operators may not use (live or stylized) images, familiar through the media, in such a way that the distinction between editorial or program content, and the advertising message to boost sales of the relevant foodstuff, becomes blurred.[62]
- It is prohibited to create a sense of urgency or minimize the price inappropriately.[63]
- The ad may not undermine the role of parents or of other adults responsible for the care of children concerning the choice of diet and lifestyle. In addition, it may not directly incite children to lobby their parents or

60 Flemish Decree of 27 March 2009 on radio and television broadcasting, *Official Belgian Gazette*, 30 April 2009, Art. 77.

61 See *supra* I.1.2.

62 Code on the Advertising of Foodstuffs, http://www.jep.be/media/pdf/sectoriele_code/FEVIA_nl.pdf, Art. 5.

63 Code on the Advertising of Foodstuffs, Art. 6.

other adults responsible for their care, to purchase the relevant advertised foodstuffs.[64]

- When an advertisement is set up in the form of a contest or the offering of a gift, it is important that the advertising is explained in language that children understand and that the children clearly comprehend what and how many products, as the case may be, are to be bought before they can receive a gift or participate in the contest.[65]

With respect to the advertising of foodstuffs directed at children and young persons, (the age limit is, however again, not specified):

- The use of fantasy including animation may not take advantage of children's and young persons' imaginations so as to mislead them about the nutritional advantages of the relevant foodstuff.[66]
- The ad may not make allusion to the status or popularity between peers, success at school, in sports or to intelligence.[67]

In 2012, another self-regulating initiative, known as '*The Belgian Pledge*[68], was set up by the Belgian Federation of the Food Industry[69], the Union of Belgian Advertisers[70] and Comeos.[71] The European Pledge largely inspired this Pledge.[72] Food business operators who have voluntarily signed up for this Belgian Pledge have made the following commitments:[73]

64 Code on the Advertising of Foodstuffs, Art. 7.

65 Code on the Advertising of Foodstuffs, Art. 8.

66 Code on the Advertising of Foodstuffs, http://www.jep.be/media/pdf/sectoriele_code/FEVIA_nl.pdf, Art. 9.

67 Code on the Advertising of Foodstuffs, Art. 10.

68 http://belgianpledge.be

69 FEVIA – www.fevia.be

70 UBA – www.ubabelgium.be

71 Association that represents Belgian trade and services.

72 http://www.eu-pledge.eu/

73 http://belgianpledge.be

- No advertising for food and beverage products to children under the age of twelve on TV, print and internet, except for products which specifically fulfil nutritional criteria based on accepted scientific evidence and/or applicable national and international dietary guidelines.
- No communication related to products in primary schools, except where specifically requested by, or agreed with, the school management for educational purposes.

ii. Advertising of alcoholic beverages directed at minors

(a) Legislation

As regards audiovisual media, the Flemish and German speaking communities[74] are, so far, the only ones to have implemented the following restriction set by the Audiovisual Media Services Directive[75]: audiovisual commercial communications for alcoholic beverages shall not be aimed specifically at minors and shall not encourage immoderate consumption of such beverages.

The Flemish Decree on radio and television[76] goes even further and prohibits any audiovisual commercial communications that show minors consuming alcoholic beverages. In addition, a television commercial for alcoholic beverage may not be broadcasted before or after programs for children, and such programs may not be sponsored by companies whose primary activity is the production or sale of alcoholic beverages.[77]

74 Flemish Decree of 27 March 2009 on radio and television broadcasting, *Official Belgian Gazette* 30 April 2009, Art. 68 and Decree on the audio visual media services and film screenings, *Official Belgian Gazette* 6 September 2005 (of the German-speaking community), Art. 6.1 § 3.

75 Directive 2010/13/EU of the European Parliament and of the Council of 10 March 2010 on the coordination of certain provisions laid down by law, regulation or administrative action in Member States concerning the provision of audiovisual media services (Audiovisual Media Services Directive), Arts. 9 and 22.

76 Flemish Decree of 27 March 2009 on radio and television broadcasting, *Official Belgian Gazette* 30 April 2009, Art. 68.

77 Flemish Decree of 27 March 2009 on radio and television broadcasting, *Official Belgian Gazette* 30 April 2009, Arts. 83 and 94.

(b) Code of conduct

Regarding soft law, however, the Code of conduct on the advertising of alcoholic beverages contains various restrictions in the interest of protecting minors. In addition to the restrictions referred to above, which this Code also covers, a number of other restrictions are further elaborated:

- The Code contains a number of restrictions as to the media used. With respect to radio or television, the Code prohibits the advertising of alcoholic beverages five minutes before and after a program destined for minors. The advertising in newspapers or magazines is also prohibited if their audience is primarily minors. In cinemas, it is forbidden to advertise alcoholic beverages during a film that is mainly for minors. The same rule applies to digital media that is primarily focused on minors.[78]
- With respect to the content of the ad, the Code goes further than the Flemish Decree on radio and television as it prohibits any advertisement for alcoholic beverages that shows one or more minors or people who appear to be minors, irrespective of whether they are consuming alcoholic beverages or not.[79]
- The ad may not represent the consumption of alcoholic beverages as a sign of maturity or its non-consumption as a sign of immaturity.[80] This was the case on a brewer's website, where an age-check application stated: "*You cannot choose your age, but if you are younger than 18 there are many other fun stuff to do. Making figures with bread dough, coloring with crayons or dress up like a wizard. Choose!*" [81]
- It is prohibited to take advantage of the lack of knowledge, inexperience or gullibility of minors.[82]

78 Code of Conduct on the Advertising of Alcoholic Beverages, http://www.jep.be/media/Alcoholconvenant%20NL%202013.pdf, Art. 11.

79 Code of Conduct on the Advertising of Alcoholic Beverages, Art. 4.2.

80 Code of Conduct on the Advertising of Alcoholic Beverages, Art. 4.3.

81 JEP decision 2 September 2011 (NV Brouwerij Alken Maes).

82 Code of Conduct on the Advertising of Alcoholic Beverages, Art. 4.4.

- Using drawings or marketing techniques that refer to characters that are popular with or well-known to minors or using images or allegations that are essentially part of young popular culture, to advertise alcoholic beverages, is also prohibited. Application of this prohibition was sought in a case where a poster, advertising an alcoholic beverage, contained a cartoon with a butcher holding his axe ready to slaughter a rooster. Since the character and other images in the cartoon were not considered to be especially popular with or well-known to minors, the advertisement was allowed. The JEP, however, recommended the advertiser to be particularly careful when using cartoons to advertise alcoholic beverages.[83]

  An infringement of this prohibition occurred in a supermarket publicity folder. Consumers were told that they could collect cards with images of characters from DreamWorks movies such as Shrek, Kung Fu Panda, etc. when purchasing the products in the relevant folder. Amongst these products were two adverts for beer.[84]

- Ads may not incite minors to hassle their parents or others responsible for them, to purchase alcoholic beverages, nor may they seek to take advantage of the special trust minors have in their parents, teachers of others in positions of trust.[85]

- Recommending alcoholic beverages to minors as a remedy for dangerous situations is also not allowed.[86]

b. Pregnant women

As explained above, under the Code on "the advertising of alcoholic beverages" ads may not be directed towards pregnant women.[87]

83 JEP decision 31 August 2007 (Etn. P. Bruggeman).

84 JEP decision 18 August 2013 (Delhaize).

85 Code of Conduct on the Advertising of Alcoholic Beverages, Arts. 4.6 and 4.7.

86 Code of Conduct on the Advertising of Alcoholic Beverages, Art. 4.8.

87 Code of Conduct on the Advertising of Alcoholic Beverages, Art. 6.3.

c. Elderly people or people that are ill

In the interest of elderly people or people who are ill, the Code on the Advertising of Alcoholic Beverages prohibits such advertising in social institutions and health care institutions, unless the ad appears in the catering facilities.[88]

II. Misleading Advertising

1. What are the national rules on misleading advertising with respect to foodstuffs?

The Belgian rules on the advertising of foodstuffs in general are determined by legislative acts as well as by codes of conduct. This is no different with respect to misleading advertising concerning foodstuffs.

a. Legislation

As an EU Member State, Belgium has implemented the Labelling Directive[89] relating to, amongst other things, the advertising of foodstuffs. This Directive contains several provisions on misleading advertising with respect to foodstuffs that are also covered in the new Regulation 1169/2011 on the provision of food information to consumers (hereinafter 'FIC Regulation').[90]

In particular:

(1) Advertising shall not be such as could mislead the purchaser to a material degree, particularly:

88 Code of Conduct on the Advertising of Alcoholic Beverages, Art. 2.2.

89 Directive 2000/13/EC on the approximation of the laws of the Member States relating to the labelling, presentation and advertising of foodstuffs, *op cit.*

90 Regulation (EU) No. 1169/2011 of 25 October 2011 on the provision of food information to consumers, *op cit,* Art. 7.

(i) as to the characteristics of the foodstuff and, in particular, as to its nature, identity, properties, composition, quantity, durability, origin or provenance, method of manufacture or production;

(ii) by attributing to the foodstuff effects or properties which it does not possess; and

(iii) by suggesting that the foodstuff possesses special characteristics when in fact all similar foodstuffs possess such characteristics.

(2) Subject to European Community provisions applicable to natural mineral waters and foodstuffs for particular nutritional uses, advertising may not attribute to any foodstuff the property of preventing, treating or curing a human disease, or refer to such properties.

The Belgian legislator has implemented these restrictions in the R.D. on Food Advertising.[91]

The Belgian Act of 6 April 2010 on market practices and consumer protection is also often used as a legal basis in judicial proceedings against misleading advertising of foodstuffs.[92] Although not specifically targeted at foodstuffs, but rather at goods and services in general, this Act contains a number of provisions prohibiting misleading advertising, in general, which are the implementation of Directive 2005/29/EC concerning unfair business-to-consumer commercial practices in the internal market and Directive 2006/114/EC concerning misleading and comparative advertising.[93]

91 Royal Decree of 17 April 1980 concerning the advertising of foodstuffs, *op cit.*, Art. 4.

92 Act of 6 April 2010 on market practices and consumer protection, *op cit.*

93 Directive 2005/29/EC of the European Parliament and of the Council of 11 May 2005 concerning unfair business-to-consumer commercial practices in the internal market and Directive 2006/114/EC of the European Parliament and of the Council of 12 December 2006 concerning misleading and comparative advertising.

b. Codes of conduct

The inter-professional Code on the Advertising of Foodstuffs does not merely repeat the legal provisions of the R.D. on Food Advertising but further interprets them from a more practical point of view:[94]

(1) The text, sound, and image of the advertisement for foodstuffs must present the properties of the product (such as the taste, size, content, nutritional advantage or the advantage for one's health) in a correct way and may not mislead consumers with respect to any of these properties.

(2) Tests about the taste or preference of consumers may not be used in a way that creates the perception of a certain statistical value if this value is not correct.

(2) Foodstuffs that are not intended to replace a meal may not be represented as such.

2. What are the national landmark cases regarding misleading advertising of foodstuffs?

Over the years, Belgian courts have been confronted with various food law matters. From time to time misleading advertising of foodstuffs has been at issue, to which the aforementioned rules were applied.

Indication of special properties while all similar products possess them

A Belgian supermarket offered for sale a fermented, partially skimmed milk containing various fruits. The packaging contained the following statement: "*Guaranteed without preservatives*".

An authorised Belgian association for professionals filed suit against the supermarket for, amongst other things, misleading advertising.

94 Code of Conduct on the Advertising of Foodstuffs, *op cit.*, Art. 4.

Thermic treatment of milk ensures its preservation. As a consequence, the court held that the statement *"Guaranteed without preservatives"* was misleading because it was obvious that thermic-treated fermented and partially skimmed milk does not contain any preservatives because none are needed. The absence of preservatives, therefore, was not a special characteristic of that product.[95]

Misleading due to the incorrect interpretation of tasting tests

A distributor of a brand of ice tea had stated in its advertisements that: *'Traditionally, ice teas were manufactured as a soft-drink, namely through low temperature bottling (15–20°C). The procedure requires the addition of preservatives that gives the product a bitter after-taste'.* The distributor emphasised that its ice tea was bottled at a high temperature making the use of preservatives needless. Another statement was that more than 60 % of consumers prefer the distributor's brand of ice tea to competing brands.

The market leader of ice teas filed suit because the advertising was incorrect and misleading. The first statement gave the impression that the market leader's ice tea brand contained preservatives, which was incorrect and thus misleading. The statement regarding the preference of more than 60 % of consumers was also challenged. Prior to this advertising campaign, a market study was carried out with 600 consumers comparing the distributor's ice tea with the ice tea of the market leader. When analysing these statistics the court discovered that the statistical value, namely a 60 % preference, was incorrect because it did not take into account the number of consumers that expressly indicated that they had no preference. As a result, the judge held that the advertising was misleading.[96]

In view of this case, it is not surprising that the inter-professional Code on the Advertising of Foodstuffs, contains a rule that taste or preference tests on consumers may not be used in a way that creates the perception of a certain statistical value if that value is incorrect.

95 President of the Commercial Court of Brussels 25 April 1986, RW 1986-87, 885, note G.L. Ballon.

96 Voorz. Kh. Brussel 18 October 1993, Jaarboek Handelspraktijken en mededinging 1993, note F. Domont-Naert.

Misleading by omission

An alternative product for cream was advertised on television and in some magazines stating that the product *"is made of vegetable fats"*.

The court was of the opinion that in the advertisement in question, the presence of vegetable fats was *the ingredient* upon which the advertisement sought to persuade consumers to purchase the product. The statement was, however, considered to amount to misleading advertising, since in reality the product was not only made of vegetable fats but also of animal fats. Even if the advertisement did not state *'exclusively made...'* it was, nevertheless, considered to be misleading because it gave the impression that the product contained only vegetable fats, and the consumer would, therefore, have purchased the product without knowing that it also contained animal fats.

One of the defence arguments was that the advert could not be misleading as the list of ingredients indicated the presence of animal fats. However, the court disagreed since the advertisement in question was not on the package itself but on television and in a magazine where the list of ingredients was not indicated.[97]

Misleading with respect to the production method used – identification of the consumer that could be deceived

A butcher advertised his meat, both inside and outside his shop, as being 'kosher' meat. However, as the meat was not ritually prepared in accordance with Hebrew requirements, two other butchers filed suit based upon misleading advertising.

The Court of First Instance was of the opinion that, since the butcher's clientele was largely of Arabic origin, the clientele only required the meat to be halal and not 'kosher'. The advertising of the meat as being 'kosher' did not mislead his clientele.

The Court of Appeal, however, overruled the decision at first instance, and stated that Muslims might also be misled if they purchased the 'so-called'

97 Brussels, 27 March 2007, Jaarboek Handelspraktijken en mededinging 2007, 140.

kosher meat in order to serve it, for example, to orthodox Jewish guests. Moreover, a Moroccan can be a Jew, requiring his/her meat to be 'kosher'. As a result, the advertisement was held to be misleading.[98]

Reference to yogurt as an ingredient of the product

This landmark case with respect to misleading advertising is discussed under section III because the case also covers some interesting labelling issues.

Cases regarding misleading advertising of foodstuffs have not only been submitted to the Belgian courts, but also to the JEP:

Misleading because it attributes effects or properties to the relevant product which the product does not possess

A poster showed the following computation: a glass of wine (image) + a mint (image) = the name of the brand of mints. The slogan on this poster read: *"Refreshing power mint"*. The public authorities filed a claim with the JEP because the advertisement gave the impression that the mint neutralizes the alcohol, which it does not.[99] Advertising is misleading if it attributes effects or properties to the relevant product that the product does not possess.

Misleading advertising despite explicit statement

In a television commercial for a cream dessert, five pistachio nuts come running, three of which jump into the cup of the cream dessert. Upon a complaint by a consumer, the JEP decided that, despite the fact that the product packaging mentioned *"with the taste of pistachio nuts"*, there was still the risk that consumers could be misled by the television commercial into thinking that the cream dessert contains pistachio nuts when it does not.[100]

---

98 Brussels, 12 September 2000, Jaarboek Handelspraktijken en mededinging 2000, 421.

99 JEP decision 17 December 2008 (Perfetti Van Melle).

100 JEP decision 21 November 2005 (Danone).

III. Mandatory Labelling: The Issue of the Product Name

1. Belgian context

In Belgium, there is much legislation that attributes specific mandatory definitions to certain foodstuffs. While some of them merely implement European requirements, most of them are essentially national.

This is the case, for instance, for bread[101], yogurt[102], cheese[103], lemonade[104], mustard[105], dairy farm products,[106] ice cream[107], fresh minced meat[108], cream[109], mayonnaise[110] and tea[111].

In principle, these national definitions should not preclude businesses in the food industry from using the name that they legally use for their products in another Member State.[112]

101 Royal Decree of 2 September 1985 on bread and other bread products (last amended on 6 July 2009).

102 Royal Decree of 18 March 1980 on yogurt and other fermented milk based products (last amended on 20 March 2012).

103 Royal Decree of 15/12/1932 on the rules for commerce of cheese (last amended on 10 August 1999).

104 Royal Decree of 4 October 1995 on lemonades (last amended on 18 July 1997).

105 Royal Decree of 14 October 1970 Royal Decree on mustard (last amended on 2 October 1980).

106 Royal Decree of 10 January 2001 instituting the definition of dairy farm products (last amended on 20 July 2006).

107 Royal Decree of 11 June 2004 on ice cream for human consumption (last amended on 8 June 2009).

108 Royal Decree of 8 March 1985 on the production and commercialisation of fresh minced meat (specific labelling requirements are provided for equine minced meat).

109 Royal Decree of 23 May 1934 on the trade in cream.

110 Royal Decree of 12 April 1955 on the trade in mayonnaise and similar products.

111 Royal Decree of 28 April 1999 on tea and tea extracts (last amended on 20 March 2012).

112 See Chapter 1.1. (section 2.2) and Chapter 1.2. (section 3).

There is even some vertical legislation in Belgium that goes further and contains provisions that expressly exclude from their scope, food products that are otherwise legally produced and/or commercialised in another Member State (including Turkey and EFTA treaty states). In those particular circumstances, food business operators may simply disregard the requirements laid down for the relevant products. This is the case, for instance, for bread, ice cream, tea and – to a certain extent –lemonades.

Despite this, the issue of the product name may still arise and hinder the free movement of goods. Such is the case when national regulations consider that given product names are intrinsically linked to essential characteristics covered by its own definitions.

Food business operators that wish to sell and promote their food products in Belgium must, therefore, double-check that the products in question may be promoted under the name legally used in the country of production, in particular with respect to the products mentioned below.

2. The specific case of yogurt

Particular attention should be paid to the term 'yogurt'. There is no European provision that defines the characteristics of yogurt, other than the fact that it is a dairy product.[113]

However, in Belgium, as in the vast majority of the EU countries, yogurt is characterised by the presence of two specific live lactic ferments in the final product. The CJEU recognised that this condition forms an essential characteristic for consumers. Therefore, if the product does not have these live lactic ferments, the CJEU considered that the relevant Member State has reasonable grounds to prohibit the use of the name since any additional

113 Regulation (EEC) No. 1898/87 of 2 July 1987 on the protection of designations used in the marketing of milk and milk products (OJ L 182, 3.7.1987, p. 36), Art. 2(3) and Annex.

descriptive information could not be sufficient to ensure correct information for consumers.[114]

The Court of Appeal of Brussels has ruled on an interesting case referring to this issue.[115] In that case, the issue related to the advertising of a vegetable spreadable fat marketed under the commercial name 'Yogorine' pertaining to the YOGOOD range of products (including the products Yogosalad and Yogonaise).

Competitors had introduced a cease-and-desist action and claimed that the promoter was making an illegal reference to the term 'yogurt'.

The four grounds relied on in the action, can be summarised as follows:

(1) *The name of the product: YOGOOD – YOGORINE:*

The competitors bringing the action first challenged the use of the commercial name 'Yogorine – Yogood' on the grounds that it illegally gave the erroneous impression that the products were dairy products. They based their claim on an infringement of European Regulation No. 1989/87 on milk and milk products that exhaustively lists the designations that may be used for milk products, including the term yogurt. This Regulation further states that a product that is not a milk product may not refer to milk or milk products (including yogurt) unless the milk product is an essential ingredient either in terms of quantity or characterises the final product.[116]

The court held that the name 'Yogorine – Yogood' refers to a milk product since it has a similar (even identical) pronunciation to the term 'yogurt'.

114 See, in this regard, CJEU, Case 298/87, 14 July 1988 *Smanor,* ECR, 1988, 4489 which ruled on a preliminary question concerning the prohibition of the use of the name 'deep-frozen yogurt' and the follow-up interpretative communication issued by the European Commission (1991) with respect to vinegar, yogurt and caviar (Commission interpretative communication of 15 October 1991 on the names under which foodstuffs are sold [OJ, 91/C270/02]).

115 Court of Appeal of Brussels, 29 May 1996, Danone & Belgian Federation of the milk industry v. Unilever Belgium n.v.) *Jaarboek Handelspraktijken Mededinging,* 1996, 74 (the decision confirmed the judgement in first instance pronounced by the President of the Commercial Court of Leuven on 2 August 1995).

116 Regulation No. 1898/87, *op cit.,* Art. 2(3).

The court found in favour of the complainants' position and ruled that the presence of only 10 % of yogurt in the final product does not amount to the milk product being an essential ingredient in terms of quantity or characteristic.

Therefore, the use of the commercial name 'Yogorine – Yogood' was held to be illegal and the removal of its mention from all labels and promotional materials was ordered.

(2) *The indication of yogurt in the list of ingredients:*

The list of ingredients mentioned '*yogurt (10 %)*'. It is worth noting that although the live lactic ferments were present at the beginning of the manufacturing process, they were no longer live in the final product.

In the issue at hand, the question was: '*With respect to the list of ingredients, must the food manufacturer mention the ingredients as they are characterised at the time of their entry in the manufacturing process or should it identify the ingredient on the basis of the characteristics it possesses in the final product?*

In other words, when yogurt, used as an ingredient, loses its essential characteristics in the course of the manufacturing process, will the manufacturer still be authorised to refer to the term 'yogurt' in the list of ingredients?

The Court of Appeal of Brussels held that ingredients listed on the label are those which have the characteristics as identified in the final product; failure to do so could cause the consumer to be misled.

The defendant was consequently ordered to replace the term '*yogurt (10 %)*' by '*heat-treated fermented milk (10 %)*' since the ingredient no longer contained live lactic ferments and could, therefore, no longer be identified as yogurt under Belgian law.

(3) *The claim 'prepared with yogurt':*

The product bore the claim 'prepared with yogurt'. The Court made a direct link between the fact that yogurt may not be listed within the list of ingredients and the – a fortiori – misleading claim '*prepared with yogurt*'.

The manufacturer was, therefore, ordered to remove any reference to this claim from the product labels and promotional campaign.

(4) The promotional campaign

The launch of the product was accompanied by a substantial promotional campaign in which the beneficial characteristics of yogurt and dairy products were given prominence.

As indicated above, a product may not claim to be prepared with dairy products if the milk product used is not an essential part, either in terms of quantity or for characterization of the final product. In addition, European and Belgian legislation state that the labelling and methods used must not be such as could mislead the purchaser to a material degree, particularly as to the characteristics of the foodstuff.[117]

Based on the combined application of these two pieces of legislation, the Court considered that the advertising in question was misleading since it gave the false impression that the vegetable spreadable fat, Yogorine, had a significant milk product content.

3. Dairy farm products

Still, in the sector of milk and milk products (e.g. cheese and yogurt), the terms, 'farmhouse product', 'from the farm' or 'farmer' (in the French and Dutch languages: '*de ferme*' or '*fermier*'/'*hoeve*'; '*paysan*'/'*boere*'), or any derivative or similar denomination, may only be used if the final product is exclusively manufactured on the same farm as that from which the milk originates.[118]

It is worth noting that this legislation does not provide for a mutual recognition clause, *i.e.* a clause that expressly allows products legally labelled in the Member State of production to be marketed under the same name in

117 Directive 2000/13, *op cit.*, Art. 2(1)(a)(i) and Royal Decree on Food Advertising, *op cit,* Art. 2(9).

118 Royal Decree of 10 January 2001 instituting the definition of dairy farm products (last amended on 20 July 2006), Arts. 2 & 3.

Belgium. As a consequence, it is likely that Belgian courts would take the view that, if the above conditions are not met, the claim will mislead the consumer, regardless of the origin of the product (domestic or imported). Unfortunately, there is no published case law that can confirm this.

4. Mustard, or how to characterise an ordinary 'colour, smell and flavour'

Belgium has implemented specific rules on the composition of mustard and related definitions. In addition to these definitions, one strange provision stands out and deserves attention: a mustard which has a colour, flavour, or smell which is *out of the ordinary,* is considered as harmful, thus effectively banning its commercial use.[119] It is obvious, however, that what is *'out of the ordinary'* is highly subjective, and how to determine what is ordinary in matters of personal taste, remains an open question.

5. Remarks with respect to energy and sport drinks

Energy drinks and sports drinks are not defined either at the European or Belgian national levels. Food business operators, therefore, have relative flexibility when it comes to identifying their products as 'energy drinks' or 'sport drinks' in compliance with the obligation to mention the name of the product on the label (once only).

119 Royal Decree on mustard, *op cit.*, Art. 5.

Claims that such products improve energy, however, are considered as nutritional or (non-specific) health claims (depending on context) and are, until now, not authorised under the EU Claims Regulation.[120]

To resolve this contradiction, the Belgian authorities have, therefore, tended to consider that although food business operators may identify their product under the name 'energy drink' or 'sport drink' (in French and/or Dutch), they may not use such terms more than once, i.e. beyond their legal obligation to mention the name on the label. This means that a repetition of the name on the label is prohibited and that no additional claim will be allowed (such as 'recover energy').

IV. Voluntary Labelling

1. "Clean labels" – Are there any national definitions or requirements for the use of the following claims?

a. Pure, natural & fresh

Until recently (April 2012), the use of the terms 'pure' or 'natural' and their derivatives was regulated under Belgian law: one could use such terms only if the foodstuff was not refined and was free of any pesticide residue.[121]

120 It should, however, be noted that the European Commission approved one claim with respect to glucose (stating: *'Carbohydrates contribute to the maintenance of normal brain function'* – In order to justify using the claim, information must be given to consumers that the beneficial effect is obtained with a daily intake of 130 g of carbohydrates from all sources. The claim may be used for food which contains at least 20 g carbohydrates, excluding polyols, which are metabolised by humans, per quantified portion and complies with the nutrition claim LOW SUGARS or WITH NO ADDED SUGARS as listed in the Annex to Regulation (EC) No. 1924/2006. The claim cannot be used on food which is 100 % sugars); Commission Regulation (EU) No. 1018/2013 of 23 October 2013 amending Regulation (EU) No. 432/2012 establishing a list of permitted health claims made on foods other than those referring to the reduction of risk of disease and to children's development and health (O.J.24 October 2013).

121 Royal Decree of 17 April 1980, *op. cit.*, Art. 3(2) before its modification by the Royal Decree of 29 March 2012.

Practical application of these requirements, however, was not accurately understood by all food business operators, and their enforcement was even ignored.

The Belgian government, therefore, decided to withdraw these requirements from the law. The clause was replaced by a provision announcing a separate legislative act that would set out the conditions for the use of claims 'pure', 'natural' and even 'fresh'.[122] To date, however, the authorities have not taken any legal initiative, and have not even adopted guidelines, albeit unofficial, in this regard.

When using these terms, food business operators must, therefore, assess the legality of the use of these terms on the basis of the general prohibition of misleading consumers and, in particular, of suggesting that a given foodstuff possesses special characteristics when there is nothing special which distinguishes it from all similar foodstuffs.[123]

It is interesting to note that, in this regard, the JEP (Belgian advertising standards self- regulatory body – see section 1) was requested to rule on a complaint about a reference to the freshness of a product.[124]

In the absence of any legal definition or guidelines in Belgium relating to this, the JEP based its decision on the guidelines issued by the Food Standards Agency in the U.K.

The advertisement for the product in question – a pasteurised vegetable soup – invited the public to '*take advantage of the tasty fresh vegetables*' ('*geniet van de heerlijk verse groenten*').

Basically, the soup was made with vegetables that are harvested annually, and then washed and frozen. They were then added, in their frozen state, to the soup and immediately pasteurized in order to avoid deterioration and extend their shelf life.

122 Royal Decree of 29 March 2012 modifying the R.D. of 17 April 1980 on Food Advertising, Art. 3.

123 See Directive No. 2000/13, *op cit.*, Art. 2. For more detail, see the introductory chapter of this book, *Advertising food in Europe: Setting the scene.*

124 JEP 5 March 2008 (Unilever [Knorr]).

The JEP considered that the claim used in the ad was misleading for consumers regardless of the fact that they are usually reasonably well-informed, observant and circumspect and should, therefore, know that the product contains preservatives. It stated that the manner in which the claim was presented was too absolute since, once the vegetables have undergone a specific processing, they can no longer be referred to as 'fresh'.

The JEP based its reasoning on that adopted by the Food Standard Agency in its guidelines on criteria for the use of the terms fresh, pure, natural, and other similar claims.[125]

The JEP took the following criteria into account:

- *The term can also be helpful when used to identify products that have not been processed. In these cases it is important to be clear what is meant by processing: excluding the use of chill temperatures and other controlled atmospheres for the delayed ripening and/or extended storage of fruit and vegetables or washing and trimming would seem unnecessarily restrictive.*
- *The term "fresh" is now used generically to indicate that fruit and vegetables have not been processed, rather than that they have been recently harvested. This is acceptable provided it is not used in such a way as to imply the product has been recently harvested (e.g. "fresh from the farm" or "freshly picked") if this is not the case.*
- *The term "fresh" may be used to describe fruit and vegetables that have been washed and/or trimmed, provided that the fact they have been washed and/or trimmed is also indicated.*

b. Homemade ('artisanal') / Grandmother's recipe

Again, the use of the term 'homemade' in Belgium is characterised by the lack of legal requirements.

125 Criteria for the use of the terms fresh, pure, natural, etc. in food labeling – see, in particular, provisions 18, 25 and 26; available on the FSA website at: http://www.food.gov.uk/multimedia/pdfs/markcritguidance.pdf.

It is only vey recently that the Belgian legislator defined an 'artisan's' activity (Belgian act of 14 March 2014).[126] The aim of this legal text is to protect artisan professions and to lay down the conditions that will apply to their activities. It is worth noting that, as a result of industry lobbying, that legislation expressly excludes from its scope any impact on the definition of 'homemade' or 'artisanal' claims with respect to food products.[127]

As a result, when referring to the homemade character of their products, food business operators must go back to basics and assess the legality of such claims in the context of the general prohibition of misleading consumers.

The JEP had the opportunity of giving a ruling on a TV-spot made by a well-known multi-national.[128] The advertising at issue showed 'vintage images' of a woman preparing a vanilla flavoured pudding. The ad mentioned, amongst other things, the manufacturer's 'unrivalled technique' ('*inimitable tour de main*'/'inimitabel *handbeweging*'). The JEP considered that this referred to the producer's know-how rather than, in this context, to a particular human gesture. It added that the consumer could not be misled into thinking it referred to the industrial method of production since the manufacturer in question is a well-known multi-national, from which the consumer could not expect to purchase a 'homemade' product.

This decision displays a clear link between the degree of knowledge that the average consumer may have about the advertiser/manufacturer and his perception of a particular advertisement. It should be noted that the reasoning, based on this link, is contrary to the one adopted by the JEP concerning the 'freshness' claim referred to above.[129]

126 Belgian act of 19 March 2014 on the definition of 'artisan (Belgian Gazette, 15.04.2014, p. 32311).

127 See the opinion of the Council of State dated 18 October 2013 which defines the scope of the legislation as follows: 'This act *defines the notion of artisan or artisanal enterprise. It does not aim to define the home-made character of products or services*'..

128 JEP, 23 November 2010 (Nestlé Belgilux [La Laitière]).

129 See section 4.1(a) above – JEP 5 March 2008 (Unilever [Knorr]).

c. Farmhouse products

With respect to milk and milk products (e.g. cheese and yogurt), the terms 'farmhouse product', 'from the farm' or 'farmer' (in French/Dutch languages: '*de ferme*' or '*fermier*'/'*hoeve*'; '*paysan*'/'*boere*') or any derivative or similar denomination, may only be used if the final product is manufactured exclusively on the same farm as that from which the milk originated.[130]

The relevant legislation makes no provision for a mutual recognition clause, i.e. a clause that expressly allows products, legally labelled in the Member State of production, to be marketed under the same name in Belgium. It is therefore likely that Belgium will consider that if the above conditions are not met, the claim could mislead consumers.

d. Other similar claims related to "clean labels" (e.g. 'additive-free')

The claims such as '**additive-free**' or '**preservative free**' are not specifically regulated in Belgium. When using these terms, one must refer to the general prohibition of misleading consumers and, in particular, of suggesting that the foodstuff in question possesses special characteristics when in fact all similar foodstuffs possess those characteristics.

This may be the case for products where the adjunction of additives is illegal such as, for example, in the case of most organic foodstuffs or honey.

With respect to clean labelling, food business operators also tend to surf on the wave of '**palm oil-free**'. Depending on the context of the claim, this may refer either to an environmental claim (reference to the sustainable method of production) or to the nutritional benefit of the product. In the latter case, the Belgian authorities consider that the claim falls under the scope of the EU Claims Regulation and has the same meaning for consumers as the nutrition claim 'Low Saturated Fat'. Therefore, a product which claims to be 'palm oil-free' must – in addition to being free of palm oil – also contain a maximum of 1,5 g of saturated fatty acids and trans-fatty

130 Royal Decree of 10 January 2001 instituting the definition of dairy farm products (last amended on 20 July 2006), Arts. 2 & 3.

acids per 100 g of solids or 0,75 g/100 ml for liquids and, in either case, the sum of saturated fatty acids and trans-fatty acids must not account for more than 10 % of the energy.[131]

2. Nutrition & health claims

a. Within the list of health claims authorised pursuant to Regulation 1924/2006, are there any related substances that are prohibited or considered as a medicinal substances within your jurisdiction?

Although the classification of a substance has to be determined on a case-by-case basis, products containing the following substances are generally regarded as medicinal products in Belgium[132]:

- **Lactulose**: The related claim is '*Lactulose contributes to an acceleration of intestinal transit*'. The claim may, however, be made only for food which contains 10 g of lactulose in a single quantified portion.[133] In these quantities, lactulose is generally regarded as a medicinal product in Belgium.
- **Melatonin**: The claim authorised by the European Commission with respect to the melatonin is '*Melatonin contributes to the reduction of time taken to fall asleep*'.[134]

---

131 Regulation No. 1924/2006, *op cit.*, Annex.

132 Source: Federal Public Service Health, Food Chain Safety and Environment, available on the Internet through: http://www.health.belgium.be/eportal/foodsafety/advertising/index.htm?fodnlang=fr.

133 In order to justify using the claim, information must be given to consumers that the beneficial effect is obtained with a single serving of 10 g of lactulose per day – See Commission Regulation (EU) No. 432/2012 of 16 May 2012 establishing a list of permitted health claims made on foods, other than those referring to the reduction of the risk of disease and to children's development and health, as recently amended by Commission Regulation (EU) No. 1018/2013 of 23 October 2013.

134 See Regulation No. 432/2012, *op cit.*

b. Are there any national laws and regulations permitting food business operators to make reference to recommendations or endorsements by national associations, medical, nutrition or dietetic professionals, and health-related charities?

References to recommendations or statement of health professionals are allowed to the strict extent that such recommendations or statements relate to claims that have been duly authorised under the EU Claims Regulations.[135]

c. Are there any national laws or regulations regulating the use of nutrition or health claims on non-pre-packaged food?

Belgium has not added any other requirement concerning the use of nutritional or health claims made on non-pre-packaged food.

As a consequence, when a food business operator claims the nutritional or health benefit of a non-pre-packaged foodstuff in Belgium, it is not required to provide nutritional information to consumers, nor state the importance of a varied and balanced diet and a healthy lifestyle and the quantity of the food and pattern of consumption required to obtain the claimed beneficial effect (as would be the case for pre-packaged food).

d. Is there a notification procedure required prior to/for marketing foodstuffs bearing nutritional or health claims?

As indicated in Chapter 2, the EU Claims Regulation enables Member States to require that the manufacturer or the person placing the relevant product on the market, give prior notification of the product labels bearing nutrition or a health claims.

To date, Belgium has not put such a system in place.

135 See R.D. on food advertising – to be read in combination with Articles 12(3) and 11 of the EU Claims Regulation.

Such prior notification procedure, however, exists with respect to fortified foods[136] and food supplements[137] when it is intended to place them on the Belgian market. As the authorities will verify, amongst other things, the labels to be placed on these products effectively constitutes a monitoring of the intended nutrition or health claims for the product.

V. Enforcement of Food Law and Self-regulating Bodies

1. Which actions may one risk in case of non-compliance with the labelling or advertising requirements?

a. Public authorities

When a food business operator is in violation of food labelling or advertising requirements, it exposes itself to a broad spectrum of sanctions that can be imposed by officials of the Federal Agency for the Safety of Food Chain (hereinafter the 'FASFC'), officials of the Federal Public Service Economy (hereinafter 'FPS Economy') and the criminal courts. The spectrum of sanctions is spread over the following legislative acts:

- The Belgian Penal Code;
- Act of 24 January 1977 concerning the protection of the health of consumers with respect to foodstuffs and other products, *Official Belgian Gazette* 8 April 1977;
- Royal Decree of 17 April 1980 concerning the advertising of foodstuffs, *Official Belgian Gazette* 6 May 1980;

136 Royal Decree of 3 March 1992 on the market placement of nutrients and foodstuffs where nutrients have been added (last amended on 5 August 2006).

137 Royal Decree of 3 March 1992, *op cit.* and Royal Decree of 29 August 1997 on the manufacturing and marketing of foodstuffs consisting of or containing plant or plant preparations (last amended on 19 March 2012).

- Royal Decree of 22 February 2001 on the organisation of the inspections performed by the FASFC[138] (hereinafter the 'R.D. on FASFC inspections'); and
- Act of 6 April 2010 concerning market practices and consumer protection, *Official Belgian Gazette* 12 April 2010 (hereinafter the 'Act on MPCP').

When the officials of the FASFC or FPS Economy discover or become aware of a violation of food labelling or advertising requirements, they will draft an official report in this respect.[139]

i. Warning

At their own discretion, the FASFC or FPS Economy officials can give the infringing food business operator a warning with a request to cease the infringement.[140] From the nature of this action, it can be understood that a warning will generally be sent for minor and or first infringements.

In case the officials deem a warning to be appropriate, they will communicate it together with the official report and provide the infringer a period to cease the infringement. If the warning is being ignored, the official report on the infringement will be communicated to the official authorised to impose an administrative fine (see *supra* V.1.1(b)) and even the public prosecutor will be informed thereof.[141]

138 Royal Decree of 22 February 2001 on the organisation of the inspections performed by the FFSA, *Official Belgian Gazette* 28 November 2001 (hereinafter the 'R.D. on FFSA inspections').

139 Act on MPCP, Art. 133 and R.D. on FASFC inspections, Art. 5.

140 Act on MPCP, Art. 123 and R.D. on FASFC inspections, Art. 5.

141 Act on MPCP, Art. 123 and R.D. on FASFC inspections, Art. 5.

ii. Administrative fines

Instead of a warning or when the food business operator ignores the warning it received, the authorised officials of the FASFC or FPS Economy can impose an administrative fine.[142] By paying the administrative fine the food business operator avoids prosecution. Absence of payment will result in the transfer of the file to the public prosecutor.[143]

The amount of the administrative fine will be determined by the authorised official, but must be between the minimum and maximum set by law, namely between 25 EUR and 100,000 EUR.[144]

However, it is important to bear in mind that, in Belgium, the amounts of all criminal fines are subject to surcharges. As a result, a criminal fine of 'minimum 100 EUR and maximum 2,000 EUR' has to be multiplied by six[145] and will thus be a criminal fine of 'minimum 600 EUR and maximum 12,000 EUR'. This multiplication should also be taken into account when calculating the amount of the administrative fine.[146]

This type of sanction is common practice not only for the enforcement of food labelling or advertising requirements but also for food law in general. In more than 80 % of the food law cases that are dealt by the FASFC per year, an administrative sanction is proposed. The graphics below are based on the annual reports of the FASFC.[147]

142 Act on MPCP, Art. 136 and R.D. on FASFC inspections, Art. 7.

143 Act on MPCP, Art. 136 and R.D. on FASFC inspections, Art. 7.

144 Act on MPCP, Art. 136, Royal Decree of 27 April 1993 concerning the settlement of the infringement of the Act on the market practices and on the information and protection of the consumer and R.D. on FASFC inspections, Art. 7.

145 As from 1 January 2012 the amounts of the criminal fines have to be multiplied by 6 (Act of 5 March 1952 on surcharges on criminal fines).

146 Such calculation is not required for the administrative fine under the Act on Market Practices and Consumer Protection, *op cit.*, Art. 136.

147 http://www.afsca.be/publications-en/annualreport.asp

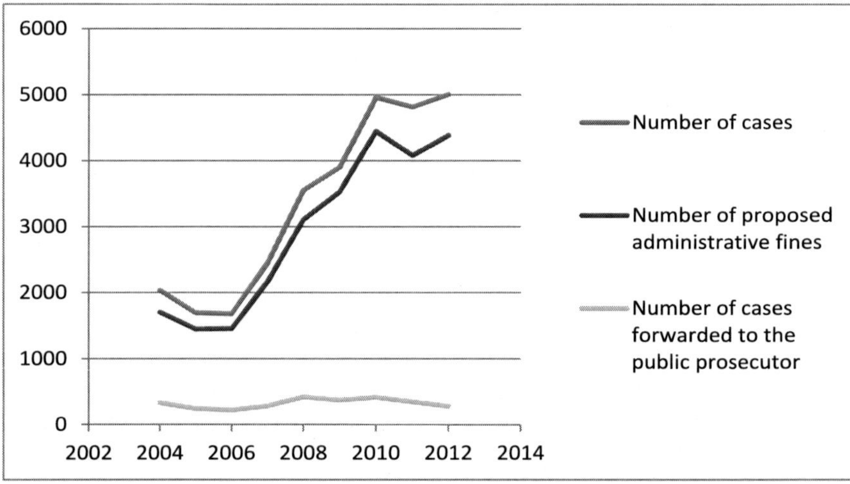

Over the years, the number of FASFC cases with respect to food law in general has increased. As the number of proposed administrative fines has also increased in a similar way, it not surprising that the total amount of proposed administrative fines has also increased (see graphic below). Over the last eight years, the average administrative fine proposed per case has fluctuated between 505 EUR and 666 EUR, but it remains difficult to assess whether such an average adequately represents the value of administrative fines that are usually imposed by the FASFC.

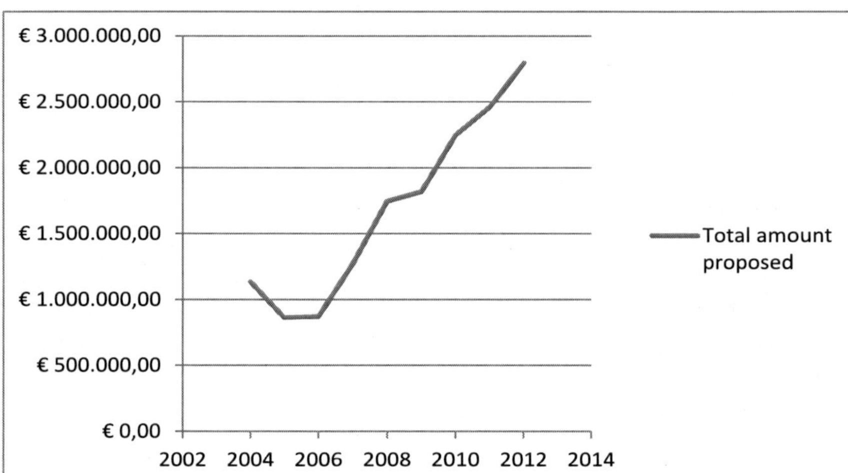

iii. Criminal sanctions

As indicated above, only the timely payment of the proposed administrative fine avoids the risk of prosecution when the food business operator violates food labelling or advertising requirements. Depending on the type of infringement, the food business operator may risk a criminal fine and/or imprisonment. The value of criminal fines for infringements of food labelling or advertising requirements ranges between 156 EUR[148] and 120,000 EUR[149] (including the surcharges. Imprisonment, on the other hand, varies between eight days and five years. However, imprisonment is rather exceptional.

If, for example, images of a dentist are used in the promotion of food[150], the food business operator may risk a criminal fine of minimum 600 EUR and maximum 90,000 EUR (surcharges included) and/or imprisonment between one month and one year. The persons involved in the distribution of the advertisement, such as a publisher, a broadcasting organisation, etc. will not be held criminally liable if they reveal the name of the person in Belgium who is the author or who took the initiative to distribute the advertisement.

iv. Preventive attachment & rendering unusable

If the products of a food business operator are, for example, incorrectly labelled, the products can be subject to preventive attachment by the FASFC officials.[151]

Depending on the situation and in the interest of public health, the products can subsequently be destroyed, processed, rendered unusable, sold or returned to the owner.[152]

148 For example, Act of 24 January 1977 concerning the protection of the health of consumers with respect to foodstuffs and other products, B.S. 8 April 1977, Art. 13.

149 For example, act on MPCP, Art. 125.

150 See R.D. on Food Advertising, Art. 2.5°.

151 R.D. on FASFC inspections, Art. 6 § 1.

152 R.D. on FASFC inspections, Art. 6 § 3.

b. Food business operators / competitors

A food business operator is often more sensitive to its competitor's advertising or labelling, certainly when the former complies with the relevant requirements while its competitor does not. Under the Belgian legal framework, various actions are available to food business operators. The strategic choice of which action to take depends on the goal, urgency, costs and whether damage or loss has been incurred.

i. File a complaint

As a food business operator, one may file a complaint with the FASFC and/or the FPS Economy. In such case the officials of the FASFC or the FPS Economy who receive the complaint will assess whether the complaint is founded. If so, they will decide whether any of the aforementioned sanctions should be imposed.

For the filing of such complaint, no fees or costs are charged by the FASFC or the FPS Economy. The downside, however, is that unless another form of action is taken in parallel, one has no control as to whether the FASFC or the FPS Economy will impose a sanction and, if so, within which timeframe. In addition, if the aim is to obtain compensation for damage or loss, filing a complaint with the FASFC or the FPS Economy will not be the proper action to take.

ii. File a criminal complaint

Aside from a complaint with the FASFC or the FPS Economy, one may also file a criminal complaint with the police or the public prosecutor's office. Later, during the criminal proceedings, the plaintiff may intervene as an 'injured' party.

If from the start, the plaintiff wishes to be indicated as an injured party due to having incurred damages, the plaintiff may directly file the criminal complaint with the examining magistrate. In this case, the examining magistrate may request a security deposit.

When holding a defendant guilty, the criminal courts may impose a criminal sanction and may grant the injured party compensation for the damage or loss incurred. The downside of filing a criminal complaint is that these are lengthy proceedings and therefore not recommended for urgent matters. In addition, once filed, one has limited control over the complaint during the various stages of the criminal proceedings.

iii. Initiate civil proceedings for damages

To claim compensation for damage or loss incurred as a result of e.g. the misleading advertising by a competitor, proceedings on the merits can be initiated. In commercial matters, the average duration of a case of first instance varies between nine and eighteen months; at the appellate level, it may take even longer. The duration strongly depends on the complexity of the matter at hand and the backlog of the relevant court.

iv. Initiate summary proceedings

These proceedings entitle the claimant to obtain an order awarding interim relief, which will remain valid until a decision on the merits is rendered. Two requirements have to be met for an interim relief order to succeed: the case must be urgent and the requested order must be provisional.

The latter means that it may not cause any prejudice to the merits of the case. An example might be the urgent appointment of an expert to record evidence of any infringement to avoid its disappearance.

v. Initiate injunction proceedings

These proceedings are common practice when confronted with issues such as misleading advertising. They entitle the claimant to obtain a decision on the merits (a cease-and-desist order) in specific matters[153] but following the rules of summary proceedings.

In addition, and to compel the losing party to abide by the injunction, the court can impose a penalty fine for non-compliance, which will be due if the losing party does not comply with the injunction in a timely fashion or

153 Such as the Act of 6 April 2010 on Market Practices and Consumer Protection. Please note that these kinds of proceedings are not open to mere contractual matters.

if it continues to perform actions in infringement of the order. In practice, such fines often range from 1,000 EUR to 50,000 EUR per infringement (per day). Another common practice in injunction proceedings is that the losing party is ordered to publish the whole, a part or a summary of the relevant judgment in a few newspapers or journals.

c. Consumers / consumer associations

Although the aforementioned actions for food business operators are also available to consumers, in practice, the actual actions of consumers are rather limited to:

(1) filing a complaint with the FASFC or the FPS Economy, and

(2) informing and requesting a consumer association to take action and file a complaint with the JEP.

Under the Belgian Judicial Code, each party to proceedings must autonomously exercise its own rights and interests.[154] Proceedings brought by consumer / (inter) professional associations are not admissible since their interest is not the personal interest of the association, but the mere sum of the personal interests of its members. However, the Act on MPCP provides an exception hereto. It allows professional organisations and recognised consumer associations to commence injunction proceedings for the benefit of the collective interest of its members, although without the right to claim damages.

In addition, consumer / (inter) professional associations can also file a claim with the JEP.

2. Are there any national self-regulating / disciplinary bodies with respect to advertising for a.o. foodstuffs?

In the past, the food industry has taken several self-regulating initiatives such as the Code on the Advertising of Foodstuffs or the Code of Conduct on the Advertising of Alcoholic Beverages. The food industry appointed

154 Arts. 17 and 18 of the Belgian Judicial Code.

the Jury for Ethical Practices on Advertising ('JEP'), an independent self-disciplinary body[155], with the task of enforcing these codes.

The JEP's remit is advertising via mass media[156] and direct mail. Its decisions are based on legislation, self-disciplinary codes (such as the aforementioned ones) and the Consolidated ICC Code on Marketing and Advertising.[157]

Proceedings brought before the JEP are initiated by way of a complaint submitted by consumers, consumer associations, socio-cultural associations, (inter) professional associations, or members or representatives of the public authorities. In addition, the President of the JEP may also initiate proceedings upon his or her own initiative or upon the initiative of one or more of the Jury members.[158]

The filing of a complaint is free of charge. However, filing an appeal against the first instance decision of the JEP requires a deposit of 500 EUR from the relevant advertiser or 30 EUR from the one who filed the complaint.[159]

When confronted with a complaint, the JEP can take three types of decisions:[160]

(1) In case of no infringement, the JEP can declare the complaint unfounded;

(2) In case of infringement, the JEP can request the advertiser to adapt or to cease the relevant advertisement. In addition hereto, the JEP can request the advertiser to present its next campaign to the JEP before launching it.

However, if the advertiser does not adapt or cease the advertisement, the JEP will request the media and/or relevant professional associations to cease the relevant advertising.

155 The JEP was created by the Council on Advertising which is an association of representative organizations of advertisers, media and publicity agencies.

156 Including television, radio, posters, Internet, etc.

157 Rules of the JEP of 2 January 2013, http://www.jep.be/media/JEP%20Reglement%20NL%202013.pdf, Art. 1.

158 Rules of the JEP of 2 January 2013, Art. 5.

159 Rules of the JEP of 2 January 2013, Art. 5.

160 Rules of the JEP of 2 January 2013, Art. 2.

(3) As it is not the JEP's intention to either censor or promote a certain taste or ideology, the JEP can formulate an advice of reservation. With such an advice the JEP leaves it up to the media and (inter)professional associations to decide.

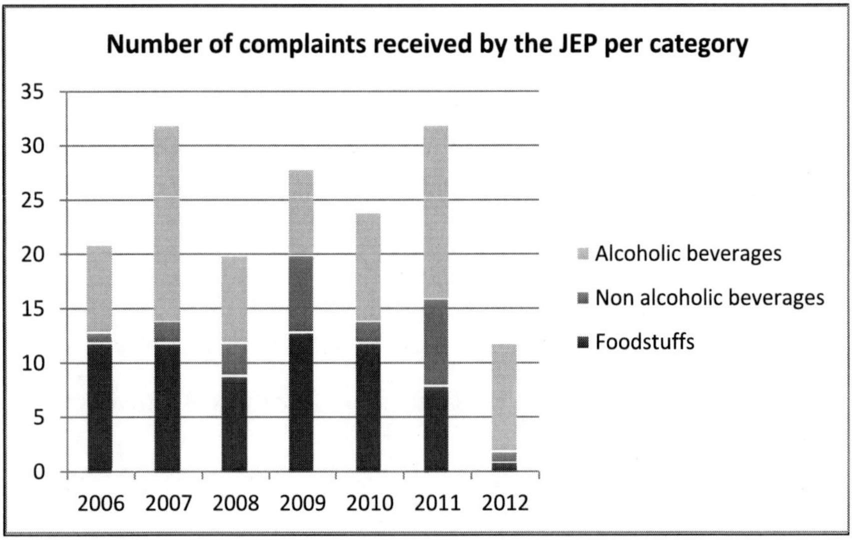

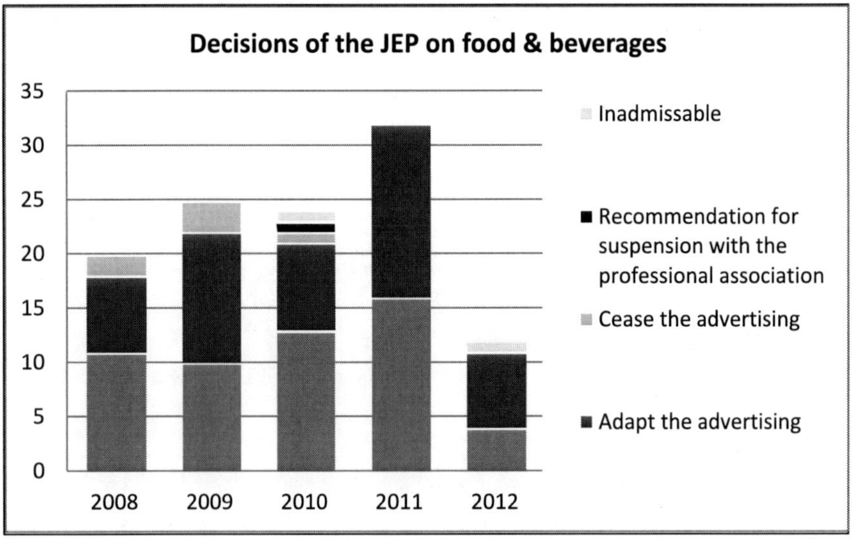

Summaries of the JEP's decisions are freely accessible on its website.[161]

In case the advertiser does not comply with the JEP's final decision to adapt or cease the advertisement, the Code of Conduct on the Advertising of Alcoholic Beverages provides for an extra sanction that is due without further notice[162], without prejudice to the actions the JEP can take:

(1) A fixed fee of 50 EUR to be paid to the JEP in case the educational slogan is missing or is not in accordance with the requirements set by the Code.

(2) A fixed fee of 1,000 EUR to be paid to the JEP per day that the advertiser does not comply with the JEP's decision. Any member adhering to the Code may initiate legal proceedings too with a view to ordering the relevant advertiser to pay this fixed fee.

Furthermore, the Code of Conduct on the Advertising of Alcoholic Beverages stipulates that in case of recidivism, the advertiser can be ordered to systematically present its future campaigns to the JEP for a period to be determined by the JEP but for a minimum of 12 months.[163]

161 www.jep.be

162 Code of Conduct on the Advertising of Alcoholic Beverages, Art.13.2.

163 Code of Conduct on the Advertising of Alcoholic Beverages, Art.13.3.

In case of doubt regarding a food advertisement, it can be helpful to seek the advice of the JEP. Such advice costs 100 EUR; however, it is a mere indication and does not guarantee that the advertising is free of risk.[164]

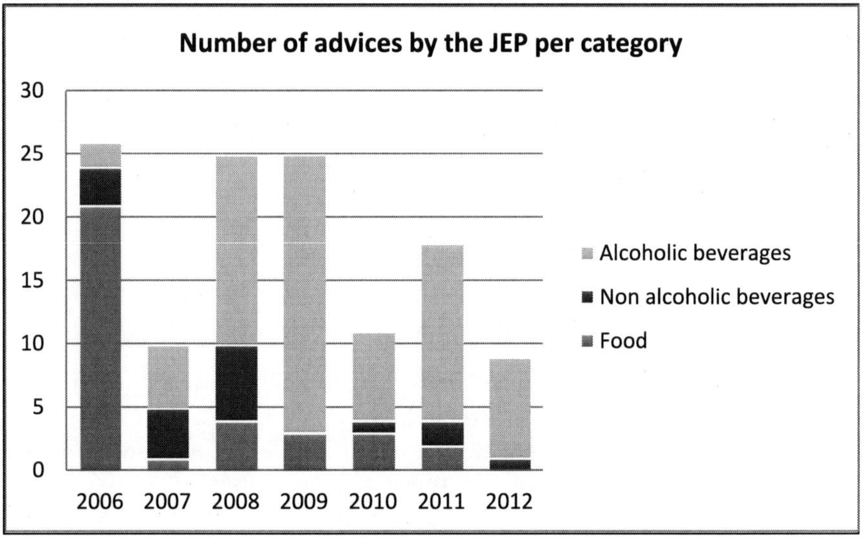

164 Rules of the JEP of 2 January 2013, Art. 13.

CHAPTER 5
Denmark

Martin Draebye Gantzhorn and
Christian Marquard Svane

DK

I. Possible Bans on Food Advertising

1. Is there any general national legislation or code of conduct regulating the promotion of foodstuffs?

a. Introduction

The advertising and promotion of foodstuffs in Denmark is subject to the horizontal provisions of the Marketing Practices Act[1] (as well as the provisions of the Danish Food Act.[2] Furthermore, with a legal basis in the Danish Food Act, the Ministry of Food, Agriculture and Fisheries of Denmark has issued a number of executive orders, which provide detailed requirements for the promotion of foodstuffs.

Also, in relation to alcoholic beverages, authorities, companies and consumers have agreed on a set of promotional guidelines.

b. The Marketing Practices Act

The Marketing Practices Act transposes the requirements of the Unfair Commercial Practices Directive (Directive 2005/29/EC) into Danish law.

Any trader who promotes goods and services towards consumers is subject to the Marketing Practices Act. As an overall principle, Section 1 of the

1 Consolidate Act no 1216 of 25 September 2013

2 Consolidate no. 250 of 8 March 2013.

Marketing Practices Act stipulates that traders must comply with the "fair trading practice" legal standard.

Furthermore, the Marketing Practices Act prohibits, e.g. the use of improper/derogatory statements on competitors and competitors' products (Section 3), unfair comparative advertising (Section 5), and the promotion of alcoholic beverages towards minors (Section 8).

c. The Food Act

The principal legislative act in Danish food law is the Danish Food Act. The Food Act sets out a number of general principles applicable to the marketing and labeling of foods. Furthermore, the Food Act provides a legal basis for a number of executive orders on the labeling, promotion and composition of foods.

Section 14 of the Food Act prohibits the use of misleading claims (and other types of misleading advertising) in the course of promotion of foodstuffs. Please note that Section 14 of the Food Act is subordinate to Article 16 of Regulation 178/2002 and that Section 14 is applicable only insofar as Article 16 of Regulation 178/2002 is inapplicable to a specific measure. De facto and de jure, the scope of application of Section 14 of the Food Act is limited to misleading advertising in business-to-business relations.

d. The Executive Order on Labelling of Foodstuffs

The principal legislative act on the promotion of foodstuffs is the Executive Order on labelling of foodstuffs.[3] The Executive Order on labelling of foodstuffs, which transposes a number of food labelling directives (including Directive 2000/13) into Danish law, contains horizontal requirements applicable to, e.g. trade names, mandatory information, lists of ingredients, aromas, additives, etc.

3 Executive Order no. 1308 of 14 December 2005 (as later amended).

DK

2. Is there any specific national restriction or prohibition (mandatory legislation and code of conduct)?

a. Certain substances

Pursuant to Section 2(1)(b) of the Danish Medicines Act[4], a product is to be classified as a medicinal product if it may be administered to human beings with a view to making a medical diagnosis or to restoring, correcting or modifying physiological functions in human beings, i.e. if a product has a "medicinal effect", it is a medicinal product.

The Danish Health and Medicines Authority, which is responsible for (administratively) enforcing the Medicines Act, follows an administrative practice according to which the existence of certain substances in a product may lead to the product being classified as a medicinal product.

According to this administrative practice, the presence of the following substances in a product will establish a prima facie assumption of the product having a medicinal effect: glucosamine, ephedrine, pancreatic enzymes and melatonin.

Furthermore, it is the administrative practice of the Danish Health and Medicines Authority that a reclassification from foodstuff to medicinal product is permanent, and it is therefore not possible to reintroduce the same product as a foodstuff, unless the product is completely rebranded as a new and separate product.

i. Foods for Particular Nutritional Purposes (PARNUTS)

Pursuant to the Executive Order on Foods for Particular Nutritional Purposes[5], foods for particular nutritional purposes (PARNUTS) may only be marketed in Denmark if a prior notification has been submitted to the Danish Veterinary and Food Administration.

4 Consolidate Act no. 506 of 20 April 2013.

5 Executive Order no. 1102 of 26 November 2012.

ii. Sweets and soft drinks

Pursuant to Section 21 of the Executive Order on TV Commercials, etc.[6], TV, radio and on-demand advertisements relating to sweets, chocolate, soft drinks, snacks, etc. may not contain any claims that these products may replace ordinary meals.

iii. Infant formulae

Pursuant to the Executive Order on Infant Formulae, etc.[7], infant formulae may only be promoted towards health care professionals. It is not allowed to advertise infant formulae directly at consumers.

iv. Fortified foods

Pursuant to Executive Order on the Addition of Nutrients to Foods[8], foods enriched with vitamins and minerals may only be marketed in Denmark if a notification has been submitted to the Danish Veterinary and Food Administration six months prior to the introduction of the product. During the six-month delay, the Danish Veterinary and Food Administration will assess whether the product may be legally marketed in Denmark or not.

Please note that the Danish Veterinary and Food Administration have issued "general approvals" for the addition of certain vitamins and minerals to specific types of foodstuffs, e.g. the addition of up to 40 mg per 100 ml of Vitamin C in fruit juices. When such general approvals exist, there is no requirement of a six-month delay, and the product may be marketed upon prior notification to the Danish Veterinary and Food Administration, cf. Sections 5 and 6 in the Executive Order on the Addition of Nutrients to Foods.

6 Executive Order no. 801 of 21 June 2013.

7 Executive Order no. 1198 of 9 October 2013.

8 Executive Order no. 1104 of 26 November 2012.

Pursuant to the Executive Order on the Addition of Other Substances than Vitamins and Minerals to Foods[9], foods enriched with other nutrients than vitamins and minerals (e.g. caffeine) may only be marketed in Denmark if a notification has been submitted six months prior to the Danish Veterinary and Food Administration. During the six-month delay, the Danish Veterinary and Food Administration will assess whether the product may be legally marketed in Denmark or not.

Please note that the Danish Veterinary and Food Administration has issued "general approvals" for the addition of certain "other substances" to specific types of foodstuffs, e.g. for the addition of up to 32 mg/100 ml of caffeine in soft drinks. When such general approvals exist, there is no requirement of a six-month delay, and the product may be marketed upon prior notification to the Danish Veterinary and Food Administration, cf. Section 7 in the Executive Order on the Addition of Other Substances than Vitamins and Minerals to Foods.

The updated lists of general approvals are available on the Danish Veterinary and Food Administration website.

v. The guidelines on promotion of alcoholic beverages (Self-regulation)

With regards to the marketing and promotion of alcoholic beverages, the Guidelines on Promotion of Alcoholic Beverages apply to the promotion of alcoholic beverages with an alcohol content of at least 2,8 % by volume. The guidelines were drafted in cooperation with the Ministry of Health, the Ministry of Business and Growth and consumer and business representatives with a view to apply the concept of "fair marketing practices" from Section 1 of the Danish Marketing Practices Act to the promotion of alcoholic beverages. The requirements contained in the Guidelines on Promotion of Alcoholic Beverages are commonly accepted as the minimum level of compliance.

9 Executive Order no. 991 of 9 August 2013.

The general principle of the Guidelines on Promotion of Alcoholic Beverages is that alcohol advertising should be less "aggressive" than advertising for non-alcoholic beverages or other foodstuffs. Furthermore, the advertisements may not indicate that alcohol is harmless or that a moderate alcohol intake may promote a healthy lifestyle.

If an alcohol advertisement utilizes fashion models or actors, these models or actors must appear to be older than 25 years. Also, it is not allowed to promote alcoholic beverages in relation to sporting activities or to promote alcoholic beverages in work places or educational institutions (e.g., at universities).

Consumers and traders may submit complaints to the Alcohol Advertisement Board. The remedies available to the Alcohol Advertising Board are to express criticism or to forward the complaint to the Danish Consumer Ombudsman. The Danish Consumer Ombudsman may then initiate legal proceedings under the provisions of the Danish Marketing Practices Act.

b. Is the promotion of (certain) foodstuffs towards a specific section of the population restricted or prohibited by any national mandatory and/or soft laws?

i. Alcoholic beverages

Pursuant to Section 8(2) of the Marketing Practices Act, marketing directed at children and young people must not directly or indirectly incite them to use intoxicants (including alcohol). Furthermore, pursuant to Section 8(3) of the Marketing Practices Act, marketing directed at minors (under 18) may not mention alcohol, contain references to alcohol, or portray images of alcohol products.

Also, pursuant to the Guidelines on Promotion of Alcoholic Beverages (Section 6), promotion of alcoholic beverages (with an alcohol content exceeding 2,8 % (volume)) may not in any way be marketed towards minors, and advertisements may not be used in media if more than 30 % of readers, listeners or viewers are – or must be assumed to be – minors.

DK

ii. Foodstuffs with added caffeine

Pursuant to Section 46 of the Executive Order on Labelling of Foodstuffs[10], any foodstuff with added caffeine must carry the following information: "Contains caffeine. Not to be ingested by children or pregnant women".

It follows that these products should not be advertised towards children or pregnant women.

iii. Food supplements

Pursuant to Section 6 of the Executive Order on Food Supplements[11], food supplements should always carry the following information on the label: "Only to be used by infants or pregnant women under the supervision of medicinal doctors or health visitors".

It follows that these products should not be advertised towards infants or pregnant women.

II. Misleading Advertising

1. What are the national rules on misleading advertising with respect to foodstuffs?

As mentioned in section I.1, the Marketing Practices Act prohibits the use of misleading claims in advertising of goods and services towards consumers. In addition to the general ban on misleading advertising, Danish food law prohibits misleading advertising of foodstuffs both in business-to-business relations (pursuant to Section 14 of the Danish Food Act) and in business-to-consumer relations (pursuant to Article 16 of Regulation 178/2002).

The detailed provisions on misleading advertising (in relation to the promotion of foodstuffs) are provided in the Executive Order on the

10 Executive Order no. 1308 of 14 December 2005.

11 Executive Order no. 1440 of 15 December 2009.

Labelling of Foodstuffs. As a supplement to the Executive Order on the Labelling of Foodstuffs, the Danish Veterinary and Food Administration has published a Guidance on the Labelling of Foodstuffs (in Danish – "Mærkningsvejledningen"), which reflects the Danish Veterinary and Food Administration's administrative practice.

Pursuant to Section 75 of the Executive Order on Labelling of Foodstuffs, it is always considered misleading to claim a beneficial property for a foodstuff if all similar products have the same property or if all similar products are required by law to have the same property (e.g., it is not allowed to claim the beneficial effects of the content of iodine in table salt since all table salts are required to contain iodine).

Also, pursuant to Section 76 of the Executive Order on Labelling of Foodstuffs, it is not allowed to use endorsements by health care professionals or to claim that a foodstuff may prevent, alleviate or treat diseases or to use claims or other promotional measures, which may instil fear in consumers.

Pursuant to the Guidance on the Labelling of Foodstuffs, when assessing whether a claim is misleading, the Danish Veterinary and Food Administration will assess whether the claim could mislead the average, well-informed and diligent consumer. The Danish Veterinary and Food Administration will consider a number of elements and factors (apart from the claim itself), including illustrations, colours and typography, as well as the environment in which the product is promoted and the company's profile.

Any and all promotional material will be taken into account including text, illustrations and content not placed on the label, such as content from company websites.

2. What are the national landmark cases regarding misleading advertising for foodstuffs?

The Danish Veterinary and Food Administration has the competence to enforce the prohibition on misleading advertising of foodstuffs. When the Danish Veterinary and Food Administration have rendered a decision, the food business operator may lodge a complaint with a special complaints unit within the Ministry of Food, Agriculture and Fisheries.

Only a very limited number of cases reach the Danish courts, and the cases that do indeed reach the ordinary courts are often criminal proceedings. We have listed a number of judgments below, which may be considered as landmark cases on misleading advertising of foodstuffs.

"Real juice" [12]

Since the early 1970s, a Danish company has marketed a well-known line of fruit juices (made from concentrate) under the trade name "Real Juice". In 1998, the Danish Veterinary and Food Administration ruled that the trade name "Real Juice" was misleading because the company did not differentiate its juice from other fruit juices (i.e. the juice had the same fruit content as competing juices).

The company brought legal proceedings in the High Court of Eastern Denmark, and in 2001 the High Court ruled that the trade name "Real Juice" was not misleading. The High Court placed particular importance on the fact that the term "Real" had been used for more than 30 years and assessed that the term "Real" therefore no longer carried any specific meaning as to the quality or contents of the product. Therefore, the company could continue its use of the term "Real".

For the sake of good order, we note that in 2010, the company changed the name of the juice on a voluntary basis.

"Home-made chocolates" [13]

Since the mid-1940s, a company had marketed its chocolates as home-made. It produced the chocolates in a production facility owned by the company,

12 The High Court of Eastern Denmark's judgment of 7 June 2001 in case no. B-0828-99.

13 The High Court of Eastern Denmark's judgment of 15 January 2002 in case no. B-0354-01.

and sold them in eight of the company's own retail shops. The chocolates had always carried the claim "home-made".

In 1998, the Danish Veterinary and Food Administration ruled that the use of the claim was misleading. According to the Veterinary and Food Administration, the claim "home-made" could only be lawfully used if the foodstuffs were produced in the particular retail shop, i.e. the fact that the chocolates were produced in another facility rendered the claim "home-made" misleading. The company was therefore ordered to cease its use of the claim. The company filed a complaint with the Ministry of Food, Agriculture and Fisheries. The complaints unit upheld the Veterinary and Food Administration's decision.

The company then brought legal proceedings against the Ministry. The High Court of Eastern Denmark ruled in favour of the company. The court attached particular importance to the fact that the chocolates had been produced according to the recipes, which had been used since the 1940s and that the chocolates were mainly produced by hand. The Danish Veterinary and Food Administration were therefore forced to change its administrative practice.

Healthy Smoothies (Administrative action)

Pursuant to Section 76 of the Executive Order on Labelling of Foodstuffs, it is not allowed to claim that a foodstuff may prevent, alleviate or treat diseases. Historically, the Danish Veterinary and Food Administration has applied a very strict interpretation of this prohibition.

"Joe and the Juice" is a Danish chain of juice bars selling freshly squeezed juices and smoothies with names such as "Go Away Doc", "Stress down" and "Hangover Heaven".

In line with its settled practice, the Danish Veterinary and Food Administration had ordered "Joe and the Juice" to change its marketing of some of the claims used, including "Stress down" and "Hangover Heaven", because these were regarded as unsubstantiated, general, non-specific health claims cf. Article 10, sec. 3 of Regulation 1924/2006.

Further in line with its practice, the Danish Veterinary and Food Administration ordered "Joe and the Juice" to change its marketing of "Go

Away Doc" on the grounds that the product name indicated a medical effect, cf. Section 76 of the Executive Order on Labelling of Foodstuffs.

DK

The Danish Veterinary and Food Administration was then subject to widespread criticism from pundits and politicians, which caused it to retract its decision and declare that it would "rethink" its administrative practice for the assessment of such claims.

In 2012 the Danish Veterinary and Food Administration issued a new decision according to which the product names "Stress down", "Hangover Heaven" and "Go Away Doc" were not deemed to constitute health or disease claims. The Agency has since published a memo on the assessment of borderline health or disease claims and has expressed that its administrative practice on the assessment of health or disease claims is now, more or less, aligned with the interpretation of other competent authorities. Nonetheless, the Danish Veterinary and Food Administration's administrative practice is still regarded as very strict.

III. Mandatory labelling – Name of the product

Are there any national definitions of a foodstuff that could hamper the marketing of an imported food product?

1. Energy drinks

No formal definition exists, but the Danish Veterinary and Food Administration defines "energy drinks" as soft drinks with added caffeine, taurine, glucoronolacton and vitamins or minerals.

According to the Executive Order on the Addition of Other Substances than Vitamins and Minerals to Foods[14], energy drinks may contain up to 32 mg of caffeine per 100 ml.

14 Executive Order no. 991 of 9 August 2013.

2. Sports drinks

No formal definition exists, but according to the administrative practice of the Danish Veterinary and Food Administration, drinks containing electrolytes are likely to be classified as sports drinks.

3. Yogurt

Pursuant to Section 23 of the Executive Order on Dairy Products[15], "yogurt" is defined as dairy milk made sour with symbiotic cultures of "Streptococcus thermophiles" and "Lactobacillus delbrueckii subsp. bulgaricus". These cultures must be present in the minimum amount of 10 million pr. ml. when the product's shelf life expires.

4. Cheese

Pursuant to Section 4 of the Executive Order on Dairy Products[16], "cheese" is defined as a matured or non-matured (fresh) milk product, with or without rind or coating, and in which the ratio between whey protein and casein does not exceed the ratio in milk, and which is produced by either:

(1) coagulation in whole or in part of the protein in milk, skimmed milk, fat standardized milk, cream or buttermilk or a combination of these, by means of rennet or other suited coagulants and with partial separation from the whey, resulting in a concentration of milk protein, or

(2) any processing technique, involving coagulation in whole or in part of milk protein in dairy milk or other milk products, which results in a finished product, which has the same physical, chemical and sensory properties, as a product produced in accordance with the process described in 1).

15 Executive Order no. 2 of 1 April 2013.

16 See above.

IV. Voluntary Labelling

1. "Clean Labels": Are there any national definitions or requirements for the use of the following claims: (a) natural, (b) pure, (c) home-made/"grandmother" recipe or (d) and other similar claims

a. Natural

Danish food law does not contain any definition or explicit requirements for the use of the claim "natural". Instead, the Danish Veterinary and Food Administration will assess whether the use of the claim is misleading for the foodstuff in question.

Pursuant to the Guidance on the Labelling of Foodstuffs[17] (in Danish – "Mærkningsvejledningen"), the claim "natural" will (as a main rule) not be considered misleading if the foodstuff/ingredient is present in its natural form and has not been processed or has undergone only minor processing.

b. Pure

Danish food law does not contain any definition or explicit requirements for the use of the claim "pure" (or claims carrying the same meaning, e.g. 100 %). Instead, the Danish Veterinary and Food Administration will assess whether the use of the claim is misleading for the foodstuff in question.

Pursuant to the Guidance on the Labelling of Foodstuffs[18] the claim "pure" will (as a main rule) not be considered misleading if the product consists of only one single ingredient. Please note that it is not allowed to use the claim "pure" for foodstuffs, which are, by law, required to consist of only one ingredient (e.g. milk).

17 Guidance Document no. 9017 of 14 January 2013.

18 See above.

c. Home-made / "grandmother recipe"

Danish food law does not contain any definition or explicit requirements for the use of the claims "home-made" or "grandmother recipe". Instead, the Danish Veterinary and Food Administration will assess, whether the use of the claim is misleading for the foodstuff in question.

Pursuant to the Guidance on the Labelling of Foodstuffs[19], the claim "home-made" (or claims carrying the same meaning) will (as a main rule) not be considered misleading if the foodstuff has been produced according to a proprietary recipe and if the product is made without the use of semi-fabricated ingredients.

In 2002 the High Court of Eastern Denmark ruled that the claim "home-made" could be used for chocolates, which had been produced in a factory. The High Court of Eastern Denmark attributed particular importance to the fact that the chocolates were produced in accordance with a 50-year-old recipe and that the chocolates were mainly produced by hand.[20]

Pursuant to the Guidance on the Labelling of Foodstuffs[21], the claim "grandmother recipe" will be considered misleading if the foodstuff has not been produced according to an "old recipe". Old recipe is understood to be a recipe that is no longer commonly used by producers of the food in question.

d. Other similar claims related to "clean labels" (e.g. "additive-free")

i. "Fresh"

Danish food law does not contain any definition or explicit requirements for the use of the claim "fresh". Instead, the Danish Veterinary and Food Administration will assess whether the use of the claim is misleading for the foodstuff in question.

19 See above.

20 The High Court of Eastern Denmark's judgment of 15 January 2002 in case (16th dep.), docket no. B-0354-01).

21 See note 15.

Pursuant to the Guidance on the Labelling of Foodstuffs[22], the claim "fresh" may only be used for products with a short shelf life. If a preservative agent has been added to a foodstuff, the foodstuff may only be claimed to be fresh in the period of time in which the foodstuff would have been fresh, had the preservative agent not been added.

For example, in relation to coffee, the Danish Veterinary and Food Administration has previously assessed that the claim "freshly ground" was misleading since the coffee had a shelf life of 12 months. In relation to fruit juice, the Danish Veterinary and Food Administration has previously assessed that the claim "freshly squeezed" was misleading because the product had a shelf life of up to six months.

In relation to bread, it is the administrative practice of the Danish Veterinary and Food Administration to consider the claim "freshly baked" is not misleading if the product is sold within the same day as it is baked. In relation to the concept "bake-off" (i.e. breads which have been pre-baked and then frozen), the Danish Veterinary and Food Administration will consider the claim "freshly baked" to be misleading.

ii. Fruit illustrations

Danish food law does not contain any definition or explicit requirements for the use of illustrations of fruits. Instead, the Danish Veterinary and Food Administration will assess whether the use of the illustration is misleading for the foodstuff in question.

As a clear starting point, labels should only contain illustrations of fruits if the foodstuff contains fruits. Furthermore, even though the foodstuff does indeed contain the fruit (which is depicted on the label), there must be a correlation between the amount of fruit in the product and the number of fruits depicted.

Please note that fruit illustrations are allowed for foodstuffs that contain "natural aromas". If the foodstuff contains both natural and artificial aromas, the natural aromas should be the "main" aroma if fruit illustrations are used.

---

22 See note 15.

2. Nutrition & health claims

a. Within the list of health claims authorised pursuant to Regulation 1924/2006, are there any related substances which are prohibited or considered as a medicinal substance within the analysed jurisdiction?

The Danish Health and Medicines Authority considers melatonin to be a medicinal substance.

b. Are there any national laws and regulations permitting food business operators to make reference to recommendations or endorsements by national associations, medical, nutrition or dietetic professionals, and health-related charities?

Pursuant to Section 76 of Executive Order on Labelling of Foodstuffs[23], it is prohibited to utilize recommendations from healthcare professionals in the marketing of foodstuffs. Furthermore, according to the administrative practice of the Danish Veterinary and Food Administration, it is not allowed to depict anyone wearing, e.g. a doctors' coat because this may give the consumers the impression that the person endorsing the product is a medical doctor.

Furthermore, according to the administrative practice of the Danish Veterinary and Food Administration, it is not allowed to make reference to endorsements from nutritional or dietetic professionals or organizations consisting of such professionals.

c. Is the use of nutrition or health claims on non-prepackaged food further regulated at the national level?

Non-pre-packaged foods are subject to the same requirements as pre-packaged foods.

23 Executive Order no. 1308 of 14 December 2005.

d. Is a notification procedure required prior to/for marketing foodstuffs bearing nutritional or health claims?

There is no such notification procedure, although food supplements and fortified foods may only be marketed upon prior notification to the Danish Veterinary and Food Administration.

V. Enforcement of Food Law and Self-regulating bodies

1. Which actions may one risk in case of non-compliance with the labelling or advertising requirements?

a. Public Authorities

i. The Danish Veterinary and Food Administration

The Danish Veterinary and Food Administration is the authority with the primary responsibility for enforcing food legislation. Pursuant to Section 52 of the Food Act, it may order food business operators to perform or abstain from certain actions.

Administrative sanctions

The administrative sanctions available to the Danish Veterinary and Food Administration are the following:

(1) warnings,

(2) orders (e.g. on recall or destruction),

(3) prohibitions (e.g. on the marketing of a product),

(4) imposing administrative fines,

(5) recall of special approvals (e.g. for the sale of organic food), and

(6) recall of the permission to conduct business as a food business operator.

The Danish Veterinary and Food Administration publishes administrative sanctions on its website. With regards to the size of fines it follows an administrative practice. Breaches of the labelling requirements are, as a starting point, sanctioned with a fine of DKK 10.000 (~ EUR 1.350).

In the case of wholesalers who process foods, the fines will be increased by 50 % (i.e. DKK 15.000 ~ EUR 2.000) if the company has more than 10 employees and by 100 % (i.e. DKK 20.000 ~ EUR 2.700) if the company has more than 49 employees.

In case of wholesalers who do not process foods and retailers, the fines will be increased by 50 % (i.e. DKK 15.000 ~ EUR 2.000) if the company has more than 10 employees and by 100 % (i.e. DKK 20.000 ~ EUR 2.700) if the company has more than 24 employees.

Criminal sanctions

If the Danish Veterinary and Food Administration impose an administrative fine and the company is not willing to pay, or in cases where the breach is sufficiently serious, the Danish Veterinary and Food Administration may file a complaint with the police.

Pursuant to Section 60 of the Food Act, food law related offences are subject to a fine. Nonetheless, in cases of intentional offences, food business operators (and their management) risk imprisonment for a period of up to two years, if either of the following occur:

a) the actions have endangered consumers or the actions have posed a risk or endangered consumers, **or**

b) if the food business operator or a third party has profited (or intended to profit) from the actions.

Also, pursuant to Section 75 of the Danish Penal Code[24], the Danish courts may, in criminal proceedings, seize all profits stemming from criminal actions.

24 Consolidate Act no. 1028 of 22 August 2013.

DK

ii. The Danish Consumer Ombudsman

Pursuant to Section 27 of the Marketing Practices Act[25], the Consumer Ombudsman may issue orders (e.g. an order to cease using a specific claim) directed at an individual company if it determines that the company has clearly violated the Marketing Practices Act. The company on which the order has been imposed may ask the Consumer Ombudsman to initiate legal proceedings against the complainant in order to have the dispute settled in court.

The Marketing Practices Act also contains a legal basis for imposing fines for violations of a number of its provisions.

b. Competitors

Pursuant to Section 27 of the Marketing Practices Act[26], anyone (including competitors) affected by the actions of a trader may initiate legal proceedings against the trader for violations of the Marketing Practices Act, with a view of banning a promotional action (e.g. the use of a comparative claim). These lawsuits, which are not uncommon, often include a claim for damages. Also, it is not uncommon for companies to lodge complaints with the Danish Veterinary and Food Administrations against each other.

c. Consumers / (consumer) associations

Pursuant to Section 27 of the Marketing Practices Act[27], anyone (including consumers) affected by the actions of a trader may initiate legal proceedings against the trader for violations of the Marketing Practices Act. Also, it is not uncommon for consumers to lodge complaints with the Danish Veterinary and Food Administrations against companies.

25 Consolidate Act no. 25 September 2013.

26 See above.

27 See above.

2. Are there any national self-regulating bodies with respect to advertising for foodstuffs?

The Alcohol Advertisements Board

The Alcohol Advertisement Board enforces the Guidelines on Promotion of Alcoholic Beverages against companies promoting alcoholic beverages (with an alcohol content exceeding 2,8 % volume).

Consumers and traders may submit complaints to the Alcohol Advertisement Board. The remedies available to the Alcohol Advertising Board are to express criticism or to forward the complaint to the Danish Consumer Ombudsman. The Danish Consumer Ombudsman may then initiate legal proceedings for non-compliance with the Danish Marketing Practices Act.

CHAPTER 6
France

Joseph Vogel and Christophe Nussbaumer

FR

I. Possible Bans on Food Advertising

1. Is there any general national legislation or code of conduct regulating the promotion of foodstuffs?

There is no general legislation that specifically regulates the promotion of all foodstuffs.

In 2009, the advertising professionals signed a charter aiming to promote diet and physical activity favourable to health in programmes and advertisements broadcast on television, with the objective of contributing to preventing unbalanced nutritional behaviour among the youngest viewers.

According to the terms of this charter, which the *Conseil Supérieur de l'Audiovisuel* ("CSA") is responsible for implementing, the television channels undertake to do the following:

- grant preferential prices to the "national institute for prevention and education in health" (French acronym INPES) for broadcasting collective campaigns to promote its health messages; and
- broadcast programmes on food and physical activity and make them available to young viewers.

Following the signing of this charter, the *Autorité de Régulation Professionnelle de la Publicité* ("**ARPP**") published in September 2009 a new Recommendation on eating habits and behaviour ("*comportements alimentaires*"). The ARPP analyses draft advertisements pertaining to foodstuffs submitted by its members for opinion in accordance with this Recommendation.

Between 2010 and 2011 the ARPP considered only four advertisements to be non-compliant with this Recommendation.

The activity of the ARPP and its associated bodies is further developed in Section 5–2 below.

1. Is there any specific national restriction or prohibition (mandatory legislation and code of conduct)?

a. Restrictions relating to certain products in particular

i. Alcohol

The promotion of alcohol is restricted by the Evin Law[1], which was subsequently completed in 2009 by the Bachelot Law.[2] These laws are codified in Articles L.3323-2, among others, of the Public Health Code ("*Code de la Santé Publique*").

The following restrictions apply:

- Alcohol advertisements are prohibited on television and in cinemas;
- Alcohol advertisements on the radio are only allowed between midnight and 7:00 on Wednesdays and between midnight and 17:00 all other days;
- Alcohol advertisements are limited to the indication of the degree of alcohol, the origin, name and composition of the product, the means of production and consuming methods, the name and address of the manufacturer;
- All advertisements must carry a health warning specifying that "*alcohol abuse is bad for your health*";

1 Law No. 91-32 of 10 January 1991 regarding the fight against smoking and alcoholism ("*Loi Evin*").

2 Law No. 2009-879 of 21 July 2009 on hospital reform, patients, health and territories.

- Sponsorship campaigns by alcohol producers are prohibited (except if free of charge [*"mécénat"*]).

In addition to this legislation, the ARPP published a Recommendation regarding alcohol advertisements in June 2010. A decision was handed over by the *Jury de Déontologie Publicitaire* ("**JDP**") whereby it considered that an advertisement did not comply with the relevant legislation and the Alcohol Recommendation for two reasons[3]:

- the person in the advertisement was not identified as someone intervening in the elaboration, distribution or presentation of the product to the consumer, since the ad shows a man wearing a cap and t-shirt pointing at a sign which states, "Vignerons 100 % Caromb" (i.e. Winegrower 100 % from Caromb (town in France)); and
- the advertisement did not include the health warning imposed by the Evin Law.

ii. Drinks with added sugar, salt or artificial sweeteners/ manufactured food products

The promotion of drinks with added sugar, salt or artificial sweeteners and manufactured food products (in particular, those containing such substances) is restricted by Decree n°2007-263 of 27 February 2007[4] and an Order of 27 February 2007.[5] These rules are codified in Articles L.2133-1 and R.2133-1 of the Public Health Code.

It is provided that all advertisement for such goods must carry the following health warnings:

- *"For your health, eat at least five fruits and vegetables per day"*;
- *"For your health, engage in a regular physical activity"*;

3 Cave Saint-Marc La Provence – No. 30/09, JDP, 16 November 2011.

4 Decree No. 2007-263 of 27 February 2007 on relating to adverts and promotional messages for certain foods and drinks and amending the Public Health Code.

5 Order of 27 February 2007 establishing the terms and conditions relating to health information that must accompany adverts or promotional messages for certain foods and drinks.

- *"For your health, avoid eating too fatty, too sugary, too salty"*; and
- *"For your health, avoid snacking between the meals"*.

These four warnings must appear alternately and proportionally on all advertisements.

It is possible to avoid such restrictions by paying a contribution to the *Institut national de prevention et d'éducation pour la santé* ("**INPES**"). The contribution is equal to 1.5 % of the investments made for the advertisement.

These restrictions do not apply, amongst others, to the following:

- tea, coffee, milk and fruit juice that do not contain added sugar, salt or artificial sweeteners;
- alcohol (the public health message provided by legislation regarding alcohol is enough); and
- products available on their natural basis (e.g. fresh fruits, vegetables and spices) natural foodstuffs only packed (e.g. eggs and honey), sliced or minced products, frozen food, or canned food without any additives.

Moreover, these restrictions do not apply in the case of sponsorship and sales promotion in stores.

iii. Foodstuffs benefiting from an agricultural label

An Order of 3 July 1996[6] provides that the information to the consumer on the price of the foodstuffs benefiting from an agricultural label provided outside the place of sale must include the following:

- the red label logo;
- the complete name of the product and, if necessary, the fact that it is a farm product ("fermier");

6 Order of 3 July 1996 on the information to the consumer on the price of the foodstuffs benefiting from an agricultural label.

- the name of the association which owns the label; and
- the method of feeding in the case of meat products (including poultry and rabbit) and aquaculture products.

iv. Energy drinks

The commercialization of energy drinks was prohibited in France in 1996. In 2008, in the absence of a formal demonstration of an identified risk, and despite suspicions of risks, the commercialization of energy drinks was authorized in accordance with the free movement of goods legally manufactured or commercialized in the European market.

The *Syndicat National des Boissons Rafraîchisantes* ("**SNBR**" = national association for refreshing drinks) has implemented a Best Practices Code. This Code provides that the indications "*consume with moderation*" and "*not recommended for children, pregnant women and nursing mothers*" must be present on the labelling.

The Code also provides that (i) no communication or advertisement should be targeted towards children under 12 years old, (ii) no advertisement should promote the consumption of such drinks with alcohol, and (iii) no allegations similar to sport drinks regarding rehydration should be made.

b. Restrictions relating to a specific section of the population

i. Alcohol

The Evin Law provides that alcohol advertisements are prohibited in youth press/magazines and on websites dedicated to youth and sports.

The Bachelot Law provides that alcohol cannot be sold to children (under 18 years old).

ii. Drinks with added sugar, salt or artificial sweeteners/ manufactured food products

Decree n°2007-263 of 27 February 2007 and an Order of 27 February 2007 provide that for advertisements during youth programs, the messages can be directed using informal pronouns (i.e. use of "tu").

Moreover, all advertisements for cereal based products for young children and baby products must carry the following health warning:

- *"Teach your child not to snack between the meals"*; and
- *"Moving, playing is essential to the development of your child"*.

In conclusion, all advertisements for follow-on formulae products must carry the following health warning:

- *"In addition to milk, water is the only essential drink"*; and
- *"Moving, playing is essential to the development of your child"*.

iii. Drinks and foodstuffs

Automatic vending machines have been prohibited in schools since the 1st of September 2005.[7]

The ARPP published the Diets for children under 3 years of age Recommendation and the Child Recommendation in November 2000 and June 2004, respectively.

- The **Diets for children under 3 years of age Recommendation** provides the following rules:

  The advertisement should not suggest that everyday consumer products meet the specific nutritional needs of young children.

7 Law No. 2004-806 of 9 August 2004 on public health policy, article 30.

However, if in the same visual, are represented everyday consumer products and products for children under three years of age, no confusion should exist as to the nature of these products.

Advertising of foods from organic agriculture (organic products) must not disparage, directly or indirectly, foods for children under three years which are subject, statutorily, to greater safety obligations.

All advertising highlighting the absence of ingredients prohibited by regulation (e.g. *"no colouring"*, *"no preservatives"*, etc.) is prohibited, except if very clearly specified *"in accordance with the relevant regulations"*.

Any medical or scientific backing appropriating regulatory, health or nutritional claims is prohibited.

- The **Child Recommendation** completes the relevant legislation and focuses on several issues such as, among others, children's eating habits and behaviours.

  It provides the following rules:

  Advertising showing a consumer situation, such as a snack or meal, must ensure that the food represented corresponds to a balanced diet.

  Advertising must not encourage children to consume a product excessively.

  Advertising must not encourage children to eat unreasonably throughout the day. Snacking should not be presented as substitutable for a meal.

  Advertising should not suggest that the only consumption of product induces optimal performance and maximum success in a particular artistic activity, school or sports.

iv. Energy drinks

The sale and use of energy drinks are prohibited in schools (Official Bulletin, State Education n° 31 of July 31, 2008).

II. Misleading Advertising

1. What are the national rules on misleading advertising with respect to foodstuffs?

Article R. 112-7 of the French Consumer Code is the mere transposition of Directive 2000/13:

European law	French law
Article 2(1) of Directive 2000/13 1. *The labelling and methods used must not:* (a) *be such as could mislead the purchaser to a material degree, particularly:* (i) *as to the characteristics of the foodstuff and, in particular, as to its nature, identity, properties, composition, quantity, durability, origin or provenance, method of manufacture or production;* (ii) *by attributing to the foodstuff effects or properties which it does not possess;* (iii) *by suggesting that the foodstuff possesses special characteristics when in fact all similar foodstuffs possess such characteristics;* (b) *subject to Community provisions applicable to natural mineral waters and foodstuffs for particular nutritional uses, attribute to any foodstuff the property of preventing, treating or curing a human disease, or refer to such properties.*	**Article R. 112-7 of the French Consumer Code** *The labelling and the manner in which it is done must not be likely to create confusion in the mind of the buyer or the consumer, particularly in regard to the characteristics of the foodstuff including its nature, identity, properties, composition, quantity, durability, origin or provenance, or its method of manufacture or production.* *The labelling must not include any wording which might suggest that the foodstuff has special characteristics when all similar foodstuffs have those same characteristics.* *Without prejudice to the provisions applicable to foodstuffs intended for a specific diet or to natural mineral waters, the labelling of a foodstuff must not claim that it has properties which could prevent, treat or cure a human ailment, or refer to such properties.* *The above prohibitions or restrictions also apply to the advertising and displaying of foodstuffs, particularly in regard to the form or appearance given to them or their packaging, the packaging material used, the manner of their presentation and the environment in which they are displayed.*

2. What are the national landmark cases regarding misleading advertising for foodstuffs?

a. Geographic origin

FR

Paris Court of Appeal, Havana Club International (Pernod SA), 10 May 2012[8]

Even though it produced its rum in the Bahamas, the labelling of the Matusalem bottles of 1872 Holding VOF included various references to Cuba such as "Santiago de Cuba", "Original Cuba formula", and "Spirit of Cuba". Such references could also be found on the company's website and on its advertising materials.

The Paris Court of Appeal considered that these references, despite the more discrete reference to the production in the Bahamas, were misleading and contributed to the confusion of not only consumers, but also professional distributors.

Court of Cassation, 3 September 2002[9]

An egg producer marketed its eggs using packaging that had a representation of Mont Saint-Michel, with an address in this location, as well as the drawing of corn cobs and wheat and terms such as "tradition" and "like in the old days".

According to the court, such marketing is misleading advertising because the eggs appear to be linked to a prestigious site while the production sites were unrelated to Mont Saint-Michel and the laying hens were not fed with grain of maize but with industrially elaborated foods.

8 Paris Court of Appeal, Havana Club International v. 1872 Holdings VOF, 10 May 2012, n° 10/04016.

9 Court of Cassation, 3 September 2002, n° 01-86.760.

b. Misleading advertisement on the characteristics of the foodstuffs

Court of Cassation, Danone v. Andros, 12 January 1999[10]

This case is of particular interest because the Court of Cassation explains how an advertising campaign should be analysed in connection with the concept of misleading advertisement.

Andros brought an action against Danone to have it withdraw its advertisement presenting a product under the designation "fresh compote" which it considered to be misleading. Danone counterclaimed alleging that Andros was guilty of misleading advertising.

Dismissing Danone's counterclaim, the Versailles Court of Appeal found that each element of the advertising campaign of the company Andros, taken in isolation, was not likely to mislead the consumer as to the "fresh" character of the product. However, the Court of Cassation considered that the advertising campaign as a whole, and not each element taken in isolation, should be analysed in order to determine whether it is misleading. The Court of Appeal should have checked if the whole advertising campaign of Andros was creating an ambiguity of the exact nature of the products that could have led to "confusion in the mind of the consumers", by indicating a long use-by date and mentioning "fresh compote".

Paris Court of Appeal, La Laitière, 8 December 2010[11]

Nestlé marketed La Laitière branded yogurts with the sayings "coffee flavoured yogurt", "coconut flavoured yogurt", "lemon flavoured yogurt", etc. The packaging of these products also included realistic representations of fruits or other vegetables on the label.

Following a claim brought by Andros, the Paris Court of Appeal ruled that such labelling was misleading with regards to the yogurts' true characteristics since such a presentation could lead the consumer to think that the products contained natural flavours from the fruits or other vegetables

10 Court of Cassation, 12 January 1999, n° 97-13.801.

11 Paris Court of Appeal, Andros v. Nestlé, 8 December 2010, n° 09/03571.

represented on the labels. Yet, these products hardly contained any of these fruits or other vegetables, and the flavours were exclusively artificial.

Regarding the "coffee flavoured yogurt", the Court of Appeal considered that the sentence "0,7 coffee extract" in the ninth position on the label was misleading since such a percentage was insufficient to give the yogurt a taste of coffee, a taste which necessarily came from the artificial coffee flavouring mentioned in the seventh position on the label.

Paris Commercial Court, Artificial sweeteners, 10 May 2007 [12]

The McNeil Group sells a range of sucralose-based artificial sweeteners under the brand "Splenda".

Its competitor, the Group Merisant, which markets a similar product under the brand name "Canderel" brought an action before the Commercial Court of Paris for deceptive and misleading advertising following the promotional campaign of the Splenda brand. The campaign referred repeatedly to the French verb for "sweeten" and to the expression "comes from sugar and tastes of sugar", while a sweetener does not provide the other properties of sugar, whether nutritional or functional and technological.

The Court stated that consumer surveys showed that, as a result of the repeated use in its advertising and on the packaging of Splenda products, the expressions, shortcut and verb indicated that it created the impression of a close proximity between the Splenda product with sugar in the minds of a significant number of consumers.

Therefore, the Court considered that there was a risk of misleading consumers as to the intrinsic qualities of the product and that the advertisement violated the provisions of Article L. 121-1 of the Consumer Code.

Nonetheless, the Paris Commercial Court found that the product's labelling and packaging was not misleading and therefore did not infringe Article R. 112-7 of the Consumer Code on the labelling of foodstuffs because the average consumer was able to understand that Splenda was a sweetener, given that the word "sweetener" appeared in a systematic manner, immediately below the brand name Splenda.

12 Paris Commercial Court, 10 May 2007, n° 2006072035.

III. Mandatory Labelling: Name of Product

Are there any national definitions of a foodstuff that could hamper the marketing of an imported food product?

Apart from the vertical harmonization directives, which have been transposed into French law by various decrees and orders (specifically with regard to cocoa and chocolate products, jams, etc.), French law has a number of regulations which, at minimum, define the name under which a foodstuff is sold.

For example, *"the term 'cheese' is reserved to a product fermented or not, matured or non-matured, obtained from the following exclusively milk-based materials: milk, semi- or full-skimmed milk, cream, fat, buttermilk, used alone or mixed and totally or partially coagulated before draining or after the partial elimination of the watery part. The minimum dry matter content of the product defined must be of 23 grams for 100 grams of cheese"* (Decree No. 2007-628 of 27 April 2007, article 1).

Or, for instance, Decree No. 93-1074 of 13 September 1993 regarding certain categories of bread defines the following terms:

- ***"Home-made bread"*** *(article 1): entirely kneaded bread made and cooked on the place of sale to the end customer.*
- ***"French tradition bread"*** *(article 2): bread which (1) has not been frozen during its elaboration, (2) contains no additives and (3) results from the cooking of a pastry presenting the following characteristics:*
  - *An exclusive mix of wheat flour bread-making, drinking water and household salt;*
  - *Fermented with baking yeast and/or yeast; and*
  - *Eventually contain, in comparison with the total weight of the flour, a maximum proportion of 2 % of soybean flour, 0,5 % of soy flour and 0,3 % of malted wheat and rye flour.*
- ***"Leavened bread"*** *(articles 3 and 4): the breads described above presenting a maximum pH of 4,3 and a concentration of endogenous acetic acid of the crumb of at least 900 parts per million (ppm).*

The question at issue is all the more important for France since failure to comply with the regulations incurs sanctions.

In effect, a trader who puts pre-packaged foodstuffs on the market in France must meet the requirements of Articles R. 112-14 and R. 112-14-1 of the Consumer Code. Article R. 112-14 defines the requirements applicable to domestic products and products imported from third countries. Article R. 112-14-1 concerns products imported from other Member States of the European Union.

Failure to comply with those requirements can constitute the offense of deception.[13]

Further, under Article R. 112-14 of the Consumer Code, where there is no specific regulation on fraud prevention in force, the name by which a foodstuff must be called is that fixed by trading practice. The Court of Cassation applied those provisions to the letter in holding the offence of deception to have been committed for the marketing of a product under the name "prime ham" when it was composed of a proportionally high amount of pork shoulder and additives favouring water retention and may not, in light of practices in the trade, use that name.[14]

In contrast, the resale in France of Italian salami, whose H.P.D. rate (humidity of skimmed product) is higher than the rate allowed by the Code of Practice for cured and preserved meat products (but is consistent with the Italian standards), has been considered lawful in France because the label clearly stated the origin of the product.[15]

13 Court of Cassation, criminal division, 7 Oct. 1998, No. 97-84.270; Court of Cassation, criminal division, 10 March 1987, No. 86-94.291; trout described as salmon trout whereas they have never lived free-range nor eaten shell fish, Court of Cassation, criminal division, 10 March 1987, No. 86-94.291; CA Versailles 11 Feb. 1988; non-fattened chicken weighing less than 1,8 kg described as a fattened hen (poularde), CA Paris 20 June 1986; organic foodstuff not prepared according to the applicable regulations, Court of Cassation, criminal division, 4 June 1985, No. 84-95.955.

14 Court of Cassation, criminal division, 15 May 2001, No. 00-84.279.

15 Tribunal de grande instance [District Court], Creteil, 11th chamber, 5 May 1987.

However, the European Court of Justice has not hesitated to describe as measures having an equivalent effect to quantitative restrictions on imports those national regulations fixing the characteristics of products, where such products have been lawfully manufactured and marketed in the exporting Member State.

Accordingly, the definition of certain foodstuffs falls under Article 34 TFEU:

- **MILK POWDER (ECJ Case 216/84 Commission v. France [1988] ECR p. 793, judgment of 23 February 1988):**

  Article 1 of the Law of 29 June 1934 relative to the protection of dairy products (OJ 1 July 1934) stated: "*it is forbidden to produce ..., sell, import ... 3° under the name 'powdered milk', 'condensed milk' whether or not qualified subsequently, or under any fancy name whatsoever, a product which looks like powdered or concentrated milk intended for the same use which is not exclusively made from the concentration or desiccation of milk or skimmed milk whether sweetened or not, the addition of foreign fats being prohibited in particular*" (version abridged on 19 May 2011).

  For the Court of Justice, an absolute prohibition on the importation and sale of milk substitutes is not necessary in order to protect consumers.[16] Therefore, by prohibiting the importation and sale of powdered and concentrated milk substitutes under any name whatsoever, France had failed to fulfill an obligation under Article 30 of the Treaty.[17]

16 **Point 13 of the judgment**: *"It follows that an absolute prohibition on the importation and sale of milk substitutes is not necessary in order to protect consumers and hence the French Government's first susbmission must be rejected".*

17 **Point 23 of the judgment**: *"It appears from all the foregoing that it is established that there has been a failure to fulfil obligations. It must therefore be held that, by prohibiting the importation of substitutes for milk powder and concentrated milk under any name whatsoever and the sale of such imported products, the French Republic has failed to fulfil an obligation incumbent upon it under Article 30 of the EEC Treaty".*

FR

- **FROZEN YOGURT (ECJ Case 298/87 Smanor [1988] ECR p. 4489, judgment of 14 July 1988):**

  Unlike the French Council of State (*Conseil d'État*) which held Decree No. 82-184 of 22 February 1982[18], prohibiting the sale of frozen yogurt under the name 'yogurt' in France, to be a regulatory measure enacted "*in the interest of consumers*" not constituting a "measure having equivalent effect"[19], the Court of Justice ruled the decree to be incompatible with Article 28 EC (now Article 34 TFEU). The ECJ in effect found that the characteristics of frozen yogurt were not substantially different from fresh yogurt and the consumers could be adequately informed by proper labelling including a best-before date.

  § 32: *"As the deep-freezing of a product is expressly mentioned in that provision, it must be concluded that a Member State cannot refuse to permit a certain name to be used for a given product on the sole ground that that product has undergone deep-freezing treatment, so long as it continues to satisfy, after undergoing such treatment, the other conditions laid down by the national rules for the use of the name in question.*

  § 33: *"Whether yogurt, once it has been deep-frozen, still complies with the other conditions laid down by the French rules for authorization to use the name 'yogurt' is a question of fact which is for the national court to decide".*

18 *"The name 'yogurt' shall be used to designate only fresh fermented milk obtained, in accordance with proper and usual practices, from the growth solely of the specific lactic, thermophile bacteria known as lactobacillus bulgaricus and streptococcus thermophilus, which must be introduced at the same time and must be alive in the product put on sale at the rate of at least 100 million bacteria per gram.*
The milk used in the manufacture of the yogurt [...] cannot have been subject to reconstitution. However milk powder, whether skimmed or not, may be added to it to a maximum dose of 5 grams of powder for 100 grams of milk used.
After coagulation of the milk, the yogurt must not be subjected to any treatment other than refrigeration, and possibly stirring.
The quantity of free lactic acid contained in the yogurt [...] must not be less than 0.8 gram per 100 grams at the time of sale to the consumer".

19 Conseil d'État, 29 Oct. 1986, Nos. 41.852 and 45.416.

- **SUGAR versus ARTIFICIAL SWEETENERS (ECJ Case C-241/89 SARPP v. Chambre syndicale des raffineurs et conditionneurs de sucre de France, ECR 1990 p. I-4695, judgment of 12 December 1990):**

  In this case, the Paris Tribunal de Grande Instance referred to the Court for a preliminary ruling a question on the interpretation of Article 30 of the EEC Treaty with a view to determining whether the French rules on the labelling of artificial sweeteners are compatible with the aforementioned article of the Treaty.

  Article 10(1) of Law No. 88-14 of 5 January 1988 on legal actions brought by approved consumers' associations and on the provision of information to consumers prohibits all statements alluding to the physical, chemical or nutritional properties of sugar or to the word 'sugar' in the labelling of sweeteners that are sweeter than sugar but do not have the same nutritional qualities, in the labelling of foodstuffs containing such substances, as well as in the sale and presentation of such substances and foodstuffs and in the information supplied to consumers on them.

  The Court considers that "*the provisions of Directive 79/112 [...] must be interpreted as meaning that they preclude the application to national and imported products of national rules which prohibit any statement in the labelling of artificial sweeteners alluding to the word 'sugar' or to the physical, chemical or nutritional properties which artificial sweeteners also possess*" (point 25).

- **FOIE GRAS (ECJ Case C-184/96 Commission v. France ECR 1998 p. I-6197, judgment of 22 October 1998):**

  A Member State which adopts legislation relating to preparations with foie gras as a base, reserving certain trade descriptions to products possessing particular qualities[20], and without including a mutual recogni-

20 Decree n°93-999 of 9 August 1993, Article 2: The Decree applies in particular to the following descriptions: whole foie gras, foie gras, blocks of foie gras – with either goose or duck foie gras as a base –, liver parfait, liver medallions or paté, galantine of liver or liver mousse with goose foie gras as a base, or duck foie gras, or goose and duck foie gras.

tion clause for products coming from other Member States and complying with the rules enacted by those States, fails to fulfil its obligations under Article 30 of the Treaty.

Point 18: *"In those circumstances, national legislation prohibiting a product from a Member State which complies with the rules laid down by that State but which does not fully satisfy the requirements imposed by that legislation from being marketed under a given trade description must be regarded as capable of hindering, at least potentially, inter-State trade".*

- **EMMENTHAL (ECJ Case C-448/98 Guimont ECR 2000 p. I-10663, judgment of 5 December 2000):**

Hearing a reference for a preliminary ruling concerning the interpretation of Articles 3(a) and Articles 30 et seq. of the Treaty of Rome [now Art. 3, § 1, a) and Art. 34 TFEU)], the ECJ held that, *"Article 30 of the Treaty precludes a Member State from applying to products imported from another Member State, where they are lawfully produced and marketed, a national rule prohibiting the marketing of a cheese without rind under the designation 'Emmenthal in that Member State."*

In that case, the technical manager of a dairy had been prosecuted for having sold or offered for sale emmenthal with deceptive labelling pursuant to Article R. 112-7 of the Consumer Code according to which labelling should not create confusion in the minds of consumers, *"particularly in regard to the characteristics of the foodstuff"*. However, the "characteristics of the foodstuff" called *"emmenthal"* within the meaning of the French regulations are defined in Article 6 and the annex of Decree No. 88-1206 of 30 December 1988, implementing the Law of 1 August 1905 on frauds and falsifications relating to products or services and the Law of 2 July 1935 concerning the organisation and sanitation of the milk market as regards cheese. Article 6 of the Decree of 1988 provides that *"the designations listed in the Annex are reserved for cheeses which meet the requirements relating to the manufacture and composition which are described in said Annex"*. In the Annex, Emmenthal cheese is described as *"a firm cheese produced by curing, pressing and salting on the surface or in brine; of a colour between ivory and pale yellow, with holes of a size between a cherry and a walnut; hard, dry rind, of a colour between golden yellow and light brown"*.

However, the Court found that the name "Emmenthal" does not appear to be a designation of origin but simply a type of cheese, widely used within the European Union without any requirement related to the presence of a rind, which is not the result of any difference in the maturing method.

Point 33: "*Therefore, even if the difference in the maturing method between Emmenthal with rind and Emmenthal without rind were capable of constituting a factor likely to mislead consumers, it would be sufficient, whilst maintaining the designation 'Emmenthal', for that designation to be accompanied by appropriate information concerning that difference*".

Point 34: "*In those circumstances, the absence of rind cannot be regarded as a characteristic justifying refusal of the use of the 'Emmenthal' designation for goods from other Member States where they are lawfully manufactured and marketed under that designation*".

As a result, the French regulation cannot prevent the import of Emmenthal cheese without a rind and the European Court of Justice ruled that the French law was contrary to the principle of the free of movement of goods.

IV. Voluntary Labelling

1. "Clean labels" – Are there any national definitions or requirements with respect to claims such as 'natural', 'pure', 'home-made', 'additive-free'?

There are a number of legal and regulatory provisions governing the specifics of consumer information affixed on a voluntary basis by economic operators. Such information must comply with those conditions, subject to the discretion of the courts, and also with the following:

– general legal requirements, in particular related to the prohibition of misleading commercial practices or the prohibition of information which may cause confusion, and the protection of certain terms (e.g. designations of origin, specific sales descriptions, and protection of the terms 'milk' 'dairy product'); and

- specifically defined requirements such as for nutritional labelling or of nutrition and health claims or even certain claims such as the terms "fresh" or "homemade".

FR

Under those provisions the French administrative authorities have the power to regulate products placed on the market within the limits of the prohibition under EU law of measures having equivalent effect to quantitative restrictions on trade between Member States.

The following terms are defined under the French rules:

"Natural": Product coming directly from nature or which received a maximum of one slight treatment (e.g. pasteurisation, cooling, etc.), but without additives, residues or foreign objects.

- For the DGCCRF (General Directorate for Competition, Consumer Affairs and Fraud Control), the term 'natural' on the labelling of foodstuffs can only be used for *"product[s] found in nature or as close as possible to [their] original environment, non-treated and only containing normal ingredients, without additives, or residues or foreign bodies"* (**Avis DGCCRF Opinion no. 92-141, 25 Feb. 1992, BID 1992**). The requirements for use of the term *"natural"*, *"100 % natural"* and any other similar expression on the labels of foodstuffs are now defined in the **DGGCCRF's information leaflet** (Information Note of the DGCCRF) **No. 2009-136 of 18 August 2009**. It clearly states that the acceptability of such claims must be assessed both with regard to their possible misleading nature but also their possible unfair nature. Two types of claims are in fact taken into account: those claiming the product is actually natural and those claiming the product has a natural origin.
- Thus, the marketing of individually pre-packaged "brioches" labelled "natural products" when, in fact, the product contained calcium propionate, soy lecithin, ascorbic acid and salt containing potassium ferrocyanide, constitutes deception in respect of the essential characteristics of the good. The manufacturer received a suspended prison sentence of two months and was fined 10,000 FF (approximately EUR 1,500).[21]

21 TGI Saumur, June 10, 1993, BID 1994, NO 7, pp. 33–34, no. 94-274.

"Pure": Only for certain products such as oils, orange juice, liquorice, honey, etc.

"Home-made" / "grandma's recipe": The product must be made on the point of sale from ingredients which traditionally form the recipe.

- Thus, factory-produced biscuits made from typically industrial ingredients such as soy lecithin, citric acid, palm oil and ammonium bicarbonate that cannot even be found in stores or hypermarkets cannot be qualified as "homemade".[22]

"Artisanal": The product must be made by an "*artisan*" registered with the crafts and trades register.

"Old fashioned" / "traditional recipe" (*à l'ancienne / traditionnel*): The product must be made with products according to identified age-old practices. It excludes the presence of additives.

"Local produce" (*du terroir*): Use of raw materials that come from a specific geographic zone.

"Fresh": There are three conditions:

- manufactured less than 30 days earlier;
- must present the same characteristics at the moment of the sale than at the moment of the production; and
- cannot be conserved by a special treatment (except refrigeration and pasteurization) or contain conservatives.

  When a product is labelled as "fresh", it must not have undergone any process of filtration, binding, or pasteurization, with the exception of dairy products. A fruit compote having undergone pasteurization cannot therefore be described as "fresh" in the sense of the freshness of the product, as there is no specific exemption available for compotes.[23]

22 Paris Correctional Tribunal, 3rd Chamber, 4 Dec. 1995.

23 Commercial Court, Nanterre, 16 Dec. 1993, Quot. Jur. 1994, No. 73, p. 8.

"New": This claim is valid for up to a year. If it is an existing product, the modification must be substantial.

"Country" / "farm produce" / "farmer's" (*campagne/fermier/paysan*): Guaranties that the product is manufactured on the site itself, at a non-industrial scale and according to traditional techniques.

In this respect, the methods of exploitation of agro-food products are highly regulated by the public authorities. In 2007, the DGCCRF carried out an investigation into claims enhancing the attractiveness of products related to the use of the term "*fermier*" (farm-produce) at the end of which it had inspected 1251 producers (at factories, farms, roadsides, canning factories, open-air markets or on the Internet) and at retailers' premises (delicatessens, grocery stores, camp-site stores, organic goods stores, hypermarkets, butchers' shops, caterers, *rotisseries*, and restaurants).

The investigation resulted in 18 charges, 45 reminders of the regulations and 71 notifications of regulatory information. The offences found were mainly in respect of misleading advertising and deception.

With regard to the designations of origin, the ECJ deemed that by maintaining the national protection granted to the designations: "Salaisons d'Auvergne" (Auverge cured meats) as well as the labels designating regions "Savoie", "Franche-Comté", "Corsica", "Midi-Pyrénées", "Normandy", "Nord-Pas-de-Calais", "Ardennes de France", "Limousin", "Languedoc-Roussillon" and "Lorraine", France had failed to fulfill its obligations under Article 28 EC [Art. 34 TFEU]. Indeed, according to the ECJ and the Commission, protection for designations of origin and geographical indications may be afforded only within the framework laid down by the Regulation No. 2081/92.[24]

"Montagne" [Mountain]: A last example concerns the use of the description "montagne" [mountain]: the French legislation reserved the use of the description "mountain" to products manufactured on the national territory and made from domestic raw materials. The Court of Justice held that the measure was discriminatory in respect of goods imported from other Member States that could never use the term "mountain" and held that

24 ECJ Case C-6/02 Commission v. France ECR 2003 p. I-2389, judgment of 6 March 2003.

the application of the national measure could also have effects on the free movement of goods between Member States.[25]

2. Nutrition & health claims

a. Within the list of health claims authorised pursuant to Regulation 1924/2006, are there any related substances that are prohibited or considered as a medicinal substance?

Although it may be authorised by Regulation No. 1924/2006, a substance can be considered as a medicine in France. It cannot therefore be freely marketed, e.g. lactulose and melatonin are considered to be drugs and can only be sold in pharmacies.

The question posed has been the subject of much litigation in France concerning food supplements.

Under the terms of Decree No. 2006-352 of 20 March 2006, food supplements are "foodstuffs the purpose of which is to supplement the normal diet and which constitute a concentrated source of nutrients (vitamins and minerals) or other substances with a nutritional or physiological effect, alone or combined, marketed in dosage form, such as capsules, tablets [...] and other similar liquid or powdered forms intended to be taken in small quantities of measured dosages".

To determine whether a substance can be deemed to be a food supplement or a medicine, the court must a carry out a concrete assessment. On the one hand, a product is a medicine by virtue of its presentation when it is presented as possessing curative or preventive properties with regard to human illnesses and, on the other and, by virtue of its function, which when examined on a case-by-case basis, taking into account all its characteristics, including its composition, its use, the risks related to its use, its pharmacological properties, immunological or metabolic disorders, it is

25 ECJ Case C-321/94Pistre and others, ECR 1997 p. I-2343, Judgment of 7 May 1997.

capable of restoring, correcting or modifying physiological functions in a manner that is significant.[26]

Similarly, Vitamin C 1000 mg and magnesium associated to Vitamins B1, B2 and B6 are regarded as medicines in France.[27]

Lastly, "when, having regard to the whole of its characteristics, a product is likely to respond to both the definition of medicinal products and to that of food supplement resulting from the Decree of 20 March 2006, it is, in case of doubt, regarded as a medicinal product".[28]

b. Are there any national laws and regulations permitting food business operators to make reference to recommendations or endorsements by national associations, medical, nutrition or dietetic professionals, and health-related charities?

There is no specific regulation expressly prohibiting references to the recommendations of doctors or specific health-care professionals and associations.

It is essential, according to the CNA[29], that the relevant authorities in conjunction with consumer associations, scientists and representatives of economic operators, can establish criteria enabling the definition of the types of national professional associations in the medical, nutritional or dietary sectors and philanthropic bodies active in the field of healthcare to which it is possible to make reference in the context of claims made [in respect of products] (Opinion No. 58 CNA, 28 June 2007, JO 12 August 2007).

26 e.g. Court of Cassation, criminal division of 29 June 2010, case No. 09-86.608: for products DHA Brainbooster, Chondrosteo and Forticalcium regarded as medicines; 21 September 2010, case No. 09-82.844: medicinal plants authorised in food supplements in application of Decree of 20 March 2006 but considered as medicines; 3 May 2011, case No. 09-88.525: vitality complex legally marketed in Belgium under reference NUT PL 702/03 but considered to be a medicine in France.

27 Court of Cassation, criminal division, 22 February 2011, case No. 10-81.742.

28 Court of Cassation, criminal division, 19 May 2009, case No. 08-83.747.

29 Conseil national d'alimentation [National Food Council].

c. Is the use of nutrition or health claims on non-prepackaged food further regulated at the national level?

There are no regulations on nutritional or health-related claims specifically targeting non-prepackaged foodstuffs.

d. Is there a notification procedure required prior to / for marketing foodstuffs bearing nutritional or health claims?

For substances that are not on the list of health claims authorised pursuant to Regulation 1924/2006, food supplements remain subject to the internal rules that must be applied in respect of Articles 34 and 36 TFEU. Now, Decree 2006-352 relating to food supplements and enacting into national law Directive 2002/46/EC provides for:

- A mandatory declaration to DGCCRF of the placing on the market of new food supplements; and
- A procedure of "mutual recognition" which allows an application to be made for authorisation to use food supplements of which at least one ingredient is not allowed in France, but is legally used in another Member State.

A draft decree laying down the list of plants authorised in food supplements and their conditions of use has been notified to the Commission on December 2012. This draft decree has not been published in France yet. The plants that will not appear in the list will still be subject to the notification procedure described above.

In this regard, the Commission has criticised France for not providing for a simplified procedure, enabling a substance to be included in the national list of authorised additives, which is necessary if they are to be marketed in France.

The Advocate General relied on the example of the drink manufacturer Red Bull where the applicant waited nearly seven months for acknowledgement of receipt of its application and more than two years to be informed of the decision to refuse it. For the ECJ, the French Republic had effectively failed to fulfil its obligations under the Treaty by failing to provide for a procedure which could be completed within a reasonable time and which could, when it is refused, be challenged before the courts.[30]

Accordingly, and after having made a reference to the ECJ for a preliminary ruling[31], the criminal chamber of the Court of Cassation quashed a conviction for forgery pronounced by a court of appeal which, on the one hand, did not examine specifically if the excess of the RDAs of vitamins was dangerous to health and which, on the other hand, had not verified if the national authorization procedure offered all the necessary guarantees to protect the rights of importers (the case concerned meal substitutes and food supplements which were freely available in other Member States[32]).

More recently, the Court of Justice has held that France failed to fulfil its obligations under former Article 28 EC (now Art. 34 TFEU) by laying down, for processing aids (substances used in the process of elaborating or manufacturing a foodstuff, and the aim of which is to obtain a certain technical effect during that process) and foodstuffs whose preparation involved the use of processing aids from other Member States where they are lawfully manufactured and/or marketed, a prior authorisation scheme not complying with the principle of proportionality.[33]

30 ECJ Case C-24/00 Commission v. France, ECR 2004 p. I-1277, judgment of 5 February 2004.

31 ECJ, 5 February 2004, C- 95/01.

32 Court of Cassation, criminal division 27 March 2007, No. 06-82.257.

33 ECJ Case C-333/08, Commission v. France ECR 2010 p. I-757, judgment of 28 January 2010.

V. Enforcement of Food Law and Self-regulating Bodies

1. Which actions may one risk in case of non-compliance with the labelling or advertising requirements?

<table>
<tr><td>→ Non-compliance with the labelling requirements</td><td>→ Articles L.214-1 and R.112-7 of the Consumer Code</td><td>Maximum administrative fine of 450 € per item.</td></tr>
<tr><td>→ Misleading advertisement
→ Misleading labelling</td><td>→ Articles L.120-1 and following of the Consumer Code</td><td rowspan="2">Criminal sanction: two years imprisonment and a € 37,500 fine. The fine can be doubled if the prohibited practice results in use of merchandise dangerous to human or animal welfare.
The amount of the fine can be brought to 50 % of the expenses linked to the advertisement or prohibited practice.
Moreover, the judge can order the following:
– removal of the product (article L.121-3); and
– publication of the decision and eventually, at the expense of the convicted party, the publication of one or more corrective statements (article L.121-4).</td></tr>
<tr><td>→ Deception
→ Fraud</td><td>→ Articles L.213-1 and L.213-2 of the Consumer Code</td></tr>
<tr><td>→ Absence of labelling
→ Inadequate labelling</td><td>→ Article 121-3 of the Criminal Code</td><td>Deliberate endangering of others is a misdemeanour.
The direct exposure of another person to an immediate risk of death or injury likely to cause mutilation or permanent disability by the manifestly deliberate violation of a specific obligation of safety or prudence imposed by any statute or regulation is punished by one year's imprisonment and a fine of € 15,000 (article 223-1 of the Criminal Code).</td></tr>
</table>

→ Absence of labelling → Inadequate labelling	→ Article 221-6 of the Criminal Code	Causing the death of another person by clumsiness, rashness, inattention, negligence or breach of an obligation of safety or prudence imposed by statute or regulations, in the circumstances and according to the distinctions laid down by article 121-3, constitutes manslaughter punished by three years' imprisonment and a fine of € 45,000.

Please note that non-compliance with advertising and labelling requirements can also give rise to civil actions by competitors on the basis of unfair competition. This is especially the case in the event of misleading advertisement or labelling.

2. Are there any national self-regulating bodies with respect to advertising for foodstuffs?

a. Autorité de Régulation Professionnelle de la Publicité ("ARPP")

The ARPP is the main self-regulating body in France for advertising. It carries out actions in favour of fair advertising, in the interest of consumers, the public and advertising professionals.

Its mission is to achieve an adequate balance between the freedom of expression and the respect of consumers. Maintaining this balance between creativity and responsibility is at the heart of advertising self-regulation.

The ARPP's actions are the following:

- development of recommendations;
- compliance check before publication;
- interventions for failure after diffusion;
- interface with the public for advertising; and
- development of professional regulation.

The ARPP is assisted by three other bodies: **the CEP, CPP and JDP**.

b. Conseil de l'Ethique Publicitaire ("CEP")

Created in 2005, the CEP's mission is to enlighten the ARPP on rapidly changing sensitivities and fragmentation of values in society. Composed of equal numbers of independent experts and professionals, the CEP is a forum for critical reflection on the ethics linked to advertising.

The CEP's mission is to examine, *ex ante*, advertisements and to produce public opinions on two types of questions:

- a reflection on emerging ethical issues in advertising;
- an evaluation of the efficiency of self-regulation in itself.

Therefore, the CEP has been designed to continuously improve the self-regulation of advertisement.

This type of body is, to our knowledge, quite unique in Europe.

c. Conseil Paritaire de la Publicité ("CPP")

The CPP is a consultation body within which consumer and environmental associations can voice their opinion on problematic advertising trends and ethical rules.

This body allows professional regulation to take advantage of the expertise of associations to better integrate their concerns as early as possible and, more broadly, to promote the process of working together to reduce the problems encountered in the field of advertising ethics.

This body has the following functions:

- participation in the development of ethical standards: the program of work ethics and professional rules decided by ARPP, subject to prior consultation and opinion of the CPP, published on its website;
- exchange of expertise between professionals and consumer associations; and

- drafting of an annual Review to establish an annual evaluation of the implementation of the ARPP rules on sensitive issues.

d. Jury de Déontologie Publicitaire ("JDP")

The JDP comprises nine independent and impartial members recruited on the basis of their competence and integrity.

The Jury's mission is to speak out publicly on complaints made against advertisements or campaigns that may violate professional rules relating to advertising.

All decisions of the JDP are published and may lead to sanctions such as requesting the media to immediately stop the transmission of the advertisement.

The publication of the JDP's decisions is indexed according to the gravity of the offense and the response brought by the professional (depending on whether or not the latter accepts to withdraw or amend its advertisement):

- the first stage of publication is to publish the decisions online;
- the second level of publication is to send a press release, quoting the brand name of the advertiser and the agency responsible for the breach;
- in cases where the violation of ethical rules is particularly serious, the publication of an insert in the press can be decided.

CHAPTER 7
Germany

Andreas Meisterernst and Leonie Evans (Née Kirchner)

DE

I. Possible Bans on Food Advertising

1. Is there any general national legislation or code of conduct regulating the promotion of foodstuffs?

Advertising of foodstuff is regulated by § 11 of the German Food and Feed Act (LFGB) dealing with the protection from deception and misleading advertising and § 12 of the Food and Feed Act prohibiting disease related advertising. These provisions transport the Labelling Directive 2000/13/EC into German law. However, deviating from EU law, in Germany foodstuffs must not give the appearance of medicinal products (§ 11 (1) no 4 Food and Feed Act).

In addition, § 12 (1) Food and Feed Act includes the following prohibitions:

No. 2 – references to medical recommendations and medical reports;

No. 3 – medical records or references to them;

No. 4 – third-party statements, in particular letters of thanks, of appreciation or recommendation in so far as they refer to the curing or abatement of diseases as well as references to such statements;

No. 5 – depiction of persons wearing professional clothing or pursuit of the business of qualified health care practitioners or traders of medicinal products;

No. 6 – statements which are suitable to create or exploit fear; and

No. 7 – written statements that suggest using food to treat diseases.

These prohibitions clearly go beyond the EU prohibition of disease related advertising in Article 2 (1) (b) Labelling Directive 2000/13/EG. The ECJ ruled in *Douwe Egbert*[1] that a national provision prohibiting references to medical recommendations, attestations, declarations and opinions or to statements of approval, other than a statement that a foodstuff is not to be consumed against medical advice, violates EU law. However, it does not follow necessarily from this decision that § 12 (1) nos. 1–7 Food and Feed Act violate EU law too. In contrast to the German provisions of § 12 (1) nos. 1–7 Food and Feed Act on disease related advertising, the Belgian provision subject to the EJC decision *Douwe Egberts* applied to health related advertising. The Court of Appeals Karlsruhe[2] interpreted § 12 (1) no. 1 Food and Feed Act in the light of the ECJ's decision in *Douwe Egberts* to the effect that § 12 (1) no. 1 Food and Feed Act only applies if the statement in question is misleading. Drawing this conclusion from the *Douwe Egberts* decision is not coercive either. EU law rather demands a teleological reduction of § 12 (1) nos. 1–7 Food and Feed Act to the effect that there must be a disease related reference.[3] Thus, § 12 (1) nos. 1–7 Food and Feed Act are merely concrete examples of § 12 (1) no. 1 Food and Feed Act.

The prohibition of disease related advertising does not apply to advertising directed to qualified healthcare practitioners (§ 12 (2) Food and Feed Act). This exception originates from Article 6 (2) Directive 89/398/EEC on foodstuffs intended for particular nutritional uses. It has been implemented in general German food law and therefore applies to the advertising of all foodstuffs.

Advertising for infant formulae is regulated by § 25 (a) German ordinance on dietetic foodstuff that transports Directive 2006/141/EC on infant formulae and follow-on formulae into German law. According to Article 14 (1) (2) Directive 2006/141/EC the Member States may further restrict or prohibit such advertising. The German provision of § 25 (a) ordinance on dietetic foodstuff goes beyond the directive as well. Several prohibitions concern-

1 Case-239/02, Douwe Egberts, 15 July 2004.

2 Court of Appeal Karlsruhr « Kollagen Hydrosolat », Judgment 8 March 2006, 6 U 126/05.

3 Sosnitza in Meyer/Streinz, LFGB, BasisVO, HCVO, 2nd edition, C.H.Beck § 12 LFGB, para. 12.

ing the labelling of infant formulae and follow-on formulae also apply to advertising, and § 25 (a) ordinance on dietetic foodstuff establishes further prohibitions for advertising infant formulae.

In addition, food advertising must not amount to an unfair commercial practice violating the Act Against Unfair Competition, which transports Directive 2005/29/EC into national law.

There used to be a provision prohibiting claims that refer to slimming or weight-reducing effects of a food (§ 6 German ordinance in nutrition labelling). This provision violates EU law and must not be applied any more.

European law	German law
Article 2(1) Directive 2000/13 1. *The labelling and methods used must not:* *(a) be such as could mislead the purchaser to a material degree, particularly:* *(i) as to the characteristics of the foodstuff and, in particular, as to its nature, identity, properties, composition, quantity, durability, origin or provenance, method of manufacture or production;* *(ii) by attributing to the foodstuff effects or properties which it does not possess;* *(iii) by suggesting that the foodstuff possesses special characteristics when in fact all similar foodstuffs possess such characteristics;* *(b) subject to Community provisions applicable to natural mineral waters and foodstuffs for particular nutritional uses, attributed to any foodstuff the property of preventing, treating or curing a human disease, or refer to such properties.*	**§ 11 German Food and Feed Act (LFGB)** *It is prohibited to place food on the market under a misleading name, claim or presentation or to advertise food in general or in a particular case with a misleading description or other statements. It is misleading in particular, if* 1. *names, claims, presentations, descriptions or other statements, on characteristics, in particular on the nature, properties, composition, quantity, durability, origin, provenance, method of manufacture or production which can be misleading are used for a food,* 2. *effects are attributed to a food which it does not possess according to sciences or which are not sufficiently scientifically proven;* 3. *suggested that a food possesses special characteristics when in fact all similar foodstuffs possess such characteristics;* 4. *a food is given the appearance of a medicinal product.*

3. The prohibitions or restrictions referred to in paragraphs 1 and 2 shall also apply to: *(a) the presentation of foodstuffs, in particular their shape, appearance or packaging, the packaging materials used, the way in which they are arranged and the setting in which they are displayed;* *(b) advertising.*	**§ 12 German Food and Feed Act (LFGB)** *When dealing with food and advertising food it is prohibited in general or in a particular case to use* *1. statements which refer to curing, abatement or prevention of a disease;* *2. references to medical recommendations and medical reports;* *3. medical records or references to them;* *4. third party statements, in particular letters of thanks, appreciation or recommendation in so far as they refer to the curing or abatement of diseases as well as references to such statements;* *5. depictions of persons wearing professional clothing or pursuit of the business of qualified health care practitioners or traders of medicinal products;* *6. statements which are suitable to create or exploit fear;* *7. written statements suggesting to use food to treat diseases.* *2. The prohibitions of subparagraph 1 do not apply to advertising directed to qualified health care practitioners.*

2. Is there any specific national restriction or prohibition (mandatory legislation and code of conduct)?

a. Restrictions relating to certain products, in particular alcoholic beverages

Only two German provisions deal with advertising restrictions relating to alcoholic beverages. There is a prohibition of advertising of alcoholic beverages in cinemas before 6 p.m. (§ 11(5) Act on the protection of minors). Secondly, advertising of alcoholic beverages on the radio and TV must neither be directed or particularly appeal to minors nor depict minors consuming alcohol (§ 6 (5) State Treaty on the protection of minors in media).

In addition, there are self-regulatory rules on advertising by the German Advertising Standards Council (*Deutscher Werberat*). These rules are not binding, but public service broadcasters commit to follow the voluntary Code of Conduct. They include, for example, the following rules[4]:

- Commercial communication for alcoholic beverages shall not promote abusive consumption of alcoholic beverages or trivialise such consumption.
- There must be no 'flat-rate' and 'all you can drink' offers.
- There must be no presentation of high alcohol content as a positive quality of a brand.
- There must be no promotion of drinking of alcoholic beverages by minors.
- There must be no association between the consumption of alcoholic beverages and driving.
- There must be no claim relating to the elimination or relief of anxiety.
- There must be no claim relating to improvement of physical performance and social or sexual success.

b. Restrictions relating to a specific sections of the population, e.g. children

Recital 18 and Article 5 (3) of Directive 2005/29/EC on unfair business to consumer commercial practices dictate that commercial practices that are specifically aimed at a group of consumers who are particularly vulner-

4 See http://www.werberat.de/sites/default/files/uploads/media/dw_code_of_conduct_alcoholic_beverages_2009_en.pdf.

able, such as children, shall be assessed from the perspective of the average member of that group. This principle echoes in § 3 (2) Act Against Unfair Competition which states that commercial practices towards consumers shall be illegal in any case where they do not conform to the professional diligence required of the entrepreneur concerned and are suited to tangible impairment of the consumer's ability to make an information-based decision, thus inducing him to make a transactional decision which he would not otherwise have made. Here reference shall be made to the average consumer or, when the commercial practice is directed towards a particular group of consumers, to the average member of that group. Reference shall be made to the perspective of the average member of a group of consumers who are particularly vulnerable and clearly identifiable because of his/her mental or physical infirmity, age or credulity, if it is foreseeable for the entrepreneur that his commercial practice will affect the latter group only.

In addition, including in an advertisement a direct exhortation to children to purchase the goods or services marketed, or to persuade their parents or other adults to do so, is always illegal according to § 3 (3) Annex No. 28 Act Against Unfair Competition. This provision, which is based on Directive 2005/29/EC, was recently the subject of a decision of the Federal Court of Justice.[5] The court ruled that advertising which uses language directly addressing people in the second person singular and employing terms typical for children is considered as advertising mainly directed at children. Terms such as "get yourself..." in a child related advertising violate this provision.

Furthermore, self-regulatory rules on advertising by the German Advertising Standards Council (*Deutscher Werberat*) provide principles for advertising with and directed at children.[6] There shall be, for example, none of the following:

- No direct invitation to children to buy or make their parents buy the product;
- No statements by children about the special advantages and features of the product that do not conform to the natural utterances of the child;

5 Federal Court of Justice, "Runes of Magic", Judgment, 17 July 2013, I ZR 34/12.

6 See http://www.werberat.de/sites/default/files/uploads/media/dw_adv_with_and_for_children_en.pdf.

- Aleatory advertising media (e.g. free raffles, prize competitions and puzzles, etc.) should not mislead the potential purchaser, should not allure by the offer of excessive advantages, should not exploit gambling instincts and should not indulge in touting;
- Examples of infringements include (1) "Try it" in a commercial showing children consuming the advertised product; (2) "Get the new issue" spoken with a child's voice; and (3) "You can now learn the nicest Christmas songs with this product".

DE

II. Misleading Advertising

1. What are the national rules on misleading advertising with respect to foodstuffs?

Rules on misleading advertising are laid down in § 11 German Food and Feed Act (LFGB) dealing with protection from deception and misleading advertising that transports the Labelling Directive 2000/13/EC into German law. A comparison to Article 2 (1) Directive 2000/13/EC is provided in section 1.1 above.

2. What are the national landmark cases regarding misleading advertising for foodstuffs?

Contrary to what exists in many other EU countries there are hundreds of cases on misleading advertising for foodstuffs in Germany. Some interesting decisions on the following topics will be outlined.

a. Country of Origin Labelling

Dutch chocolate[7]

The Supreme Court of the German Reich ruled in 1929 that a product named "Dutch Chocolate" must be produced in Holland. It does not suffice if the product is produced in a factory in Germany under the direction of a Dutch company and with Dutch raw materials.

Black Forest wine[8]

A fruity wine carrying references and pictures indicating it originates from the Black Forest was held misleading because it was neither produced in the Black Forest nor did the berries come from there.

Chiabatta bread[9]

A bread named 'Ciabatta' with the Italian national colours green, white, red not in the form of a flag on the packaging was held not misleading because the label also beared the claim 'Italian style'.

b. Composition and characteristics of the food

Near-water mango-orange-flower[10]

A soft drink named "Near-water mango-orange-flower" which shows a picture of an orange flower but does not contain orange flower or essence of it was held misleading. The depiction of an orange flower creates the consumer expectation that the soft drink would contain orange flower or parts of it. According to the guidelines on soft drinks, which were held not

7 RG JW 1929, 1215.

8 VG Karlsruhe 9 August 1999, 14 K 1009/99.

9 OLG Koblenz 12 June 2001, 4 U 1573/00.

10 OLG Karlsruhe, 14 March 2012, 6 U 12/11.

binding but should be taken into account to determine consumer expectations, lifelike depiction of fruit may only be used for products containing fruit juice or fruit puree. Neither the mere description as a "low calories soft drink with mango and orange flower flavour" nor the list of ingredients suffices to correct this unfounded consumer expectation.

Pork roast[11]

A ready-to-eat meal named "pork roast" made of tumbled meat without reference to the fact that it consists of assembled pork meat was found misleading. According to the guidelines on meat, which were consulted to determine the consumer expectation, the name "roast" may only be used for a product that consists of one natural piece if the name clearly indicates that the meat is not naturally grown. Thus, use of the name "pork roast" was illegitimate.

Nut-triangle[12]

A non-prepackaged bakery product named "nut-triangle with couverture and cocoa compound coating" was held misleading regarding the component "with couverture" because the average consumer would expect a separate share of couverture as well as cocoa compound coating. The average consumer does not understand the term "with couverture and cocoa compound coating" as a list of ingredients of a single coating but he expects two different coatings and has a higher quality of the coating in mind. Since the nut triangle had one single coating and not couverture and cocoa compound coating, which the consumer expects because of the name "nut-triangle with couverture and cocoa compound coating", this name was held misleading.

11 VG Berlin, 20 November 2011, 14 K 43.09, LRE 64, 22.

12 BVerwG, 20 June 2012, 3 B 87/11, LRE 64, 17.

Frikadelle[13]

A meatball named "Frikadelle" which contains 65 % pork, 15 % beef, 5 % mechanically recovered poultry and 15 % other ingredients was held not misleading because the list of ingredients showed 5 % poultry meat. Starting material for a "Frikadelle" is pork and beef according to the German Guidelines on meat and meat products.

Slim whilst sleeping[14]

A bread high in protein was advertised with the slogan "Slim whilst sleeping" in a leaflet. This slogan was determined misleading because it creates the consumer expectation that the bread itself has a slimming effect. However, the inside of the flyer makes clear that the bread itself does not have any slimming effect but that it is part of a concept to lose weight. Nonetheless, the court concluded that this note does not suffice to clarify the wrong impression that the bread has a slimming effect.

Ginger beer[15]

A soft drink called "Ginger beer", which is not beer, was held misleading because consumers expect beer in the drink. Due to the presentation of the product and the meaning of the word "beer", the consumer expects the product to be beer. The food business operator did not manage to prove the opposite.

13 OVG Nordrhein-Westfalen, 7 August 1996, 13 A 7606/95, LRE 33, 400.

14 Schleswig-Holsteinisches OLG, 21 June 2012, 6 W 1/12, LRE 64, 25.

15 KG Berlin, 12 October 2012, 5 U 19/12, WRP 2013, 224.

III. Mandatory Labelling: Name of Product

1. Are there any national definitions of a foodstuff that could hamper the marketing of an imported food product?

a. Energy and sports drinks

Energy drinks are defined as "soft drinks containing caffeine and one or more of the following substances: taurine, inositole, glucuronolactone" according to the German ordinance on fruit juice and soft drinks. Provisions on marketing and labelling are provided by the German ordinance on fruit juice and soft drinks.

There is no definition for sport drinks.

b. Yogurt

Yogurt is defined by the German ordinance on milk products as "made of milk or cream while the end product contains specific thermophile ripening cultures, whose growing optimum is at 42 degrees Celcius".

c. Cheese

Cheese is defined by the German ordinance on cheese as "fresh products or products which are in different stages of ripeness and which are made of curdled cheese milk".

d. Bread

Bread is defined by the guidelines on bread and small baked products as "made from grain and/or grain products by adding liquids and other foodstuffs (e.g. potato products) by kneading, forming, loosening, baking or hot extracting the dough. Bread contains less than 10 % fat and/or sugar per 90 % grain".

There are a lot of other guidelines on different products, e.g. meat, fine bakery products, vegetable juices, tea, etc. containing definitions and provisions on the composition and labelling of the foodstuff.

IV. Voluntary Labelling

1. "Clean labels" – Are there any national definitions or requirements with respect to claims such as 'natural', 'pure', 'home-made', 'additive-free'?

Matters of "clean labelling" are decided on a case-by-case basis. In particular, the notion 'natural' confronts us with many obstacles with regard to labelling products and/or ingredients. Thus, the German approach to this popular claim will be outlined in the following section.

There is neither a general legal definition of 'natural' nor a specific national provision on 'naturalness'. The former provision of § 17 (1) (4) Former Food and Feed Act (LMBG), which stated that the term "natural" must not be used for food which contains authorised food additives or residues of pesticides or substances with a pharmacological effect, has not been transferred to the current Food and Feed Act (LFGB) because of the ECJ decision "d'arbo naturrein".[16] As such, the crucial issue is the general prohibition of misleading advertising. The consumer does not expect a food bearing the term "natural" to be totally unprocessed.

"Natural" ingredients may be processed but no extensive chemical processes should have taken place. A reference point to understand this issue is Regulation (EU) No. 1334/2008 on flavourings. Article 3 (2) lit. c) Regulation (EC) 1334/2008 gives conclusive evidence as parts of it refer to traditional food preparation processes listed, and Article 3 (2) lit. k) sets out certain criteria for an "appropriate physical process", while Annex II provides a list of traditional food preparation processes. Most importantly, Article16 Regulation (EC) 1334/2008 provides specific requirements for the use of

16 C-465/98, d'arbo naurrein, 4 April 2000.

the term "natural" to describe certain flavouring in the sales description. According to Article 16 Regulation (EC) 1334/2008 the term 'natural' may only be used for the description of flavouring if the flavouring component comprises only flavouring preparations and/or natural flavouring substances. The term 'natural flavouring substance(s)' may only be used for flavourings in which the flavouring component contains exclusively natural flavouring substances. With respect to flavouring, the term 'natural' may only be used in combination with a reference to a food, food category or a vegetable or animal flavouring source if the flavouring component has been obtained exclusively or by at least 95 % by w/w from the source material referred to.

The Court of Appeals Hamburg opted for a different reference point in a recent decision concerning infant formula.[17] It remarked that any recourse to the Flavouring Regulation when deciding on the term "natural" for a food is not convincing because the consumer expects a flavouring to be extracted from a base product implying that processing has taken place and that the term "natural" does not refer to the absence of any processing but to the naturalness of the base product. The court referred instead to the provision of § 2 (3) (2) (1) Food and Feed Act which differentiates between "natural substances", "substances of natural origin" and substances which are "chemically equal" to natural substances. The court asserted that the relevant public expects "natural lactic acid culture", which was in question in the case, to be "taken from nature" and that the biochemical composition has not been altered in a laboratory. Since the lactic acid culture which was advertised as "natural" had not been taken from nature as it is but its biochemical composition had been changed by an enzymatic selection process, the court held the advertising to be misleading.

However, this is just one decision of many decided on a case-by-case basis. As already mentioned above the justification for using the term "natural" when advertising foodstuffs always depends on the particular facts of the case.

17 Court of Appeals Hamburg, 29 August 2013, 3 U 12/12.

2. Nutrition & health claims

a. Within the list of health claims authorised pursuant to Regulation 1924/2006, are there any related substances that are prohibited or considered as a medicinal substance within your jurisdiction?

The substances Melatonin, Activated Charcoal and Lactulose, for which health claims have been authorised by Regulation (EU) No. 432/2012, are considered medicinal substances by German authorities. Upon the initiative of Germany, Recital 17 was integrated in Regulation (EU) No. 432/2012, according to which any decision on a health claim in accordance with Regulation (EC) No. 1924/2006, such as inclusion in the list of permitted claims referred to in Article 13(3) thereof, does not constitute an authorisation of the marketing of the substance on which the claim is made, a decision on whether the substance can be used in foodstuff, or a classification of a certain product as a foodstuff. However, the categorisation as medicinal substances by German authorities is not binding, and there is no case law on this issue. The crucial criterion for demarcation is the dosage. The authorisation of a health claim implies that the respective substance is considered a food in some Member States if the conditions of the claim, especially the dosage, are followed. Room for deviating qualification only remains regarding medicinal products by presentation.[18]

b. Are there any national laws and regulations permitting food business operators to make reference to recommendations or endorsements by national associations, medical, nutrition or dietetic professionals, and health-related charities?

No, there are no provisions permitting food business operators to make such references. In contrast § 12 (1) (2) Food and Feed Act prohibits references to medical recommendations and medical reports when dealing with and

18 Meisterernst and Haber, *Praxiskommentar Health & Nutrition Claims* Behr's Verlag Article 1 para. 60.

advertising food. For detailed information on the prohibition of disease related advertising, please refer to section 1.1.

c. Is the use of nutrition or health claims on non-prepackaged food further regulated at the national level?

DE

No, there is no national legislation or case law on this issue.

d. Is there a notification procedure required prior to / for marketing foodstuffs bearing nutritional or health claims?

No, there is no notification procedure for food except for food supplements and certain dietetic foodstuff in Germany. These notifications are required regardless of the use of nutrition or health claims.

V. Enforcement of Food Law and Self-regulating Bodies

1. Which actions may one risk in case of non-compliance with the labelling or advertising requirements?

a. Public authorities

Prosecution of infringements is a complex issue because Germany is a federal republic with 16 federal states. According to § 38 Food and Feed Act, the federal states are competent to prosecute food law infringements including infringements regarding food info and advertising. The supreme authorities of the states coordinate and organise the reinforcement of food control administration, and the administrative authorities exercise the actual supervisory tasks. Food inspectors, food chemists and veterinarians may take samples and start the necessary actions. They enforce the national provisions in the case of an infringement, and state laboratories that provide scientific reports support their work. Furthermore, the Federal Office of Consumer Protection and Food Safety (BVL) coordinates actions, and the Federal Institute for Risk Assessment (BfR) exercises scientific risk evaluations.

The legal basis for actions that administrative authorities may take are stated in §§ 38 to 49 Food and Feed Act and in Article 54 Regulation (C) No. 882/2004 on official controls performed to ensure the verification of compliance with feed and food law, animal health and animal welfare rules. The most important measures that supervisory authorities may take are laid down in § 39 Food and Feed Act. According to this provision authorities may take necessary measures to prevent dangers for human health and risks of misleading behaviour. In particular, authorities can temporarily prohibit the placing on the market of a product or prohibit the production, use and marketing of a product. In addition, Article 19 Regulation (EC) No. 178/2002 regulates the withdrawal of a product. In comparison to this EU provision, § 39 (2) Food and Feed Act allows further action because it is not restricted to food safety issues.

Furthermore, § 40 (1) Food and Feed Act states that within the framework of Article 10 of Regulation (EC) No. 178/2002, the competent authority may inform the public of the name of the food or animal feed and the name or trade name of the food or animal feed manufacturer, processor or distributor. Where doing so is better able to prevent risks, it may also release the name of the operator responsible for placing the product on the market. A public information measure, within the meaning of and in accordance with the above rules, may also be taken in the following cases: no. 4 where food, which is not injurious to health but is unfit for human consumption in particular because it is nauseating, is or has been distributed in significant quantities or where, because of its specificity, it has been distributed only in small quantities but over a relatively lengthy period of time. This provision was subject to the recent ECJ case *Karl Berger/Freistaat Bayern.*[19] The ECJ ruled that Article 10 of Regulation (EC) No. 178/2002 must be interpreted so as not to preclude national legislation allowing information to be issued to the public mentioning the name of a food and the name or trade name of the food manufacturer, processor or distributor, in a case where that food, though not injurious to health, is unfit for human consumption.

19 Case C-636/11, Karl Berger/Freistaat Bayern, 11 April 2013.

Thus, the authority lawfully informed the public about the food unfit for human consumption.

Another German provision currently attracting a lot of attention is § 40 (1a) Food and Feed Act according to which the competent authority may inform the public of the name of the food or animal feed and the name or trade name of the food or animal feed manufacturer, processor or distributor, if there is a reasonable suspicion that statutory threshold values, maximum levels or maximum amounts have been exceeded. The competent authority may do the same in case of infringements of provisions on consumers' health safety or deception or compliance with hygienic requirements and a severe or repeated infringement and where a monetary fine of 350 € was assessed. After several German courts[20] expressed their doubts about the constitutional compliance of this provision, the federal states no longer enforce it. This issue will be of further concern for sure.

Regarding criminal procedures §§ 59 to 60 Food and Feed Act contain criminal sanctions on almost all food law infringements. Most of them are punished as misdemeanours.

Criminal provisions on infringement of labelling and advertising requirements

Non-compliance with labelling requirements	1. § 59 (1) (21 a) Food and Feed Act, § 10 (1) Ordinance on food labelling Labelling as "defrosted" missing, food beyond date of minimum durability sold.	1. Up to one year imprisonment or monetary fine.
	2. § 60 (1) Food and Feed Act, § 10 (2) Ordinance on food labelling No. 1 committed negligently.	2. Misdemeanour punished by a monetary fine up to 50.000 €.
	3. § 60 (2) (26 a) Food and Feed Act, § 10 (3) Ordinance on food labelling Selling food that does not contain mandatory labelling requirements.	3. Misdemeanour punished by a monetary fine up to 50.000 €.

20 Administrative Court of Baden-Württemberg, Bavaria and Münster.

Non-compliance with labelling requirements	4. § 60 (2) (26 a) Food and Feed Act, § 5 Ordinance on lot labelling Selling food without a lot number.	4. Misdemeanour punished by a monetary fine up to 50.000 €.
	5. § 59 (2) (3) Food and Feed Act, Regulation (EC) No. 1924/2006 Infringement of Health Claims Regulation.	5. Up to one year imprisonment or monetary fine.
	6. § 59 (1) (21 a) Food and Feed Act, § 26 (5) (1) Ordinance on dietetic food Incorrect labelling and advertising of dietetic food.	6. Up to one year imprisonment or monetary fine.
	7. § 60 (2) (26 a) Food and Feed Act, § 26 (7) (3) Ordinance on dietetic food Inadmissable advertising of infant formulae.	7. Misdemeanour punished by a monetary fine up to 50.000 €.
Misleading labelling Misleading advertisement	1. § 11, 59 (1) (7) (8) (9) Food and Feed Act.	1. Up to one year imprisonment or monetary fine.
	2. 60 (1) (1) Food and Feed Act Selling and advertising food with misleading name, statement or presentation.	2. Misdemeanour punished by a monetary fine up to 100.000 €.
	3. § 60 (1) (2) Food and Feed Act No. 2 committed negligently.	3. Misdemeanour punished by a monetary fine up to 50.000 €.
	4. § 60 (2) (1) Food and Feed Act Infringement of the prohibition of disease related advertising	4. Misdemeanour punished by a monetary fine up to 50.000 €
Fraud	§ 236 Criminal Code Fraud	Up to seven years imprisonment or monetary fine

b. Competitors actions

Actions by competitors are very common in Germany, and the country has a very distinct practice of unfair competition law and unfair practices. A typical scenario starts with a warning letter to cease and desist. The competitor is asked to discontinue the advertising and sign a declaration of discontinuance with a penalty clause. The parties might negotiate about omitting the advertising or parts of it in the future if they agree for one party to sell the products in stock until a certain date. At the same time the warned party usually draws a caveat, which is a protective brief explaining the factual and legal situation from its point of view. It is sent to the court where the applicant is expected to apply for an interim injunction. Interim injunctions are usually ordered without oral hearing, and the caveat serves the purpose of explaining the respondent's point of view before the court makes a decision. An interim injunction can be granted within a couple of days and is immediately enforceable, meaning that the advertising must cease immediately. If the label is concerned, the product cannot be sold any more. An interim injunction is only valid for six months. Thus, the summary proceeding is often followed by a lawsuit.

Due to this elaborate competitive law system, and because Germans prefer to go to court to have a matter decided by the judicial system, the objections of the authorities play a much smaller role in Germany compared to other EU states.

c. Consumer associations

There are no class actions in Germany. Actions by one single consumer are rare.

However, there are several consumer associations in Germany, which are qualified to bring actions on behalf of consumer interests. Their standing is based upon § 8 (2) no. 3 Act Against Unfair Competition, which has its origin in Directive 98/27/EC on injunctions on the protection of consumers' interests. Consumer associations can bring actions against entities that they believe are perpetrating unfair commercial practices if they are included in the list of qualified entities. Qualified entities are, e.g. the consumer associations of the federal states, Foodwatch e.V., and the German *Verbraucherschutzverein*.

2. Are there any national self-regulating bodies with respect to advertising for foodstuffs?

There is the German Advertising Standards Council (*Deutscher Werberat*), which sets rules on advertising. These rules are not binding, but the media, including the public service broadcasters in particular, exercise responsibility and are therefore obliged to follow the Code of Conduct.

In the case of a complaint the German Advertising Standards Council asks the company to change or discontinue the advertising and threatens to issue a public reprimand. In 96 % of the cases the company withdraws the advertising and no public reprimand is issued. In four decades 18.000 cases have appeared before the Advertising Standards Council, and 7.700 campaigns were objected towards the company while 114 public reprimands have been issued.[21] As these figures illustrate, the role of this self-regulating body is rather small.

21 See http://www.werberat.de/beschwerdefaelle-aus-40-jahren.

CHAPTER 8
Italy

Giorgio Rusconi

IT

I. Possible Bans on Food Advertising

1. Is there any general national legislation or code of conduct regulating the promotion of foodstuffs?

There is no general national legislation specifically applicable to foodstuffs. There is only general legislation on advertising that also regulates this matter. Furthermore, advertising is regulated by *Codice di Autodisciplina della Comunicazione Commerciale* (Marketing Communication Self-Regulation Code or the "Code").[1] The self-regulatory system was set up in Italy in 1963, with the creation of the *Instituto dell'Autodisciplina Pubblicitaria* (the Italian Self-Regulation Organization, or IAP), in order to ensure that all marketing communication be honest, truthful and proper and carried out as a service for the information of consumers. Amongst IAP's main responsibilities are the formulation and updating of the rules of the Code and the appointment of members to the *Giurì*[2] and the Review Board.

IAP is a self-regulation body made up of associations which undertake to comply, and make sure their members comply, with the Marketing Communication Self-Regulation Code laid down by the same. IAP members also undertake to cause all their associated entities to insert in their contracts a clause of agreement with the Code and the *Giurì* decisions, so that even the commercials of the user, agency or professional that do not

1 (58th edition – effective as of 27 March 2014, available on the Internet at <http://www.iap.it/about/the-code/?lang=en&lang=en>).

2 The *Giurì* is composed of members appointed by IAP, and chosen from among experts in law, consumer affairs and communication" (the Code, Article 29); it "examines the marketing communication submitted to it and judges it according to the provisions of this Code" (the Code, Article 32).

belong to the above associations, are subject to the Code. Thus, although it is a self-regulating text, it governs most commercial communications in Italy.

2. Is there any specific national restriction or prohibition (mandatory legislation and code of conduct)?

a. With respect to certain foodstuffs

As regards *infant feed for babies*, Decree No. 82 of 9 April 2009 by the Ministry of Labour, Health and Social Policies, implementing Directive No. 2006/141/EC, specifically regulates the advertising of newborn and infant feed, specifically distinguishing between infant age groups, namely 0-6 months *(**"alimenti per lattanti"**)* and over 6 months of age *(**"alimenti di proseguimento"**)*.

As regards **alcoholic beverages**, Act 125/2001 (subject to the specific restrictions dealt with in the following paragraph) prohibits advertisements attributing therapeutic effectiveness or indications that are not expressly recognised by the Ministry of Health. Article 22 of the Code regulates the matter in detail. It does not impose a total ban on advertising alcohol and highlighting its characteristics and qualities, but rather aims at protecting the consumer from any advertising which may encourage the harmful abuse of alcohol or its consumption driven by illusory expectancies, such as obtaining greater physical efficiency or achievements in one's social life. Marketing communications regarding alcoholic beverages should not contrast the need to enhance the establishment of models of consumption inspired by moderation, fair behaviour, and responsibility. The main intent is to protect the primary interests of people, and especially infants and teenagers, from the consequences connected with the abuse of alcoholic beverages.

In particular, marketing communications should not:

- encourage excessive, uncontrolled, and hence harmful consumption of alcoholic beverages;
- depict an unhealthy attachment or addiction to alcohol, or generally lead people to believe that resorting to alcohol can solve personal problems;

- address or (even only indirectly) refer to minors, and show them (or people who clearly appear to be minors) consuming alcohol;
- use any signs, drawings, characters and/or real people that are directly and mainly related to minors and that may arouse the direct interest of minors;
- associate the driving of vehicles with the consumption of alcoholic beverages;
- lead the public to believe that the consumption of alcoholic beverages promotes clarity of mind and enhances physical and sexual performances, or that failure to consume alcohol implies physical, psychological, or social inferiority;
- depict sobriety and abstention from drinking alcohol as negative values;
- induce the public to disregard the different drinking styles that should be considered in relation to the specific features of individual products and the consumer's personal conditions;
- stress the high alcoholic content of a beverage as the main theme.

The issue of the prohibition to address, or even only indirectly refer to, minors was dealt with by a decision by the *Giurì,* which banned a communication inviting parents to give their children an egg-based liqueur with energy properties (*Giurì* Case 71/84 – *Comitato di Accertamento v. Wax & Vitale spa* – 27 November 1984).

As regards **food supplements** that are likewise subject to specific restrictions laid down in Legislative Decree No.169/2004, under Article 7 of said Decree, when supplements are anyhow advertised as coadjutants in low-calorie diets aimed at weight loss, the commercial must in no way make reference to any weight loss time schedule or amount of weight lost as a consequence of the product's use. On the other hand, it should point out the need to in any case follow an adequate low-calorie diet and abandon excessively sedentary life styles. Moreover, the commercial cannot mention the details of the notification procedure to the Italian Health Ministry of the food supplements advertised.

Article 23-bis of the Code further regulates the advertising of food supplements in greater detail. In particular, commercial communications regarding these kinds of products should not claim properties that are not consistent with the specific features of the products or that the products do not really possess.

Moreover, without prejudice to the provisions of Regulation (EC) no. 1924/2006, the commercial should be conceived so as not to induce consumers to make poor nutritional choices and must avoid references to any recommendation or endorsement of a medical character.

In particular, as to marketing communications regarding food supplements proposed for weight control or loss and other specific typologies of supplements, IAP issued a specific Regulation (*"Regulation concerning marketing communication relating to food supplements")* setting forth rules on the advertising of such products.

b. With respect to specific sections of the population

Under Act 125 of 30 March 2001 it is forbidden to advertise alcoholic beverages and spirits within programmes addressing minors as well as in the fifteen minutes preceding and following their transmission, or to broadcast TV commercials showing children consuming alcohol or portraying the consumption of such beverages in a positive light.

In addition, alcoholic drinks (whether hard or light) cannot be directly or indirectly advertised in places mainly attended by children under the age of 18 years, in the daily and periodic press targeted at minors and in theatres where films mainly intended for children are shown.

The TV and Minors Self-Regulation Code issued on 29 November 2002 by the Telecommunications Ministry specifies that advertisements for alcoholic beverages generally should not portray minors drinking alcohol, whereas during the time slot for programmes specifically devoted to children (i.e., from 4:00 pm to 7:00 pm), commercials of alcoholic beverages and spirits should be avoided.

II. Misleading Advertising

1. What are the national rules on misleading advertising with respect to foodstuffs?

Legislative Decree No. 109 of 27 January 1992, as modified by Legislative Decree No. 181 of 23 June 2003 implementing Directive 2000/13/EC, generally provides that the labelling, presentation and advertising of foodstuffs must not be such as to:

(i) mislead the purchaser as to the characteristics of the foodstuff and, in particular, as to its nature, identity, quality, composition, quantity, durability, origin or provenance, method of manufacture or production;

(ii) attribute to the foodstuff effects or properties which it does not possess;

(iii) suggest that the foodstuff possesses special characteristics when in fact all similar foodstuffs possess such characteristics;

(iv) attribute to any foodstuff the property of preventing, treating or curing a human disease, or refer to such properties.

2. What are the national landmark cases regarding misleading advertising for foodstuffs?

The instances envisaged by the provisions outlined above on several occasions have been further specified by the relevant authorities' (and particularly self-regulatory) decisions. Thus:

- where the type of product the consumer is purchasing is misrepresented, especially where there exist specific provisions linking a definite designation to specific product characteristics, the relevant authority found that the consumer had been misled as to the product's nature or identity and consequently inflicted a sanction. In Case 26/08 the *Giurì* ruled on a new product defined as "mayonnaise" which, however, did not contain one of the fundamental ingredients included in the traditional (although not regulatory) recipe, that is, egg-yolk. According to the *Giurì,* the average consumer identifies mayonnaise with a sauce in the composition of which egg-yolk is essential. Therefore, (s)he will expect that if a product is called mayonnaise, it will contain egg-yolk[3];

- the discrepancy between what is declared and the product's actual composition has been at the heart of frequent complaints of misleading advertising. This is the case especially with so-called "negative adjectivations", namely, marketing communications that aim at distinguishing their products from those of the same kind on account of the absence of definite substances which are often disliked by consumers. The decision by the Italian Supervisory Authority for Competition and the Market, or AGCM ("AGCM"), in Case PI4344 – *Ditta C.a.r.n.j. – Turkey sausage* –5 February 2004, *Ruling No. 12881, Bollettino n.6/2004,* stating that "the noun *'salsiccia'* (sausage), which in the Italian language identifies *'minced pork or beef stuffed into an intestine casing'*", may, in any case, represent a designation of use generally associated with pork only where it is not, as in the case at hand, accompanied by further specifications as to the product contents. In the AGCM case, however, it appears undisputable that the designation *"salsiccia [sausage]* followed by the indication *"di tacchino" [of turkey,* hence, *turkey sausage]* suggests that the product has a different composition from that of typical pork sausages, and basically consists of turkey stuffed into an intestine casing. *[...]* Moreover, it may be reasonably held that *[...]* failure to provide adequate information as to the actual percentages of turkey and pork in the product, may mislead the consumer to infer, that the product is composed to a greater extent of turkey than pork, whereas in fact the product contains turkey and pork in nearly equivalent percentages". Likewise AGCM, in Case PI5977 – *Omogeneizzato Plasmon alla banana* [Plasmon Banana Homogenised Food] – 10 October 2007, *Ruling No. 17473, Bollettino n.38/2007,* sanctioned a homogenised product bearing the indication "100 %" followed by the name of the fruit on the packaging, despite the fact that it contained a high percentage of another fruit (as attested by the ingredient list). On that occasion AGCM stated that "the modes how the product is presented to the public, and particularly its packaging (which is the first thing to influence the purchaser and

3 *Giurì* Decision 26/08 – *Unilever Italia S.r.l. v. Kraft Foods Italia S.p.A.* -17 April 2008.

therefore the main factor of appeal to the consumer), does not give the consumer the exact perception of the actual composition of the homogenised food since, by portraying and mentioning only the fruit mainly contained in the same package, it misleads the consumer into believing that such fruit is the only product component, and thus fails to convey accurate, transparent information. Actually, the presence of apple (36 %) and de-acidified concentrated apple juice (4 %), due to their aggregate relevant quantity as compared to the total banana and plum contents, determines a substantial difference not only in respect of the food product composition but also with regard to its characteristics and identity, and is apt to mislead consumers". Absolutely similar is also the decision in Case PI5216 – *Paté di fegato d'anatra Jensen's* [Jensen's Duck liver paté] – 8 March 2007, *Ruling No. 16588, Bollettino n.10/2007,* which states that "the designation *'paté'* followed by the indication *'fegato d'anatra'* [duck liver] as well as the representation of the same bird on the front of the package, leads the consumer to believe that the product composition is characterised by *'duck liver'*, although as a matter of fact, from the documents gathered during the procedure and the percentages of the ingredients reported on the label, the product results to be composed to a definitely prevailing extent by other types of meat. Nor can such misleading information be considered 'mitigated' by the product low price [...]. *Held,* the commercial in contention, through the designation *'Paté di fegato d'anatra'* [duck liver paté], is apt to mislead consumers in respect of the product nature and composition, since it leads consumers to believe that, contrary to the truth, the product mainly contains said ingredient"[4];

- as regards deception as to the product origin, labels and advertisements that concerned products the indication of origin of which was apt to arise confusion in consumers have been sanctioned. In this regard, see AGCM decisions in Case PI2351 – *Cavazzutti G. & figli* – 15 April 1999, *Ruling No. 7107, Bollettino n.15/1999* on *"Salsiccia di Pollino" [Sausage of Pollino]* and in Case PI5468 – *Filù Ferru di L.s.m.* – 26 April 2007, *Ruling No. 16785, Bollettino 17/2007,* whereby the indications relating to the place of production and bottling, reported on only the front la-

4 See also AGCM Case PI3614 – *Preparazione di frutta Zuegg* [Zuegg fruit preparation] – 27 March 2002, *Ruling No. 10591, Bollettino n.13/2002.*

bel of the product and in reduced types, as opposed to the whole set of images and symbols recalling the region of Sardinia, *per se* do not amount to an element apt to inform the consumer that the product is a type of aqua vitae lacking said geographic characterization. In light of the above elements, the message was found apt to mislead consumers as to the product provenance and processing characteristics, thus prejudicing consumers' economic behaviour. Such a violation further brings prejudice to competitors, who are undeniably harmed by the diversion of customers provoked by the error incurred by the recipients of the message reported on the label when making their purchasing choices. Likewise, in Decision No. 85/2009 the *Giurì* deemed that the claims *"L'unico latte romano"* [The only Roman milk], *"romano al cento per cento"* [100 % Roman], *"arriva sulla tavola dei romani prima degli altri"* [arrives on the Romans' tables before the others], *"il più fresco"* [the freshest], *"nessun altro può offrire una simile garanzia di freschezza"* [no other can offer such a freshness warranty], were misleading since the producer recognised that for a certain period of time the milk so advertised was actually pasteurised and packaged in a different region of Italy and for that reason cannot certainly qualify as "Roman". Giurì Case 85/09 – *Centrale del Latte di Roma S.p.A. v. Ariete Fattoria Latte Sano S.p.A.* – 26 October 2009[5];

5 See also AGCM decision in Case PI4878 – *Salamella Calabrese – Fiorucci* – 26 October 2005, *Ruling No. 14821, Bollettino n.43/2005,* where the advertisement, consisting in the label bearing the wording *"LE SPECIALITÀ REGIONALI SALAMELLA CALABRESE PICCANTE – PURO SUINO"* [i.e., REGIONAL SPECIALITIES CALABRIAN HORSESHOE PEPPERONI – PURE PORK], suggested that (contrary to the truth) the product at issue was a salami prepared in line with the quality parameters typical of the Calabrian salami manufacture tradition. Indeed, "the use of the indication *'Calabrian'* in the text and of the graphic types resulted apt to mislead the consumer into believing that the advertised product had the same qualities and features of the salamis enjoying the recognition of the protected designation of origin, particularly the 'Salsiccia di Calabria DOP' *[Sausage of Calabria PDO]"*. The advertisement, therefore, was held apt to mislead consumers creating confusion between the product it refers to and the Calabrian salamis enjoying the PDO designation (nor is the indication on the label of the place of production and packaging sufficient to exclude the misleading character of the advertisement since such indication is reported in much smaller types than the rest of the advertisement).

- the exaltation of particular features of a product, even though corresponding to the truth, has been deemed unlawful whenever such features may actually be found in all products of the same kind insofar as required by the law or falling within the very composition of the product. On this point the *Giurì* has specified that "any advertisement of a product presenting as peculiar to the same a characteristic which vice versa is common to all the products of the same kind, amounts to misleading advertising and has thus the effect of establishing an indirect comparison which very likely leads consumers to believe that the characteristic is special and, as such, possessed only by the product claiming it." Similarly, "the self-appropriation on an exclusive basis of a quality which instead is common to one's competitor's products as well", amounts to an unlawful comparison (*Giurì* decisions Nos. 116/2005 – *Granarolo S.p.A. v. Danone S.p.A.* – 25 July 2005 ; 218/1998 – *Unilever Italia Divisione Van Den Bergh v. Fabat spa* – 14 July 1998);
- particular attention has been paid to the presence in commercial communications of claims regarding the medicinal actions of a food product, clarifying that commercials concerning issues connected with people's health and referring directly to products claiming to have effects in said ambit, must be characterised by the utmost sense of responsibility: indeed, the intended recipients of these kinds of commercials must be regarded as "weak consumers", since they can only exert a limited control over advertising claims, exactly on account of the particular relevance of the benefits boasted by the same.[6]

6 See *Comitato di Controllo* Injunction 167/2004 – *Comitato di Controllo v. Latteria Sociale Merano* – 26 July 2004, whereby it is not fair to represent the food product (yogurt) in the commercial in absolute, generic terms as an instrument of protection against many diseases as if it were a medicinal drug indicated to prevent miscellaneous diseases.

As to the aspects not related to the product features, food advertisements offending the woman's dignity[7], or harmful to the person's image[8], or indecent and vulgar[9], have been found contrary to the principles inspiring the Code.

III. Mandatory Labelling

Are there any national definitions of a foodstuff that could hamper the marketing of an imported food product?

a. Energy drinks

The Italian Minister of Health National Food Safety Committee in Opinion No. 5 of 2012 (Energy Drinks and Alcoholic Drinks) defined (although the definition is not mandatory) "energy drinks" (EDs) as "*(generally alcohol-free) beverages containing stimulant substances and marketed with indications of 'positive' effects such as increased physical and mental energy and/or enhancement of sports and cognitive performances.*"

7 See *Comitato di Controllo* injunction No. 104/2011- *Comitato di Controllo v. Pasticceria Alba S.r.l.*– 25 July 2011, which sanctioned an advertisement where a female body, on display to the public as if in a shop window, is put on a par with the gastronomic products (*arancini* [croquettes of rice filled with peas, giblets and meat sauce] and brioche with ice-cream) of a renowned bakery; similarly, *Comitato di Controllo* injunction No. 13/2011 (pizza) – *Comitato di Controllo v. Metro food S.a.s.*- 28 January 2011, *Comitato di Controllo* injunction No. 15/2009 (*scamorza*) – *Comitato di Controllo v. Industria Lattiero Casearia – 23 March 2009*, and *Giurì* Decision No. 80/2008 – *Comitato di Controllo v. Montalbano Industria Agroalimentare S.p.A.* – 30 September 2008, where the mixture of levels determined by the transfer of the tastiness of artichokes on the woman's body leads to an evident commodification of the woman and degradation of her dignity.

8 See *Comitato di Controllo* Injunction 77/2011 – *Comitato di Controllo v. Dimocar S.r.l.* – 20 May 2011, whereby the man's image is represented in a demeaning manner, displayed to the public as if in a shop window, put on a par with the product advertised and thus becoming an offer and a good for consumption just as the products advertised (meat).

9 In Case 33/2009 – *Comitato di Controllo v. Saiwa S.r.l.* – 26 May 2009, the *Giurì* held that, although no repugnancy element could be found, indecency and vulgarity were definitely present in a TV commercial advertising chips showing the mimic representation of *fellatio* announced by the repeated, allusive invitation *"leccami, dai, leccami"* ["lick me, come on, lick me"].

The report by Professor Gian Vincenzo Zuccotti, attached to the above Opinion, clarifies that energy drinks are not sports drinks because these two categories are neatly distinguished by their composition. Indeed, sports drinks are *"alcohol-free, generally fruit-flavoured beverages, containing water, carbohydrates, minerals and electrolytes, plus, sometimes, vitamins and other nutrients."*

b. Yogurt

Pursuant to the Health Ministry's Circular Letter No. 2 of 4 January 1972, the traditional designation of "yogurt" is used to refer to *"milk fermented by specific acidifying microorganisms, namely* Lactobacillus bulgaricus *and* Streptococcus thermophilus". Said fermented milk is obtained by using as a raw material full cream, or semi-skimmed, or skimmed milk which then undergoes a thermal clearance (sterilization or pasteurization) before being inoculated with the specific fermentation microorganisms. The yogurt so obtained must be cooled to approximately 4°C and kept at this temperature until distributed to consumers.

c. Cheese

Pursuant to Royal Decree Law No. 2033 of 15 October 1925 the designation *"formaggio"* or *"cacio"* (cheese) is exclusively used to identify the *"product obtained from full-cream, or semi-skimmed, or skimmed milk, or from cream, following acid or presamic coagulation, also by using ferments and common salt."*

d. Bread

Under Act No. 580 of 4 July 1967, bread is the *"product obtained from the full or partial cooking of duly leavened dough, prepared using corn meal, water and yeast, whether or not with the addition of common salt (sodium chloride)."*

e. Carbonated waters

Decree by the President of the Republic (DPR) No. 719 of 19 May 1958 regards the following products as **carbonated waters**: (a) seltzer water *(acqua* *di seltz),* a designation identifying drinkable waters supersaturated with carbon dioxide; and (b) soda water *(acqua di soda),* a designation identifying drinkable waters containing sodium bicarbonate, supersaturated with carbon dioxide. Under the same Decree **alcohol-free beverages** are carbonated and still drinks packaged in bottles or other hermetically sealable containers, prepared with drinkable water or still mineral water and containing one or several of the following substances: (a) fruit juice; (b) infusions or extracts of fruit, or portion of edible, or bitter, or aromatizing plants; (c) natural essences; (d) saccharose (or dextrose up to a maximum of 10 per cent content); and (e) citric acid, tartaric acid. The designation **soda** *(gassosa)* identifies the colourless beverage prepared with carbonated drinkable water and sweetened with saccharose, possibly with the addition of citric acid, tartaric acid, and lemon essence.

f. Baked Products and products associated with festivities

By Decree of 22 July 2005, the Ministry of Productive Activities defined the designation, obligatory ingredients, and production of some baked products and products associated with certain festivities, namely:

- the designation ***panettone*** identifies a *"sweet, soft-dough baked product, obtained by natural fermentation from acid dough, having a round-base shape with a cracked, characteristically cut top crust, a spongy structure with elongated alveoli, and a characteristic acid-dough fermentation aroma"*;
- the designation ***pandoro*** identifies a *"sweet, soft-dough baked product, obtained by natural fermentation from acid dough, having the shape of a frustum with an eight-pointed star section and a non-crusty outer surface, a spongy, silky structure with tiny, uniform alveoli, and a characteristic butter and vanilla aroma"*;
- the designation ***colomba*** identifies a *"sweet, soft-dough baked product, obtained by natural fermentation from acid dough, having an irregular oval dove-like shape, a spongy structure with elongated alveoli, topped with icing and a decoration consisting of pearl sugar and no less than two percent almonds compared to the finished product and by making reference to the moment of decoration"*;

- the designation ***savoiardo*** identifies a *"confection biscuit made with eggs having a characteristic stick shape with a structure characterised by tiny, regular alveoli, an outer surface covered with sugar, and a typical vanilla and lemon aroma. The product must have a moisture percentage comprised between four and twelve per cent"*;
- the designation ***amaretto*** identifies a *"hard-and-dry pastry biscuit having a characteristic roundish shape, with crystalline, alveoli-like structure, a cracked top surface and a typical bitter almond taste, possibly with the addition of pearl sugar. The product has a moisture percentage lower than three per cent"*.

Under Act No. 96 of 10 March 1969, the designation ***pomodori pelati*** (peeled tomatoes) identifies *"long-type tomatoes deprived of their peel and obtained from fresh, sound, ripe and properly washed fruits"*. They must satisfy the following minimum prerequisites: (a) the typical red colour of sound, ripe tomatoes; (b) the smell and taste characteristic of tomatoes, without any alien smell or taste; (c) no larvae and parasites or alterations of a parasitic nature consisting in necrotic stains of whatever size affecting the pulp, no perceivable blemishes of other nature (i.e., depigmented parts, residues of mechanic injuries, or growth cicatrices) affecting the fruit outer surface, and no inner rot along the stylar axis; (d) a drained product weight not be lower than 60 % of the net weight; (e) an entire shape, or in any case such as not to show injuries altering the fruit shape or volume in no less than 70 % of the drained product weight in the case of containers with a net content not exceeding 400 grams, and no less than 65 % in the other cases; (f) no less than 4 % dry residue, net of added salt; (g) an average peel content (calculated using at least 5 containers) no greater than 3 sq cm per every 100 grams of contents; in each container the peel content cannot exceed four times said limit.

g. Beer

Under Act No. 1354 of 16 August 1962 the designation **beer** identifies the *"product obtained through the alcoholic fermentation with* Saccharomyces carlsbergensis *or* Saccharomyces cerevisiae *strains of a must prepared with (sometimes roasted) malted barley, or malted wheat, or a mixture of both, and water, and made bitter by the addition of hop, or hop derivates, or both."*

IV. Voluntary Labelling

1. "Clean labels": are there any national definitions or requirements with respect to claims such as 'natural', 'pure', 'home-made', 'additive-free'?

Other types of claims may be used for mere commercial purposes, or as appropriate to highlight certain specific merchandise features of a foodstuff.

a. "Extra"

The use of the term *"extra"* (meaning "superior", "choice" or "select") is regulated for certain products and subject to certain specific conditions, namely:

(1) *pomodori pelati extra* (choice peeled tomatoes) and *concentrato di pomodoro extra* (choice tomato concentrate);

(2) *confettura extra* (superior jam) and *gelatine di frutta extra* (superior fruit jelly), as regulated by Legislative Decree No. 50/2004 implementing Directive No. 2001/113/EC;

(3) chocolate: designations such as *extra* (select) or adjectives making reference to quality criteria, may be used, on condition that the product has a higher content in total solids compared to standard products, as regulated by Legislative Decree No. 178/2003 Implementing Directive No. 2000/36/EC

In the other cases, statements of superiority or exceptionality of a product compared to another, must not only be specified as to their contents but also backed by evidence.

b. "Pure"

"Puro" ("pure") is a term generally used to mean "only" or "exclusively".

For instance, in *Salame di pura carne suina* (Pure pork salami) and *Mortadella di puro suino* (Pure pork Bologna sausage) it means that only pork has been used in their production, with the exclusion of all other types of meat. In *Puro cioccolato* (Pure chocolate), it means that in the production of chocolate (not of its filling, if any), no vegetal fats other than cocoa butter have been used. In this last regard, on 25 November 2010 in case C-47/09 between the European Commission and the Italian Republic, the European Court of Justice stated that "*by providing that the adjective 'pure' may only be added to the sales name of chocolate products which do not contain vegetable fats other than cocoa butter, the Italian Republic has failed to fulfil its obligations under Article 3(5) of Directive 2000/36/EC of the European Parliament and of the Council of 23 June 2000 relating to cocoa and chocolate products intended for human consumption and under Article 3(1) of that directive, read in conjunction with Article 2(1)(a) of Directive 2000/13/EC of the European Parliament and of the Council of 20 March 2000 on the approximation of the laws of the Member States relating to the labelling, presentation and advertising of foodstuffs*".

c. "Fresh"

"Fresco" ("fresh") is one of the terms the use of which is regulated in connection with specific products, including among others:

(1) "fresh pastas" (DPR No. 187/01): the sole parameters considered to use this designation are moisture and free water activity in the prepackaged product;

(2) "pasteurised fresh milk" and "high quality pasteurised fresh milk": use of these designations is subject to compliance with the parameters laid down in Decree-Law No. 157 of 24 June 2004 enacted (with amendments) by Act No. 204 of 3 August 2004;

(3) "fresh fishery products" (Regulation (EC) No. 853/04): used for fishery products that have not undergone any treatment other than chilling;

(4) *"formaggi freschi a pasta filata"* (i.e., "spun-paste" or "stretched-curd" fresh cheese): used to identify products that have not undergone any preservation treatment, must be consumed within a few days, and are subject to the obligation of prepackaging at the origin.

d. "Natural"

The term "naturally/natural" is currently governed by European Parliament and Council Regulation (EC) No. 1924/2006 of 20 December 2006 (*OJ L404)* on nutrition and health claims made on foods, the Annex of which establishes that, if a food naturally meets the condition(s) laid down in the same Annex for the use of a nutritional claim, the term "naturally/ natural" may be used as a prefix to the claim.

The term "natural" may then be used, in certain specific cases, for purposes different from nutritional ones. Indeed, it is currently an integral part of the following designations:

(1) the trade description *"acqua minerale naturale"* (natural mineral water) established by Legislative Decree No. 176 of 8 October 2011 implementing Directive 2009/54/EC on the exploitation and marketing of natural mineral waters, *OJ L164*;

(2) the designations of *"aromi naturali"* (natural aromas) which satisfy the specific provisions laid down for the use of the term "natural";

(3) the designations *"sardine al naturale"* or *"tonno al naturale"* (sardines or tuna in brine/*au naturel)* when the covering medium used is the natural juice (liquid exuding from the fish during cooking), or a saline solution or water, possibly with the addition of herbs, spices or natural flavourings (Council Regulations (EEC) Nos. 2136/89, *OJ L 212* and 1536/92, *OJ L 163*).

2. Nutrition & health claims

a. Within the list of health claims authorised pursuant to Regulation 1924/2006, are there any related substances which are prohibited or considered as a medicinal substance within the analysed jurisdiction?

No, within the list of health claims authorized pursuant to Regulation (EC) No. 1924/2006 or pursuant to Regulation (EU) No. 432/2012 there are no substances that are prohibited or considered as medicinal substances in the Italian jurisdiction.

b. Is the use of nutrition or health claims on non-prepackaged food further regulated at the national level?

No.

c. Are there any national laws and regulations permitting food business operators to make reference to recommendations or endorsements by national associations, medical, nutrition or dietetic professionals, and health-related charities?

In Italy, Act 283 of 30 April 1962 prohibits the sale or advertising of a food product or foodstuff that adopts improper designations or names, advertising claims or mottos, quality or authenticity marks or certifications by whoever issued, or illustrative drawings that deceive or mislead purchasers as to the nature, substance, quality or nutritional properties of the food substances, or claiming particular medicinal actions.

More generally, Article 23 (d) of the Consumers' Code regards as misleading any commercial practices consisting in (falsely) asserting that a professional or his/her commercial practices or product(s) have been authorized, accepted or approved by a public or private organisation, or that the conditions necessary for the authorization, acceptance or approval received, have been satisfied.

The Italian Supervisory Authority for Competition and the Market (AGCM) had the chance to clarify the point stating that, where a commercial operator wishes to boast the approval or endorsement of any public or private organisation, it is necessary that the activities aimed at obtaining such approval or endorsement have actually been carried out according to objective criteria, verifiable by third parties (i.e., professionals and consumers), and that the approval or endorsement sought has been granted on the basis of non-discriminatory criteria. In Cases PS411 – *Ovito – Magicannuccia Approvati FIMP* –31 July 2008, *Ruling No. 18700* and PS411B – *Ovito – Magicannuccia Approvati FIMP* – 3 July 2008, *Ruling No. 18572* the commercial practice consisting in the use of the FIMP logo with the claim *"Approvato dalla FIMP – Federazione Italiana Medici Pediatri"* ("As approved by FIMP (the Italian Federation of Paediatricians)") is in contrast with the Consumers'

Code requirements insofar as, in view of crediting the products it refers to, it is apt to induce consumers to erroneously rely on their supposed special characteristics, so as to cause them to perceive such products as possessing further, better prerequisites compared to other goods belonging to the same category. In particular, the factual circumstance relating to the presence of the term "approved" leads the consumer to assume the existence of a product verification and controlling procedure, subject to the respect of definite conditions, carried out by the national professional organisation representing paediatricians, elements which inevitably lead to an interpretation as to the particular quality and fitness of all children products bearing the FIMP logo, exactly on account of the reliance generally made by parents on paediatricians.

The claim *"Approvato dalla FIMP – Federazione Italiana Medici Pediatri"* ("As approved by FIMP (the Italian Federation of Paediatricians)") evoked by and contained in the logo in the case in hand presupposes not a quality certification obtained through the successful completion of a specific approval procedure but rather a commercial agreement made for a profit and concerning the sponsorship of a product by FIMP on an exclusive basis for a definite term. By giving particular emphasis to the existence of the FIMP endorsement, the affixation of the FIMP logo on packages and the related promotional campaigns acquires a deceptive, ambiguous value as it suggests to the average consumer that the products having this claim on their packages has a *quid pluris,* i.e. additional special characteristics making them particularly apt (in terms of safety, high quality, excellence, non-toxicity, etc.) to satisfy children's needs, while they have not.

Recently, the Ministry of Health, Veterinary Healthcare, Nutrition and Food Safety Department, on 21 February 2011 issued a Note concerning the use of logos and/or testimonials on food product labels, specifying that *"...the criterion to establish the accuracy of such statements is to establish that they come from one of the associations under Article 11 of Regulation (EC) No. 1924/2006, and that the truthfulness of the assertion made can be checked from a scientific point of view."* In particular, in the event of mere attestations by associations of medical specialist and health-related charities ("commended/recommended by...", "endorsed by...", logos of associations, etc.), in case of controls the operator may be asked to provide evidence of the tests made to support the assertion.

The above Note further states that *"as far as concerns the use of cryptographic attestations/logos on labels, again they are admissible when they consist in images that the average consumer would perceive as not particularly suggestive advertising messages and not such as to mislead the final consumer on the assumption that the label in any case reports the actual nutritional indications of the product."*

d. Is a notification procedure required prior to/for marketing foodstuffs bearing nutritional or health claims?

In Italy there is no specific notification procedure for products bearing nutritional or health claims. Yet, under Legislative Decree 169 of 21 May 2004 the placing on the market of a food supplement is subject to the procedure of notification to the Ministry of Health, which assesses its compliance with applicable laws and provisions so as to guarantee product safety and correct information to consumers.

Foodstuffs supplemented by vitamins and minerals referred to in Regulation (EC) No 1925/2006 are likewise subject to a notification procedure. For monitoring purposes, the foods containing the following functional substances fall within this procedure: caffeine (for addition to energy drinks); coenzyme q (for addition to beverages); glucuronolactone (for addition to energy drinks); luteine; taurine (for addition to energy drinks).

V. Enforcement of Food Law and Self-Regulating Bodies

1. Consequences resulting from non-compliance with the labelling or advertising requirements

Non-compliance with labelling and/or advertising requirements exposes the infringer to a series of sanctions and actions. In addition to the criminal sanctions laid down in Articles 5151[10] and 5161[11] of the Criminal Code and the possibility for the competitor to petition the Civil Court to obtain an *interim* measure to enjoin the infringer and seek damages for breach of competition rules (Article 2598 Civil Code[12]), violation of food products labelling requirements under Article 2 of Legislative Decree 109/1992 is punished by a fine of 3,500.00 up to 18,000.00 Euro. The same Decree punishes violation of the label content requirements by a fine of Euro 1,600.00 up to 9,500.00 Euro.

With reference to the advertising sector more generally, the Supervisory Authority for Competition and the Market (AGCM) can start proceedings even of its own motion (that is, without receiving a prior report or complaint) regarding unfair commercial practices or misleading and comparative ad-

10 Article 515 Criminal Code – Trade fraud: "Whoever, in the exercise of a commercial activity or in a shop or other point of sale open to the public, delivers to the purchaser a good or chattel in lieu of another, or a good or chattel having a different origin, provenance, quality or quantity than what declared or agreed, shall be punished by imprisonment for up to two years or by a fine of up to 2,065 euro, unless the act committed amounts to a more serious criminal offence."

11 Article 516 Criminal Code – Sale of not genuine foodstuff as genuine: "Whoever sells or however markets not genuine foodstuff as genuine shall be punished by imprisonment for up to six months or by a fine of up to 1,032 euro."

12 Article 2598 Civil Code – Unfair competition acts: "Without prejudice to the law provisions protecting distinctive signs and patents, whoever commits the following acts:
(1) using names or distinctive signs apt to generate confusion with the names or distinctive signs lawfully used by others, or slavishly imitating a competitor's products, or committing by any other means acts apt to generate confusion with a competitor's products and activity;
(2) disseminating news and comments on a competitor's products and activities apt to discredit the latter, or taking undue advantage from the qualities of a competitor's products or business;
(3) directly or indirectly using any other means not consistent with fair professional principles and apt to prejudice the competitor's business;
shall be liable for unfair competition."

vertising. AGCM has investigation powers, including having access to any relevant document, requesting anybody to provide relevant information and documents (with the authority to inflict sanctions in case of refusal or of transmission of untruthful information and/or documents), benefitting from the services of Revenue Officers (*Guardia di Finanza*), and ordering and obtaining expert reports.

If AGCM establishes that there has been an infringement, it can enjoin its discontinuation, order the publication of rectifications at the expense of the enterprise liable for the violation, and inflict a fine ranging between 5,000.00 and 500,000.00 Euro. If the infringing practice concerns dangerous products or indirectly threatens the safety of minors, the fine will amount to 50,000.00 Euro as a minimum. In case of non-compliance with AGCM's orders, the infringer will be liable for a fine ranging between 10,000.00 and 150,000.00 Euro.

However, the institute of commitments is envisaged: in other words, except in particularly serious and manifestly unfair instances, if the infringing enterprise commits to remove the unfair aspects of its commercial conduct, AGCM may give up the infringement assessment procedure.

With reference to advertising self-regulation, a distinction must be drawn between the activity of the Control Committee *(Comitato di Controllo)* and that of the *Giurì*. The Control Committee, following reports from consumers, consumers' associations or in pursuit of the monitoring activity carried out by the members of the Committee and IAP Secretariat, submits to the *Giurì* the commercials and marketing communications that are deemed not to comply with the Code provisions protecting the citizen-consumer. It may invite the infringing operator to modify the commercial or marketing communication that is deemed non-compliant with the Code, issue cease-and-desist injunctions in respect of commercials evidently contrary to the Code principles and, at the request of the concerned party, give its prior opinion on commercials and marketing communications prior to their diffusion. Vice versa, the *Giurì* examines the commercials and marketing communications that are submitted to it (either by the Committee or by enterprises) and passes its decisions on the same in accordance with the Code. The *Giurì*'s decisions are final. If the *Giurì* establishes that a commercial is contrary to the Code, it orders the concerned parties to immediately cease and desist from broadcasting it and can order the publication of an excerpt of the decision. Failing compliance with the decision, the *Giurì* will order that the public be informed of such failure.[13]

The table below summarises the main sanctions:

Type of sanction	Rule breached	Sanction	Authority
Criminal	Article 515 Criminal Code – Trade fraud	Imprisonment for up to two years or a fine of up to 2,065.00 Euro	Criminal Court
	Article 516 Criminal Code – Sale of not genuine foodstuff as genuine	Imprisonment for up to six months or a fine of up to 1,032.00 Euro	
Civil	Article 2598 Civil Code – Unfair competition	Civil court enjoining measure and possibly damages	Civil Court
Administrative	Article 2 Legislative Decree 109/92 – Unfair competition	Fine from 3,500.00 to 18,000.00 Euro	Regions, Municipalities, or other administrative authorities instructed by Regions
	Misleading commercial practices (Articles 20 and ff. Consumers' Code)	Cease-and-desist injunction and a fine from 5,000.00 to 500,000.00 Euro	Supervisory Authority for Competition and the Market
Self-regulation	Article 2 Marketing Communication Self-Regulation Code	Enjoining order	IAP *Giurì* and Control Committee

13 The relevance of these sanctions should be considered in several different respects, namely: *(i)* the prejudice deriving from failure to exploit an advertising campaign; *(ii)* the damage caused to the infringer's commercial activity: think, to make but an example, of "seasonal" (in the broad sense of the word) products, a far from infrequent case; *(iii)* the moral implications of the decision, with the ensuing effects on the company's image; and *(iv)* the additional sanction, applied in the worst cases or in the event of relapse, and consisting in the publication of an excerpt from the decision on the media indicated by the *Giurì* in its decision.

2. Are there any national self-regulating bodies with respect to advertising for foodstuffs?

The often quoted advertising self regulation system (which is not limited to foodstuff advertising) is a complex, purely and typically juridical phenomenon and the result of a voluntarily undertaken body of rules, whereby a number of entities agree (and cause their members or associates to agree) to comply with the provisions established by the same and laid down in the Marketing Communication Self-Regulation Code (the 57th edition of which has been in effect as of 6 April 2013), to circulate the decisions rendered by the Advertising Self-Regulation Organization (IAP), and to adopt adequate measures *vis-à-vis* IAP members not respecting them. Member organisations further undertake to ensure that each of their own members or associates insert in their contracts and agreements a specific clause subscribing to the Code and undertaking to comply with the *Giurì*'s decisions, so that also the commercials and marketing communications of the user, agency or professional that are not members of the above associations are subject to and comply with the Code all the same. Thus, although the latter is the result of a collective self-regulating effort, a large share of the Italian commercials and marketing communications are subject to the same.

CHAPTER 9
Luxembourg

Véronique Hoffeld and Claudia Lenertz

I. Preliminary Remark

The Luxembourg legislation on food law is based on the European regulations and inspired by the European directives. However, the particularity of the Luxembourg legal environment on food law is the absence of published case law regarding the advertisement of foodstuffs.

II. Possible Bans on Food Advertising

1. Is there any general national legislation or code of conduct regulating the promotion of foodstuffs?

a. Introduction

The promotion of foodstuffs in Luxembourg is regulated by the amended Grand-ducal Regulation of 14 December 2000 on labelling, presentation and advertising of foodstuffs (the *"Advertising Regulation"*[1]) which transposed the Directive of the European Parliament and the Council, 2000/13/EC[2] on the approximation of the laws of the Member States relating to the labelling, presentation and advertising of foodstuffs.

According to the Advertising Regulation, the advertising of a foodstuff is defined as any communication disseminated in the direct or indirect scope

1 Grand-Ducal Regulation of 14 December 2000 on labelling, presentation and advertising of foodstuffs

2 Council Directive 2000/13/EEC on the approximation of the laws of the Member States relating to the labelling, presentation and advertising of foodstuffs, OJ 2000 L 109/29.

of promoting the sale of foodstuffs, whatever the means of communication used. The information put on the label also falls under the scope of this regulation.[3]

b. General prohibitions referring to health in its broad sense

According to Article 16 of the Advertising Regulation, the promotion and advertising of foodstuffs, which contains the following references to health, are prohibited in food labelling[4], without prejudice to Regulation No 1924/2006 concerning the nutrition and health claims made on food ('EU Claims Regulation'):

- the name of an illness and any allusion to an illness or to a person suffering from an illness;
- the names or representations, even stylised, of organs or circulatory and nervous systems of the human body which may evoke the belief that the foodstuff will have an effect on these organs or systems;
- representations of persons, clothes or devices evoking medical, pharmaceutical or health professions;
- references or recommendations, declarations or medical advices, except for the mention that a foodstuff is not suitable for a specific diet;
- references to the Ministry of Health or other services, public servants, regulations or advices of the Ministry of Health or of other bodies involved in the health field;
- references to weight loss;
- any other indication relating to health, such as "*comforting*", "*strengthening*", "*energising*", "*for your health*", "*tonic*" for foodstuffs or for products consumed for recreational purposes containing alcohol; and

3 Grand-Ducal Regulation of 14 December 2000, op cit., Art. 19.

4 Grand-Ducal Regulation of 14 December 2000, *op cit.,* Arts. 16 and 17.

- claims which could provoke or exploit the feelings of fear or anxiety and attempt to discredit foodstuffs which are similar or not.
- references to an effect of the foodstuff on health or on the metabolism if this claim cannot be proven.

c. General prohibitions that aim to prevent misleading information:

In addition, it is forbidden to use on the labelling of foodstuffs the following information[5]:

- claims involving objective and measurable elements that cannot be justified;
- indications relating to the addition of vitamins and pro-vitamins if these substances have been added for technological or organoleptic purposes;
- indications related to the absence of a specific additive if the foodstuff contains another additive of the same group[6]; and

2. Is the promotion of certain foodstuffs restricted or prohibited by any national mandatory and/or soft laws (e.g. code of practice, case law)?

In addition, the Luxembourg legislation provides for several specific restrictions as regards the promotion of certain foodstuffs. Amongst them, we may identify restrictions/market bans with respect to alcoholic beverages.

5 Regulation of 14 December 2000, supra note 1 at p. 1, Art. 17.

6 It should be noted that this prohibition was previously also applicable in Belgium but has since been removed because it was considered too general and too restrictive with respect to the objective (which is to avoid misleading the consumer).

Luxembourg has implemented the rules laid down by the *"Audiovisual Media Services Directive"*[7] in Article 4 of the amended Grand-Ducal Regulation of 5 April 2001, which provides that television advertising for alcoholic beverages shall comply with the following restrictive criteria[8]:

- it may not be aimed specifically at minors or, in particular, depict minors consuming these beverages;
- it shall not link the consumption of alcohol to enhanced physical performance or to driving;
- it shall not create the impression that the consumption of alcohol contributes to social or sexual success;
- it shall not claim that alcohol has therapeutic qualities or that it is a stimulant, a sedative or a means of resolving personal conflicts;
- it shall not encourage immoderate consumption of alcohol or present abstinence or moderation in a negative light; and
- it shall not place emphasis on high alcoholic content as being a positive quality of the beverages.

In addition, according to the Grand-Ducal Regulation of 14 December 1970, the sale of absinthe is forbidden. Therefore, the advertising of such beverage is prohibited in Luxembourg.

7 Directive 2010/13/EU of the European Parliament and of the Council of 10 March 2010 on the coordination of certain provisions laid down by law, regulation or administrative action in Member States concerning the provision of audiovisual media services (Audiovisual Media Services Directive), repealing Council Directive 89/552/EEC of 3 October 1989 on the coordination of certain provisions laid down by Law, Regulation or Administrative Action in Member States concerning the pursuit of television broadcasting activities, OJ 1989 L 298/23.

8 Grand-Ducal Regulation of 5 April 2001 on the rules applicable to the advertising, sponsoring, teleshopping and self-promotion in television programmes, Art. 4.

3. Is the promotion of (certain) foodstuffs towards a specific section of the population restricted or prohibited by any mandatory and/or soft laws?

In Luxembourg, the law of 22 December 2006 on the sale of alcoholic beverages to minors below the age of 16, provides that it is forbidden for all bars, shops and public places, to sell alcoholic beverages or a mix of alcoholic beverages with other beverages that contain more than 1,2 % of alcohol by volume, to minors under the age of 16.[9]

In the event that one of these establishments breaches this provision, a fine ranging from 251 to 1.000 € will be applicable.

III. Misleading Advertising

1. What are the national rules on misleading advertising with respect to foodstuffs?

As far as misleading information is concerned, Luxembourg has accurately implemented[10] the rules provided by Directive 2000/13/EC.[11] The FIC Regulation, which goes into effect on 13 December 2014, reiterates the same principles. The latter will be directly applicable in all Member States.

2. What are the national landmark cases regarding misleading advertising for foodstuffs?

As indicated in the introductory section of this chapter, Luxembourg is characterised by the absence of judicial activity when it comes to mislead-

9 Luxembourg Law of 22 December 2006 on the sale of alcoholic beverages to minors

10 Grand-Ducal Regulation of 14 December 2000 supra note 1 at p. 1, Art. 15.

11 Council Directive 2000/13/EEC supra note 2 at p. 1 – See Introductory Chapter 1.1 of the Book – Section 3.

ing advertising on foodstuffs. There is indeed no published case law in Luxembourg related to misleading advertising of foodstuffs.

IV. Mandatory Labelling: Name of the product

Are there any national definitions of a foodstuff that could hamper the marketing of an imported food product?

The Luxembourg Advertising Regulation expressly allows the use of the name under which the product is legally manufactured and marketed in the Member State of production.

However, as this is stated by European legislation, where the application of the other provisions of the Advertising Regulation would not enable Luxembourg consumers to know the true nature of the foodstuff and to distinguish it from foodstuffs with which they could confuse it, the sales name used for the foodstuff must be accompanied by other descriptive information which must appear in proximity to the name under which the product is sold.

In exceptional cases, where the sales name of the Member State of production designates a foodstuff which is so different, as regards its composition or manufacture, from the foodstuff known under that name in Luxembourg that the provisions above mentioned are not sufficient to ensure the correct information for consumers in Luxembourg, the sales name of the Member State of production is not permitted in Luxembourg.

Specific legislation provide for definitions with respect to certain foodstuffs:

a) **Energy drinks:** There is no national definition in Luxembourg for energy drinks. However, according to Article 16 of the Advertising Regulation[12], the promotion and advertising of foodstuffs containing references to health such as *"energising"*, is forbidden for foodstuffs containing alcohol.

12 Grand-Ducal Regulation of 14 December 2000, supra note 1 at p. 1.

b) **Sports drinks:** There is no national definition in Luxembourg for sports drinks.

c) **Yogurt:** According to the Grand-Ducal Regulation of 13 January 1994[13] on the production and placing on the market of raw milk, heat-treated milk and milk-based products, the terms *"yoghourt", "yaort"* or *"joghourt"* are defined as the fermented milk obtained by the action of lactic acid bacteria, notably *Streptococcus thermophilus* and *Lactobacillus bulgaricus* after inoculation with these bacteria which must be present in live form and in abundant amounts (greater than or equal to 10 exponent 7 per gram) in the final product. These conditions have been recognised by the Court of Justice of the European Union as being essential characteristics for the consumers. Therefore, if the product does not have these live lactic ferments, the CJEU considered that the relevant Member State has reasonable grounds to prohibit the use of the name since any additional descriptive information could not be sufficient to ensure correct information for consumers.

d) **Cheese**: According to the Grand-Ducal Regulation of 13 January 1994[14] on the production and placing on the market of raw milk, heat-treated milk and milk-based products, cheese is defined as the fresh or matured product, solid or semi-solid obtained by coagulating milk, skimmed milk, partially skimmed milk, cream, whey or buttermilk, solely or in combination, by the action of rennet or other suitable coagulating agents, and partially draining of lactoserum resulting from such coagulation or by using manufacturing techniques involving the coagulation of milk and/or milk substances, in order to obtain a final product with the same essential physical, chemical and organoleptic characteristics as the product defined above.

The Luxembourg cooked liquid cheese *"concoillotte/ kach keiss"* and quark curd cheese (*"fromage blanc"*) shall only contain the ingredients of milk, enzymes and cultures of microorganisms necessary for their manufacture. For the manufacture of certain common varieties, the use

13 Grand-Ducal Regulation of 13 January 1994 on the production and placing on the market of raw milk, heat-treated milk and milk-based products.

14 Grand-Ducal Regulation of 13 January 1994, supra note 14, at p. 10.

of certain technologically essential substances and ingredients normally used in the manufacture of these varieties is allowed.

e) **Bread:** According to the Grand-Ducal Regulation of 30 May 1967 on the sale of bread, bread weighing five pounds, three pounds or one pound is called *"pain de ménage"*. The bread called *"pain de ménage"* is baked using flour that meets specific standards referred to as "*legal flour*" ("*farine légale*").

f) The bread called *"pain de ménage"* can only be baked, sold and advertised as loaves corresponding to the above-mentioned weights. However, a difference of 50 grammes per loaf from the required weight is tolerated. However, in a batch of ten loaves chosen at random, if it appears to the seller that six of these loaves weigh 50 grammes less than the required weight, the aforementioned tolerance no longer applies.

g) Bread weighing less than 400 grammes baked using flour called legal flour ("*farine légale*"), as well as all breads of any weight baked with plain white flour or special flour, are defined as novelty breads. These breads can be baked without any weight restrictions.

h) Breads called "*French baguettes*", baked with flour called legal flour ("*farine légale*"), also qualify as novelty breads.

According to Article 5 of the above-mentioned regulation, breads are only sold to the consumer in authorised establishments called *"boulangeries"* or *"pâtisseries"* (i.e. bakeries). However, they may also be sold in other shops of foodstuffs provided that there is a special and separate place for their presentation and conservation.[15]

15 Grand-Ducal Regulation of 30 May 1967, supra note 28, Art. 5.

V. Voluntary Labelling

1. "Clean labels" – Are there any national definitions or requirements for the use of the following claims? If so, please provide the definition and relevant legal source(s) including any case law.

a) **Natural & Pure:** According to Article 18.2 of the Advertising Regulation, it is forbidden to use the word, expression or claim *"natural" or "pure"*, and other similar terms if they are used as culinary terms. A foodstuff may also not contain detectable amounts of residues of pesticides, additives, or other chemical products other than those arising naturally. The foodstuff may not be refined.

b) **Homemade/grandmother recipe:** there is no national definition of such claim.

c) **Made in Luxembourg**: This label may be used for goods as well as foodstuffs that are *"Made in Luxembourg"*.[16] The label is used to identify and emphasise products and services in Luxembourg that have as a common characteristic their Luxembourg origin. Products which are wholly manufactured in Luxembourg or where the last, substantial transformation, which was economically justified, took place in Luxembourg are considered to be Luxembourgish goods. This label of origin may be an additional method of promoting national products.

d) ***"Gesond iessen, Méi bewegen"*:** On 5 July 2006, the Ministry of Health, the Ministry of National Education, the Ministry of Family and Integration and the Ministry of Sport signed a joint declaration to promote physical activity and healthy eating, entitled *"Gesond iessen, Mei bewegen"* [17] (i.e. Eat healthily, Be more active). The main objectives of this campaign are to create awareness and information about the importance of a lifestyle which is favourable to physical, mental and

16 Regulation of 18 July 1984 concerning the use and control of the Luxembourgish label of origin, according to Article 22 of the uniform Benelux law on trademarks and products.

17 Ministry of Health www.sante.public.lu

social well-being, to a healthy and balanced diet and to increase the quantity and quality of physical activity of the national population, including children and adolescents.

As an example, based on this label, some primary schools in Luxembourg have decided to charge a lower price for water than soft drinks in the vending machines, have prohibited the isolated sale of French fries in canteens, and have increased the distribution of fresh nutritional products.

2. Nutrition & health claims

a. Within the list of health claims authorised pursuant to Regulation 1924/2006, are there any related substances that are provided or considered as a medical substance within your jurisdiction?

According to the Ministry of Health there are internal discussions regarding some authorised health claims that might be considered as medical substances. Indeed, the Ministry considers that if a substance has a therapeutic effect, the foodstuff might be dangerous within the meaning of Article 14 of Regulation 178/2002.[18]

However, since for the moment the discussions are ongoing, we may not confirm which substances are considered as medical substances.

18 Council Regulation (EC) No 178/2002 laying down the general principles and requirements of food law, establishing the European Food Safety Authority and laying down procedures in matters of food safety.

b. Are there any national laws and regulations permitting food business operators to make reference to recommendations or endorsements by national associations, medical, nutrition or dietetic professionals, and health-related charities?

In Luxembourg, there are no regulations permitting food operators to make such reference. As far as food labelling and advertising goes, Article 16 of the Advertising Regulation prohibits the use of references, recommendations, declarations or medical advices, except for the mention that a foodstuff is not adapted to a special diet.

c. Are there any national laws or regulations regulating the use of nutrition or health claims on non-prepackaged food?

Luxembourg has not added any other requirements concerning the use of nutritional or health claims made on non-prepackaged food.

As a consequence, when a food business operator claims the nutritional or health benefit of a non-prepackaged foodstuff in Luxembourg, it is not required to provide nutritional information to consumers, nor state the importance of a varied and balanced diet, a healthy lifestyle and the quantity of food and pattern of consumption required to obtain the claimed beneficial effect (as would be the case for prepackaged food).

d. Is there a notification procedure required prior to / for marketing foodstuffs bearing nutritional or health claims?

Luxembourg law does not provide for a specific notification procedure prior to the marketing of foodstuffs bearing authorised nutritional or health claims. However, there is a control procedure *a posteriori* which is organised by the *"Organisme pour la sécurité et la qualité de la chaîne alimentaire"* which is a body competent for controlling that the foodstuffs placed on the Luxembourg market which contain nutritional or health claims comply with the applicable national and European provisions.

VI. Enforcement of Food law and Self-Regulating Bodies

1. Which actions may one risk in case of non-compliance with the labelling or advertising requirements?

In the event that a business operator commercialises foodstuffs without complying with the labelling and advertising requirements of the Luxembourg Law, it may risk various sanctions from the following entities:

a. Public authorities

i. Control Bodies

Within the meaning of Article 4 of Regulation (EC) 882/2004[19] the Luxembourg Ministry of Health is the national competent authority that performs official controls to ensure the verification of compliance with feed and food law, animal health and animal welfare rules.

Indeed, Article 5 of the Grand-Ducal Regulation of 25 April 2008 implementing measures of EC Regulation 882/2004 provides that the Ministry of Health shall control all stages related to the manufacturing, transformation and distribution of foodstuffs and thus is also competent to monitor the advertisement of the foodstuffs placed on the national market.

In order to help the Ministry of Health to ensure that foodstuffs comply with the applicable national and European provisions, two bodies have been created:

1. *"L'Organisme pour la Sécurité et la Qualité de la Chaîne Alimentaire" (OSQCA):* according to Article 2 of the aforementioned Grand-Ducal Regulation, the Ministry of Health and Ministry of Agriculture have created this national organisation which is charged with controlling the safety and quality of the food chain in Luxembourg;

---

19 Council Regulation (EC) No 882/2004 on official controls performed to ensure the verification of compliance with feed and food law, animal health and animal welfare rules, OJ 2004 L 191/1.

2. *"Le Laboratoire National de Santé":* pursuant to the law of 7 August 2012[20], this body is a public institution which has several departments competent in the food chain, such as the department called *"division du contrôle des denrées alimentaires"* which is the inspection authority competent, amongst others, for compliance control of the labelling of foodstuffs placed on the Luxembourg market.

ii. Penalties

- General criminal penalties if breach of any food requirement:

  According to Article 24 of the Advertising Regulation, any breach of the provisions of the regulation are punished according to Article 2 of the amended Law of 25 September 1953 concerning the reorganisation of the control of foodstuffs, beverages and common products[21], notwithstanding the provisions of Article 9, the provisions of the Criminal Code or any other law.

Article 2 of the aforementioned law provides that an infringement of the regulations related to the manufacturing, preparation, transformation, commercialisation and distribution of foodstuffs and beverages are punished by a fine ranging from 251 to 2,000 €, per violation.

- *Criminal penalties in case of falsification & misleading information.*

  In addition, Article 9 of the law of 25 September 1953 concerning the reorganisation of the control of foodstuffs, beverages and common products provides that breaches made by the following persons are punished by a prison sentence of between eight days and one year and/or by a fine ranging from 500 to 15.000 €, per violation:

1. those who have falsified, or made falsified, counterfeited or made counterfeit foodstuff or beverages for human or animal use;

20 Luxembourg Law of 7 August 2012 creating a public institution called Laboratoire National de Santé.

21 Luxembourg Law of 25 September 1953 concerning the reorganisation of the control of foodstuffs, beverages and common products.

2. those who have sold, exposed for sale, stored or transported for sale or delivery, foodstuffs or beverages for human or animal use, knowing that they were falsified, counterfeited, spoiled or corrupted;

3. those who maliciously or fraudulently, have revealed or recommended methods of falsification of foodstuff or beverages for human or animal use;

4. those who falsified or made counterfeit trademarks or signs;

5. those who used, directly or through an intermediary, indications or signs which were likely to mislead on the nature, the composition, the method of manufacture, the origin or the weight of foodstuffs or beverages or to improperly attribute to such foodstuffs special properties or characteristics.

However, in the event that the infringement provided under numbers 2 and 5 was committed by lack of precaution the fine will range from 50 to 250 € and a prison sentence of between one to seven days.

Further, if a business operator has been convicted of a crime (misdemeanor or felony) and sanctioned for any of the causes specified in the abovementioned Article 9, the courts may decide to close the business operator's retail premises or may oblige the operator to cease business activities for a period that may not exceed ten years.[22]

In the event of a breach of these measures, the shop or business premises will be immediately closed and sealed off for a period of time equal to that fixed in the judgment, and the business operator will be punished by a prison sentence ranging from eight days to two months and by a fine ranging from 500 to 10.000 €, per violation.[23]

Further, any person who personally or by an intermediary, manufactured, produced, prepared, transformed, sold or distributed foodstuffs or beverages although there was a prohibition, shall be sentenced to a prison sentence ranging from eight days to two months and to a fine ranging from 251 to

22 Luxembourg Law of 25 September 1953, supra note 40 at p. 22, Art.17.

23 Luxembourg Law of 25 September 1953, supra note 40 at p. 22, Art.16.

5.000 €. The objects used for the manufacture, preparation, transformation, commercialisation or distribution will be confiscated, and the police will immediately close the business premises.[24]

In the event of repeated serious offences (felonies) before the expiry of a five-year term from the date of the first conviction, the courts may prohibit the business operator, permanently or for a term of five to ten years, from the manufacture, preparation, transformation, commercialisation or distribution of foodstuffs.

In addition, a business operator who refuse the visits, inspections, sampling, sequestration or seizure by the competent officers will be subject to a fine ranging from 251 to 2.000 €, per violation. In the event of a repeated offence within two years from the last conviction for an offence punishable as mentioned above, the court may raise the fine to 4.000 €, per violation, and may impose a prison sentence ranging from 8 days to 1 year.

The courts may order that the judgment shall be displayed, in whole or in part, in public places and for the length of the time that they determine and that the judgment shall be notified by newspapers or published at the expense of the convicted person. The courts may also order that the objects referred to in Article 9 be confiscated.

b. Competitors

According to the amended law of 30 July 2002 concerning commercial practices and sanctioning unfair competition, any person who carries out a commercial activity or an industrial, craft or liberal professional activity, who acts contrary to fair commercial, industrial, craft or liberal professions practices, or who commits an act contrary to contractual obligations, who removes or attempts to remove from her/his competitor(s) a part of their clientele or undermines or attempts to undermine their ability to compete, will be liable for unfair competition.

24 Luxembourg Law of 25 September 1953, supra note 40 at p. 22, Art.18.

In the event that a business operator does not comply with the advertising requirements, a competitor may take legal action against him for the infringement of the aforementioned law that prohibits misleading advertising.

According to Article 17 of the law of 2002, the term *"misleading advertisement"* means any advertising which in any way, including its presentation, deceives or is likely to deceive the persons to whom it is addressed or whom it reaches and which, because of its misleading character, is likely to affect their economic behaviour or which, for those reasons, prejudices or is likely to prejudice a competitor.

In the event of a misleading advertisement, according to Article 23 of the law of 2002[25], the competitor may request the President of the District Court competent for commercial matters to order that the business operator cease all misleading advertisements or any acts contrary to such law, even in the absence of proof of loss or actual damage to the competitor or the intention or negligence of the business operator. The judge may also order that the decision be displayed outside the business premises of the operator and at the latter's costs or the judge may also order that the judgment be published, in full or in part, in any or all newspaper(s).

In the event of breach of the injunctions or prohibitions of a definitive judgment which may not be appealed, the business operator will be liable for a fine ranging from 251 to 120.000 €, per violation.

c. Consumers associations

Consumers associations may also request the District Court competent in commercial matters to order an injunction to cease any practice that is contrary to the Consumer Code, such as an unfair, misleading or aggressive commercial practice. In the event of such practices being used by a business operator, the latter may, according to Article L.122-8 of the Consumer Code, be sentenced to a fine ranging from 251 to 120.000 €, per violation.

25 Luxembourg Law of 30 July 2002, supra note 24 at p. 21.

2. Are there any national self-regulating bodies with respect to advertising for a.o. foodstuffs?

Since 2009, Luxembourg has established a "Commission Luxembourgoise pour l'Ethique en Publicité (CLEP)" which handles complaints from consumers only (not from competitors).

The Advertising Council of Luxembourg ("Conseil de la Publicité du Luxembourg") and the Commission for Ethics in Advertising (CLEP) aim at the promotion, development, and defense of advertising and freedom, as well as the implementation of self-regulating advertising on the basis of a Code of Ethics.

LU

The CLEP investigates consumers' complaints and handles the requests for prior examination of the advertisements that may be submitted by advertisers, agencies and media.

CHAPTER 10
The Netherlands

Remco Bäcker, Kim Lucassen, Joanne Zaaijer and Victor van Ahee

I. Possible Bans on Food Advertising

NL

1. Is there any national legislation (or national codes of conduct) on the promotion of foodstuffs?

a. Dutch Civil Code

The Dutch Civil Code (DCC) pertains to general rules of civil law in the Netherlands. The rules of civil law pertaining to misleading advertising are also included in the DCC. These rules of civil law also apply to the advertising of foodstuffs. The relevant articles of the DCC provide protection against misleading advertising for consumers (Article 6:194 DCC) and for competitors (Article 6:193a and others of the DCC). The provisions pertaining to the protection of consumers against misleading advertising is the implementation of (a part of) the Unfair Commercial Practices Directive (Directive 2005/29/EC).[1] This is set out in more detail under II.1 below.

b. Commodities Act

The Commodities Act (*Warenwet*)[2] is a framework act that provides for general principles and conditions pertaining to foodstuffs and consumer products. Express conditions pertaining to foodstuffs are set out in more detail in specific decrees, so called Commodities Act Decrees (*Warenwetbesluiten*).

1 Directive 2005/29/EC of the European Parliament and of the Council of 11 May 2005 concerning unfair business-to-consumer commercial practices in the internal market.

2 Wet van 28 december 1935, houdende voorschriften betreffende de hoedanigheid en aanduiding van waren., described in more detail in II.1 sub b.

These Commodities Act Decrees can include so called *horizontal legislation*, pertaining to all foodstuffs (such as the Preparation and Processing of Foodstuffs Commodities Act Decree[3]), but can also include so-called *vertical legislation*, pertaining to specific foodstuffs (such as the Dairy Produce Commodities Act Decree[4]).

The Commodities Act contains a general rule pertaining to the promotion of foodstuffs in Article 20. This article states that it is prohibited to professionally advertise commodities (such as foodstuffs) in a way that the advertiser knows or reasonably should know that such advertising is in conflict with certain provisions of the Commodities Act and certain Commodities Act Decrees that pertain to foodstuffs.[5]

c. Self-regulation

In the Netherlands various self-regulatory codes apply regarding the promotion of foodstuffs. The self-regulatory framework in the Netherlands is predominantly included in the Dutch Advertising Code (*Nederlandse Reclame Code*) that contains a general part and a specific part with particular advertising codes. The general part deals with issues such as misleading advertising, and the specific part contains targeted advertising codes such as the Advertising Code for Foodstuffs and the Advertising Code for Alcoholic Beverages, which are described under Section II.2 below.

The Dutch Advertising Code Foundation is the self-regulatory body that adopts the Dutch Advertising Code and the individual advertising codes. Certain organisations of consumers, producers, advertisers and media participate in this foundation. Furthermore, the Dutch Advertising Code Foundation is linked with the Dutch Advertising Code Committee, which will be described further in V.2 below.

3 *Besluit van 10 december 1992, houdende vaststelling van het warenwetbesluit bereiding en behandeling van levensmiddelen.*

4 *Besluit van 25 oktober 1994, houdende het Warenwetbesluit Zuivel.,* please see III.1 sub (d) of this chapter.

5 As described in Article 8 sub a through e of the first subparagraph of the Commodities Act.

2. Is the promotion of certain foodstuffs restricted or prohibited by any national mandatory and/or soft laws?

In the Netherlands the promotion of certain foodstuffs is restricted and in some cases prohibited by mandatory law and by soft law. Mandatory law contains restrictions regarding the promotion of alcoholic beverages, and infant formulae and dietary products. Soft law of the Netherlands contains restrictions on the promotion of alcoholic beverages, confectionary, and energy drinks.

NL

a. Alcoholic beverages

The promotion of alcoholic beverages in the Netherlands is restricted by mandatory law as well as by soft law.

i. Mandatory law

The promotion of alcoholic beverages is restricted under the Alcohol Licensing and Catering Act 2013[6] (*Drank- en horecawet 2013 or "ALCA"*). The ALCA provides for the possibility to impose rules through a governmental decree that can govern, along with others, the content of the promotion of alcoholic beverages, the target group of such promotion as well as the time, means and medium of the promotion. Such governmental decree is not currently in force since the government prefers to have the promotion of alcoholic beverages governed by self-regulation. If the self-regulation of the alcoholic beverages industry does not follow government policy, it can adopt a governmental decree in accordance with the ALCA.

The Media Act 2008[7] (*Mediawet 2008*) governs the promotion of alcoholic beverages through television and radio communication. This Act prohibits advertisements or teleshopping spots for alcoholic beverages through any media (defined as any audio-visual electronic broadcasting medium) be-

6 *Wet van 7 oktober 1964, tot regeling van de uitoefening van de bedrijven en de werkzaamheid, waarin of in het kader waarvan alcoholhoudende drank wordt verstrekt.*

7 *Wet van 29 december 2008 tot vaststelling van een nieuwe Mediawet.*

tween 06:00 – 21:00 hours. Also, the product placement of alcoholic beverages in programs is not permitted between 06:00 – 21:00 hours. This time restriction applies to promotion through public media services as well as through commercial media services.

The Media Act 2008 further states that if a certain program on commercial television or radio is sponsored by a sponsor that produces or sells alcoholic beverages, such sponsoring shall only be effectuated by a neutral mention or display of the sponsor's name or figurative trademark.

ii. Self-regulatory

The self-regulation of the promotion of alcoholic beverages is laid down in the Advertising Code for Alcoholic Beverages[8] (*Reclamecode voor Alcoholhoudende Drank or* "ACAB"). The ACAB has been adopted by the Campaign for Sensible Drinking Foundation (*Stichting Verantwoord Alcoholgebruik*) and certain trade organisations and so-called 'Product Boards'. A Product Board is a public organization of companies within the same production chain. A Product Board has public law status and therefore has the power to establish certain rules. At the same time it acts as an interest group for businesses in the industry and as an advisory body for the government. The current government is considering whether to abolish the Product Boards in 2014 in which case the Ministry of Economic Affairs would carry out their duties from then on.

The ACAB is part of the Dutch Advertising Code (*Nederlandse Reclame Code or* "DAC") and provides for certain general restrictions regarding the content of the advertisement and its suggestions. The ACAB contains rules that apply to alcohol promotions during events and sponsoring. The ACAB also provides for an obligation to include either a warning slogan or logo pertaining to alcohol use in advertisements for alcoholic beverages. A breach of the ACAB can lead to a complaint with the Dutch Advertising Code Committee (*Reclame Code Commissie*) as described under V.2 below.

8 Available in Dutch at www.reclamecode.nl.

b. Confectionary

The Confectionary Code (*Code voor Zoetwaren*) is also a part of the Dutch Advertising Code and provides for certain general rules regarding the contents of advertisements for confectionary. Pursuant to the Confectionary Code an advertisement of confectionary products shall not be misleading regarding responsible use of confectionary. Furthermore, in advertisements for confectionary products a specific picture of a toothbrush is prescribed. Ice cream, soft drinks and sandwich filling are not governed by the Confectionary Code. The promotion of these products is therefore not restricted by the Confectionary Code.

NL

c. Energy drinks

No national Dutch law restricts the advertising of energy drinks in the Netherlands. The trade association for soft drinks, water and juices or *Nederlandse vereniging voor frisdranken, waters en sappen* is a member of the UNESDA, the Union of European Soft Drink Associations, which has adopted a code for the Labelling and Marketing of Energy Drinks[9] and a code for the Labelling and Marketing of Energy Shots.[10] These codes stipulate principals regarding the sales and marketing of energy drinks and shots and are guidelines that directly apply to the members of UNESDA.

Amongst other things, the UNESDA code for energy drinks contains the principle that the promotion of the benefits of energy drinks (and their ingredients) shall not include references to alcohol in combination with energy drinks. The UNESDA code for energy shots contains, for example, the principles that (i) energy shots should not be sold in packages of more than 100 ml and (ii) such energy shots are not placed next to energy drinks (but preferably in the food supplements section), so as to avoid leading the consumer to believe the two drinks belong to the same category.

9 UNESDA Code for the Labelling and Marketing of Energy Drinks, revised by the UNESDA Board, 25 May 2012, Oslo, available at www.unesda.org.

10 UNESDA Code for the Labelling and Marketing of Energy Shots, revised by the UNESDA Board, 25 May 2012, Oslo, available at www.unesda.org.

d. Other

Dutch law also prohibits the promotion of infant formulae other than in publications specialising in baby care and scientific publications. This prohibition follows from Commission Directive 2006/141/EC[11] and is implemented in Dutch law in the Commodities Act Decree Infant Formulae[12] (*Warenwetbesluit Zuigelingenvoeding 2007)*. The implementation in Dutch law did not result in any deviation from the relevant directive, neither did the implementation of Directive 2009/39/EC on foodstuffs intended for particular nutritional uses. The prohibition of the use of the adjectives 'dietetic' or 'dietary' for the promotion of foodstuffs for normal consumption is implemented in the Commodities Act Decree for products for particular nutrition (*Warenwetbesluit Producten voor bijzondere voeding*).[13]

3. Is the promotion of (certain) foodstuffs towards a specific section of the population restricted or prohibited by any national mandatory and/or soft laws?

The Media Act 2008 (*Mediawet 2008*) provides that advertising during or around programs intended for children up to the age of twelve years can be governed in more detail by a governmental decree. Such decree is not currently in force. No other Dutch law provides for regulation of advertisements to specific target groups.

The Dutch Advertising Code (*Nederlandse Reclame Code* or DAC), however, does provide for certain restrictions on advertising to specific target groups. The Advertising Code for Alcoholic Beverages (ACAB)[14], for example, does not allow advertisements for alcoholic beverages to be aimed specifically at pregnant women or children (under the age of 18). The explanatory notes

11 Commission Directive 2006/141EC of 22 December 2006 on infant formulae and follow-on formulae.

12 *Regeling van de Minister van Volksgezondheid, Welzijn en Sport van 15 mei 2007, nr. VGP/VV 2769236, inzake volledige zuigelingenvoeding en opvolgzuigelingenvoeding*

13 *Besluit van 16 april 1992, houdende Warenwetbesluit Producten voor bijzondere voeding.*

14 *Reclamecode voor Alcoholhoudende Drank.*

to the ACAB state that expressions in advertisements for alcoholic beverages that specifically attract children/youth, such as teenage idols, toys or 'young'/'modern' language, are not allowed.

More in general the ACAB prohibits advertisements for alcoholic beverages to be made to a public that consists of more than 25 % minors (under 18). Such advertisements are not allowed to be aired during or around radio/tv-programs that are followed or viewed by a public consisting of more than 25 % minors. Radio/tv-stations directed at minors, youth magazines or youth websites may also not advertise for alcoholic beverages.

The ACAB also prohibits the advertising of alcoholic beverages on (the clothing of) sportsmen/sportswomen or sports teams (or on objects used by them).

The Advertising Code for Foodstuffs (*Reclamecode Voor Voedingsmiddelen)* provides for a prohibition of advertisement of foodstuffs that target children under the age of seven[15], unless the government or a relevant (governmental) authority approves of such advertisement. Furthermore, advertising of foodstuffs to children is not allowed in day care centres or at (primary) schools. Foodstuffs may not be advertised using a teenage idol for advertising purposes.

Advertising and promotion of foodstuffs in secondary schools is only allowed if regular packages are promoted (e.g. no king-size or XXL packages) and if such promotion does not encourage excessive use of that particular food product.

The Confectionary Code[16] prescribes that the emblem of the toothbrush must be displayed in a larger size on advertisements that will be viewed by a public audience of which it is reasonably expected to predominantly consist of children under the age of 14.

Finally, there is a specific code pertaining to advertising to youths and children, the Children and Youth Advertisement Code (*Kinder- en Jeugdreclamecode),* that provides general rules governing advertising to chil-

15 According to a generally accepted market survey.

16 *Code voor Zoetwaren* mentioned under I.2 (b) above.

dren (under 12) and youths (under 18). These rules pertain to the recognisability of the product and whether or not the advertisement is misleading.

Certain restrictions apply for advertising of energy drinks to specific groups. As mentioned under I.1 (c) above, the UNESDA has adopted codes for the Labelling and Marketing of Energy Drinks and for the Labelling and Marketing of Energy Shots. In the code pertaining to energy shots it is prescribed that advertisement for energy shots should be aimed at an adult audience and that the (composition of) energy shots should be designed to appeal to the adult market. It is therefore not allowed to advertise for energy shots near primary or secondary schools. Also, manufacturers have to recommend to retailers not to place energy shots near toys or confectionary that specifically target children.

The UNESDA code that pertains to energy drinks prescribes that *'no marketing communications concerning energy drinks will be placed in any media with an audience of which more than 35 % is under 12 years of age'*. Also, no sampling of energy drinks is allowed in the proximity of primary or secondary schools or comparable institutions aimed at that age group.

II. Misleading Advertising

1. What are the national rules on misleading advertising with respect to foodstuffs?

a. Dutch Civil Code

The general rule of civil law pertaining to misleading advertising is implemented in the Dutch Civil Code (DCC). Article 6:194 DCC provides that it is unlawful to make public – or cause to make public – information regarding goods or services (including foodstuffs) which are offered in the conduct of a profession or business and that information is misleading to another person acting in the conduct of his business. The information is considered misleading if it is misleading in respect of aspects such as nature, composition, origin, volume of stocks, or price. A non-exhaustive list of these aspects is included in this article. Article 6:194 of the DCC only applies to the unlawful act of a 'professional' party against another 'professional' party. Consumers cannot make a claim on the basis of article 6:194 of the DCC.

Consumers are protected under Article 6:193a – 6:193j DCC, which provides for protection of the consumer against a trader who engages in an unfair commercial practice. Such practice is considered an unlawful act towards the consumer. This provision is the implementation of the relevant provisions of the Unfair Commercial Practices Directive (Directive 2005/29/EC).[17]

b. Administrative law

In the Netherlands the general regulatory framework act regarding inter alia foodstuffs is the Commodities Act[18] (*Warenwet*). Article 20 of the Commodities Act contains the general rule that it is prohibited to trade in foodstuffs (whether professionally or not) that contain a statement or representation that implies that the product cures, treats or prevents certain human diseases (unless it is qualified and approved as a medicine).

The Commodities Act provides for a framework that can be integrated into specific areas through governmental decrees. Such governmental decrees are called Commodities Act Decrees (*Warenwetbesluiten or* "CAD"). Specific CADs govern areas or products such as protein products, food supplements and sugar.

Specific rules regarding misleading advertising with respect to foodstuffs are included in the Food Labelling Commodities Act Decree[19] (*Warenwetbesluit etikettering van levensmiddelen or* "Food Labbeling CAD"). The Food Labelling CAD is based upon the Commodities Act and implements Directive 2000/13/EC.[20]

---

17 Directive 2005/29EC of the European Parliament and of the Council of 11 May 2005 concerning unfair business-to-consumer commercial practices in the internal market.

18 *Wet van 28 december 1935, houdende voorschriften betreffende de hoedanigheid en aanduiding van waren.*

19 *Besluit van 10 december 1991, betreffende Warenwetbesluit Etikettering van levensmiddelen.*

20 Directive 2000/13/EC of the European Parliament and of the Council of 20 March 2000 on the approximation of the laws of the Member States relating to the labelling, presentation and advertising of foodstuffs.

The Dutch Advertising Code (DAC)[21] (see II.1 above) provides for certain conditions regarding misleading advertising. This is included in the 'General Conditions' of the DAC and therefore also applies to every specific advertisement code that is part of the DAC.

Article 7 DAC stipulates that advertisements shall not be unfair or dishonest. This article is in line with the text of Article 5 of the Unfair Commercial Practices Directive[22] (Directive 2005/29/EC) and considers advertising as unfair when it is contrary to the requirements of professional diligence and can materially distort or materially distorts the economic behaviour of the average consumer whom it concerns or to whom it is directed with regard to the relevant product. In particular, misleading and aggressive advertising is considered unfair. The DAC also contains conditions regarding misleading and aggressive commercial practices in line with the Unfair Commercial Practices Directive.

2. What are the national landmark cases regarding misleading advertising for foodstuffs?

The case law regarding misleading advertising is mainly based upon Article 7 of the Dutch Advertising Code (*Nederlandse Reclame Code or* "DAC") and the civil law equivalent included in the Dutch Civil Code (DCC) as mentioned under II.1 above. If a Dutch court finds a certain advertisement unlawful, that would be a ground for a claim based upon the unlawful act of the advertiser. Based upon the DAC people can file a complaint with the Dutch Advertising Code Committee (DACC)[23] (as described in V.2). Therefore, case law regarding misleading advertising can be found both in the case law of the Dutch courts and in case law of the DACC. Some of the national landmark cases specifically pertaining to misleading advertising for foodstuffs are the following:

21 *Nederlandse Reclame Code.*

22 Directive 2005/29/EC of the European Parliament and of the Council of 11 May 2005 concerning unfair business-to-consumer commercial practices in the internal market.

23 The Dutch Advertising Code Committee (*Nederlandse Reclame Code Commissie*).

'Mussels from Zeeland': A 'producer' of mussels labelled the packages with the description 'mussels from Zeeland' (*Zeeuwse mosselen*) when the mussels were actually from Denmark. A group of competitors brought a claim based upon misleading advertising to the Dutch court, stating that the reference to Zeeland (a Dutch seaside province) is misleading and harmful to their reputation. The Dutch court ruled that although 'mussels from Zeeland' is not a protected designation of origin or geographical indication, this does not imply that an indication of the origin cannot be misleading. In this case the indication of the mussels as being from Zeeland (while they were caught in Denmark) was considered to be a misleading advertisement based upon Article 6:194 DCC because there was no link at all between the (capture and processing of) the mussels and Zeeland.[24]

'Hypo-allergenic infant formulae': A producer of infant formula brought a claim to the Dutch court against a competitor for misleading advertisement and stating health claims in breach of the Nutrition and Health Claims Regulation (Regulation 1924/2006/EC).[25] As a counterclaim, the competitor brought similar claims to the court against the primary claimant.

The argument of the competitor that the claimant was unlawfully advertising its infant formulae was, however, accepted by the Dutch court. The claimant advertised the relevant product claiming that the product 'is the infant formula most comparable to breast feeding' and that the product 'approaches breast feeding optimally'. The court ruled on these claims that given the sensitivity of the product (infant formulae), extra caution will have to be observed when comparing it to breast feeding. Given this standard, the advertising of the claimant is considered misleading.

The Dutch court deferred most decisions on the claims and counterclaims because the relevant health claims pertaining to infant formulae were still under investigation by the European Food Safety Authority. However, this case 'backfired' unexpectedly for the claimant, because the court accepted one of the competitor's counterclaims (of the 'primary' claimant) regarding

24 Middelburg Court, 2 July 2008, ECLI:NL:RBMID:2008:BD6027.

25 Regulation (EC) No 1924/2006 of the European Parliament and of the Council of 20 December 2006 on nutrition and health claims made on foods.

the claim that the relevant infant formulae was comparable to or optimally approaching breast feeding, while it dismissed all the claimant's claims.[26]

'Fresh spinach': An advertisement claiming 'no spinach is fresher than the relevant deep-frozen spinach' was not considered misleading because – if the advertisement is considered in its entire context – the advertisement suggests that deep-frozen spinach maintains more vitamin C than 'fresh' spinach because 'fresh' spinach loses 14 % vitamin C a day whereas deep-frozen spinach holds most of the vitamin C. The average consumer will understand the advertising of deep-frozen spinach as the 'freshest' spinach in this context.[27]

'Fruit bars': In this case an advertisement was used for a snack that is a bar with a grain cover and a filling with fruit (a fruit bar). The relevant advertising for the fruit bar claimed that the fruit bar has 46 % 'fruit filling'. In fact the 'filling' of the fruit bar consisted mainly of fructose (corn sugar) and only 6,7 % of fruit.

The Dutch Advertising Code Committee did not consider the advertising statement misleading as the average consumer would not expect the fruit bar to consist of 46 % pure fruit since the advertisement uses the term '46 % fruit filling' – and not '46 % fruit'. It is therefore considered that a consumer realises that fruit is an ingredient of the 'filling' of the fruit bar. Should a consumer expect that the 46 % refers to pure fruit filling, the list of ingredients on the back of the package would give the consumer the right information.[28] It should be noted that this surprising decision has been rendered by a self-disciplinary body and not by a judicial court.

'Soy-products': A case was brought to the court by a dairy trade association against a soy products producer regarding the slogan for soy-milk, *'your milk with or without cholesterol?'*. The claim was based upon the misleading advertising provision of Article 6:194 DCC (for competitors).

26 Amsterdam Court, 23 April 2008, ECLI:NL:RBAMS:2008:BD5728.

27 RCC, 6 May 2011, case nr. 2011/00354.

28 RCC, 20 September 2011, case nr. 2011/00543.

The court considers that the relevant slogan suggests that soy milk is a dairy product that is comparable to milk. The court considers this to be misleading, applying the definition of 'milk' in Article 2 of the Directive nr EC/1898/87 with respect to the nature and origin of the product (the Directive reserves the term yogurt exclusively for milk products).

The advertisement furthermore implies that milk is unhealthy because of its cholesterol content and soy milk is a healthy alternative. The court finds that cholesterol is a minor substance of milk and cannot be considered as a distinctive element of milk. As cholesterol has a negative connotation for the general public, the use of that particular (minor) characteristic can be considered unfair. The court therefore considers that the comparison of soy milk as a healthy alternative to milk, given its low cholesterol content, is misleading.[29]

In a different case, but involving the same parties to the previous case, summary relief was requested regarding the use of a claim by the producer of soy products. The relevant advertising campaign stated in various locations an advertisement referring to 'yogurt', while the product was made of soy and contained no specific yogurt-bacteria as described in the Commodities Act Decree Dairy Produce.

The court finds that the advertisements contain various references to yogurt-bacteria that are characteristic of yogurt – as prescribed by the Commodities Act Decree Dairy Produce. In these references words were used like 'yogurtvariation' and 'yogurtcultures' and 'yogurtcategory'. The court considers this an implicit and unfair reference to 'real' yogurt. The soy products producer was ordered to cease the use of references to yogurt(-bacteria).[30]

'Trappistbread': In a somewhat older case, before 'Trappist' was registered as a trademark, a claim was made by a Trappist monastery against a producer of bread that claimed its bread was Trappistbread. The producer was not able to show that its bread was actually made in a Trappist monastery or according to Trappist recipe.

---

29 Breda Court, 25 October 2006, ECLI:NL:RBBRE:2006:AZ0888.

30 Breda Court, 30 May 2012, case nr. 248734/KG ZA 12-218, LJN: BW6807.

The court ruled that the advertising of the bread as Trappistbread was misleading because the bread was referring to the methods of bread making by Trappist monks, without actually using such sorts of methods. The Trappist monastery was considered harmed by the advertising because the misleading advertisement harms the 'goodwill' of an ecclesiastical institution like a Trappist monastery that it is considered to have. Given the 'goodwill' of a Trappist monastery, it is unfair and misleading to use that description when the particular product is not made by that monastery or according to its recipe.[31] It should, however, be noted that the term Trappist is currently protected by a collective trademark.

III. Mandatory Labelling: Name of the Product

Are there any national definitions of a foodstuff that could hamper the marketing of an imported food product?

a. Energy drinks

There is no general definition under Dutch law of the term "Energy drinks". Energy drinks fall under the definition of "soft drinks". The Commodities Act (*Warenwet)* states that soft drinks, including energy drinks, may not contain more than 350 mg/l of caffeine. For other functional ingredients (taurine, glucuronolactone and inosiet) Dutch law does not hold any maximum concentration values.

b. Sports drinks

Dutch law does not contain a definition of "Sports drinks".

31 Breda Court, 30 November 1993, ECLI:NL:RBBRE:1993:AM2035.

c. Yogurt

Pursuant to Article 8 of the Dairy Produce (Commodities Act) Decree (*Warenwetbesluit Zuivel)*, the designation "yogurt" may only be used for liquid dairy products that are obtained from cow's milk by microbial acidification by yogurt cultures, and which have the following characteristics:

(1) big amount of living micro-organisms;

(2) fat percentage of at least 2,95 %;

(3) content of milk protein of at least 2,8 % with at least 33 % milk protein in fat free dry matter; and

(4) maximum pH amount of 4,5;

to which before, during or after the acidification only protein concentrate or caseinates are allowed to have been added.

If the product contains added caseinate or whey protein concentrate, the label should include an indication that shows which percentage of these ingredients are added.

Given this definition, for example, "Biogarde"[32] cannot be named "yogurt" because the product is acidified with cultures (lactic acid bacteria) other than the ones prescribed in Article 8 of the Dairy Produce (Commodities Act) Decree. Also, yogurt products made of soy cannot be named "yogurt" since they are not obtained from cow's milk.[33]

d. Cheese

Pursuant to Article 9 of the Dairy Produce (Commodities Act) Decree (*Warenwetbesluit zuivel)*, the designation "cheese" can only be used for the dairy product that has been obtained by:

32 Biogarde is a typical Dutch product name for a yogurt product with a milder taste than "normal" yogurt (due to the different micro-organisms that are used).

33 Breda Court, 30 May 2012, case nr. 248734/KG ZA 12-218, LJN: BW6807.

(1) coagulation of cow's milk only, regardless of whether any milk ingredients are added or removed;

(2) removal of meadow; and

(3) maturation until the product is ready for consumption.

Further, Article 9 of the Dairy Produce (Commodities Act) Decree determines that for cheese, certain specific names can be used (listed in an annex to this Decree, and in Chapter 2, Section 2 of the Animal Products Regulation), provided that the nature and composition of the cheese satisfies the relevant cheese standard, or meets certain specific requirements as set out in the Animal Products Regulation. These names include *"Goudse kaas"*, *"Edammer kaas"* and *"Commissie kaas"*.

Pursuant to Article 2, paragraph 11 of the Dairy Produce (Commodities Act) Decree, it is forbidden to place the foodstuffs that are mentioned in this Decree on the market in Dutch territory, without complying with the requirements under this Decree.

Further, the Agricultural Quality Act (*Landbouwkwaliteitswet*) also contains rules regarding the use of the names *"Goudse kaas"* and *"Edammer kaas"*. "Cheese" made from, for instance, goat or sheep milk are separately regulated in the Dairy Produce (Commodities Act) Decree (*Warenwetbesluit zuivel).*

e. Bread

Article 1, paragraph 1d of the Meal and Bread (Commodities Act) Decree (*Warenwetbesluit Meel en brood*), defines "bread" as baked foodstuffs with the following characteristic elements:

- water or milk;
- no leavening (*rijsmiddel)* other than baker's yeast or sour dough; and
- either reduced or crushed fruits from grain or seeds from buckwheat and kitchen salt, to which a bread improver has been added or not.

Pursuant to Article 8 of this Decree, the word "bread" can only been used for bread with a humidity percentage of less than 20 % and a percentage of kitchen salt of less than 2,1 %, calculated on dry matter.

Furthermore, the Meal and Bread (Commodities Act) Decree (*Warenwetbesluit Meel en brood*) prescribes the following more specific definitions for different types of bread:

- The designation "white bread" (*wittebrood)* can only be used if it indicates bread that (Article 9):
  - contains a humidity percentage of at least 20 %;
  - contains a maximum percentage of kitchen salt of 2,1 % of dry matter;
  - has wheat flour as the main flour component; and
  - does not contain brans that are visible with the naked eye.
- The designations "brown bread" (*bruinbrood)* or "wheat bread" (*tarwebrood)* can only be used if they indicate bread that (Article 10):
  - contains a humidity percentage of at least 20 %;
  - contains a maximum percentage of kitchen salt of 2,5 % of dry matter;
  - the main flour component is not mixed with cracked wheat and wheat flakes; and
  - contains brans that are visible with the naked eye.
- The designation "milk bread" (*melkbrood)* may only be used for bread (Article 11):
  - with a humidity percentage of at least 20 %;
  - with a maximum amount of kitchen salt of 2,5 % of dry matter; and
  - to which milk ingredients in their natural proportions have been add ed, which makes the milk fat content at least 1,5 % of the dry matter.
- The designation "currant bread" (*krentenbrood)* should only be used for bread with at least 30 % currants (Article 12).
- The designation "plum loaf" (*rozijnenbrood)* should only be used for bread that consists of at least 30 % raisins (Article 13).

Please note that these restrictions do not apply to foodstuffs that are legitimately produced or placed on the market in another EU Member State.[34]

34 Article 1, paragraph 2 of the Meal and Bread (Commodities Act) Decree.

For this reason, the requirements do not constitute an obstacle to trade, except for products that are imported from a third-country.

f. Other relevant definitions not defined under EU law

Other relevant definitions of (particular Dutch) food products are laid down in specific Commodities Act Decrees, amongst which are the following.

The Cocoa and Chocolate (Commodities Act) Decree (*Warenwetbesluit cacao en chocolade).* Pursuant to this Decree, the designation "chocolate sprinkles" and/or "chocolate flakes" (*"chocoladehagelslag of chocoladevlokken")* can only be used for chocolate products that are presented in the form of granules or flakes and which contain a total of at least 32 % cocoa solids, including not less than 12 % cocoa butter and not less than 14 % fat cocoa solids. There is no provision in the Cocoa and Chocolate (Commodities Act) Decree stating that this restriction does not apply to foodstuffs that are legitimately produced or placed on the market in another EU Member State. For this reason, these requirements could arguably constitute an obstacle to trade, although the mutual recognition principle should apply.

Further, the Fishery Products, Snails and Frog Legs (Commodities Act) Decree (*Warenwetbesluit Visserijproducten, slakken en kikkerbillen)* lays down the requirements relating to (for instance) the designations "new herring" (*Nieuwe haring*), "Dutch new" (*Hollandse nieuwe*) and "new mates" (*Nieuwe maatjes*), all relating to the first Dutch herring of the season that is suitable for consumption. These requirements also seem to apply to imported products[35] and could therefore raise an obstacle to trade.

Reserved designations are not only laid down in the context of the Commodities Act. Also, certain Product Boards[36] (*productschappen)* have established regulations that relate to (names of) consumer products. For

35 Article 2 of the Fishery Products, Snails and Frog Legs (Commodities Act) Decree.

36 A Product Board is a public organization of companies within the same production chain. A Product Board has a public law status and therefore also has the power to establish certain rules. At the same time it acts as an interest group for businesses in the industry and as an advisory body for the government. The current government is considering abolishing the Product Boards in 2014. The Ministry of Economic Affairs will then carry out their duties.

instance, the Product Board on Alcoholic Beverages (*Productschap Drank*) has issued a regulation in which the conditions are set for the use of definitions of domestic spirits such as "Jenever" and "Advocaat" (a traditional Dutch alcoholic beverage made from eggs, sugar and brandy).[37] The rules laid down in this Regulation are binding for (in short) all natural persons and/or legal entities that operate a business or carry out activities within the field for which the Product Board has been established. This means that imported products should in principle also comply with these rules.[38]

NL

IV. Voluntary Labelling

1. "Clean Labels" – Are there any national definitions or requirements for the use of the following claims: (a) natural, (b) pure, (c) home-made / grandmother recipe or (d) other similar claims?

Beyond the general requirements on false or misleading labelling there is no specific Dutch legislation in place regarding the use of the claims "natural", "pure", "home-made / family recipe / grandmother recipe" or similar claims.

The Netherlands, however, does recognize a wide variety of quality marks (*keurmerken*), indicating claims that are similar to the ones mentioned above, or specifying certain aspects of the composition of the product ("100 whole wheat", "dolphin-friendly tuna"), health related aspects of the product ("healthy choice" – *gezonde keuze* or "I choose conscious" – *ik kies bewust*) or the preparation method of the product. For instance, "EKO", "Eco" or "Better life" are quality marks that indicate that a product is made with special attention to animal welfare and/or the environment. Also, the

37 Source: http://opmaatwaarenwet.sdu.nl/opmaatlevensmiddelenrecht/show.do?type=gen&key=ELM_03).

38 See, for example, Article 2 of the packaging regulation of the Product Board on Alcoholic Beverages.

indication "Halal" is considered a (religious) quality mark. Further, there are quality marks related to the packaging material of the foodstuff or the origin of the product ("official regional product" – *erkend streekproduct*), or specific product (group) bound quality marks (for instance, "fairtrade" or "free-range eggs" – *scharreleieren).*

Quality marks are not formally regulated in Dutch law, but are mostly an initiative of expert organizations or self-regulating bodies, setting their own requirements regarding the use of their respective quality marks.

2. Nutrition & health claims

a. Within the list of health claims authorized pursuant to Regulation 1924/2006, are there any related substances that are prohibited or considered as a medicinal substance within your jurisdiction?

To date, there are no related substances that are prohibited or officially considered as a medicinal substance pursuant to Dutch law. There is, however, a discussion going on regarding the question of whether Melatonin (with a dosage of 0,3 mg or more) should be considered a food supplement or a medicine, while the list of authorized health claims recognizes Melatonin with a dosage up to 0,5 mg still as a foodstuff. The outcome of this discussion is currently still unclear.

b. Are there any national laws and regulations permitting food business operators to make reference to recommendations or endorsements by national associations, medical, nutrition or dietetic professionals, and health-related charities?

Article 11 of Regulation 1924/2006 provides that 'in the absence of specific Community rules concerning recommendations of or endorsements by national association of medical, nutrition or dietetic professionals and health-related charities, relevant national rules may apply in compliance with the provisions of the Treaty'.

The Netherlands has, however, not implemented any national rules based on Article 11 of Regulation 1924/2006. As a consequence, under Dutch law, it is prohibited to use a (health) claim that makes reference to recommendations of individual doctors or health professionals and other associations.

c. Are there any national laws or regulations regulating the use of nutrition or health claims on non-prepackaged food?

There are no specific national laws or regulations in the Netherlands that regulate the use of nutrition or health claims on non-prepackaged food. Therefore, only the rules provided by the EU Claims Regulation apply.

d. Is there a notification procedure required prior to / for marketing foodstuffs bearing nutritional or health claims?

In the Netherlands, there is no notification procedure required prior to / for marketing foodstuffs bearing nutritional or health claims. The same applies for claims that are made with respect to food supplements and/or fortified food (food with added vitamins and minerals). Although these kinds of foodstuffs always bear at least a nutrition claim, under Dutch law there is no mandatory national prior notification procedure in place for these products.

V. Enforcement of Food Law and Self-regulating Bodies

1. Which actions may one risk in case of non-compliance with the labelling or advertising requirements?

In case of non-compliance with the labelling or advertising requirements, the following parties can take (enforcement) actions in the Netherlands:

a. Public authorities

In case of a violation of one of the provisions of the Commodities Act (*Warenwet*) or one of the underlying Decrees, the *Dutch Food and Consumer Product Safety Authority* ("NVWA") can take either administrative or criminal enforcement actions.

The NVWA is an independent agency falling under the supervision of the Ministry of Economic Affairs and the Ministry of Health, Welfare and Sports. The objective of the NVWA is to safeguard human and animal health and welfare. In this respect, the NVWA monitors the safety of food and consumer products.

The enforcement strategy of the NVWA is based on a so-called "risk-based-approach", based on knowledge and cooperation with the sector and on the influencing of behaviour. According to its website the NVWA's approach to businesses and consumers is characterized by the principle "trust, unless ...".[39] The method or methods of enforcement that the NVWA can use are, for instance, repressive supervision or investigation. Depending on the sector or the business that is under supervision, the relevant method is chosen. The NVWA works according to a differentiated approach for different "target groups". This involves determining the enforcement method to be used, depending on the risks, compliance behaviour and developments within the sector.

i. Administrative enforcement measures

Possible administrative enforcement measures are (i) imposing an administrative fine, (ii) imposing periodic penalty payments or (iii) enforcing an administrative order.

(1) *Administrative fine*

The NVWA can impose administrative fines for a violation of the provisions of the Commodities Act (Decrees).[40] The fines can amount up

39 See www.nvwa.nl

40 Pursuant to Article 32(a) of the Commodities Act (*Warenwet*).

to EUR 2,100 per violation, depending on (i) the type of violation and (ii) the size of the business (the fines are twice as high for businesses with more than 50 employees).[41] The NVWA can also decide to increase this fine up to a maximum of EUR 4,500 if the natural person or legal entity to which the offense can be attributed has been fined for a similar offense within the past two years. Further, also the severity of the offence, the extent to which the natural person or legal entity can be reproached for the offense and/or the circumstances in which the offence took place, can give rise to an increase of the fine.

Where a violation constitutes a significant risk to the health or safety of persons, the maximum fine will be imposed. An example of this is a violation of the requirements regarding the production of baby food.

Recently, the Dutch government has approved a bill that amends the Commodities Act, and leads to (among others things) an increase of the maximum amount of an administrative fine up to EUR 78,000 per violation.[42]

(2) *Periodic penalty payments*

A periodic penalty can be imposed to take away an acute health threat for the short term.[43] The amount of a periodic penalty is not fixed, but depends on the circumstances. Relevant circumstances are, for instance, the impact of the violation and the intended effect of the penalty (both the severity of the offense and the financial benefit that was obtained by the offender through committing the offense should be taken into account).

(3) *Administrative orders*

Several administrative orders can be enforced.[44] These include the recall of products, the decision to confiscate or destruct products, or setting

41 Based on the Administrative Fines (Commodities Act) Decree (*Warenwetbesluit bestuurlijke boeten*).

42 It is currently unclear when the amended Commodities Act will enter into force.

43 Pursuant to Article 32 of the Commodities Act (*Warenwet*).

44 Based on Articles 32(k) to 32(m) of the Commodities Act (*Warenwet*).

a temporary ban on the marketing of certain products, in case there are indications that these products endanger the safety or health of human beings. The costs relating to the confiscation and/or destruction of products are borne by the offender.[45]

ii. Criminal enforcement measures

Criminal enforcement measures usually only occur in serious cases, for instance when repeat offenders are involved or in cases where parties deliberately and attributably act against the applicable laws. In those situations, the NVWA may hand over the case to the public prosecutor who will start/continue with the criminal proceedings.[46] The NVWA itself also has the authority to take criminal enforcement measures through its Information and Investigation Service (the "NVWA-IOD").

Criminal enforcement measures can either be based on the Economic Offences Act (*Wet op de Economische Delicten)* or on the Dutch Criminal Code (*Wetboek van Strafrecht)*.

(1) *Economic Offences Act*

Article 1 under 4° of the Economic Offences Act (*Wet op de Economische Delicten)* provides that a violation of the Commodities Act (*Warenwet)* is considered an economic offense. Such violations qualify as an offense (Article 2, paragraph 4 of the Economic Offences Act). Pursuant to Article 6, paragraph 1, under 4° of the Economic Offences Act, an offender can be punished for an offence with (i) imprisonment (up to six months), (ii) community service or (iii) a fine of the fourth category (which is currently EUR 19,500). However, if the economic benefit of the offence is higher, a steeper fine of the fifth category can be imposed (which is currently EUR 78,000).

45 Pursuant to Article 32(n) of the Commodities Act (*Warenwet*).

46 Taking into account the Guidelines for the Prosecution of Offences under the Commodities Act (*Richtlijn voor strafvordering Warenwet (2011R033)*).

Also, additional penalties and/or measures can be imposed by the (economic divisions of the) courts.[47] Such additional punishments can include the complete or partial shutdown of a food production company for a maximum period of one year (based on Article 7c), the obligation to pay an amount to the government that is similar to the total benefit of the offence (Article 8c) or, for instance, the publication of the judgment (Article 7g).

(4) *Dutch Criminal Code*

The Dutch Criminal Code (*Wetboek van Strafrecht)* applies to violations of the food safety regulations. These violations are qualified as an offence under general criminal law. Examples include forgery and fraud.

NL

The maximum penalty for such offenses follows from the relevant provisions of the Dutch Criminal Code. For example, if forgery of documents is committed, an imprisonment of a maximum of six years or a fine of EUR 78,000 can be imposed. In case a legal entity is involved, the fine can even be increased to a maximum of EUR 780,000 (if that would be considered an appropriate punishment). Also, the Dutch Criminal Code provides that the offender can be required to pay an amount to the government that is similar to the total benefit of the offence.

b. Competitors

Enforcement actions can also be competitor-initiated, mainly based on their desire to preserve the "level playing field" in the market where they believe consumers are misled through non-compliant labelling and/or advertising of their competitors.

Competitors can inform the NVWA about these situations or file an official enforcement request, after which the authorities can decide to start an investigation or impose enforcement measures. Competitors can also start legal proceedings, for instance by stating that their competitor has conducted a

47 Pursuant to Articles 7 and 8 of the Economic Offences Act (*Wet op de Economische Delicten*).

wrongful act (for example, due to false, misleading or comparative advertising, based on Article 6:194 – 6:196 of the Dutch Civil Code).

c. Consumers / (consumer) associations

Consumers can instigate enforcement actions, for instance by informing the competent authorities of any misconduct, or by filing an enforcement request.

Consumers can also start civil proceedings against the food production companies. Their complaints could, for instance, be based on a breach of the product liability provisions in the Dutch Civil Code or consumers can state that the food production companies have conducted a wrongful act.

2. Are there any national self-regulating bodies with respect to advertising for foodstuffs?

In the Netherlands, there are several self-regulating bodies with respect to the advertising of foodstuffs. The two bodies with most influence are the following:

a. Dutch Advertising Code Committee

The Dutch Advertising Code Committee (*Reclame Code Commissie*) is the self-regulating body that evaluates whether advertisements are in conformity with the Dutch Advertisement Code. Part of the Dutch Advertisement Code are the Advertising Code for Alcoholic Beverages (*Reclamecode voor Alcoholhoudende Drank),* the Confectionary Code (*Code voor Zoetwaren*), the Advertising Code for Foodstuffs (*Reclamecode Voor Voedingsmiddelen*) and the Children and Youth Advertisement Code (*Kinder- en Jeugdreclamecode*), which are mentioned before in paragraph II.1 (a) and (b) and paragraph II.2.[48]

48 Dutch Advertising Code part B, pages 29, 117, 113 and 118.

Any party that believes that an advertisement is inconsistent with the Dutch Advertising Code can use the straightforward and inexpensive mechanism of filing a complaint at the Dutch Advertising Code Committee. Appeals against the Dutch Advertising Code Committee's ruling are referred to the Appeals Board, which issues a definitive ruling.

If the Dutch Advertising Code Committee and/or the Appeals Board determine that a complaint is justified, it can either make a 'recommendation' (i.e. to recommend to discontinue this way of advertising) or it can deliver an 'opinion without commitment'. The most far-reaching measure is the decision to distribute a decision as an "ALERT", which means that it is brought to the attention of the public through either a press release and/or on the website of the Dutch Advertising Code Committee.

b. KOAG-KAG

The KOAG/KAG organization is a self-regulating body that consists of the Inspection Board for the Public Promotion of Medicines (*Keuringsraad Openlijke Aanprijzing Geneesmiddelen,* KOAG) and the Inspection Board for the Promotion of Health Products (*Keuringsraad Aanprijzing Gezondheidsproducten,* KAG).

The KOAG-KAG monitors compliance with the legal requirements regarding public advertising of medicines and health products based on Articles 19 and 20 of the Commodities Act (*Warenwet),* the Code for the Promotion of Medicines, and the Code for the Promotion of Health Products. The KOAG-KAG has (among other things) great expertise in the assessment of claims for food supplements that are at the interface between medical claims and health claims.

In the event of a violation of the above-mentioned rules, the KOAG-KAG can either file a complaint at the Dutch Advertising Code Committee or bring a case before the Dutch civil court.

CHAPTER 11
Norway

Marie Vaale-Hallberg and Nina Charlotte Lindbach

I. Possible Bans on Food Advertising

1. Is there any general national legislation or code of conduct regulating the promotion of foodstuffs?

NO

There is general legislation in Norway on the promotion of foodstuffs. The Norwegian Food Act of 19 December 2003 ("Food Act"), further detailed in the Regulation on labelling of 21 December 1993, outlines the core principles, which state that promotion shall not be misleading and that all information must be correct and adequate.[1] It follows from this legislation that the promotion shall not mislead the consumer with regard to the *"characteristics of the foodstuf, particularly with regard to its nature, identity, quality, composition, quantity, durability, origin or place of origin, the manufacturing or production means."*[2] It is further detailed in the Regulation that the following will always be illegal: (i) claiming that the foodstuff has certain effects or properties that it has not, (ii) giving the impression that the foodstuff has special characteristics when all similar foodstuffs possess the same properties, (iii) claiming or otherwise creating the impression that a food product prevents or heals illnesses, and (iv) using the words "dietetic", "the diet" or the like, either alone or in conjunction with other words, unless permitted by regulations on foodstuffs intended for particular nutritional requirements or regulations on production and sales, etc.

1 The new EU Regulation 1169/2011 on the provision of food information to consumers will be implemented to the Norwegian legislation and is estimated to come into force on 13 December 2014. The regulation will be implemented in a new Norwegian "Regulation on food information to consumers" which will replace amongst other the above mentioned Regulation on labelling of 21 December 1993.

2 Regulation on labelling article 5.

The above-stated rules apply to all types of promotion, such as advertisements and packaging/labelling.

In addition to legislation particularly applying to foodstuffs, also the general rules on marketing, as set out in the Marketing Control Act of 9 January 2009 ("Marketing Control Act"), may be found to be applicable. Although the starting point in both acts is ensuring that consumers are not mislead, the general rules contain principles regarding unfair business practises that may be found to have a broader scope than the Food Act. Furthermore, the Marketing Control Act has specific rules in order to protect children, cf. section 1.3 below. While the Food Act is controlled by the Norwegian Food Safety Authority it is the Consumer Ombudsman that principally enforces that the general rules on marketing towards consumers are complied with.

2. Is the promotion of certain foodstuffs restricted or prohibited by any national mandatory and/or soft laws (e.g. code of practise, case law)?

There are no limitations to promoting foodstuffs in Norway in general, save from the promotion of alcoholic beverages. The Act on the Sale of Alcoholic Beverages of 2 June 1989, section 9-2, prohibits the marketing of alcoholic beverages as such and illustrates the strict polities in place in Norway to protect citizens' health – in this regard reducing the intake of alcoholic beverages. The ban is further detailed in the Regulation of 8 June 2005, Chapter 14, which places restrictions on the use of trademarks and brand names used for alcoholic beverages. Should a trademark or brand name be used for both non-alcoholic and alcoholic beverages, the advertisement of the non-alcoholic beverage is also restricted unless the latter uses its own distinct trademark. There are a few minor exemptions, such as advertisements in foreign magazines, giving information on point of sale and service and having information signs of small size in direct connection with the sale or serving.[3]

3 Cf. Regulation on the sale of alcoholic beverages etc. of 8 June 2005, Chapter 14, section 14-3.

3. Is the promotion of (certain) foodstuffs towards a specific section of the population restricted or prohibited by any national mandatory and/or soft laws?

In Norway, none of the legislation or regulations on food restricts or prohibits promotion towards a specific section of the population. The food law is lex specialis to the general rules on marketing applying to all businesses; however, the general legislation on marketing establishes certain rules protecting specific sections of the population, which the food industry must also abide by.

NO

Firstly, marketing towards children has for many years been restricted both in the current Marketing Control Act and the preceding acts. Children are considered to be a particularly vulnerable group because of their innocence and lack of experience, whereby the lack of critical attitude towards advertising makes them easy to influence. When Directive 2005/29/EC, concerning business to consumer unfair practises ("UPC Directive"), was incorporated into Norwegian law, the government drafted particular rules to protect children (children defined as persons below 18 years of age).[4] Up till this point the particular protection of children was deduced from the general rules on marketing and detailed in the practise of the Consumer Ombudsman and the Market Council.

When drafting the new act, the Ministry wanted to maintain the protection already established by practise, thus the act codified the principles already developed. The Ministry intended that the act would create better predictability and also raise awareness about the need to protect children, following a possible enhanced normative effect. One example is that the act outlines that not just the promotional activities aimed directly at children must abide by these rules, but also activities that may be seen or heard by children. The law must consider children's lack of experience, natural

4 Norway is not a member of the EU; however, Norway is a member of the European Free Trade Association (EFTA excl. Switzerland). EU and EFTA entered into the European Economic Area Agreement (EEA Agreement) in 1992, uniting the countries as one internal market. As a part of the EEA Agreement, EFTA member states are obliged to incorporate EC law on the four freedoms into their domestic laws. But prior to this, the EEA Council must take the formal decision to include new EC regulations applying to the EFTA states.

credulity and the fact that they are easily swayed. Another example is the prohibition of direct request for purchase aimed at children, which includes messages that would inspire children to persuade their parents to buy the products in question.[5] It also, however, follows from no. 20 on the UPC Directive's "black list" that such direct exhortation is deemed an illegal and aggressive commercial practice.

The rules outlined in the Marketing Control Act apply to all marketing activities regardless of media type.

Secondly, the Broadcasting Act of 4 December 1992, section 3-1 states in general that it is not allowed to broadcast commercials during children's programs, and this prohibition will also apply to foodstuffs. Moreover, it prohibits advertisements that are specifically targeted at children, incorporating much stricter requirements than what is outlined in the Marketing Control Act, which does not impose a ban as such. Marketing restrictions towards children are further outlined in the Regulation on Broadcasting of 28 February 1997 section 3-6: It is illegal to broadcast advertisements for any product (including foodstuffs) or service that is of particular interest to children and young people if the advertisement involves people or characters that, for example, within the past 12 months have appeared regularly as a substantial part of a program aimed at children or young people and broadcasted either on television or radio. Furthermore, it provides some guidelines on what factors are relevant when assessing whether the advertising is specifically targeted at children. It is of relevance whether the advertisement relates to a product or service of particular interest to children, at what time during the day the advertisement is broadcast, if children under the age of 13 are playing a part in the commercial or if the advertisement has an animation or content that particularly appeals to children.

In sum, the regulation on broadcasting offers a rather strict protection, but EU Directive 2010/13/EU of 10 March 2010 on the coordination of certain provisions laid down by law, regulation or administrative action in Member States concerning the provision of audio-visual media services (the Audiovisual Media Services Directive) implies a loophole in practice for TV channels based in EU countries with less strict rules than Norway.

5 Cf. the Marketing Control Act, section 20.

This Directive demands freedom to provide broadcasting services within the Community and imposes the "country of origin principle", see article 3. Thus, only the originating country's legislation will apply even though it is less strict than the equivalent Norwegian rules. The minimum requirements in, e.g. the Directive's articles 9 (1) (g) and 9 (1) (e) will, in any case, apply to all EU/EEA countries, but the Norwegian legislation appears to be considerably stricter.

Thirdly, the Education Act of 17 July 1998, section 9-6, aims at reducing the marketing pressure on pupils. The Act, section 9-6, states that pupils shall not be exposed to advertisements that *might create a commercial pressure* or *that can substantially influence the pupils' attitude, behaviour and values.* These restrictions apply to advertisements in the school areas, in text books as well as other learning material used in the education.

Fourthly, the Norwegian food industry has developed its own guidelines since 2007 in order to reduce the marketing pressure of unhealthy food aimed at children. Although in compliance with many entities, the authorities did not see them as sufficient. In 2012 the authorities proposed a full ban on marketing of unhealthy food aimed at minors/children (below 18 years of age).[6] The industry massively criticized this proposal, alleging non-compliance with the EEA-principles of free movement of goods. A revised proposal was launched in 2013 addressing parts of the criticism raised.[7] Eventually, the industry managed to come up with a self-regulatory regime that was deemed appropriate by the Ministries. These new guidelines came into force on 1 January 2014 applying to any entity marketing foodstuffs falling within the scope of the guidelines. Should, however, this self-regulatory regime not have the desired effect, then the second proposal may be brought into effect.

The guideline establishes that all food defined as "unhealthy" should not be marketed directly at children (below 13 years of age).

6 See http://www.regjeringen.no/nb/dep/hod/dok/hoeringer/hoeringsdok/2012-2/horing---forslag-til-ny-regulering-av-ma/horingsbrev.html?id=684713

7 See http://www.regjeringen.no/nb/dep/hod/dok/hoeringer/hoeringsdok/2013/horing---revidert-forslag-til-forskrift-.html?id=727092

The crux of the matter is to clarify which foods fall within the term "unhealthy" and what marketing activities may be seen as aimed "directly at children". As regards the latter, the guidelines make it clear that one must perform an overall assessment in order to decide whether the marketing is particularly aimed at children. To give some further guidance, it is emphasized that the assessment should take into account the following aspects: a) To what extent does the type of media that is used appeal particularly to children? b) To what extent does the means that are used appeal particularly to children? c) To what extent do the promoted products appeal particularly to children? No doubt there is a resemblance to the legislation referred to above involving broadcasting, which gives a certain predictability.

Unhealthy food is defined as certain energy-dense, salty, sweet or nutrient-poor food, all exhaustively defined in the guidelines, which include, e.g. chocolate, biscuits, snacks, soft drinks and different kinds of fast food.

Marketing is defined as any promotional sales act, however, the guidelines clarify that the following are not considered to be marketing: a) The product itself, including the packaging; b) General presentation of products at retail outlets; and c) Sponsorship which only involves the use of the sponsor's name, the sponsor- or a product's trademark, or sampling of products if a parent or other responsible adult has consented to the sampling. Furthermore, television advertisements sent after 21:00 are not considered to be marketing to children. The guidelines apply to all types of media sources and channels.

Should the guidelines not be complied with, any entities, NGOs or private persons may complain to the Complaint Commission of the Food Industry ("Matvarebransjens Faglige Utvalg"). The proceedings are confidential, but the decision will be made public. Moreover, the respondent will not be informed about who the plaintiff is. A complaint must provide 1) information allowing identification of the plaintiff and the respondent and 2) written presentation of the matter, including documentation. The respondent will have 14 days to comment, and the Commission will thereafter assess the complaint.[8]

8 As of July 2014 the Complaint Commission of the Food Industry has handled 5 cases, and their decisions have been made public on their website: http://www.mfu.as/39306-Vedtak-i-MFU.

It follows from the guidelines that with regard to children over 13, the industry is obliged to take into account both age and maturity when marketing food categorized as unhealthy.

Fifthly, when assessing whether a marketing practise is in agreement with the Marketing Control Act, the average consumer test will apply as interpreted by the European Court of Justice. However, should the commercial practise, as the case may be, be directed at a particular group of consumers, then an average member of *that group* will be the benchmark (and not the average consumer). Thus, other particular groups of society will enjoy stricter protection should their mental or physical infirmity or credulity require it. This will also apply to food.

II. Misleading Advertising

1. What are the national rules on misleading advertising of foodstuffs?

Norway has implemented Directive 2000/13/EC concerning labelling, presentation and advertising of foodstuffs, but the Norwegian legislation appears to be somewhat stricter than the Directive when comparing the clauses about prohibiting misleading advertising of food. While the wording in clause 2(1) of the Directive states that the advertisement must not "be such as could mislead the purchaser to a material degree" (our emphasis), the Norwegian legislation has not adopted the "material degree" requirement as it simply states that the advertisement shall not mislead.[9] This incompatibility has presumably little practicable impact because Regulation 178/2002 on the general principles and requirements of food law does not include the same material degree requirements.[10] Furthermore, EC Regulation 1169/2011 on the provision of food information to consumers clause 7, soon to become effective, outlines that "food information shall not be misleading".

9 cf. Food Act section 10 and Regulation on labelling of 1993, clause 5.

10 cf. Articles 8 and 16.

Evidently, the concept of misleading will be determined by an overall assessment of the advertisement in question. There are however certain actions that, according to the Regulation on Food Labels, will always be regarded as misleading, and equivalent rules follow from Directive 2000/13/EC relating to the labelling, presentation and advertising of foodstuffs and are therefore not repeated here.

2. Are there any national landmark cases regarding misleading advertising of foodstuffs?

Except for the cases referred to below, there are no national landmark cases regarding misleading advertising of foodstuffs in Norway. In general, cases revolving food law are seldom brought before the Norwegian courts. Instead, cases are normally solved in dialog with the authorities or the business in question simply decides to abide by the decisions made. Case law illustrating the line to be drawn between misleading, and thus prohibited, advertisements and legal advertisements is therefore sparse. Two judgments, nevertheless, are of interest even though both focus mainly on trademark law.

In 1995 the Norwegian Supreme Court assessed the legality of the trademark "Mozell" used on a soft drink.[11] One of Norway`s leading soft drink producers had registered "Mozell" as a trademark and used this trademark along with a label rendering a landscape that could be perceived as a German river landscape of vineyards. The label was later changed and eventually pictured a landscape that might as well be a Norwegian landscape. Wine producers from the "Mosel" district in Germany, Deutscher Weinfonds, claimed that the name Mosel was entitled to a special protection and, moreover, that the trademark and label used by the soft drink producer – even after having changed the image on the label – implied a misleading and unlawful allusion to Mosel.

The Supreme Court stated that it was decisive whether consumers would be misled to believe that the soft drink derived from Mosel. Since the trademark was applied to a non-alcoholic beverage, the Supreme Court concluded

11 Rt. 1995 s. 1908.

that the trademark registration was valid, and it also emphasized that no consumer would be led to believe that the soft drink was Mosel wine. Moreover, there was only a small risk that they would believe that the soft drink in any way originated from the Mosel district.

In 2008, the Norwegian restaurant "Champagneria" was sued by the the French Institut National de L'Origine et de la Qualite and Comite Interprofessionnel du Vin Champagne. They claimed that the use of "Champagne" in the restaurant's name was misleading because the restaurant not only served sparkling wine originating from the region Champagne-Ardenne in the North of France, but also sparkling wine originating from Spain (Cava) as well as serving tapas, and thus consumers would be misled with regards to Champagne's geographic origin. The Court of Appeal[12] stated that since "Champagneria" is the name of a service, rather than a product, it was less likely that consumers would be misled and associate the name of the restaurant with the restaurant's Spanish products.

Further, the Court of Appeal stated that it would be obvious to the consumers that in addition to selling Champagne the restaurant would also offer other kinds of beverages including Cava since it is normal for all restaurants in Norway to offer a broad selection of beverages. Also, the Court of Appeal underlined the fact that "Champagneria"'s staff informed their customers about the difference between Champagne and Cava, and thus contributed to making consumers well-informed rather than misled. Furthermore, in this case both parties benefitted financially from the business of "Champagneria" as "Champagneria" contributed to the increase of Champagne sales and knowledge about Champagne – thus the court found that the use of the name was not misleading.

Contrary to other countries, there are no current and updated Norwegian guidelines available to assist the industry in assessing when food advertisements might be deemed illegal. However, the Norwegian authorities will normally emphasise the guidelines from, e.g. the food authorities in Sweden and Denmark.

12 LB-2008-117063.

Despite the lack of case law, the general public regularly debates misleading advertising and, in particular, labelling. During the fall of 2012 the Consumer Counsel of Norway published a report after reviewing more than 60 different products available in most grocery stores.[13] Regardless of the fact that the ingredient lists were presumably correct, according to the Consumer Counsel, the information on the labels was misleading to the consumers. This report was later followed up by the Norwegian Food Safety Authority which published the report "Villedende merking – Kampanje 2013" ("Misleading labelling – Campaign 2013") in the spring of 2013 after having conducted a survey of 195 foodstuffs, checking whether the food was correctly labelled and not misleading. Out of 195, the Norwegian Food Safety Authority found that 94 of the foodstuff labels were not in compliance with the law. The Norwegian Food Safety Authority has informed that it will conduct review of labels annually.

III. Mandatory Labelling: Name of the Product

Are there any national definitions of a foodstuff that could hamper the marketing of an imported food product?

a. Energy drinks

There is no particular definition of so-called "energy drinks", but in practise the term refers to beverages with a high content of caffeine. However, energy drinks may also, as the case may be, have added amino acids, amino-acid substances, vitamins, minerals and/or various extracts of herbs. For purposes of completeness it should be mentioned that any fortification through vitamins, minerals and amino acids must obtain prior approval from the authorities.[14]

13 See http://www.forbrukerradet.no/_attachment/1133792/binary/9145.

14 cf. Regulation on fortification foodstuffs through Vitamins, Minerals and certain other substances to foodstuff of 26 February 2010, no. 246, clauses 4 and 6.

The domestic application procedure will prevail until the maximum levels of vitamins and minerals are set at the EU level and made effective in Norway. The application for prior approval for fortification through amino acids will apply unrestricted, and the food safety authority is generally reluctant to give its approval due to safety concerns.[15]

b. Sports drinks

There is no national definition of "sports drinks" in Norway, but the term is generally used for liquid products that are specially designed for use before, during and after physical activity and, as such, aims at meeting certain nutritional needs under the PARNUT-legislation.[16] Sports drinks may fall within the scope of PARNUTs regulation to the extent that the drink is intended for particular nutritional purposes because 1) the nature, special composition or process of the drink differs significantly from other food; 2) it is suitable to meet specific nutritional needs; and 3) it is intended for this purpose.

These products may be sold on the Norwegian market provided that they are safe and otherwise in compliance with applicable regulations. There is no approval or notification scheme on sports products as opposed to other PARNUTs products such as products for infants.[17]

c. Yogurt

According to the Norwegian Regulation on the quality of milk and cream of 17 July 1953, section 4, "Yogurt" is defined as sour milk that is produced by using yogurt culture and at least 2,5 % content of milk solids. The Regulation

15 The Norwegian Scientific Committee for Food Safety has made a risk assessment of 30 types of amino acids, categorizing the amino acids into high, moderate and low risk. Due to the lack of scientific documentation, it was not possible to draw a conclusion for several of the acids. http://www.vkm.no/dav/fcf209d537.pdf

16 cf. Regulation on Food Intended for Particular Purposes of 21 January 1993, no. 1382 and the Regulation on Dietary Foods for Special Medical Purposes of 8 November 2001, no. 1279.

17 Cf. Regulation on Dietary Foods for Special Medical Purposes of 8 November 2001, section 19.

does not explicitly require that live lactic bacteria must be present when sold to the final consumer, but this follows from branch practise. This regulation is old and there is now a pending draft regulation (launched on 1 November 2013) under assessment. The draft currently available does not contain a definition of yogurt.[18] It follows from the draft that the definition "yogurt" must only be used for a dairy product, but the draft makes it clear that it is possible to use the term also for non-dairy products, e.g. in order to describe a characteristic feature of the product. The legislator has not yet provided any borderline examples; however, taking into account that the overall aim of the regulation is to prevent consumers from being misled, the use of "yogurt" for non-dairy products must be in a manner that is not likely to mislead.

d. Cheese

The Regulation relating to the manufacturing, labelling and sale of cheese of 24 August 1956, no. 9632 ("Cheese Regulation") defines "Cheese" as products made from milk, cream or mixtures thereof, and where either the whey is partially removed from the milk coagulated proteins or by partial concentration of whey. Clause 1 of the current Cheese Regulation explicitly states that it is illegal under Norwegian law to sell products as cheese if they are not made from raw milk materials or if they contain fat that is not derived from milk. In addition, the authorities must approve any cheese term or description.[19] Moreover, the Cheese Regulation demands that approval must also be obtained for fantasy names, including trademarks, which are used as additional terms for a cheese designation.

Like yogurt, the scheme on cheese is old and is now being revised. The authorities' current suggestion is to consolidate the various quality requirements into one regulation and remove, e.g. the duty to apply for pre-approval of cheese designations.

18 See http://www.mattilsynet.no/mat_og_vann/merking_av_mat/generelle_krav_til_merking_av_mat/utkast_til_forskrift_om_kvalitet_paa_melk_og_meieriprodukter.11602/binary/Utkast%20til%20forskrift%20om%20kvalitet%20på%20melk%20og%20meieriprodukter.

19 cf. clause 2 of the Cheese Regulation.

In Europe, several types of cheese are protected as geographical indications and designations of origin for agricultural products and foodstuffs. These schemes are not part of the EEA Agreement, and Norway has established its own scheme for the protection of, e.g. designations of origins, geographical indications and traditional specialities in the Regulation of 5 July 2002. At present there are no other agreements between Norway/EFTA and the EU ensuring mutual and automatic acceptance and grant of protection, and so far one must apply the two schemes in parallel in order to enjoy protection in the EU and Norway. Protection of foreign geographical designations of origins and geographical indications is possible and may be registered. For example, Parmigiano Reggiano enjoys protection as designation of origin under the Regulation on the protection of Parmigiano Reggiano of 20 April 2012.

In addition, it follows from the Cheese Regulation that the terms roquefort, gorgonzola and pecorino romano, in addition to parmigiano reggiano, may not be approved as principal or supplementary designations for cheese or otherwise be used in connection with the naming of cheese made in Norway. However, foreign designations other than the ones listed above may be used provided that the cheese in question has the same properties, shape, size, look and is listed in the same fat group as the original and the word "NORWEGIAN" appears as a prefix.

e. Bread

There is no national definition of bread; however, the bread producers have developed their own standard called the "Bread Scale". This standard classifies the various *types* of bread in four different categories depending on how much whole grain flour, whole grains and bran the bread contains:

0 – 25 % "Fint" ("white")

25 – 50 % "Halvgrovt" ("semi whole grain")

50 – 75 % "Grovt"("whole grain")

75 – 100 % "Ekstragrovt" ("extra whole grain")

Figure 1: The Bread Scale

In May 2013 the results of a survey of breakfast products, conducted by The Food Safety Authority, revealed i.a. that the Bread Scale could have misleading effects. Firstly, the Food Safety Authority found that some of the breads labelled with the Bread Scale were incorrectly labelled. Secondly, quite a few of the breads labelled "whole grain" had just a little bit above 50 % of whole grain. This is compliant with the Bread Scale, but the Food Safety Authority found this to "be bordering on misleading" because the consumer, looking at the Bread Scale, would believe that the bread contained 75 % whole grain.

This example is illustrating some of the challenges faced when the industry develops their own standard – which in time also was endorsed by the authorities. Although the aim of the breadscale was giving consumers an easy method to pick bread containing the desired amount of grain, the method chosen proved to be problematic. Since the Food Safety Authority was sceptical, the industry undertook measures to develop the scale accordingly. It appears that one of the measures might be to provide the actual percentage of wholegrain on the package (close to the picture of the scale).

f. Other relevant definitions not defined under EU law

Norway has several "quality regulations" to ensure that manufacturers promote their products in an honest manner and in a way that prevents consumers from being misled, and these regulations contain definitions of several foodstuffs. Some of these regulations are based on equivalent EU legislation, and some are independently developed.

In the Regulation regarding fruit juices and similar products of 13 May 2013 no. 509, which implements Directive 2001/112/EC (amended by Directive 2012/12/EC) concerning fruit juices and certain similar products intended for human consumption, Norway as well as Denmark have added a special national provision which defines the product "Eplemost", an apple juice which does not contain added sugar.

Further, the Regulation regarding jam and similar products of 12 July 2003, implements the Directive 2001/113/EC concerning, amongst others, jam. Both the Directive and the Norwegian Regulation require 350 grams of fruit per 1,000 grams of finished product. The Norwegian regulation has however included an alternative in order for the manufacturers to be able to provide jam that contains less sugar. Should the jam consist of less than 60 % of soluble solids, then the product must contain at least 400 grams of fruit per 1000 grams of finished product.

The Regulation on vegetable conserves of 1 January 2001 is a regulation with no equivalent EU legislation. This regulation defines certain quality provisions for preservation, but moreover includes some particular rules to prevent consumers form being mislead. To be allowed to use photos and images to illustrate what a product contains, the manufacturer must ensure that the indication corresponds with the actual content. For example, in order to market a product as "lemonade" the manufacturer must ensure that the product contains at least 8 % raw lemon.[20] The authorities have recently suggested deleting this regulation in whole without replacing it with new legislation. The reasoning is that the regulation is outdated and/ or to some extent the content is already being addressed by other regulations. Rather than create an unwanted complex legal framework the intent is to simplify the rules.

The Regulation on the manufacturing, labelling and marketing of edible ice of 15 April 1977 is also a regulation with no equivalent EU legislation. This regulation defines what constitutes edible ice, and provides definitions for different kinds of ice cream. Also, this regulation is now being reviewed, and the current draft implies that it will be deleted and not replaced by new legislation. Further, the Regulation on the manufacturing, labelling and sale of butter and butter fat of 16 November 1962, which does not have any equivalent EU legislation, defines "butter" as a fatty product exclusively made from milk. Further, when selling Norwegian butter the

20 cf. Article 13.

product must be labelled with one of these designations in order for the consumer to be able to identify the location where the butter was produced: "dairy butter"/"butter" (both produced at a dairy) or "mountain- or farm butter (alpine or farm produced). Butter that is fully or partially made of whey shall be titled "whey butter".

It has now been suggested that the rules on butter should be altered and replaced by a regulation covering all types of dairy products.

IV. Voluntary Labelling

1. "Clean labels"- Are there any national definitions or requirements for the use of claims?

a. General comment

We will now comment on certain "clean labels" such as "natural", "pure", and "homemade" as well as a few similar claims, cf. clause d) below. To start, there are no clear definitions of these terms in Norwegian law, and we must base our assessment fully on the concept of misleading food information, as detailed above in section 2.1. Therefore, whether a specific claim is considered to be misleading depends on an individual assessment of each case. Unlike in other countries, there are no national guidelines available to assist the industry in assessing these claims.

Based on our experience, the Norwegian Food Safety Authority will consult the Danish and Swedish guidelines, both of which provide some guidance on the use of clean labels. However, the Food Safety Authority will not be bound by them and may, as the case may be, find reason not to emphasize them. Given the lack of other guidance, the guidelines from the Danish and Swedish authorities[21],[22] are referred to below, it should be noted that

21 "Veiledning om mærkning av fødevarer" of January 2013 ("Danish guideline").

22 Vägledning til Livsmedelsverkets föreskrifter (LIVSFS 2004:27) om märkning och presentation av livsmedel" ("Swedish guideline").

these guidelines represent the *position* of the authorities and thus it is not clear that Norwegian courts will draw the same conclusions. Obviously, the assessment will be made on a case-by-case basis, taking into account all relevant aspects in each particular case.

b. Natural

When used on food, the word "natural" and similar words normally give the consumer the impression that a product is more or less taken directly from nature or is at least minimally processed. When it comes to processed food as such it will be difficult to claim that it is more or less derived directly from nature, but despite this, such phrases are often used on products available in Norway. Whether this practice is approved by the Norwegian Food Safety Authority remains uncertain as decisions on the phrase "natural" are not made publicly available, and thus one should generally ensure that the claim "natural" is explained or specified, e.g. "natural ingredients". Further, the Norwegian Food Safety Authority may also emphasize the following:

It follows from the Danish guidelines that it is relevant to assess the type of foodstuff and the way the foodstuff is manufactured. If a product or ingredient is labelled "natural", the ingredient or foodstuff must appear as it exists in nature or be minimally processed. The guidelines do not detail the exceptions, save the "natural colouring agents" that are produced by a simple manufacturing process and derived from a vegetable or animal substance.

The Swedish guidelines are generally in line with the Danish ones, but also explicitly state that compound foodstuff may never be called natural. They further detail that if the wording "natural ingredients" is employed, then all ingredients used must adhere to the main rule referred to above.

c. Pure

In the same way as for the term "natural" there exists no clarifying practices with regards to the use of "pure" in Norway, and hence one will have to look to the foreign guidelines. Highlighting features like "pure" and "genuine" suggests that there is a counter party, that is un-pure or non-genuine food. For certain types of food, such as honey, the counter product to the "pure" or "genuine" one will not exist. To underline qualities such as the above-stated on such products may be deemed misleading. Underpinning such features may mislead the consumer into thinking that this is a special feature of this particular product and thus give it an unfair competitive advantage. In line with this, the Swedish guidelines state that the claim "pure" is misleading if no counter product exists. The guidelines also use the following examples to illustrate misleading labelling: "100 % juice", "Real Cheese" and "True orange juice".

The Danish guidelines focus on expressions such as "free of" and "no additives". The assessment is more or less the same as for the term "natural", cf. above, but the guidelines also include an example on the use of "no additives". The authorities accepted the use of "no additives" on a soy beverage because similar drinks contained the additive E 270 (lactic acid).

d. Home-made/'grandmother recipe'

Industrial food production claiming to be "home made" constitutes normally a natural contradiction; the products are normally produced in factories by assistance of machines not found in private homes. There are however products made in the stores and products more or less made by hand, both of which could legitimate such a claim. Claiming that the food is «home made», when in reality it is produced industrially, will normally be incorrect and thus not in line with the Food Act, section 10. However, it is not certain that the same claim is misleading as the use of the claim may be found to be an exaggeration also obvious for the consumers. As for the other claims also here one will have to look to foreign guidelines for guidance.

It follows from the Danish guidelines that when assessing claims such as "homemade" it will be necessary to consider the production method, whether the recipe is the owner`s old and original recipe and whether the product is made from scratch.

The Danish authorities noted a court case involving chocolate produced at a factory sold as homemade. The chocolate was based on an old recipe (50–60 years) that had not been altered. The court found that the term "home made" was not misleading, taking into account the character of the product, the production – which took place at only one factory, and mainly was carried through by hand, and the sales and marketing methods. Overall it seems like the court emphasized the fact that even though the chocolate had been through an industrial process the process did not have a distinctive industrial character. Furthermore, it was not required that the product was sold at the production plant or that the chocolate had to be manufactured in the shops where it was available for sale.

e. Other similar claims

There are no other claims related to "clean labels" specifically; however, there are certain labelling systems that are closely related to "clean" claims and therefore referred to below.

Firstly, there is the voluntary labelling system of the *keyhole,* and the rules applying to it can be found in the Regulation of 17 June 2009 concerning the voluntary labelling of foods with the keyhole (see figure 2 below). The regulation is national, but it is based on a collaboration between Norway, Sweden and Denmark.

Figure 2 The Keyhole Label

The objective of the arrangement is to make it easier for consumers to choose the healthiest alternative within a certain category of food. Products that are labelled with a keyhole contain less fat, salt and sugar and more fibre compared to other products within the same food category. The Food

Safety Authority and the Directorate of Health are responsible for the keyhole labelling system.

Secondly, DEBIO is an administrative body that controls and approves ecological food production, fishery and aquaculture. Entities that apply for approval and comply with the applicable requirements are entitled to use the DEBIO label in their marketing. Also, imported products may use the label, provided certain requirements are met. Information on procedures and requirements are available on the Debio homepage.[23]

Thirdly, suppliers may use a labelling system called the Swan-label if they meet the applicable requirements. The aim is to help consumers choose environmental-friendly products. In order to be allowed to put a Swan-label on a product, the manufacturer has to prove that the product meets all the environmental standards set forth by the Stiftelsen Miljømerking (The Eco Labelling Foundation) for the relevant product group. The label was initially intended for non-food products only, but it has been assessed whether the Swan-label will be made available for bakeries and bakery products as well, which would be the first time that the label applies to food. The review conducted late 2013 concluded that such inclusion was not appropriate under the current regime.

Fourthly, EU Directive 2005/29/EC concerning business to consumer unfair practises includes an exhaustive list of what kinds of business practices will be considered unfair in Norway. The Directive is implemented in Norway by the Regulation on unfair commercial practices of 1 June 2009. Section 1, nr. 2 states that if a business uses a label without having met the requirements, it will always be considered as an unfair practice since the use of the symbol without the necessary permit will mislead consumers.

Finally, the use of "clean labels" referring to the environmental impact of the product should take into account the Norwegian Consumer Ombudsman's position, which is detailed in two general guidelines available in Norwegian and English at www.forbrukerombudet.no. The guidelines set out rather strict requirements for entities desiring to highlight environmental friendly

23 For information about Debio label and requirements, see http://www.debio.no/forsiden/information-in-english.

aspects of their products. The courts have not yet had occasion to rule on any aspect of the guidelines.

2. Nutrition & health claims

a. What legislation, including case law, regulates the use of nutrition or health claims on foodstuffs?

Norway has incorporated Regulation (EC) no 1924/2006 and subsequent regulations, and the Norwegian rules in the area of nutritional and health claims are therefore harmonized with the applicable EU rules and thus not detailed further herein.

In Norway it is the Norwegian Medicines Agency ("NMA") that has the authority to decide which substances are to be considered medical. Should an approved health claim involve a foodstuff that contains substances that in Norway are considered to be medical, then the use of these substances will need approval from the NMA regardless of the approved health claim. Such a case has not been publicly discussed in Norway thus far, and whether the NMA objects to substances relevant for approved health claims is uncertain.

b. Are there any national laws and regulations permitting food business operators to make reference to recommendations or endorsements by national associations, medical, nutrition or dietetic professionals, and health-related charities?

There is no national law or regulation prohibiting the use of recommendations or endorsements by, e.g. national associations and medical, nutrition or dietetic professionals as long as they comply with the general rules on marketing.

Having medical or nutritional experts comment on or recommend a particular kind of food could potentially be deemed as claims falling under Regulation 1924/2006 on nutrition and health claims made on food, incorporated into Norwegian law in the Regulation on health and nutrition claims of 17 February 2010, no. 187.

c. Are there any national laws or regulations regulating the use of nutrition or health claims on non-prepackaged food?

Norway has not adopted any particular rules on health and nutrition claims for non-prepacked food.

d. Is there a notification procedure required prior to/for marketing foodstuffs bearing nutritional or health claims?

There are currently no national notification procedures required prior to/ for marketing foodstuffs bearing nutritional or health claims. There will however be a notification procedure in place for food supplements in the future, but the effective date is not clear.[24]

V. Enforcement of Food Law and Self-Regulating Bodies

1. Which actions may one risk in case of non-compliance with the labelling or advertising requirements?

a. Public authorities

In principle, both the Consumer Ombudsman and the Food Safety Authority may take action, the latter being the most likely. The Food Safety Authority is authorized to make any decision *required* in order to ensure compliance within the scope of the Food Act and the regulations attached thereto. Thus, depending on the degree of severity of the missing or misleading labelling/advertisement, the Food Safety Authority will decide what sanction is deemed most appropriate and effective in each case.[25]

The most common form of sanctioning is an injunction that requires amendment of the labelling/advertisement, or an injunction that requires the

24 Regulation on Food Supplements of 20 May 2004, no. 755, Article 10.

25 Cf. Food Act of 19 December 2013, section 23.

manufacturer to change the foodstuff's content so that it corresponds with the current labelling. The Food Safety Authority may also issue compulsory fines for each day that the company does not comply with such injunctions, but this happens rarely and (when it happens) the fines are normally low, i.e. approximately NOK 2.000 to 20.000. Severe cases may be reported to the police, but prosecution is normally reserved for serious violations concerning animal welfare and food safety.

Further, if the company does not comply with the imposed injunctions, the Food Safety Authority may prohibit the sale, or impose withdrawal of the foodstuffs from the market. Moreover, the Food Act provides a legal basis for criminal prosecution, i.e. criminal fines and imprisonment. However, such reactions are reserved for the more serious cases that the Food Safety Authority is responsible for handling, e.g. cases of animal maltreatment. Therefore, the government will usually not prosecute on criminal charges cases involving non-compliance with labelling and advertisement requirements.

When the authorities issue sanctions, the entity is normally entitled to comment, and, moreover, the sanctions also designate a complaint procedure. The case may thereafter be brought before the courts.

Should the Consumer Ombudsman take action,[26] the Ombudsman will primarily seek a solution based upon negotiation with the entity in question. In certain cases the Ombudsman is authorized to take decisions involving prohibition, injunction, penalty and/or administrative fines, but such decisions are usually taken by the Market Council, which is an administrative council with similar functions to the regular courts. Appeal is not possible, but the decisions may be brought before the courts.

b. Competitors

A company may bring a case against its competitors if it is "entitled to sue" the company in question according to the Dispute Act of 17 June 2005. In order to be entitled to sue, the company must have a "legal interest" in the

26 cf. the Marketing Control Act, chapter 7.

matter, meaning there must be a genuine need to have the claim determined against the defendant. Furthermore, before initiating legal proceedings, a party must file a warning letter containing information about the claim, giving the opposite party the opportunity to respond and notifying it about the basis of the claim before the lawsuit is filed.

Competitors may, however, notify the authorities of the non-compliant activities of other companies. As regards activities that do not comply with the new Guideline to reducing marketing pressure of unhealthy food to children[27], any entity is entitled to complain.

The industry has further established the Committee for Unfair Competition to assess whether activities are compliant with the Marketing Control Act, Chapter 6, which focuses on competition between entities (not consumer perspective). The dispute system offers quick and low-cost proceedings, and even though the opinions are not legally binding, the parties will normally comply with them.

c. Consumers / consumer associations

Consumer rights are quite similar to the rights of competitors. Normally a consumer will file a complaint with the Consumer Ombudsman, but the Consumer Council also ensures the position of the consumers and brings cases of principal interest before the courts.

2. Are there any national self-regulating bodies with respect to advertising for a.o. foodstuffs?

There are two possible examples that are of interest. First, the Complaint Commission of the Food Industry cf. section I 1. above, and secondly the Committee for Unfair Competition referred to above in section V 1. b).

27 cf. section 1.2 above.

CHAPTER 12
Poland

Sylwia Paszek

I. Possible Bans on Food Advertising

1. Is there any general national legislation or code of conduct regulating the promotion of foodstuffs?

PL

a. National legislation

There is no specific national legislation that regulates the promotion of foodstuffs. The only relevant legislation is the Polish implementation of the prohibition on misleading advertising, i.e., Article 2 of **Directive 2000/13/EC** (current Article 7 of Regulation N° 1169/2011 on the provision of food information to consumers; see in more detail point 2.

Still, the other legal acts like Act on the radio and television[1] and Press law[2] may give additional guidance as to the rules of advertising. Although these acts are addressed to and are binding on media broadcasters and press publishers, they also directly impact how advertisement is to look like and what content it should have.

For example, the following type of advertising cannot be broadcasted on the radio or TV:

- addresses juveniles to encourage them to buy certain products;
- encourages juveniles to sustain pressure on their parents or other adults so that they purchase advertised goods;

1 Act dated 29 December 1992 on the radio and television (Journal of Laws 2011.43.226 as amended).

2 Act dated 26 January 1984 – Press law (Journal of Laws 1984.5.24 as amended).

- takes advantage of the trust the juveniles have in their parents, teachers and other persons;
- shows juveniles in dangerous situations, without good reason;
- influences man's mind in latent ways;
- humiliates;
- contains discriminative content (due to gender, race, nationality, ethnic origin, etc.);
- hurts people's religious and/or political beliefs;
- is to the detriment of juveniles' physical, psychic and moral development;
- supports behaviors that are a threat to human health, safety and the environment.

Also, programs addressed to juveniles should not be accompanied by advertisements promoting foodstuffs and beverages containing ingredients that the excessive consumption of which is not recommended on a daily basis. Regulation of a list of these products and strict rules of promoting them on radio/TV is expected. As there is no regulation yet, the broadcasters currently feel free to set up program schedules at their convenience.

b. Self-regulation

Other rules of advertising come from the Code of Ethics of Advertising.[3] The Code has been drafted, popularized and enforced by the Council of Ethics of Advertising. The Council is a self-regulatory body that gathers companies from all industry branches; foodstuffs manufacturers are widely represented too.[4] Members of the Council and signatories of the Code voluntarily commit to advertise their goods and services in compliance with the rules set forth in the Code. The Council resolves any claims that are raised by third

3 See http://www.radareklamy.pl/kodeks-etyki-reklamy.html

4 See http://www.radareklamy.pl/samoregulacja/sygnatariusze.html

parties (consumers, institutions, etc.) with regard to advertising ordered by signatories of the Code.

The Code does not contain any rules that would bring specifically detailed and developed regulations relevant to foodstuff advertising. In general, it repeats the rules quoted in the national legislation.

Another self-regulation is the Code of Ethics of Advertising to Children, drafted by the Polish Confederation of Food Manufacturers and Employers' Association.[5] The Code is very brief and actually not well known. The works are pending on redrafting thereof.

2. Are there any specific national restrictions or prohibitions (mandatory legislation and code of conduct)?

a. Restrictions relating to certain products in particular

i. Alcoholic beverages

Prohibition on public promotion

The Act dated 28 October 1983 on sobriety and counteracting alcohol addiction prohibits the public promotion of alcoholic beverages.[6] The regulation provides two exceptions. Alcoholic beverages can be promoted within:

- areas of the wholesale or retail sales of alcoholic beverages (i.e., separated areas within retail or wholesale stores), and
- places of immediate consumption (bars and restaurants).

5 See http://www.pfpz.pl/index

6 Act dated 28 October 1983 on sobriety and counteracting alcohol addiction (Journal of Laws 2012.1356 as amended)

In addition to the general prohibition, it is prohibited to do the following:

- promote products and services if the name, trademark, graphic design or packaging uses or is analogous to a depiction of an alcoholic beverage or another symbol that clearly identifies an alcoholic beverage;
- promote businesses, or any other entities, that use the name, trademark, graphic design or packaging related to an alcoholic beverage as a marketing image;
- for producers or distributors whose main business is the production or distribution of alcoholic beverages of 8 % to 18 % alcohol to sponsor mass events (which includes sports events and concerts); on those occasions the name of the company and the trademark can only be disclosed in materials strictly related to the event, e.g., press announcements or visual advertisements, billboards, tickets, etc.; TV/radio advertisements of the events can include the name of the producer/distributor or the trademark, or both, however, advertisement cannot involve a person;
- for producers or distributors of alcoholic beverages containing more than 18 % alcohol to sponsor mass events.

Exception for beer

The other exception is beer which can be promoted when specific conditions are met, viz:

- advertising is not addressed to juveniles;
- advertising does not include juveniles;
- advertising does not create association between beer consumption and physical fitness or driving;
- advertising does not contain any claims that beer acts as a treatment (medicinal), stimulant, sedative, or a means to solve personal conflicts;
- advertising does not encourage excessive consumption;
- advertising does not present abstinence or moderate consumption negatively;

- advertising does not create an association between a high percentage of alcohol in a product and superior quality of the product;
- advertising does not cause associations with sexual attraction, relaxation and leisure, studying and work, professional or life success.

Beer cannot be advertised using the following media:

- the radio or TV, at cinemas or theatres – between 6 a.m and 8 p.m., except for advertising by the organizer of a sports event within the duration of the event;
- videotapes or other carriers;
- in press addressed to children or juveniles;
- the covers of magazines;
- billboards or other public displays, unless 20 % of a visual advertisement (display) consists of a warning of the harmfulness of drinking alcohol;
- when advertising involves juveniles.

PL

Non-public (private) promotion

Since the regulation prohibits public promotion of alcoholic beverages, producers and distributors seek alternatives to draw consumer attention. Some apply techniques that they categorize as *private promotion*, i.e., promotions intended to make the consumer proactive and seek information about the alcoholic beverage, addressing a request to a producer or distributor, usually by subscription to a newsletter.

Consensus is that such practice is private – not public – promotion and, therefore, is to be permitted. The courts have not yet ruled on this issue.

Entities involved in promotion

It is interesting that promoters of alcoholic beverages must pay to the Minister of Sport specific amounts of promotional revenue to the Minister of Sport. The funds are used for the popularization of sports among juveniles.

ii. Parnuts

Promotion of certain categories of parnuts (infant food, products intended for weight loss, food supplements, etc.) is subject to detailed regulation.[7]

Infant food[8]

In addition to the EU legislation, infant food can, in Poland, only be promoted in scientific publications or publications intended to promote the knowledge of baby care and must be limited to information that has been scientifically proven. Information in an advertisement cannot suggest that feeding the products to babies is adequate or better than breastfeeding.

The producers or distributors of infant food may provide informational and educational materials of their products, free of charge, if:

- an interested party requests them, and they are then supplied through healthcare units or pharmacies;
- they contain i.a. the following: information on the benefits of breastfeeding and superiority over infant food, information on proper nutrition and preparation for breastfeeding women;
- they do not contain brand names of products; they (optionally) can include the name of a producer or distributor of infant food.

It is prohibited to promote infant food in the following situations:

- at places of retail sale;
- by giving free samples of infant food or devices intended for feeding babies, vouchers, coupons, or applying promotional sales or tied sales;

7 Regulation of the Minister of Health dated 16 September 2010 on foodstuffs for particular nutritional purpose (Journal of Laws 2010.180.1214); Regulation of the Minister of Health dated 9 October 2007 on composition and labeling of food supplements (Journal of Laws 2007.196.1425 as amended).

8 Infant food means "infant formulae" as defined in Article 2 (c) of Directive 2006/141/EC of 22 December 2006 on infant formulae and follow-on formulae.

- by offering or supplying, by producers or distributors, infant food or devices intended for feeding babies, samples thereof, or other products promoting infant foods – to consumers and, specifically, to pregnant women, breastfeeding women or members of a family, free of charge or at a reduced price, either directly or through healthcare units.

Products for weight loss

Products for weight loss must be labeled and indicate the use of a product, depending on the product, i.e., *"Foodstuff intended to substitute daily food consumption, for weight loss"* or *"Foodstuff intended to substitute a meal, for weight loss"*.

Certainly, other requirements on labelling of parnuts must be present in a presentation and advertisement.

PL

Food supplements

Food supplements must be labeled "food supplements" next to a brand name; presentation or advertising cannot claim that a well-balanced diet cannot satisfy all nutritional requirements. Other requirements on labelling of food supplements must appear in a presentation and advertisement. The legislation is the mere implementation of Directive 2002/46/EC on the approximation of the laws of the Member States relating to food supplements.

b. Restrictions relating to specific sections of the population

i. Alcoholic beverages – beer

As already described, beer can be promoted provided that an advertisement is created in accordance with strict rules that are aimed to protect juveniles and is then broadcasted in a manner that it is unlikely to reach juveniles.

ii. Infant food

Pregnant women, breastfeeding women, and parents of the babies, cannot be the targets of the promotion of infant foods; specifically, they cannot be offered infant foods, samples or products, free of charge, either directly or through healthcare units.

II. Misleading Advertising

1. What are the national rules on misleading advertising with respect to foodstuffs?

Polish legislation directly implements Article 2 of Directive 2000/13[9] relating to the labelling, presentation and advertising of foodstuffs, which is currently included in Article 7 of Regulation 1169/2011 on the provision of food information to the consumer.

2. What are the national landmark cases regarding misleading advertising for foodstuffs?

a. Overview : Inspections of trade inspectorate?

Reliability of claims on products, i.e. product composition and quality, either by means of labeling or a presentation, seems to be the most problematic.

The results of a series of country-wide inspections by the trade inspectorate are that frequently foodstuffs are falsified. In one year the quality of butter was inspected; in another year, cheese quality, etc.

Producers apply three main presentation and advertising techniques:

(1) **Creating the impression that a product falls within a certain product group when it does not**

The name or presentation of a product is manipulated in an attempt to give that impression.

The best examples are the following:

- *Drinking Chocolaate "Sweet Moment"* (double "a" in the name; the product did not contain any chocolate), and

9 Act dated 25 August 2006 on safety of food and nutrition (Article 46) (Journal of Laws 2010.136.914 as amended).

- *18 % Świetna* (product meant to be cream – *"śmietana"* – but not containing enough milk fat).

(2) **Creating the impression that a product possesses special characteristics when, in fact, all similar foodstuffs possess such characteristics**

The message is that the product is superior to the other products of the same group on the market while there is no justification for such a claim. A good example is *100 % juice with no sugar added* while sugar cannot be added to that type of product, by law.

Another example is an advertisement of tomato concentrate that referred to the numbers of kilos of tomatoes used to produce each package of concentrate and, thereby, implied a higher content of tomatoes and better concentrate than others. Tomato concentrates have a similar product specification, so the advertisement was impermissible.

PL

(3) **False declarations on products composition**

In such matters it is impossible to rely on the labeling, as the information provided by the producer is deliberately untrue.

b. Court judgment: Fresh products

A Warsaw administrative court held on 18 August 2011 that a foodstuff that has undergone heat treatment (pasteurization, freezing, etc.) or the like cannot be presented as being "*fresh*" (VI SA/Wa 828/11). It is also impermissible to indicate fresh eggs in an ingredient list when, in fact, pasteurized egg pulp is used (judgment of the same court dated 29 September 2011, VI SA/Wa 1449/11).

c. Court judgment: Butter

A Warsaw administrative court held on 18 November 2011 that the name "butter" can only be used for labeling and presentation of products that cumulatively meet the following conditions: (i) a product is made only from milk, (ii) substances that were added must have been crucial for production and were not added to replace milk, (iii) the product must contain no less than 80 % and no more than 90 % of milk fat, (iv) the product must contain no more than 16 % of water, (v) the product must contain no more than 2 % of non-fat milk dry pulp (VI SA/Wa 1425/11).

d. Court judgment: Polish product

A Warsaw administrative court held on 9 February 20913 that it is impermissible to label and present a foodstuff as a "Polish product" when it was produced in Poland from entirely, or a majority, of foreign products (e.g., tropical fruit) (case number VI SA/Wa 2141/11).

III. Mandatory Labelling: Name of the Product

Are there any national definitions of a foodstuff that could hamper the marketing of an imported food product?

The Polish government has adopted EU legislation on quality standards of certain foodstuffs. Product conformity to these standards is also a precondition to apply certain names to certain types of products.

These regulated products are the following: certain types of alcoholic beverages, certain types of cocoa and chocolate products, certain processed fruit products (juices, nectars, jams, marmalades, etc.), products containing caffeine, and chicory or honey.[10]

Polish law does not provide for specifically Polish definitions of foodstuffs that would supplement the EU system.

10 Regulation of the Minister of Agriculture and Rural Development dated 10 July 2007 on labeling of foodstuffs (Journal of Laws 2007.137.966).

IV. Voluntary Labelling

1. "Clean labels" – Are there any national definitions or requirements for the use of claims such as 'natural', 'pure', 'home-made', 'additive-free'?

Polish food law neither defines nor regulates the use of claims such as natural, pure, home-made/'grand-mother's recipe', or other "clean labels" (e.g., "additive-free").

Therefore, in terms of regulatory laws, use of them is neither permitted nor restricted in any way.

However, the use of such labels needs analysis under regulations on combating unfair competition or counteracting unfair market practices. Failure to comply with the regulations could mean that competitors or consumers could file a claim against the advertiser.

If a claim is against the collective interest of consumers, the Polish competition authority (*Urząd Ochrony Konkurencji i Konsumentów* – "UOKIK"[11]) could prohibit advertisement and impose a penalty of up to 10 % of the revenue in the preceding year.

UOKIK decision: "natural mineral water" versus mineral water with preservatives

UOKIK acted for a breach of collective consumers interests because of a TV advertisement comparing "natural mineral water" consisting of water and fruits only to other flavored mineral waters presumably containing preservatives, which are therefore harmful. The advertisement showed a person to be radioactive after drinking regular flavored water, presumably with preservatives. UOKIK found that the advertisement caused unjustified fear in consumers. Preservatives are legal and permitted food additives, and, therefore, consumers should not be afraid to consume products with preservatives and should not be unjustifiably frightened with the idea of

11 See www.uokik.gov.pl.

health deterioration. As a result UOKIK imposed a fine of PLN 240,000 (approx. EUR 57,000).

Court judgment: Homemade pasta

A Warsaw administrative court held on 29 September 2011 that it is impermissible to label and present pasta as being "homemade pasta" when the ingredients include pasteurized egg pulp (instead of fresh eggs), coloring, aroma, and flavorings; those ingredients are not customarily used for homemade pasta (VI SA/Wa 1449/11).

2. Nutrition & health claims

Polish law supplements Regulation 1924/2006 only to the extent that it is necessary for execution thereof (e.g., indication of the authorities responsible within the claims authorization procedure).

Therefore, Polish regulations do not add anything extra as to the use of nutritional and health claims. Marketing foodstuffs bearing nutritional or health claims is permitted provided the claims meet the requirements set forth in Regulation 1924/2006. No specific notification related to the claim is required prior to marketing these foodstuffs. Certainly, if the product is a parnut or food supplement, general notification on introduction of such product onto the market is required.

The use of nutrition or health claims on non-prepackaged food is not regulated in any way.

Polish law does not regulate a food businesses' right to refer to recommendations or endorsements by national associations, medical, nutritional, or dietetic professionals, or health-related charities.

In practice, such recommendations by associations or health institutions are used. The other options are references to "doctors' choice" or "consumers' prize" or other "medals". If so, the trade inspectorate investigates the reliability of such references, i.e., whether the references are based on actual, existing, and institutionalized competitions with firm rules or on reliable market research or medical research, etc. If the references are fair and well justified, the trade inspectorate does not dispute the use thereof, as a rule.

Court judgment: Result of the tests or trials

A Warsaw administrative court held on 4 March 2009 that the advertisement clauses, "*if you want to have healthy joints*" and "*over 74 % of users have reported noticeable reduction of pain in joints*" are permissible because they demonstrate the results of medical tests. Therefore, these statements are not prohibited and can be used (VII SA/Wa 1901/08).

Regardless of whether such a claim would be permissible under up-to-date claims regulations or with regard to those products, the court held the rule that materials, information, and data that provide true and reliable information on the effect of a product on health can be attached to the product.

PL

V. Enforcement of Food Law and Self-Regulating Bodies

1. Which actions may one risk in case of non-compliance with the labelling or advertising requirements?

a. Public authorities

i. Administrative sanctions (applied by the trade inspectorate) – applying to a business

	Non-compliance with labeling requirements	**Non-compliance with advertising requirements**
Remedies	Order to: (i) eliminate non-compliance (e.g., prepare and use relabeling); (ii) cease marketing, (iii) recall product.	Order to: (i) eliminate non-compliance (e.g., stop advertising); (ii) cease marketing.
Penalties	Penalty up to PLN 106,000 (approx. EUR 25,000) – no more than 5 x the value of the foodstuff inspected and questioned by the inspection.	Penalty up to PLN 106,000 (approx. EUR 25,000) – no more than 5 x the value of the foodstuff inspected and questioned by the inspection.

The trade inspectorate always intervenes when it identifies non-compliance (usually within the inspection). Remedies are applied by means of administrative decisions; financial penalties are moderate and adjusted to the degree of seriousness of non-compliance.

ii. Penal sanctions – applying to natural persons (responsible for a business)

	Non-compliance with labeling requirements	**Non-compliance with advertising requirements**
Penalties	Producing/marketing falsified foodstuff (labeling does not provide actual information on a product, ingredients, or quality) is an offence. Penalties: (i) a fine up to PLN 1,080,000 (approx. EUR 260,000), (ii) limitation of liberty up to 12 months, (iii) imprisonment up to 1–2 years; If a graded offence (when an offence is a regular business or when an offence affects a foodstuff of significant value, i.e., of a value exceeding PLN 200,000, approx. EUR 47,000) more severe penalties apply (e.g., imprisonment up to 3–5 years).	Promoting parnuts in breach of regulations is a petty offence. Penalties: (i) a fine up to PLN 5,000 (approx. EUR 1,200); (ii) forfeiture of materials and products/destruction at the cost of the business.

If a trade inspectorate identifies an offence, a prosecutor is notified.

It is rare to impose penalties other than a fine (unless non-compliance affects safety).

b. Competitors

For breach of food regulations or unfair competition rules, competitors whose interests were affected or threatened can sue in a civil court.[12]

The claims include an order to:

(i) cease unfair competition,

(ii) rectify the negative effects of an act/practice committed,

(iii) make a public announcement in the form and content ordered by the court,

(iv) pay damages to the competitor under general rules of civil law,

(v) surrender unfair benefits,

(vi) pay a penalty to cause in support and protection of the Polish culture (only if the act was through fault),

(vii) dispose of assets related to the act itself, e.g., destroying products, packaging, advertising materials.

Civil actions related to food advertising are not very frequent; however, businesses are now becoming more aware of the effectiveness of such measures and litigation can be expected to increase.

c. Consumers / (consumer) associations

Consumers whose interests have been breached or merely threatened can sue in a civil court for unfair market practice.[13]

The claims include an order to:

(i) cease unfair market practice,

12 Act dated 16 April 1993 on combating unfair competition (Journal of Laws 2003.153.1503 as amended).

13 Act dated 23 August 2007 on counteracting unfair market practices (Journal of Laws 2007.171.1206 as amended).

(ii) rectify negative effects,

(iii) make a public announcement in the form and content ordered by the court,

(iv) pay damages to the consumer because of the act/practice (mainly, withdrawal from a contract and refund of the price paid),

(v) pay a penalty to cause in support and protection of the Polish culture (only if the act was through fault).

The ombudsman and consumer organizations/associations can also make the claims listed in points (i), (iii), and (v).

Claims based on unfair market practice are rare.

d. Competition authority (UOKIK)

If promotion of foodstuffs is unfair competition or an unfair market practice then, depending on the facts and extent thereof, that could also be categorized as a violation of collective consumer interests[14] and be prohibited. A sum of interests of separate consumers is not automatically "collective consumer interest", but can be if a "group of consumers" is identified, e.g., a group that has an interest in obtaining information on the foodstuffs at issue.

The President of the UOKIK investigates violations of collective consumer interests. Anyone may notify the president of the UOKIK about a potential violation. The president can prohibit and order other remedies, and impose a fine of up to 10 % of the preceding year's revenue.

14 Act dated 16 February 2007 on competition and consumers protection (Journal of Laws 2007.50.331 as amended).

2. Are there any national self-regulating bodies with respect to advertising for foodstuffs?

There is a number of food business associations. The most important are the following:

- Polish Confederation of Food Manufacturers and Employers' Association (PZPF, http://www.pfpz.pl/index/) – member of FoodDrinkEurope, European Dietetic Food Industry Association and Union of European Soft Drinks Association; and
- Meat manufacturers' associations.

Their main task is to actively participate and lobby in the legislative proceedings, either at the domestic level or at the EU level.

They are not very active in drafting self-regulations. PZPF is an author of the Code of Ethics of Advertising to Children mentioned.

CHAPTER 13 Portugal

Ana Menéres and Margarida Brito da Cruz

I. Possible Bans on Food Advertising

1. Is there any general national legislation or code of conduct regulating the promotion of foodstuffs?

PT

Food law is still an emerging area of law in Portugal. The legislative process has been developed in line with the law of the European Union (EU), mostly through Regulations, which are directly applicable in the Portuguese legal system. The promotion of foodstuffs is not regulated by a specific document. The main national legislation regarding promotion and advertising of foodstuffs are the Portuguese Advertising Code[1] and Decree-Law 560/99 of 18 December[2], which transposed into national law Directive 97/4/EC of the Council of 27 January and Directive 1999/10/EC of the Commission of 8 March on the approximation of legislation of the Member States with respect to the labelling, presentation and advertising of foodstuffs intended for the final consumer and also Decree-Law 57/2008 of 26 March[3] regarding unfair commercial practices.[4] The Portuguese Advertising Code does

1 Decree-Law 330/90 of 23 October, published in the Official State Gazette, 1st Series, No 245, 1990, last amended by Law 8/2011 of 11 April.

2 Decree-Law 560/99 of 18 December, published in the Official State Gazette, 1-A Series, No 239, 1999, last amended by Decree-Law 156/2008 of 7 August.

3 Decree-Law 57/2008 of 26 March, published in the Official State Gazette, 1st Series, No 60, 2008.

4 These Directives amended Directive 79/112/EEC of 18 December 1973 on the approximation of laws of the Member States relating to the labelling, presentation and advertising of foodstuffs for sale to the ultimate consumer. Directives 97/4/EC, 1999/EC and 79/112/EEC were later codified by Directive 2000/13/EC of the European Parliament and of the Council of 20 March 2000 on the approximation of laws of the Member States relating to the labelling, presentation and advertising of foodstuffs.

not have specific provisions regarding foodstuff, however it clearly states that *"all advertising which is considered to be misleading under the terms of Decree-Law 57/2008 of 26 March"* is forbidden[5], providing specific provisions for alcoholic beverages, medicinal products and the health and safety of consumers. Finally, Decree-Law 560/99 specifically provides that the indications included in the labelling shall not be presented in a misleading way to the consumer, which is applicable to the advertising of foodstuffs as well.[6]

2. Is the promotion of certain foodstuffs restricted or prohibited by any national mandatory and/or soft laws (e.g., code of practice, case-law)?

The Portuguese Advertising Code establishes restrictions on the advertising of certain foodstuffs (i.e. alcoholic beverages). Article 17 of the mentioned Code limits the advertising of alcoholic beverages, only authorizing it in specific circumstances, namely whenever it does not (i) specifically target minors of age and does not show them consuming alcoholic beverages; (ii) encourage excessive consumption; (iii) disregard consumers; (iv) promote the idea of success, social benefit or special abilities as a result of the consumption; (v) suggest the existence of therapeutic qualities or stimulant effects; (vi) connect the consumption of alcohol related to sports or driving activities; and (vii) promote the alcoholic level as something positive. Advertising of alcoholic beverages on TV from 7:00 am until 9:30 pm is prohibited.

Furthermore, any type of advertising that encourages behaviors that cause damage to the consumer's health and security, namely as a result of lack of information regarding the danger the product may cause or of the specific ability of causing accidents, as a result of the use of the product, is not allowed.[7]

Concerning codes of practice in particular, ICAP – Instituto Civil da Autodisciplina da Comunicação Comercial – a Portuguese self-regulatory

5 Art. 11 of Decree-Law 330/90 of 23 October.

6 Art. 23 of Decree-Law 560/99 of 18 December.

7 Art.13 (1) of Decree-Law 330/90 of 23 October.

Association for the advertising area, has a Code of Conduct regarding Advertising and other Commercial Communications establishing specific provisions concerning alcohol as well. The provisions of the Code of Conduct bind the members of this particular Association (ICAP), which has now over one hundred companies as members (such as Beiersdorf, Coca-Cola, GSK, L'OREAL, and Vodafone, among others.)

The Portuguese Advertising Code does not provide any other specific provisions regarding foods. Decree-Law 57/2008 of 26 March, on misleading commercial practices, prohibits any commercial practices likely to contain false information that may mislead the consumer regarding the characteristics of a certain good, including foodstuffs.[8]

The relevant case law is the one issued by ICAP regarding the application of the legal provisions applicable to the advertising of foodstuffs.

3. Is the promotion of (certain) foodstuffs towards a specific section of the population restricted or prohibited by any national mandatory and/or soft laws?

The Portuguese Code of Advertising prohibits the advertising of alcoholic beverages to minors of age (18 years old). Article 17(5) states that any commercial communications and advertising of any events where the participants are minors, namely sports, culture, and recreational activities must not mention, implicit or explicitly, the brand or brands of alcoholic beverages.

Furthermore, the Portuguese Code of Advertising establishes that advertising addressed to minors of age should always take into account their psychological vulnerability and it should not (i) encourage them to purchase a specific good (which includes foodstuffs) or service based on their inexperience and credulity, or (ii) encourage them to persuade their parents to buy a certain product.[9]

8 Art. 7 of Decree-Law 57/2008 of 26 March.

9 Art. 14 of of Decree-Law 330/90 of 23 October.

The mentioned Code also prohibits any kind of advertising which may be harmful to the health and security of the consumer (including foodstuff), stating that this shall be taken into account, in particular, regarding advertising aimed at children, adolescents, elderly people or handicapped persons.[10]

II. Misleading Advertising

1. What are the national rules on misleading advertising with respect to foodstuffs?

In Portugal, the specific national provisions ruling misleading advertising with respect to foodstuffs are similar to the ones established at the EU level and are included in Decree-Law 560/99 of 18 December.

The rules concerning labelling indications apply to the presentation and advertising of foodstuffs, its form or looks, package size, way in which foodstuffs are put up, as well as the environment to which they are exposed.[11]

Moreover, advertisements that attribute prevention, treatment and curative properties to foodstuffs or mention such properties are forbidden.[12]

The Portuguese Advertising Code establishes the principle of truth in article 10, stating that advertising must be truthful and not distort facts. According to the same article, all facts relating to the nature, composition, characteristics and purchasing conditions of the advertised goods must be accurate and likely to be evidenced at any moment by the competent authorities. As previously mentioned[13] the same Code expressly forbids misleading advertising.

10 Ibid, Art. 13.

11 Art. 23 (3) of Decree-Law 560/99 of 18 December.

12 Art. 23 (2) of Decree-Law 560/99 of 18 December.

13 *Vide* 1.1.

2. What are the national landmark cases regarding misleading advertising for foodstuffs?

The Court case law regarding misleading advertising for foodstuffs in Portugal is not abundant. However, Portugal has a self-regulatory organization for advertising – Civil Institute for Self-Regulation of Commercial Communication (ICAP) – that takes decisions regarding litigation on advertising matters. The complaints addressed to ICAP are based on the breach of the advertising legislation in force and ICAP's Code of Conduct, which is very similar to the Portuguese Code of Advertising, however, not legally binding, only binding the associates of ICAP.

In 2011, ICAP issued a decision[14] regarding a litigation proceeding between two companies of the food industry (ANID and LACTOGAL) on misleading advertising. ANID considered that LACTOGAL breached the principle of truth due to misleading advertising. In the advertisement at stake, LACTOGAL compared its milk to other kinds of milk (but not naming other brands) and advertised certain characteristics of its milk, such as mentioning the milk's flavor as a distinct element and the milk's capacity to better preserve nutrients, which were considered as misleading advertising by ICAP. In fact, ICAP considered that the idea of exclusivity of LACTOGAL's milk, implicated by the advertisement, created the impression that LACTOGAL's milk was superior to the other brands. Moreover, ICAP further considered that LACTOGAL did not prove that its milk was more fresh, had more nutrients and was more beneficial to children under 12 months as when compared to the mainstream milk of consumption. In this sense, ICAP considered that LACTOGAL's advertisement breached both the Advertising Code and Decree-Law 57/2008 of 26 March regarding unfair commercial practices, since the advertising in question was misleading to the consumer.

In 2010, there was another litigation[15] concerning the advertising of Tunacol canned tuna, where the producer of Tunacol, Ramirez & Cª, had included a health claim in the advertisement, stating that Tunacol reduced bad choles-

---

14 Proceeding 4J/2011, 2nd Section of ICAP's Ethical Committee of 3 March 2011.

15 Proceeding 27J/2010, 1st Section of ICAP's Ethical Committee of 21 December 2010.

terol up to 15 %. The complaint was presented by APIFARMA (Portuguese National Association of the Pharmaceutical Industry), arguing that the health claim in the advertisement was not substantiated by any studies and that there was a breach of the EU Regulation 1924/2006 of 20 December 2006 on nutrition and health claims made on foods.[16] ICAP concluded that the advertisement's health claim was not proved and could mislead consumers as regards the characteristics of the good (Tunacol). ICAP further added that the characteristics advertised (reduction of cholesterol) were similar to an advertisement for a medicinal product. Therefore, ICAP's Ethical Committee decided that Tunacol's advertisement was in breach of ICAP's Code of Conduct, of the Portuguese Advertising Code and of the legal provisions on unfair commercial practices (Decree-Law 57/2008 of 26 March).

III. Mandatory Labelling: Name of the Product

Are there any national definitions of a foodstuff that could hamper the marketing of an imported food product?

Mandatory labelling legislation in Portugal is harmonized by EU legislation. The national applicable law regarding foodstuff labelling in general is Decree-Law 560/99 of 18 December, previously mentioned, in conjunction with European Regulations (Regulation (EU) 1169/2011 of 25 October, Delegated Regulation (EU) 1155/2013 of 21 August, Implementing Regulation (EU) 1337/2013 of 13 December and, most recently, Delegated Regulation (EU) 78/2014 of 22 November). There is also specific national legislation regarding nutritional labelling, namely Decree-Law 167/2004 of 7 July and Decree-Law 136/2003 of 28 June, concerning food supplements.

There are no legal definitions of "energy drinks", "sport drinks" or cheese in our national law or arising from case law.

16 Please note that this decision has been pronounced before the adoption of the union list establishing the authorised functional health claims (Regulation N° 432/2012).

Regarding "yogurt" specifically, Ministerial Order 742/92 of 24 July[17] provides the following definition: *"Yogurt – the curdled product obtained from lactic fermentation due to the exclusive action of Lactobacillus delbrueckii subsp. bulgaricus and Streptococcus thermophilus on the milk and other milk products (...), and the flora shall be live and abundant in the final product".*[18]

The legal definition of "bread" is provided in Decree-Law 289/84 of 24 August[19] which establishes the characteristics of the different types of bread and related products and regulates certain aspects of its commercialization. "Bread" is defined in article 2 as *"the product obtained from the pressing, fermentation and cooking in adequate conditions, of the wheat flour, rye, triticale or corn, pure or mixed, according to the types legally established, clean water and ferment and yeast, as well as the possibility of use of other ingredients, such as additives, and also processing aids within the conditions legally established".*

There is no vertical legislation in Portugal not harmonized at the European level regarding the naming of food products that is likely to hamper the marketing of foodstuffs.

IV. Voluntary Labelling

1. "Clean labels" – Are there any national definitions or requirements for the use of claims such as 'natural', 'pure', 'home-made', 'additive-free'?

The Portuguese legislation does not provide rules regarding clean labels specifically, nor any similar claims related to clean labels, such as "natural", "pure", "home-made", etc. There are only indirect references in the law. For

17 Ministerial Order 742/92 of 24 July, published in the Official State Gazette, 1-B Series, No 169, 1992.

18 The Ministerial Order is still in force.

19 Decree-Law 289/84 of 24 August, published in the Official State Gazette, 1st Series, No 196, 1984.

instance, Decree-Law 120/2011 of 28 December[20] provides a definition of "non-transformed foodstuffs" stating that these types of foodstuffs were not submitted to a treatment likely to cause a substantial amendment of their original state but which may, however be divided, separated, sliced, or sold boneless, minced, peeled, trimmed, grated, selected, clean, tailored, quick-frozen, frozen, under low temperatures, crushed or shelled, packaged or not. This definition does not match the claim "natural", but it is the closest one in the Portuguese legislation. Furthermore, there is no relevant case law on "clean labels".[21]

2. Nutrition & health claims

a. Within the list of health claims authorised pursuant to Regulation 1924/2006, are there any related substances that are prohibited or considered as a medicinal substance within your jurisdiction?

Regulation 1924/2006 is directly applicable in Portugal, and, therefore, the prohibitions included in this Regulation are applicable within the national jurisdiction. Portuguese legislation does not prohibit any of the substances listed in Regulation 1924/2006 or consider those substances as medicinal products.

b. Are there any national laws and regulations permitting food business operators to make reference to recommendations or endorsements by national associations, medical, nutrition or dietetic professionals, and health related charities?

Recommendations or endorsements by food business operators are not specifically regulated by Portuguese legislation and, consequently, there is no prohibition *de per se*. Such recommendations or endorsements may

20 Decree-Law 120/2011 of 28 December, published in the Official State Gazette, 1st Series, No 248, 2011.

21 As previously mentioned, there is little case law on foodstuff, in general.

be regarded as a mean of advertising within the Portuguese Advertising Code in case they are included in the advertising definition of article 3 of the Code, which provides that advertising consists in *"any mean of communication undertaken by public or private entities within a commercial, industrial, artisanal or liberal activity with, to direct or indirectly promote (...) ideas, principles, initiatives or institutions"*, and, consequently, should comply with the advertising principles established by the Code, namely the principle of veracity. However, in some cases, depending on the context in which the recommendations or endorsements are used, such recommendations or endorsements may be regarded as purely informative and not regarded as advertising under article 3 of the aforementioned Code, in which case advertising rules will not be applicable. There are some examples of recommendations and endorsements by food business operators in Portugal: for example, Danone, a famous Portuguese brand of yogurts, explicitly refers to medical societies and associations (Portuguese Society of Cardiology and the Portuguese Diabetics Association, among others) on its website (http://www.danone.pt/saude/). Becel's website in Portugal contains an indirect recommendation from the Portuguese Foundation of Cardiology stating *"FCP recommends the consumption of food of plant origin in order to reduce cholesterol"* and displays this message and the foundation logo next to Becel products.[22]

PT

c. Are there any national laws or regulations regulating the use of nutrition or health claims on non-prepackaged food?

Non-prepackaged food is ruled by Decree-Law 560/99 of 18 December. However, in what concerns nutrition or health claims, there are no specific rules.

d. Is there a notification procedure required prior to/for marketing foodstuffs bearing nutritional or health claims?

No, there is no national procedure required for marketing of foodstuffs bearing nutritional or health claims.

22 http://www.becel.pt/proactiv/sobre-a-gama-pro-activ/shots-becel-proactiv.aspx

Food supplements are subject to a notification procedure in Portugal. Food supplements are ruled by Decree-Law 136/2003 of 28 June[23], which transposed Directive 2002/46/EC into the national law. Food supplements will be classified as medicinal products only if they are covered and fall within the legal definition of medicinal product. Otherwise, food supplements are in the category of foodstuffs. In order to place food supplements on the market, the manufacturer or the person responsible for placing on the market (i.e. the distributor)[24] must proceed with a notification to the Governmental Entity supervising that area. This notification must be submitted to the Portuguese Food and Veterinary General Directorate ("DGAV") which is the national competent authority regarding food supplements. The notification should be submitted online (suplementosDSNA@dgav.pt) together with a copy of the label.[25] Fortified food is not subject to specific national laws since Regulation 1925/2006 is directly applicable in Portugal.

V. Enforcement of Food Law and Self-Regulating Bodies

1. Which actions may one risk in case of non-compliance with the labelling or advertising requirements?

a. Public authorities

Whoever does not comply with labelling or advertising requirements may be subject to a misdemeanor procedure, either as a result of an inspection or the participation of a competitor. According to Decree-Law 560/99 of 18 December, the following events constitute infringements, sanctioned with fines that may range from € 99 up to € 3.740,98 for physical persons, and up to € 44.891,81 for legal persons:

23 Decree-Law 136/2003 of 28 June, published in the Official State Gazette, Series I-A, No 147, 2003, last amended by Decree-Law 296/2007 of 22 August.

24 Art. 9 of Decree-Law 136/2003 of 28 June.

25 Information available at http://www.dgv.min-agricultura.pt.

(i) The lack, inaccuracy or deficient badge indication or of the mandatory indications in the labelling of foods;

(ii) Indications in the labelling which are not allowed or are likely to mislead the consumer;

(iii) The commercialization of foods in relation to which the "use-by" date has elapsed or is in breach with the legal requirements established for pre-packaged food for immediate sale;

(iv) The commercialization of foods, sale or exhibition for sale to the final consumers of pre-packaged foods without a label written in the Portuguese language; and

(v) The amendment, occultation or destruction of the mandatory indications to be included in the labelling.

The attempts of the infringement or negligent conduct or omission are also punished, and the removal of foods infringing the law may also be determined as an ancillary penalty.[26]

b. Competitors and consumers

Concerning competitors and consumers or consumers associations specifically, once the Portuguese Food and Veterinary General Directorate (DGAV) was created in 2008, the Portuguese Authority of Food and Economic Safety (ASAE), which is the entity responsible for economic supervision and guaranteeing food safety, started to receive many reports both from individuals and public authorities (anonymous or identified). Until November 2013, 150.000 reports were made.

The available mean of reaction for consumers or consumer associations whenever there is a suspicion that food law was breached is to report to the ASAE or DGAV. The report shall be filed on ASAE's website, and the reporter should identify the infractor, all relevant facts and witnesses. In the

26 Art. 28 of Decree-Law 560/99 of 18 December.

specific case of food poisoning, the individual reporting the breach must contact ASAE and immediately notify a health professional.[27]

With respect to infringements of food advertising laws, complaints may be filed with ICAP identified above (a self-regulated private association), the Consumer's General Directorate (Direcção-Geral do Consumidor) or ASAE. Complaints filed by competitors or consumers consist in identifying the infringement, and the regulatory/supervising entities (such as ICAP and ASAE) will start the infringement procedure. Competitors and consumers may seek compensation for damages resulting from the infringement through civil liability actions.

2. Are there any national self-regulating bodies with respect to advertising for foodstuffs?

As mentioned above, ICAP (Civil Institute for Self-Regulation of Commercial Communication) is a self-regulating body in Portugal, which implements a self-regulating system that promotes legal, honest, truthful and adequate advertising. The majority of entities, including the Public Administration, recognize ICAP as an entity that defends the rights and interests of the civil society as well as of the industries, by promoting the credibility of advertisement speech and safeguarding the freedom of commercial expression. ICAP handles complaints from competitors, members and non-members, consumers, consumers associations, statutory bodies and other interested parties; however, the decisions are only binding for ICAP members. ICAP also provides a mediation service through a forum for the parties to meet and reach agreement about a contested advertisement.[28]

27 Information available at http://www.asae.pt/.

28 Information available at http://www.icap.pt/icapv2/icap_site/index.php.

CHAPTER 14
Slovak Republic

David Stros

I. Possible Bans on Food Advertising

1. Is there any general national legislation or code of conduct regulating the promotion of foodstuffs?

a. National legislation regulating promotion of foodstuffs

SK

In the Slovak Republic, there is no specialized act of law that focuses only on the regulation of promotion and advertising of foodstuffs.

Particular legal rules concerning the advertising, promotion and presentation of foodstuffs can be found in special legal regulations on foodstuffs. These regulations are concentrated in the Act on Foodstuffs[1] and its implementing decrees,[2] which together create the so-called Food Codex. It serves as a collection of acts of law stipulating rules for foodstuffs, in general, and for specific categories of foodstuffs on food safety, ingredients, technological processes of manufacturing, packaging and labelling, storing, placing on the market, etc. These acts also stipulate specific requirements and restrictions on the labelling of foodstuffs, their presentation and prohibition of misleading advertising..

Besides these special regulations, particular duties and restrictions can be found in several acts regulating promotion and advertising: Act on Advertising, Act on Broadcasting and Retransmission and Consumer Protection Act. These acts of law include general rules applicable to advertising irrespective of the advertised object as well as special rules for special types of food products, such as alcoholic beverages or food for infants.

1 Act No 152/2005 Coll., on foodstuffs.

2 Especially Decree No 127/2012 on labelling of foodstuffs (Note: valid until 13/12/2014).

These acts[3] have duly incorporated all relevant major Directives of the European Union on advertising, such as Directive 84/450/EEC[4] relating to the approximation concerning misleading advertising,[5] and Directive 2005/29/EC concerning unfair business-to-consumer commercial practices in the internal market,[6] or Directive 2000/13/EC on the approximation relating to the labelling, presentation and advertising of foodstuffs[7] and others.

b. Code of Conduct regulating promotion of foodstuffs

The Code of Conduct (created by the Advertising Standards Council) established higher requirements on the advertising of foodstuffs and non-alcoholic and alcoholic beverages.[8]

The advertisement of foodstuffs should comply with the following:

- truthfully present the characteristics of food, including size, shape, look, used cover material, composition, durability, content, origin, manufacturing process and benefit for consumer's nourishment and health, as well as food layout and surroundings, in which the food is shown;
- not deceive consumers regarding any characteristics of the food;

3 Act No 147/2001 Coll., on advertisement.
Act No 308/2000 Coll., on broadcasting and retransmission.
Act No 250/2007 Coll., on consumer protection.
Act No 152/2005 Coll., on foodstuffs.

4 Directive 84/450/EEC was later replaced by Directive 2006/114/EC.

5 Council Directive 84/450/EEC of 10 September 1984 relating to the approximation of the laws, regulations and administrative provisions of the Member States concerning misleading advertising, replaced by Directive 2006/114/EC concerning misleading and comparative advertising.

6 Directive 2005/29/EC of the European Parliament and of the Council of 11 May 2005 concerning unfair business-to-consumer commercial practices in the internal market, also later replaced by Directive 2006/114/EC.

7 Directive 2000/13/EC of the European Parliament and of the Council of 20 March 2000 on the approximation of the laws of the Member States relating to the labelling, presentation and advertising of foodstuffs.

8 Self-regulating body in the field of advertising, see Section V.3.

- refer to the food's nutrition and health benefits only if verified on scientific grounds;
- not encourage the consumer to consume oversized portions; size of shown food portion or soft drink portion should be adequate to featured environment and data;
- not question the promotion of a healthy and balanced diet or a healthy and active lifestyle;
- not present junk food in an advertisement in a way that encourages the consumer to consume excessive junk food or downplays or denies the nutritional or physiological effects of excessive consumption of junk food.

Special rules are recommended also for advertisement of alcoholic beverages, infant formulae and follow-on formulae and foodstuffs for particular nutritional uses and nutritional supplements.

2. Is there any specific national restriction or prohibition (mandatory legislation and code of conduct)?

a. Promotion of alcoholic beverages

Act on Advertisement stipulates restrictions concerning the advertising of alcoholic beverages, which shall not[9]:

- relate alcohol consumption to higher physical or psychical performance;
- claim that alcohol beverages have healing, stimulating or calming effects or that they help to solve personal problems;
- encourage excessive drinking or present abstinence or moderation as negative characteristics;
- accentuate the content of alcohol in beverages as a sign of their quality;

9 Act No 147/2001 Coll., on advertisement.
Act No 308/2000 Coll., on broadcasting and retransmission.

- target persons under 18 years of age, whereas no person, which could be considered under 18 years of age, can be shown in an advertisement featuring the consumption of alcoholic beverages.

Special rules for advertising of alcoholic beverages are stipulated for the purposes of and by the Act on Broadcasting and Retransmission.

b. Advertising towards children

As far as it concerns the advertising of foodstuffs towards children, the general rules of advertising set by the Act on Advertisement[10] apply.

Advertisement shall not abuse the trust of children and adolescents. Especially, it shall not:

- promote behaviour, which could threaten their health, psychical or moral development;
- picture them in dangerous situations;
- encourage the purchase of unsuitable products or products, the sale of which is prohibited to children, or purchase via telephone, telefax or electronic computer network by abusing their inexperience and gullibility;
- challenge children to directly request purchase of products from parents or other persons.

As for advertising of alcoholic beverages, it shall not focus on children and persons who could be perceived as children (under 18) and shall not show under-age people consumoing alcoholic beverages.

c. Advertising towards pregnant women

There are no special rules for advertisement of foodstuffs towards pregnant women. However, in case of special foodstuffs that are not suitable

10 Act No 147/2001 Coll., on advertisement.

for consumption by pregnant women, the products must present the necessary warning.

d. Advertising of unhealthy food

There are no explicit restrictions for the advertisement of unhealthy food, but several general regulations are applicable to this field of foodstuffs. According to the Act on Advertisement, advertisements shall not present products that are harmful to life and health without explicit and clear warnings. Advertisements shall also not claim that products are beneficial for human health if such effect has not been proved by an expert opinion.

It is only the Code of Conduct that requires that advertisements shall not question the promotion of a healthy and balanced diet or healthy and active life style, and it shall not present junk food in advertisements in a way that encourages the over-consumption of junk food or downplays or denies the nutritional or physiological effect of excessive consumption of junk food.

II. Misleading Advertising

1. What are the national rules on misleading advertising with respect to foodstuffs?

Misleading advertising is prohibited by the **Act on Regulation of Advertisement.**

The **Consumer Protection Act** implemented Directive 2005/29/EC concerning unfair business-to-consumer commercial practices in the internal market, and therefore it explicitly prohibits unfair and misleading commercial practices in relation to consumers.

According to the **Act on Foodstuffs** and its implementing decree, the following rules of advertising and labelling of foodstuffs apply: It is prohibited to place on the market any products that have misleading labelling or an offer for consumption. Misleading offer for consumption is defined as any kind of oral or written information about foodstuffs provided by the seller to the consumer, which is untrue, misleading or misrepresentative.

Information about a foodstuff is considered misleading (or misleading labelling) in the following situations:

a) if it misleads consumers, especially:

   - about the characteristics of foodstuffs, their nature, composition, properties, quantity, durability, origin of provenance or source and means of processing or manufacturing;
   - by attributing effects or properties, which the foodstuff does not possess;
   - by suggesting that the foodstuff possesses certain special characteristics, when in fact all similar foodstuffs possesses such characteristics;

b) by attributing preventive, treating or curing characteristics to the foodstuff or referring to such characteristics (unless otherwise specifically regulated by other legal regulation);

c) claiming that foodstuffs for normal consumption do not provide sufficient amounts of nutrients, such as provided by the advertised foodstuff;

d) stating an increased or special nutritional value of the foodstuff caused by adding additives or food supplements, except cases where specification of nutritional evaluation is presented with the foodstuff;

e) that the foodstuff was made in compliance with religious or ritual rules, if such fact is not confirmed by the relevant religious authorities.

Furthermore, the following statements are prohibited in respect of foodstuffs and their labelling:

- statements that the foodstuff is a source of all essential nutritional preparations (unless explicitly confirmed by a legal or administrative decision of a food-control body);
- statements that cannot be proved;

- statements that the foodstuff is suitable for targeted prevention, calming of pain, treatment or curing of disease or health disorders (unless explicitly confirmed by a legal or administrative decision of a food-control body);
- statements that could raise doubts about the harmlessness of other similar foodstuffs or which could cause consumer concern or doubt;
- statements about fast weight loss due to consumption of certain foodstuffs; and
- any statement or information that could cause confusion of foodstuffs for normal consumption with foodstuffs intended for special nutritional uses.

Misleading advertising is also considered an action in unfair competition within the field of private law, defined and further specified by the Commercial Code. The **Commercial Code** prohibits advertising that misleads or may mislead its target audience and which, due to its false nature, may impact the economic behaviour of such persons or may be to the detriment of another competitor or consumer.

The Commercial Code also prohibits the misleading labelling of products and services, which is defined as any description or labelling of goods and services that may mislead consumers and competitors that goods originate from a certain country or area, or that they are manufactured or provided by a certain manufacturer or provider, or that they have certain characteristic features, or are of a special quality. It is irrelevant whether such description appeared directly on the goods, labels, packaging, or in business documentation, etc. It is also irrelevant whether the deceitful description is disclosed directly or indirectly, as well as the manner of such disclosure.

Any incorrect description of goods or services, even if accompanied by an addendum such as "the kind", "the type", and "the method", in order to distinguish the goods' origin, shall also be treated as deceitful as long as the description is capable of misleading competitors and consumers as to the origin and characteristics of the goods or services. Description of goods and services which are commonly used in business to describe a certain kind or quality of products or services shall not be treated as deceitful unless accompanied by an addendum that may imply a mistaken assumption as to their origin, such as the words "genuine", "original", etc.[11]

2. What are the national landmark cases regarding misleading advertising for foodstuffs?

According to our knowledge, there are no specific cases which would be of significant relevance for the topic as such.

III. Mandatory Labelling: Name of the Product

Are there any national definitions of a foodstuff that could hamper the marketing of an imported food product?

Specific decrees of the Slovak Food Codex concern individual categories of foodstuffs and stipulate requirements for their processing, ingredients, packaging and storing or labelling as well. Besides categories of products defined in accordance with relevant European directives, national law recognizes additional categories and definitions of other food products, such as energy drinks or various meat or bakery products.

a. Energy drinks

Slovak food law recognizes a special category of stimulating non-alcoholic beverages, regulated by a commodity decree implementing the Food Codex for non-alcoholic beverages. Stimulating beverages are classified into a

11 Act No 40/1995 Coll., on regulation of advertisement.
Act No 250/2007 Coll., on consumer protection.
Act No 152/2005 Coll., on foodstuffs.
Decree No 127/2012 Coll., on labelling of foodstuffs.
Decree No 195/1996 Coll., on order No 981/1996-100 issuing Part One and Two, Catch Two and Three of Part Two of Food Codex.
Act No 513/1991 Coll., Commercial Code.

group and subgroup of non-alcoholic beverages as *"non-alcoholic beverage flavoured, stimulating"*. They are defined as beverages of special purpose, containing stimulating substances in amounts higher than stipulated by law, which were granted market permission by the Ministry of Health of the Slovak Republic.

Such product shall be labelled by its name according to the product classification mentioned above, and it shall meet the requirements on labelling regarding higher amounts of stimulating substances. A non-alcoholic beverage is not considered stimulating if it contains quinine or caffeine in the highest amount allowed by special law.[12]

b. Dairy products

The Slovak Republic has adopted a special law on milk and milk products, which includes products such as sour cream, yogurts and various categories of cheeses. There is also a special category of soured-milk products, such as yogurts or acidized milk. Soured-milk products are defined as products manufactured from cow, sheep or goat milk by souring it with suitable microorganisms that cause characteristic biochemical changes accompanied by a decrease in pH level, condensation of proteins and development of aromatic substances. Soured-milk products, including yogurts, are characterised by the presence of living microorganisms used for fermentation.

Yogurts are defined as soured-milk products characterized by symbiotic cultures of Lactobacillus delbrueckii subsp. bulgaricus and Streptococcus thermophilus. Acidified milk is characterized by culture of Lactobacillus acidophilus. Kephir is a soured-milk product characterized by culture created from kephir grains, Lactobacillus kephir sp. of Leuconostoc, Lactococcus and Acetobacter growing in specific conditions. Kephir grains are characterized by yeast, which does not ferment lactose (Saccharomyces omnisporus, Saccharomyces cerevisae and Saccharomyces exiguus).

12 Decree No 357/2000 Coll., on order No 2313/4/2000-100 issuing Catch of Food Codex on beverages.

The law also specifies conditions under which yogurt can be labelled as "natural" or "white".[13]

c. Cheese

The law recognizes the category of natural cheese for which the ratio of whey proteins and casein does not exceed the ratio of these proteins in milk. It is manufactured by total or partial condensation of proteins from cow, sheep or goat milk of various amounts of fat, or from butter-milk, or by their combination by affection of rennet or other suitable coagulation agents, or by lactic acid, created by biological souring of milk sugar and partial separation of whey, released during processing, or by other similar techniques containing coagulation of milk proteins, which result in products with similar physical, chemical and organoleptic properties.

There are several categories of natural cheese, such as aging or non-aged soft cheese, semi-hard, hard or extra hard product. There are also special legal definitions for fungal (blue) cheese, steamed cheese, whey cheese or lumpy cheese, as well as the national specialty, a sheep's cheese called "bryndza".[14]

d. Bread

A special legal regulation stipulates various cereal products and conditions for their manufacturing and labelling, including various types of flour, rise, pasta, bakery and pastry products.

As for bread itself, as a bakery product it is manufactured only by biological leavening. It is made from flour, water, yeast and other components, in the shape of a loaf weighing more than 400 g. If it is sliced or portioned its weight can be lower.

13 Decree No 526/2006 Coll., on order issuing Catch of Food Codex on milk and milk products.

14 Decree No 526/2006 Coll., on order issuing Catch of Food Codex on milk and milk products.

There are several types of bread, wheat, rye, wheat-rye or rye-wheat and other types, such as multigrain, wholegrain or special.[15]

e. Other products

The Slovak legal regulations also define other types of products, such as meat products[16] or mayonnaise,[17] and stipulate requirements on their labelling, ingredients, means of manufacturing, etc.

IV. Voluntary Labelling

1. "Clean labels": Are there any national definitions or requirements with respect to claims such as 'natural', 'pure', 'home-made', 'additive-free'?

SK

National requirements on labelling of foodstuffs also concern the use of claims characterizing the foodstuff, such as "natural", "identical with natu-

15 Decree No 360/2005 Coll., issuing order No 2657/2004-100 on Catch of Food Codex on eatable cereals and cereal products.

16 Meat products are divided into categories, which are further specified, in particular soft meat products, long-life meat products, boiled meat products (pâtés, meat spreads and creams, head cheese, aspic products, white and blood sausages, meat mousses), roasted meat products, salted meats (including, e.g. smoked bacon), semi-canned meat and meat cans (including, e.g. luncheon meat) and other meat products.
As for soft meat products, legal regulation also includes a definition of various types of sausages, salami or ham. For example, ham is defined as a meat product made from thighbone muscles of fatstock, poultry, rabbits or venison.
Legal source: Decree No 455/2005 Coll., issuing order No 1895/2004-100 on Catch of Food Codex on meat products.

17 Mayonnaise is a product of semi-thick consistency acquired by emulsion from vegetable oil in an egg component and in a deacidifying component. Egg component is a processed egg composition, processed yolk or processed egg-white.
Mayonnaise product is defined as mayonnaise, which contains other foodstuffs or even additives. There are also special sub-categories, such as basic mayonnaise, flavoured mayonnaise, mayonnaise sauce or mayonnaise spread and tartar sauce.
Legal source: Decree No 400/2005 Coll., issuing order No 1752/2005-100 on Catch of Food Codex on eggs, mayonnaise and mayonnaise products.

ral", and "pure", "fresh", "home-made", "vital", "genuine" or "rational". These terms can be used only if they are not misleading about characteristics of the foodstuffs or in few specific cases defined by law., These specific cases concern, e.g. natural yogurt"[18], "fresh fishery products"[19] or "natural mineral water"[20].

Claims such as grandmother recipe, among others, are not excluded from use provided that they do not mislead consumers about the character, origin or characteristics of foodstuffs.

2. Nutrition & health claims

Nutrition and health claims and conditions of their use are stipulated by Regulation (EC) No 1924/2006 on nutrition and health claims made on foods.

According to the Act on Foodstuffs and its implementing regulation[21] it is forbidden to mislead consumers about the proprieties of the foodstuff or by false labelling of foodstuffs, which attributes preventive, treating or curing characteristics to the foodstuff or refers to such characteristics. Therefore, if nutrition and health claims are presented, they shall be in compliance with Regulation No 1924/2006. The Act also applies[22] such that if the foodstuff is presented with a nutrition claim, the product labelling shall also include information about nutritional value of the foodstuff.

18 Decree No 526/2006 Coll. on Order No 2143/2006-100 issuing Catch of Food Codex on milk and milk products.

19 Decree No 171/2009 Coll. on Order No 1903/2008-100 on Catch of Food Codex on fishery products and products made from them.

20 Decree No 198/2004 Coll. on Order No 608/9/2004-100 issuing Catch of Food Codex on mineral water, spring water and bottled drinking water.

21 Decree. No 127/2012 Coll. on labelling of foodstuffs.

22 Decree. No 127/2012 Coll. on labelling of foodstuffs.

a. Within the list of health claims authorised pursuant to Regulation 1924/2006, are there any related substances which are prohibited or considered as a medicinal substance within your jurisdiction?

Within the Slovak jurisdiction, there is no special regulation of substances, which would be prohibited or considered as medicinal substances on top of Regulation 1924/2006.

b. Are there any national laws and regulations permitting food business operators to make reference to recommendations or endorsements by national associations, medical, nutrition or dietetic professionals, and health-related charities?

SK

There is no such legal act in Slovakia, which would allow recommendation or endorsement of a product using nutritional or health claims by medical, nutrition or dietetic professionals.

c. Are there any national laws or regulations regulating the use of nutrition or health claims on non-prepackaged food? If so, please provide details thereof.

There are no special national rules regulating the use of nutrition or health claims in this respect.

d. Is there a notification procedure required prior to/for marketing foodstuffs bearing nutritional or health claims?

The marketing of foodstuffs bearing nutritional or health claims does not have to be notified to local public bodies. Nevertheless, there is an obligatory notification of the marketing of food supplements on the Slovak market, where the entrepreneur is entitled to market such product only after the affirmative response of the relevant public body. The obligation of notification also applies to the marketing of foodstuffs for special nutritional purposes.

V. Enforcement of Food Law & Self-Regulating Bodies

1. Which actions may one risk in case of non-compliance with the labelling or advertising requirements?

a. Enforcement by public authorities

The State Veterinary and Food Administration Authority is charged with the supervision and enforcement of compliance with all acts of law related to foodstuffs[23] and their labelling, and there-to related protection of consumers under the Consumer Protection Act, the Act on Foodstuffs and Tobacco Products and its implementing acts, and the Act on Advertising. Slovak Trade Inspection[24] acts as the general supervisor of all consumer rights and legal regulations ordered by the Consumer Protection Act and Act on Advertising, which do not fall within the scope of special powers given to specialized public bodies, such as the State Veterinary and Food Administration Authority.

The Council for Broadcasting and Retransmission[25] supervises advertisement in the area of radio and television broadcasting and compliance with the Act on Broadcasting and Retransmission.

The Consumer Protection Act for protection of consumers' rights established the Special Committee for the evaluation of conditions of consumers' contracts and unfair commercial practices of sellers.[26] The Committee, operating under the Ministry of Justice, investigates violations of law upon its own initiative and also upon motions from consumers. It provides notification of these cases to public bodies, which are required by law to take them up.

---

23 In particular, it covers general supervision of foodstuffs´ manufacturing, in the trade network, in the field of handling foodstuffs and their placing on market.

24 See www.soi.sk.

25 See http://www.rvr.sk/en/.

26 See *Komisia na posudzovanie podmienok v spotrebite ských zmluvách a nekalých obchodných praktík predávajúcich.*

By virtue of administrative proceedings, these public bodies are authorized to impose administrative fines in an amount that varies depending on the particular case. Within the field of food law, legal regulations set the minimum and maximum fine that can be imposed for a certain offences. For violations of food law, i.e. labelling and advertising, there are no criminal sanctions or imprisonment.

The following fines can be imposed for particular violations of acts of law in the field of advertising of foodstuffs.

According to the Act on Foodstuffs, a fine of € 100 up to € 100.000 can be imposed for the manufacturing or placing on the market of the following:

- foodstuffs, which are not labelled in accordance with the law or which are unlabelled;
- foodstuffs, which are attributed with properties that the foodstuff does not possess;
- foodstuffs, which labelling is misleading or which are offered for consumption in another misleading manner.

A fine of € 500 up to € 200.000 can be imposed for the infringement of prohibition of misleading labelling or misleading advertising of foodstuffs.

A fine of € 1.000 up to € 500.000 can be imposed in the case of manufacturing or placing on the market of foodstuffs without information about their allergen components, if they are present.

The Consumer Protection Act only stipulates the general provision on fines up to € 66.388, which can be imposed for infringement of rules stipulated by this act and by directly applicable acts of the European Union in the field of consumer protection. If such infringement repeats within 12 months, the fine may reach up to € 165.970. According to the Act on Advertising, a fine up to € 165.970 can be imposed for misleading adverting.

When determining the sanction, the appropriate body shall take into account all relevant facts and circumstances of the case, such as the seriousness of the violation, length of time and the consequences for consumers, circumstances under which the law was violated (including whether the conduct was intentional or negligent), etc. Administrative proceedings on are two-instance proceedings, and the losing party can appeal the final decision by filing an action within the administrative justice system.[27]

b. Competitors and consumer associations

The Consumer Protection Act grants special rights to associations of consumers that were established for the purpose of enforcement of consumers´ rights or which are registered in the list of authorized entities administered by the European Community.

Such association of consumers is entitled to file a request for a preliminary injunction with the public body for protection from a particular infringement of collective consumers' interests if the operator has not refrained from such infringement based upon the previous request of the consumers association. A decision to impose a preliminary injunction ordering the entrepreneur to refrain from infringing the consumers´ rights shall be followed by administrative proceedings to evaluate the potential violation of law or special legal regulations.

Each consumer is entitled by the Consumer Protection Act to seek judicial protection of his or her rights with the local court. The association of consumers may also take such action in the case of the collective interests of consumers, i.e. in case of unlawful action directed against all consumers.[28]

Several associations focus on the protection of consumers, such as the Association of Slovak Consumers[29] or the Association of Consumers of Slovakia,[30] which are the most diligent in their efforts.

27 Act No 128/2002 Coll. on State control of the internal market in matters of consumer protection.
Act No 39/2007 Coll., on veterinary care.
Act No 308/2000 Coll., on broadcasting and retransmission.
Act No 250/2007 Coll., on consumer protection.
Act No 500/2004 Coll., on administrative procedure.

28 Act No 250/2007 Coll., on consumer protection.
Act No 500/2004 Coll., on administrative procedure.

29 See http://www.zss.sk/.

30 See http://www.test-magazin.sk/.

As for administrative proceedings on administrative offences and violations of law governed by public administration bodies, competitors and consumer associations may not participate as parties to these proceedings. Nevertheless, any subject can file a motion with the public administrative body on particular suspicion of a violation of law. The public bodies usually examine these notifications.

Both competitors and consumer associations are authorized to claim their rights by means of private law and to seek protection from unfair competition action under the Commercial Code.[31] As for competitors, they are authorized for such protection only if the accused subject acts in unfair competition and such action is liable to cause damage to the competitor. If certain conduct is liable to cause damage to consumers, consumer associations may also file an action for protection from unfair competition. Nevertheless, such cases are rare because of the high costs of civil proceedings.

2. Are there any national self-regulating bodies with respect to advertising for foodstuffs?

Within the field of advertising, the Slovak Advertising Standards Council (Rada pre reklamu)[32] is composed of significant entrepreneurs operating in Slovakia including media professionals, which have agreed to respect its Code of Conduct aiming at honest, decent, legal and true advertisement.

The self-regulating bodies also have a special position in respect to the enforcement of consumer rights, given by the Consumer Protection Act.

According to the Consumer Protection Act, use of unfair commercial practices may also be inspected by members of the Code of Conduct or through the creators of the Code of Conduct by other persons and associations. Such activity may be performed irrespective of court proceedings or administrative proceedings.

31 Act No 513/1991 Coll.

32 See http://www.rpr.sk/en.

In case of an alleged violation of the Code of Conduct (see section 1.1), the Committee of the Advertising Standards Council may initiate a proceeding for infringement and eventually issue a decision confirming the violation or compliance with the Code of Conduct. Such decision is not legally binding and enforceable, and the council member's disobedience may only result in its exclusion from the council.

3. Moral enforcement of food law

Recent developments show an increased interest of Slovak consumers in information about country of origin and quality of foodstuffs, as well as about their ingredients and effects on human health.

Consumers have become more sensitive to the quality of foodstuffs and the fair business practices of retail chain stores. For example, it was a consumer's initiative that created a mobile application for smartphones[33] whereby consumers can report suspicious foodstuffs. Via this application, the consumer creates a complaint on the particular foodstuff for filing with the Slovak Veterinary and Food Administration, and the application sends it directly to this public body for examination. Another consumer´s initiative created a special webpage[34] in order to raise public awareness about the quality of foodstuffs and healthy living.

Great emphasis and attention is focused on Slovak origin of foodstuffs. Based on this trend, Slovak lawmakers have stipulated new legal obligations for food retail stores to publish information about the amount (portion) of foodstuffs of Slovak origin (made in Slovakia) in grocery retail stores.

Another consumer-made webpage[35] focuses on grocery products made in Slovakia by small local producers and provides direct access to them.

It is also customary to publish cases of food law violations in the local media and to indicate which retail stores offer such "bad" foodstuffs.

33 "Better foodstuffs", see https://play.google.com/store/apps/details?id=sk.peterbartos.lepsie-potraviny.

34 See www.viescojes.sk (meaning "you know what you eat").

35 See http://www.poctivepotraviny.sk/ as "conscientious foodstuffs".

CHAPTER 15
Spain

Núria Porxas and Javier Carreras

I. Possible Bans on Food Advertising

1. Is there any general national legislation or code of conduct regulating the promotion of foodstuffs?

Spanish law, including food law, is a complex corpus of legislation in which European Union law coexists not only with national legislation, but also with the product of the extensive legislative powers that Spain's seventeen autonomous regions (*comunidades autónomas*) hold in many areas. As a consequence of this decentralised structure, even though general legislation regulating the promotion of foodstuffs is enacted at the national level, a number of specific regional regulations should also be taken into account.

ES

Regarding national legislation, the Spanish Food Code, which was enacted in September 1967,[1] was the first general provision governing the conditions to be met by food products for human consumption, including certain rules about labelling and advertising. Even though most of this code has been surpassed by subsequent Union and Spanish legislation, a large part of it remains in force.

More specifically, advertising of foodstuffs, as well as food labelling, is regulated by Royal Decree 1334/1999[2], which approves the so-called "General Rule" (*Norma General*). The General Rule implements Directive 2000/13 on

1 Decree 2484/1967 of 21 September 1967, approving the text of the Spanish Food Code (entered into force in 1974). BOE 248 of 17 October 1967, as amended.

2 Royal Decree 1334/1999 of 31 July 1999, approving the general rules on labeling, presentation and advertising of foodstuffs. BOE 202 of 24 August 1999, as last amended by Royal Decree 890/2011 of 24 June 2011.

labelling.[3] Moreover, although technically unnecessary for coding purposes, the General Rule also includes provisions taken from European regulations on food enzymes and flavourings, given their direct applicability.

Needless to say the promotion of foodstuffs is also subject to general rules governing advertising in Spain, which are essentially set out in the Spanish Unfair Competition and General Advertising Acts.[4]

On the other side, with respect to advertising self-control by the industry, the *Asociación para la Autorregulación de la Comunicación Comercial* (Autocontrol) is the main Spanish advertising self-regulating body. Autocontrol's members are bound by the Advertising Code of Conduct, which is inspired by the ICC Code of Advertising and Marketing Communications Practice and sets forth general rules applicable to all advertising, irrespective of the industry sector.

2. Is there any specific national restriction or prohibition (mandatory legislation and code of conduct)?

a. With respect to certain foodstuffs

In addition to the implementation of the prohibitions set forth in Directive 2007/65/EC, which amended the Audiovisual Media Services Directive (repealed by Directive 2010/13/EC), the Spanish General Law on Audiovisual Communication[5] (LAC) expressly forbids the advertising in audiovisual media of alcoholic beverages with an alcohol content of more than 20 %. Additionally, advertising which associates the consumption of alcohol with

3 Directive 2000/13/EC of the European Parliament and of the Council of 20 March 2000 on the approximation of the laws of the Member States relating to the labelling, presentation and advertising of foodstuffs (OJ 2000 L 109), as last amended by Regulation (EC) No 596/2009.

4 Law 3/1991 of 10 January 1991, on unfair competition (BOE 10, 11 January 1991) as amended, and Law 34/1988 of 11 November 1988, on advertising (BOE 274, 15 November 1988) as amended.

5 Law 7/2010 of 31 March 2010, on audiovisual communication. BOE 79, 1 April 2010, as amended.

an improvement in physical performance, social success or health is also banned by the LAC, which also prevents the advertising of certain products that improve one's physical appearance, such as slimming products.

The LAC also encourages media service providers to develop codes of conduct regarding inappropriate audiovisual commercial communication, accompanying or included in children's programs, of foods and beverages containing nutrients and substances with a nutritional or physiological effect, in particular those such as fat, trans-fatty acids, salt/sodium and sugars, excessive intakes of which are not recommended. In this regard, a significant part of the Spanish food industry has adhered to the PAOS Code (defined below).

Spanish law also contains specific rules on the advertising of foodstuffs for dietary and/or special uses.[6] The promotion of foodstuffs subject to these rules by means of discounts, contests or gifts is prohibited. This regulation also prohibits the payment of sales commissions to those involved in the distribution of these foodstuffs. Moreover, the advertising to the general public of dietetic food for special medical purposes (regulated by a separate provision) is prohibited.[7]

Regulations on performance-enhancing products[8] forbid measures that encourage the consumption (and, thus, advertising) in sports premises of any product containing forbidden substances that could cause a positive result in doping tests. These regulations provide for the creation of a new procedure for the declaration of food products introduced into Spain that fall under their scope and that the Spanish authorities will establish a specific program aimed at strictly regulating the advertising of these products.

6 Royal Decree 2685/1976 of 16 October 1976, approving the technical and health regulations on the manufacturing, distribution and sale of foodstuffs for dietary and/or special uses. BOE 284 of 26 November 1976, as amended. Foodstuffs containing complementary nutrients or intended for elderly people are included within the scope of these specific rules.

7 Royal Decree 1091/2000 of 9 June 2000, approving the technical and health regulations on dietetic food for special medical purposes. BOE 139 of 10 June 2000, as amended.

8 Basic Law 3/2013 of 20 June 2013, on the protection of the health of sports players and the fight against performance enhancing drugs in sports. BOE 148, 21 June 2013.

Additionally, a large number of food products are the subject-matter of specific regulations concerning the conditions of their commercialization. Even though they do not all include additional limitations to those already included in the general rules governing advertising, they are relevant for the purposes of the conditions to be met for using the name of the specific product and, thus, regarding misleading advertising.

Vertical Spanish legislation has already been considered an obstacle to the free movement of goods within the European Union. Particularly, Spanish law on medicinal herbs has been the source of a significant amount of litigation both at the national and European levels. Although these products are often used in food supplements and dietary products in certain Member States, they were excluded from the harmonization process conducted by Directive 2002/46/EC.[9] Accordingly, Spanish law only accepted certain listed vitamins and minerals as ingredients of food supplements, but not any other substance, particularly not medicinal herbs included in a list of herbs authorized to be used in medicines.[10] This legislation meant that food supplements lawfully produced and marketed in another Member State encountered obstacles in their commercialization in Spain as a result of the administrative practice of systematically classifying these products based on medicinal herbs that were not listed in the Spanish regulations as medicinal products by function. The Spanish Supreme Court[11] held that Directive 2002/46 expressly gives Member States the right to regulate nutrients or other substances with nutritional or physiological effects used as ingredients of food supplements and, therefore, upheld this administrative practice. In contrast, the High Court of Justice of the autonomous region

9 Directive 2002/46/EC of the European Parliament and of the Council of 10 June 2002 on the approximation of the laws of the Member States relating to food supplements (OJ 2002 L 183/51).

10 Royal Decree 1275/2003 of 10 October, on food supplements. BOE 246, 14 October 2003. Also the Order of 3 October 1973 approving the special registry of medicinal plant based products. BOE 247 of 15 October 1973, repealed by Royal Decree 1345/2007 of 11 October 2007, governing the process for the authorisation, registration and conditions for supplying industrially-manufactured medicinal products for human use. BOE 267, 7 November 2007.

11 Ruling of the Supreme Court (Administrative Chamber) no. 6725/2003 of 30 March 2006.

of Madrid[12] had previously found this practice to constitute a measure of equivalent effect incompatible with the principles of the free movement of goods. Following a case brought by the Commission against Spain[13], the European Court of Justice found that by withdrawing from the market any product based on medicinal herbs that was not classified and authorized as a drug, Spain had failed to fulfil its obligations under articles 28 and 30 EC Treaty.

b. With respect to a specific sections of the population

The current Spanish Law on Food Safety and Nutrition[14] (LFSN) restricts the advertising of foodstuffs designed to substitute normal eating or nutrition habits during motherhood, breast-feeding and among the young and elderly. Besides this specific limitation, the main target population of the LFSN measures are children, young people and pregnant women.

The LFSN refers to the fact that the Spanish Ministry of Health and Consumption launched a Strategy on Nutrition, Physical Activity and Prevention of Obesity (NAOS Strategy) in 2005. The Spanish Consumer, Food Safety and Nutrition Agency has coordinated its implementation. The NAOS Strategy gives priority to measures aimed at the abovementioned sectors of the population. A core element of the NAOS Strategy is the declaration of schools as advertising-free spaces. It also encourages self-regulation by the food industry as regards advertising aimed at children under 15.

In 2005 the Spanish Federation of Food and Drinks Industries (FIAB) published a code that established a set of rules to guide adhering companies through the development, implementation and dissemination of their advertising messages aimed at children under the age of 12. This first code was developed in line with the Principles of Food and Beverage Product Advertising of the EU Agro-Food Industries Confederation (FoodDrinkEurope), which was approved in February 2004. After seven years, changes in market

12 Ruling of the High Court of Madrid (Administrative Chamber) no. 1260/1997 of 25 January 2000.

13 Case 88/07 *Commission of the European Communities v Kingdom of Spain* ECR I-1353.

14 Law 17/2011 of 5 July 2011, on food safety and nutrition. BOE 160, 6 July 2011.

conditions – particularly, the increased use of electronic communications – together with the mandate included in the LFSN to protect children under 15, led the industry to enact a second version of the text in December 2012; the new *"Code of co-regulation of advertising for food products and beverages aimed at children, the prevention of obesity and protecting health"* (PAOS Code).

The PAOS Code is applicable to the advertising of food products and beverages by adhering companies operating in the audiovisual and printed media sector (labelling and packaging are expressly excluded from its scope) aimed at children under 12 years of age, as well as to any advertising on the Internet aimed at children under 15 years of age. Briefly, the PAOS Code contains a comprehensive set of rules aimed at protecting children and adolescents from advertising that takes advantage of their credulity and naivety or that promotes unhealthy food and living habits. Generally, the goals of the PAOS Code are to promote healthy diets (varied, balanced and moderate) and physical activity among children and adolescents.

Children are also protected by many other prohibitions and limitations on food advertising in Spain. For instance, the autonomous regions have their own rules on the protection of infants and young people[15] and preventing drug addiction.[16] Among other limitations, these regional rules contain stricter prohibitions and limitations on the advertising of alcoholic products than the prohibitions and limitations contained in the national regulations. Some set out specific categories of promotion and advertising: direct, indirect, hidden and surreptitious.[17]

15 For instance, Aragon Law 12/2001 of 2 July 2001, on infants and adolescents. BOE 189, 8 August 2001.

16 For instance, Basque Country Law 18/1998 of 25 June 1998, on prevention, assistance and reinsertion in relation to drug addictions, which has been amended several times, the last time by Law 1/2011 of 3 February. BOE 315, 31 December 2011, and BOE 42, 18 February 2011.

17 This is the case of Galician Law 11/2010 of 17 December 2010, on the prevention of the consumption of alcoholic beverages by minors. BOE 25, 29 January 2011. This provision granted a one-year period to adapt advertising and sponsorship agreements to its detailed provisions.

II. Misleading Advertising

1. What are the national rules on misleading advertising with respect to foodstuffs?

Misleading advertising is defined and regulated in general terms for all types of goods and services in the abovementioned Spanish Unfair Competition and General Advertising Acts. Misleading advertising with respect to foodstuffs is specifically regulated in the General Rule. This set of rules merely implements the general Union provisions (article 3 of Directive 2006/114/EC and article 2 of Directive 2000/13).

There are a myriad of additional rules that include general provisions preventing or forbidding misleading advertising, such as health regulations concerning specific foodstuffs.[18] In any case, the basic outline of the prohibition of misleading advertising is not affected by these sectorial regulations.

In August 2013, a law was enacted in Spain with the aim of improving the operation and structure of the food chain to increase the efficiency and competitiveness of the Spanish agri-food industry and to reduce the imbalance in the commercial relationships between different operators.[19] Even though most of its provisions are aimed at achieving fair competition by protecting market agents with less negotiating power, it also includes certain provisions concerning misleading and unfair advertising of food.

This law includes a general prohibition on the use of trademarks for food products in the framework of unfair competition practices, such as passing-off, trademark infringements or illegal advertising. Moreover, a specific rule concerning the communication of comparative tests of foodstuffs is also provided. In addition to specific obligations concerning the veracity and scientific and technical precision of these tests, which even apply to the

18 The national legislator is attempting to repeal a large number of health regulations concerning particular foodstuffs that are formally in force but obsolete and not always in line with EU guidelines. One of the best recent examples is Royal Decree 176/2013 of 8 March 2013. BOE 76, 29 March 2013.

19 Law 12/2013 of 2 August 2013, on measures to improve the operation of the food chain. BOE 185, 3 August 2013.

laboratories where the tests are carried out, this law also stipulates that if, as a result of comparative tests carried out on foodstuffs, legal requirements are found to be infringed, the relevant tests must be communicated to the producers or marketers of the foodstuffs in question before publishing the results, so that a new test can be requested. If there are discrepancies as to the compliance of the foodstuff, a third and final test will be carried out. The courts and authorities have yet to provide an opinion as to whether these requirements, which are probably designed to cover comparative tests published by consumer associations, will also apply to tests used in comparative advertising; nothing seems to prevent *prima facie* such an application.

As far as misleading advertising concerning geographical origin is concerned, under article 5 of the General Rule, the labelling of foodstuffs must include their place of origin or provenance. The failure to comply with the obligation to include the place of origin in the labelling may constitute misleading advertising and give rise to the applicable administrative sanction. The General Rule established an exception for products from other EU Member States, which only need to indicate the place of origin or source of the product in those cases in which the failure to do so may lead the consumer to err as to the true origin of the food product.

In addition to the applicable EU regulations, the Spanish autonomous regions have enacted their own rules on the protection of designations of origin and geographical indications for wine and other agricultural products intended for human consumption.[20] These rules, which coexist with certain national rules governing basic or related matters, include provisions concerning misleading advertising as to the origin of these products. The Constitutional Court has ruled on several conflicts of competences about designations of origin. For instance, in early 2013 it ruled on a dispute between Catalonia and the central government providing that, even though in that particular case the regional powers concerning designations of origin had been infringed to a certain degree, the State's competence to coordinate the general planning of economic activity in Spain gives it the right to intervene to some degree in the viticulture industry and its organization.[21]

20 Such as Extremadura Law 4/2010 of 28 April 2010, on designations of origin and geographical indications. BOE 120, 17 May 2010.

21 Constitutional Court judgment 34/2013 of 14 February 2013.

These dispositions concerning designations of origin coexist with the rules regulating the products themselves. If we once again take wine as an example, we find both national and regional rules governing commercialization and, thus, the prevention of misleading advertising practices concerning origin and characteristics.[22]

2. What are the national landmark cases regarding misleading advertising for foodstuffs?

As far as judicial litigation is concerned, most of the misleading advertising cases concern the geographic origin of the product. In this regard, several examples should be mentioned. For instance, in its ruling of 3 February 2010 the High Court of Galicia upheld a fine that had been imposed by the Galician public consumer protection agency on a supermarket chain for misleading advertising. The supermarket had included in its advertising materials in Galicia a table wine from a different part of Spain using the claim *"products from our land"*. The court held that the advertising was likely to be interpreted by the average consumer in Galicia as meaning that the geographical origin of the products was the autonomous region of Galicia and thus upheld the fine. Similarly, the Appeals Court of Huelva (Andalusia) found that the use of the claim *"Origin Jabugo"* used by the defendant in relation to ham and pig shoulder products was misleading because the products were not covered by the designation of origin *"Jamones de Huelva"*.

Even when issuing a decision on a case of feedstuffs, the ruling of the Madrid Appeals Court of 29 April 2008 considered an advertisement claiming the product in question to be *"the best nutrition"* and the fact that *"the best nutrition has never before had a better taste"* to be misleading. The Court considered that claims of number one status or ranking must include evidence that their results are better than those of competitors. Prior

22 State Law 24/2003 of 10 July 2003, on vineyards and wine, classifies as a serious infringement misleading advertising about the origin and characteristics of wine, and as a very serious infringement the omission of clear indications that avoid consumers erring when the same trademark is used for different degrees of protection. In addition to the basic rules provided in this State Law, the regions have enacted their own rules, such as Castilla and Leon Law 8/2005 of 10 June on vineyards and wine.

to this Court decision, Autocontrol had analyzed the same claims in the framework of a comparative advertising based on a comparative test on the palatability of feed products, which were deemed insufficient for making nutrition claims. Along these lines, Autocontrol has created a vast amount of doctrine on misleading comparative, top-parity and number one advertising claims, as well as on misleading advertising concerning the nature and characteristics of the advertised product. In relation to the later cases, Autocontrol has rendered decisions concerning a large number of food products, such as cream[23] or surimi-based products[24]. In relation to the former cases, for instance, Autocontrol has considered that the *"the milk with the best taste"* (*"la leche con el mejor sabor"*) is a claim of number one status that must come with evidence that can be compared to competitive products so as not to be misleading.[25] However, it has ruled that "milk of the best quality" (*"leche de la mejor calidad"*) is a top-parity claim that does not need to include evidence on its superiority but must show that it is a top-parity quality position in relation with quality competitive products.[26]

Since the vast majority of misleading advertising cases in the foodstuffs industry is brought before Autocontrol, some other relevant cases will be referenced throughout this article.

23 Decision of 15 December 2010, in the case Capsa vs Grupo Leche Pascual, S.A. (*"Nata en spray, líquida, líquida ligera"*).

24 Decision of 21 February 2007, in the case Mancomunidad Uribe-Kosta vs. Conservas Vitori, S.L. (*"Conservas Mendavia"*), which held the advertising of a crab and king prawn salad to be misleading as the product was only made with flavours and surimi and did not identify the specific fish products used to make the surimi.

25 Decision of 29 April 2010 in the case Grupo Leche Pascual, S.A.U. vs Corporación Alimentaria Peñasanta, S.A. (*"la mejor leche con el major sabor")*. However, in other cases Autocontrol has considered that taste is a subjective element that cannot be evidenced; for instance, in its Decision of 13 October 2011, in the case Campofrío Food Group, S.A. vs Creta Farms, S.L., *"la charcutería más sabrosa"* (*"the best tasting pork products"*).

26 Decision of 7 September 2010 in the case Corporación Alimentaria Peñasanta, S.A. vs Alimentos Lácteos, S.A.

III. Mandatory Labelling: Name of the Product

Are there any national definitions of a foodstuff that could hamper the marketing of an imported food product?

We refer you to our response to question 1.2(a) regarding certain litigation in relation to the Spanish law on medicinal herbs.

In relation to definitions of other specific foodstuffs, the Spanish quality rule for yogurt[27] not only defines "yogurt"[28] but also "pasteurized yogurt after fermentation". This second product is obtained by applying a heat process, equivalent to pasteurization, to yogurt after fermentation, so that the product loses the viability of its specific lactic bacteria while fulfilling the conditions set forth for yogurt in this regulation, unless provided otherwise. After a long dispute between the traditional yogurt industry and the main producer of pasteurized yogurt after fermentation, the Spanish Supreme Court confirmed, in its ruling of 10 October 2005, that the use of the term "yogurt" to identify this second type of product is compliant with EU regulations.

In its ruling of 19 May 2008, the Supreme Court found that the use of the claim "with yogurt" in relation to margarine and mayonnaise products produced in Germany was not misleading although these products did not have any of the bacteria that the Spanish quality rule for yogurt require for the product. Interestingly, despite this legal definition and without evaluating whether such a definition could in fact impede the free movement of goods, the court argued that Spanish consumers are not likely to believe that the term "yogurt" generally requires that bacteria colonies exist in the product.

27 Royal Decree 179/2003 of 14 February 2003, approving the general quality rules for yogurt or yoghourt. BOE 42 of 18 February 2003 as amended.

28 As a coagulated milk product resulting from the lactic fermentation of pasteurized milk, concentrated pasteurized milk, wholly or partly skimmed pasteurized milk, wholly or partly skimmed concentrated pasteurized milk, with or without added pasteurized cream, dried full fat or wholly or partly skimmed milk, whey powder, milk proteins, and/or other products obtained from milk fractionation by *Lactobacillus bulgaricus* and *Streptococcus thermophilus*. A minimum of 1 per 107 colonies per gram or millilitre of viable microorganisms producing the lactic fermentation must be present in the finished product.

Ice cream products are also legally defined in Spain.[29] Moreover, the applicable regulation also defines seven categories of ice cream: milk ice cream, cream ice cream, skimmed milk ice cream, sorbet, water ice cream, mousse and foam ice cream. The Jury of Autocontrol[30] has analysed both the definitions of ice cream and yogurt in the context of assessing possible misleading advertising and the use of health and nutritional claims concerning a special product which, unlike the frozen yogurt analysed in the past by the Court of Justice[31], is commercialized in a non-frozen form as a sweet milk product containing yogurt to be frozen. The product was commercialized using a slogan that plays with the Spanish names of the two categories: yogurt and ice cream. The Jury decided that the additional information offered in the advertisement avoided any possibility of misleading consumers about the nature and conditions of consumption of the product.

The Spanish Quality Rule for Cheese[32] provides a legal definition of this product[33]. Moreover, there are specific regulations for Iberian cheese[34] and for curds (*cuajada*)[35] that establish requirements for the use of these terms.

---

29 Royal Decree 618/1998 of 17 April 1998, approving the technical and health regulations on the manufacture and distribution of ice creams and prepared mixtures to freeze. BOE 101, 28 April 1998, as amended. This provision defines ice-cream as any processed foodstuff that has taken a solid, semi-solid or pasty form as a result of a freezing process simultaneous or subsequent to the addition of ingredients, and which has to maintain a certain degree of plasticity and freezing until it is sold to consumers.

30 Ruling of the Jury of Autocontrol of 12 September 2012 AEFH vs Danone, S.A. ("*Yolado*"), decided on appeal by a ruling of 29 November 2012.

31 Case 298/87, proceedings for compulsory reconstruction against Smanor, S.A. (prohibition of the use of the name "deep-frozen yogurt"), ECR, 14 July 1988, OJ C 215, 17 August 1988.

32 Royal Decree 1113/2006 of 29 September 2006, approving the quality rules for cheeses and melted cheese. BOE 239, 6 October 2006.

33 As the fresh or ripened product, solid or semisolid, obtained from milk, wholly or partly skimmed milk, cream, buttermilk, or from a mixture of some or all of these products, wholly or partly coagulated by rennet or another applicable coagulant, before draining off or after partially removing the watery part, with or without prior hydrolysis of the lactose, provided that the casein-serum proteins ratio is not lower than that present in milk.

34 Royal Decree 262/2011 of 28 February 2011, approving the composition and specific characteristics of Iberian cheese. BOE 59 of 10 March 2011, as amended.

35 Royal Decree 1070/2007 of 27 July 2007, approving the technical and health regulation for curds (*cuajada*). BOE 207 of 29 August 2007, as amended.

The Spanish Quality Rule for Bread[36] defines it as the product resulting from cooking dough obtained by mixing wheat flour and drinking water, with or without edible salt, fermented by the action of natural microorganisms specific to bread fermentation.

Spanish law also defines non-alcoholic beer as any beer with an alcoholic volume of less than 1 %[37], including the tolerance margins on the actual alcoholic strength by volume.

Finally, in addition to the identification of foodstuffs (meat, vegetables, legumes, tubers, cereals, fish, game birds, seafood, etc.) with their scientific binomial nomenclature in Latin, the Spanish Food Code defines many other foodstuffs. It offers definitions of fifteen types of raw, cured and processed cold meats, creams (three types), six types of oils, juices, compotes and jams (fourteen types), honey (ten types) as well as six different sauces. As already mentioned, although the Spanish Food Code itself has not been formally repealed, most of its definitions have been repealed by subsequent legislation.[38]

36 Royal Decree 1137/1984 of 28 March 1984, approving the technical and health regulation for the manufacture, distribution and sale of bread and special bread. BOE 146 of 19 June 1984, as amended.

37 Royal Decree 53/1995, of 20 January 1995, approving the technical and health regulations on the manufacturing, distribution and sale of beer. BOE 34 of 9 February 1995, as amended.

38 E.g., the current definitions of juices arise from the recent implementation (by Royal Decree 781/2013, of 11 October 2013, regulating the production, composition, labeling, presentation and advertising of fruit juices and other similar products aimed at human consumption) of Directives 2009/106/EC, 2010/33/EU and 2012/12/EU, modifying Directive 2001/112 of 20 December 2001 relating to fruit juices and certain similar products intended for human consumption. OJ L10, 12 January 2002, as amended (OJ L212, 15 August, 2009; OJ L126, 22 May 2010; and OJ L115, 27 April 2012).

IV. Voluntary Labelling

1. "Clean labels": Are there any national definitions or requirements with respect to claims such as 'natural', 'pure', 'home-made', 'additive-free'?

The Spanish Food Code prohibited, in general, the inclusion of adjectives such as "pure" or "natural" in the packaging and advertising of food products containing additives or foreign materials.

In relation to cold meats, the Spanish Food Code prohibits the use of the term "pure" if a product contains meat from different animals. This prohibition has been specifically included in the provision regulating cured pork products (*embutido curado*).[39] The Spanish regulation on Iberian cold meat[40] restricts the use of the term "pure" to products obtained from purebred Iberian pigs.

As far as "natural" is concerned, the General Rule regulates the use of the term in relation to flavours. The Regulation on Miracle Products[41], further described below, forbids the use of the term "natural" to indicate a characteristic linked to supposed preventive or therapeutic effects.

Moreover, the Spanish Ministry of Agriculture is the registered owner of the trademark "*raza autóctona*" (local breeds), a collective trademark that can be used in relation to certain foodstuffs provided the requirements set forth in the applicable regulation are met.[42]

39 Order of 7 February 1980, approving the quality provision for meat sausage cured products.

40 Royal Decree 4/2014,of 10 January, approving the technical and health regulations for Iberian pork meat, ham, pork shoulder and pork loin. BOE 264 of 11 January 2014.

41 Royal Decree 1907/1996 of 2 August, on advertising and the commercial promotion of products, activities or services with alleged health effects. BOE 189 of 6 August 1996, as amended.

42 Royal Decree 505/2013 of 28 June, regulating the use of the trademark "raza autóctona" in products of animal origin.

Most of the autonomous regions have enacted their own laws both on food quality and handicrafts which, among other matters, regulate the conditions of use of origin and clean labels. For instance, the Andalusian autonomous government is the registered owner of the Spanish trademark *"Pescado de la Costa"* (Coastal fish), a collective trademark that can be used in relation to fish provided it complies with the requirements set forth in the applicable regulation.[43] Moreover, the Galician Law on Food Quality[44] regulates the conditions of use and correlative protection for the labels "home-made" (*"artesano de casa"* or *"casero"*) and "from the mountain" (*"artesano de montaña"*), and also provides for the creation of a collective trademark to be used by all products that comply with various geographical quality indications, traditional specialties, traditionally made food products and products from bio-agriculture and integrated production, in order to offer the market a common image that helps to identify high quality Galician products.

The use of these claims has been considered to be subject to the above-mentioned general rules on the prevention of misleading advertising. For example, the Jury of Autocontrol ruled that the use of the claim *"100 % natural"* was misleading when the product (orange juice) contained small dosages of acidulant and stabilizer agents.[45] In a decision of 23 May 2013[46], the Jury found that the claim *"all natural and craftsman"* used in the promotion of cured ham was misleading. The Jury argued that consumers could interpret the claim as meaning that the cured ham was home-made and therefore found that such claim becomes misleading when industrial process are used in the manufacturing of the product.

43 Order of 13 December 2004, regulating the use of the trademark *"Pescado de la Costa"*.

44 Law 2/2005 of 18 February, on Food Quality. BOE 93 of 19 April 2005.

45 Decision of 29 July 2010, J. García Carrión, S.A. vs. Grupo Leche Pascual, S.A.U. *"Zumosol sólo zumo 100 %"*.

46 Decision of 23 May 2013, Campofrío Food Group S.A. vs. El Pozo Alimentación S.A. *"El Pozo Artesano"*.

2. Nutrition & health claims

a. Within the list of health claims authorised pursuant to Regulation 1924/2006, are there any related substances which are prohibited or considered as a medicinal substance within your jurisdiction?

It is possible that a substance for which a health claim has been authorized pursuant to Regulation 1924/2006 be included in a product classified and presented as a medicinal product. For example, there are authorized health claims in relation to activated charcoal and lactulose.[47] These two substances are, however, included in the list of active substances that may be used in Spain in over-the-counter medicinal products[48], although such inclusion does not necessarily mean that any product containing these substances is automatically considered a medicinal product. A medicinal product qualifies as such not only because of its ingredients but also because of its composition and presentation as having properties for treating or preventing human disease or being used in or administered to humans either with a view to restoring, correcting or modifying physiological functions by exerting a pharmacological, immunological or metabolic action or to make a medical diagnosis.

b. Are there any national laws and regulations permitting food business operators to make reference to recommendations or endorsements by national associations, medical, nutrition or dietetic professionals and health-related charities?

The LFSN allows endorsements from associations, corporations, foundations and institutions related to health and nutrition in direct and indirect food advertising if and only if they are non-profit organizations and the

47 Both under Regulation (EC) No 432/2012 of 16 May 2012 establishing a list of permitted health claims made on foods, other than those referring to the reduction of disease risk and to children's development and health (OJ 25 May 2012, L 136/1).

48 Order of 28 September 2000 and Order SCO/255/2007 of 3 February 2007. BOE 38, 13 February 2007.

quoted organization undertakes in writing to devote the financial resources obtained from the collaboration to activities aimed at improving health through research, development and specialized publications in relation to health and nutrition.

c. Is the use of nutrition or health claims on non-prepackaged food regulated at the national level?

The Spanish Food Code, which is also applicable to non-prepackaged food, already forbade the inclusion in the labelling and advertising of any foodstuff of indications as to the prevention, treatment or curing of human diseases or that may make the consumer believe that the foodstuff has better than normal attributes.

In the 1990s, a specific regulation was enacted to prevent the use of claims related to health effects in any kind of products[49], including both prepackaged and non-pre-packaged food. This regulation, which is popularly known in Spain as the "Regulation on Miracle Products", remained in force after the enactment of Regulation 1924/2006 since its scope is broader (it applies not only to foodstuffs but any product, material, substance, energy or method with alleged health effects).

ES

Other claims that are forbidden by this Regulation include claims suggesting specific slimming properties; using endorsements of any kind of authorisations, homologations or tests by health authorities from Spain or abroad; using the testimony of health professionals, famous people or real or supposed patients; trying to substitute normal eating and nutrition habits, especially in pregnant or breastfeeding women, children or older people; or suggesting or affirming an increase in physical, mental, sport or sexual performance.

49 Royal Decree 1907/1996 of 2 August, on advertising and commercial promotion of products, activities or services with alleged health effects. BOE 189 of 6 August 1996, as amended.

At the time of drafting these responses a draft regulation[50] has been published (but not enacted) on the information required for foodstuffs that are not pre-packaged and food packaged at the point of sale. The current wording of the draft does not include any specific rules regarding possible nutrition or health claims on pre-packaged food.

d. Is a notification procedure required prior to/for marketing foodstuffs bearing nutritional or health claims?

The "Regulation on Miracle Products" provides that the national authorities will issue the certificates or reports necessary for advertising, along with their alleged health effects, foodstuffs, dietetic or diet products and, in general, other products for human use or consumption if they are subject to specific technical and health regulations. Even though this specific provision has not been revoked following the enactment of Regulation 1924/2006 (its subject-matter is broader than foodstuffs), this procedure does not need to be followed when food products are advertised in accordance with Regulation 1924/2006.

Regulations against performance-enhancing products[51] provide that the Spanish authorities will establish a specific program aimed at strictly regulating the advertising of these products, including a new procedure for the declaration of food products brought into Spain that fall under its scope.

V. Enforcement of Food Law and Self-regulating Bodies

Misleading advertising claims made by food producers or traders that could cause serious harm to consumers may be punished as a criminal offence with up to six months' imprisonment or a fine of twelve to twenty-four

50 Draft Royal Decree approving the general rules on food information for food that is not pre-packaged for sale to the final consumer and collective consumers, food packaged at the point of sale following the request of the purchaser and food packaged by retailers.

51 Organic Law 3/2013 of 20 June 2013, on the protection of the health of sports players and the fight against performance enhancing drugs in sports. BOE 148, 21 June 2013.

months (i.e., an amount payable per day for a period of twelve to twenty-four months).[52] More serious offences concerning food regulations that put the health of consumers in danger may be punished with from one to four years' imprisonment or a fine of six to twelve months, as well as disqualification from carrying out professional activities in the foodstuffs sector for three to six years. The false use of origin labelling may be punished with six months to two years' imprisonment or a fine of twelve to twenty-four months.

Breaches of the Spanish Law on Food Safety and Nutrition (LFSN), including its provisions concerning food advertising, are food safety infractions that can be punished with fines ranging from EUR 5,000 to 600,000 depending on the existence or absence of a risk to public health. Together with the economic fine, other sanctions can be imposed, such as the closure of premises, the recall of products, the public disclosure of the sanctions and the names of those responsible. If criminal proceedings are initiated, the administrative proceedings will be suspended until the final decision of the criminal courts is rendered, although preventive measures may be adopted in the meantime.

ES

Most breaches of the restrictions on advertising provided by the General Law on Audiovisual Communication (LAC) are classed as serious administrative infringements that can lead to fines of up to EUR 500,000 if made on the TV or up to EUR 100,000 on other media. In July 2013 the Spanish Supreme Court upheld a fine of EUR 500,000 imposed on a private television channel for surreptitious advertising of several products, including product placement of alcoholic beverages.[53]

Breaches in consumer matters may be sanctioned with fines of up to EUR 600,000 or five times the value of the infringing products, whichever is higher. Very serious offences may also be sanctioned with the closure of premises for a maximum of five years.

52 The amount payable per day could range from EUR 30 to EUR 5,000 if the infringer is a legal person and from EUR 2 to EUR 400 if the infringer is a natural person.

53 Supreme Court judgment 6965/2010 of 30 July 2013.

The infringement proceedings may be initiated ex officio (generally as a result of an inspection) by the body responsible for the enforcement of these regulations (at a national or regional level) but also following a complaint filed by a consumer or a consumer association.

Autocontrol's Code of Conduct is applied by a "Jury" composed of prestigious scholars in the fields of law and advertising. The public National Consumption Institute appoints some of the Jury members. The Jury of Autocontrol also applies sectorial codes of conduct developed for certain food and beverage industries (such as wine[54], beer, spirits[55] or enteral feeding products[56]); specific target population groups (such as the abovementioned PAOS Code or the ANDI Code for the promotion of diet products for children[57]); or specific advertising support (such as the code of practice governing electronic advertising, named *Confianza Online*).

During its more than fifteen years of existence, the Jury of Autocontrol has created a voluminous body of decisions on the advertising of food. Recent decisions reveal several insights into its interpretation of Regulation 1924/2006, especially about the use of references to general, non-specific benefits of a nutrient or food for overall good health or health-related well-being [article 10(3)][58]; the use of health claims referring to slimming or

54 Self-Regulation Code for advertising and commercial communications for wine available at: <http://autocontrol.es/pdfs/pdfs_codigos/CODIGOFEV2012.pdf> (last accessed in October 2013).

55 Self-Regulation Advertising Code of the Spanish Association of Alcoholic Beverages (2012) available at: <http://autocontrol.es/pdfs/pdfs_codigos/cod_febe2013.pdf> (last accessed in October 2013). A decision enforcing one of these horizontal codes is the ruling of the Jury of Autocontrol of 12 September 2013 concerning a communication from Beefeater, which, despite showing an image of the product, was an editorial content about a course on preparing gin and tonics organized by the producer of this beverage.

56 Self-Regulation Advertising Code of the brewing industry (2009) available at: <http://autocontrol.es/pdfs/pdfs_codigos/CODCERVECEROS.pdf> (last accessed in October 2013).

57 Self-Regulation Code ANDI for the promotion of diet products for children (2012) available at: <http://autocontrol.es/pdfs/pdfs_codigos/codigoANDI.pdf> (last accessed in October 2013)

58 Among its recent decisions, rulings of 10 July and 12 September 2013 (appeal) in the case Asociación de Usuarios de la Comunicación (AUC) vs Grupo Conservas Garavilla, S.L. (*"Platos preparados abrir y listo Isabel"*) or ruling of 12 September 2013 (appeal), Font Vella, S.A. vs Grupo Leche Pascual, S.A.U. (*"Bezoya"*).

weight-control or a reduction in the sense of hunger or an increase in the sense of satiety or to the reduction of the energy available from a diet, as well as the use of related nutrition claims ("light" and "with no added sugar")[59]; or the joint interpretation of Regulation 1924/2006 with the Regulation of Miracle Products[60] or sectorial rules like those governing natural mineral water.[61]

The decisions of Autocontrol's Jury are only binding on its members. The main advertisers, agencies and media in Spain are members of Autocontrol, and it is estimated[62] that they represent approximately 70 % of advertising investment in the country. Consumer associations in Spain are active in reporting cases of non-compliance with the Advertising Code of Conduct. More than 75 % of the cases decided by Autocontrol's Jury in 2012 were initiated as a result of a complaint filed by a consumer or a consumer association.[63]

Autocontrol's Jury is also responsible for the enforcement of other sectorial self-regulation codes, such as the enforcement of the PAOS Code. Infringements of the PAOS Code by any of its members may result not only in Autocontrol's Jury ordering the withdrawal of the advertisement but also in the application of a penalty. Infringements of the PAOS Code are graded as minor, serious or very serious infringements. Among the criteria used by Autocontrol's Jury to grade an infringement are the following: the impact of the advertisement on consumers, the duration of the advertising campaign and the damage caused to the food industry as a result of the illegal advertising, or the existence of unfair competition practices. Moreover,

59 Among its recent decisions, ruling of 10 July 2013 in the case AUC vs Hida Alimentación, S.A. ("*Tomate Frito Light Hida*") and ruling of 12 September 2013 in the case AUC vs Hero España, S.A. ("*Mermeladas Light Hero*").

60 Among its recent decisions, ruling of 6 June 2013 in the case AUC vs. Mi Gimnasio Nutrición Deportiva S.L. ("Amino X").

61 Ruling of 12 September 2013 (appeal), Font Vella, S.A. vs Grupo Leche Pascual, S.A.U. ("*Bezoya*"); and ruling of 19 September 2013 (appeal), Grupo Leche Pascual vs Font Vella, S.A. ("*El agua ligera*").

62 Autocontrol, available at: www.autocontrol.es (last accessed in September 2013).

63 Autocontrol's 2012 Annual Report, available at: <http://autocontrol.es/pdfs/balance%20 12 %20AUTOCONTROL.pdf> (last accessed in September 2013).

Autocontrol's Jury may consider aggravating circumstances such as a failure to collaborate with the Jury or recidivism to impose more serious sanctions. Minor infringements may result in a penalty ranging from 6,000 to 30,000 Euros, serious infringements in a penalty ranging from 30,001 to 90,000 Euros, and very serious infringements in a penalty ranging from 90,001 to 180,000 Euros. The funds collected are allocated to a programme aimed at promoting healthy habits among children.

Similarly, infringements of the ANDI Code for the promotion of diet products for children by its members may result in a penalty ranging from 1,000 to 54,000 Euros for minor infringements, 54,001 to 108,000 Euros for serious infringements, and 108,001 to 216,000 Euros for very serious infringements.

Lastly, it should be borne in mind that precautionary measures are common in unfair competition proceedings in Spain. These measures are generally sought when a final decision on the merits could be rendered too late to guarantee its effectiveness. In exceptional cases, preliminary measures can be requested *inaudita altera parte.* This is particularly the case when, given the circumstances of the specific case, an extremely urgent resolution is required in order to guarantee the effectiveness of the court decision.[64] In any other cases, the respondent may challenge the requested measures within the course of a speedy procedure. Preliminary measures generally require that the claimant submit a guarantee that would cover any damage caused to the respondent as a consequence of carrying out the interim measure, should the claim be dismissed on the merits. Notwithstanding this, as previously highlighted, many misleading advertising cases in the foodstuffs industry are brought before Autocontrol.

64 Given that advertising campaigns may be up in the air for a short period of time, case law tends to recognize that these cases generally require a speedy resolution under *inaudita altera parte* proceedings (e.g., judgment of the Commercial Court of Madrid dated 7 October 2004, *Hola, S.A. vs. Gala Ediciones, S.L. et al.*).

CHAPTER 16
Sweden

Magnus Friberg and Lovisa Nelson

I. Possible Bans on Food Advertising

1. Is there any general national legislation or code of conduct regulating the promotion of food stuffs?

SE

In Sweden the Marketing Practices Act[1], which implements Directive 2005/29/EC concerning unfair business practices[2] is applicable to all marketing regardless of product, media used, target group (consumers or businesses), etc. Marketing in violation of other legislation such as product specific legislation like the Food Act, is also considered to be in violation of the Marketing Practices Act. Thus, for instance, a health claim that violates Regulation 1924/2006 concerning nutrition claims and health claims[3] for food is also in violation of the Marketing Practices Act either as contrary to good marketing practice[4] or misleading advertising[5] or both. It does not matter if the claim is made in advertising, TV-commercials, etc. or on the pack itself.

With regards to general codes of conduct there is the ICC Code of advertising and marketing communication practice as well as the ICC's Framework for Responsible Food and Beverage Marketing Communications,[6] which is

1 Marknadsföringslagen (Marketing Practices Act) SFS 2008:486.

2 Directive 2005/29/EC of the European Parliament and the Council of 11 May 2005 concerning unfair business-to-consumer commercial practices in the internal market.

3 Regulation (EC) No 1924/2006 of the European parliament and of the Council of 20 December 2006 on nutrition and health claims made on foods.

4 Marketing Practices Act, Section 5.

5 Marketing Practices Act, Section 10.

6 ICC Framework for Responsible Food and Beverage Marketing Communications.

applied primarily by the marketing industry's self-regulatory body, RO – Reklamombudsmannen or "the Swedish Advertising Ombudsman".

2. Is there any specific national restriction or prohibition (mandatory legislation and code of conduct)?

Aside from the legislation mentioned in 1.1 there is product specific legislation placing restrictions on the advertising of such products. This concerns, for instance, alcoholic beverages and medical products that affect the use of health claims for food and food supplements.

There are also restrictions with regard to advertising directed at children in certain age groups (e.g., TV commercials directed at children under the age of 12 and direct marketing, including the use of electronic media to children under the age of 16).

The food stuff legislation also contains restrictions concerning the use of certain protected product names (e.g., juice, milk, butter, etc.) that are, for the most part, based on EU legislation.

Apart from the ICC code mentioned above the self-care industry has adopted a self-regulatory regime with regard to food supplements.[7] The Swedish Food Federation has also adopted a self-regulatory regime concerning the use of nutrition and health claims entirely based on Regulation 1924/2006 concerning nutrition and health claims.

3. Is the promotion of certain foodstuffs restricted or prohibited by any national mandatory and/or soft laws (e.g., code of practice, or case law)?

Most foodstuffs that are permitted within the EU can be promoted freely. There are no restrictions other than the Marketing Practices Act (which implements EU Directive 2005/29/EU on unfair business practices).

7 http://www.svenskegenvard.se/index.php/information-in-english.

For some foodstuffs, for instance energy drinks, there are recommendations from the National Food Agency.

There are also restrictions with regard to certain substances, in particular substances derived from plants and herbs and or parts of plants and herbs.

a. Alcoholic beverages

The marketing of alcoholic beverages has been restricted in Sweden since the 1970s, and legislation concerns the marketing and advertising of alcoholic beverages to consumers. In essence, the marketing of spirits, wine and strong beer (3,5 % alcohol by volume) was restricted to restaurants and points of sale. Advertising in print consumer media was not permitted. Certain limited advertising in other consumer media was permitted for beer with an alcohol content of up to 3,5 % alcohol by volume but not more. Light beer and beverages with an alcohol content below 2.25 % alcohol by volume fell outside the scope of the restrictions.

SE

As a result of a landmark case[8] in 2006 the legislation became more permissive. The Swedish courts reached the conclusion that the Swedish prohibition against all other forms of consumer advertising except the above-mentioned advertising in restaurants and points of sale constituted a restriction on trade (Article 28) which could not be justified according to Article 30. As a result, print advertising for alcoholic beverages with an alcohol content not exceeding 15 % by volume was permitted. Marketing for wines and spirits above 15 % alcohol by volume remains restricted with the exception of marketing in restaurants and points of sale, e.g. the Swedish retail monopoly, *Systembolaget* and on Internet webpages.

The Alcohol Act[9] stipulates the following requirements and restrictions in relation to advertising of alcoholic beverages. All advertising must be moderate. It must not be intrusive, proactive or encourage the use of alcohol. This applies to all marketing of alcoholic beverages. Marketing of alcoholic

8 Market Court's decision 2003:5 Consumerombudsman v. Gourmet International Products Aktiebolag (GIP).

9 Alcohol Act (SFS 2010:1622).

beverages must not be directed to consumers under the age of 25 or show persons under that age. Television advertising is not allowed.

In marketing directed to consumers the pictorial may only consist of a representation of the product, produce or ingredient used in the product as well as only single or individual packages displaying the trademark, brand or equivalent mark. This is applicable to all advertising regardless of medium. It is not permissible to show people, scenery, dinner situations, food or other images other than that stipulated.

Texts about the product should be factual, balanced and avoid playing on emotions or moods. The text should focus on providing information about the product (e.g., origin, ingredients, properties and uses). Value statements and certificates should be used with caution and in accordance with the Marketing Act requirements for trustworthiness. Data from reviewers should be meaningful, balanced, relevant and not misleading. It should be noted that even quoted information taken out of context can be considered to encourage the use of alcohol and must not be misleading. It is worth noting that the advertiser is fully responsible for the veracity of the claims made in testimonials, newspaper articles, etc. that are used in the marketing. This is not part of the Alcohol Act but stipulated in the Consumer Agency's guideline to the Act[10] as well as the industry's recommendations concerning advertising.[11]

Print advertising in magazines and newspapers must not exceed 2100 mm and must also include information text concerning the health consequences of consuming alcohol, for instance: "Alcohol can damage your health"; "Alcohol is addictive"; "Alcohol can cause nerve and brain damage"; and "Alcohol can damage the liver and pancreas". This text must constitute 20 % of the entire advertisement.

10 KOVFS 2009:6 http://www.konsumentverket.se/Global/Konsumentverket.se/Best%C3 %A4lla%20och%20ladda%20ner/kovfs/2009/KOVFS_2009_6_marknadsf%C3 %B6ring_alkohol.pdf.

11 http://media.alkoholgranskningsmannen.se/2011/08/Rekommendationerna.pdf.

b. Marketing of beverages with an alcohol content higher than 15 %[12]

It should be noted that print advertising for alcoholic beverages with an alcohol content higher than 15 % is allowed in magazines distributed via restaurants or points of sale, and it is also allowed on the Internet. While television advertising is not allowed at all, this only concerns advertising via broadcasters established in Sweden. Broadcasting networks from other EU Member States whose broadcasts are directed specifically at a Swedish audience follow the advertising regulation of the country in which they are established. The same can be said for Internet webpages published by companies established in other Member States. Neither of these has to follow the Swedish Alcohol Act.

c. Snuff and chewing tobacco

Tobacco and tobacco products fall outside the scope of the EU definition of foodstuffs. However, Swedish national law regulates snuff and chewing tobacco as foodstuffs, and the supervision of these products falls under the National Food Agency.

The Tobacco Act[13] regulates the advertising of tobacco products, and the Consumer Agency has adopted guidelines for the interpretation of the marketing[14] rules in the Tobacco Act.

In principle, all forms of advertising are prohibited with the exception of advertising in points of sale. Such marketing should, if possible, be placed so that it cannot be seen from the outside or in the direct vicinity of the display of the products.

All advertising must be moderate. It must not be intrusive, proactive or encourage the use of tobacco. Inviting or persuasive advertising is not permitted. Text should contain only factual information about the product's nature

12 Alcohol Act (SFS 2010:1622), Chapter 7, Section 4.

13 Tobacco Act (SFS 1993:581).

14 KOVFS 2009:7.

and characteristics. Images should only show single packs. The packaging should be closed, and the background should be neutral.

d. Certain substances

The presence of certain substances in particular in food supplements may result in a classification of the product as a medicinal product. Such substances are glucosamine, melatonin and sildenafil. The same goes for ephedrine.

Certain substances derived from plants or herbs are considered unsuitable as ingredients in foodstuffs. Examples are ephedrine (which is classified as a pharmaceutical), synephrine, certain green-tea extracts and *Echinacea purpurea* (L.).

The National Food Agency has issued a list of substances derived from plants. The assessment of products containing these substances is made on a case-by-case basis and may result in a sales ban on the product. The Swedish National Food Agency and the Medical Products Agency monitor the market on a continuous basis.[15], [16]

e. Caffeine

Caffeine is not prohibited as an ingredient in products in Sweden. There are recommendations as to the daily intake of caffeine and cautions concerning certain products, such as energy drinks, for which there are also labeling requirements, but there are no set limits with regard to content. However, companies manufacturing, marketing or selling products containing caffeine are obviously responsible for the product being safe.

15 http://www.slv.se/upload/dokument/risker/naturliga/vaxter/volm.pdf.

16 http://www.lakemedelsverket.se/overgripande/Lagar–regler/Vagledningar/Vilken-lagstiftning-galler-for-min-produkt/Lakemedelsklassificering/.

4. Is the promotion of (certain) foodstuffs towards a *specific segment of the population* restricted or prohibited by any national mandatory and/or soft laws?

Promotion of foodstuffs towards children

The Marketing Practice Act of Sweden states that marketing practices must be consistent with generally accepted marketing practices. Marketing practices which contravene generally accepted marketing practices will be deemed unfair if they noticeably affect or are likely to affect the recipient's ability to make a well-founded commercial decision.[17] The preparatory work, case law and other legal sources define what is and is not acceptable marketing practice.

In the Marketing Practice Act there is no specific section regarding the promotion of foodstuffs to children, but the preparatory work to the Marketing Practice Act states that children should be protected from strong commercial exploitation.[18] The preparatory work also refers to the Consolidated ICC Code of Advertising and Marketing Communication Practice for guidance on what are generally accepted marketing practices,[19] and notes that the ICC, for example, states that children and young people should not be portrayed in unsafe situations or engaging in actions harmful to themselves or others, or be encouraged to engage in potentially hazardous activities or behavior.[20] Therefore, it is clear that these activities would not be accepted marketing practice in Sweden.

SE

The Radio and TV Act[21] contains regulations regarding advertisements to children under twelve years of age. For example, a TV commercial may not aim to capture the attention of children and a commercial may not be broadcasted on TV before, during or after a television broadcast that mainly

17 Sections 5 and 6 of the Marketing Practice Act (2008: 486).

18 Prop. 2007/08:115 p. 133.

19 Prop. 2007/08:115 p. 71.

20 Article 18 of the Consolidated ICC Code of Advertising and Marketing Communication Practice.

21 The Radio and TV Act (SFS 2010:696).

addresses children.[22] Product planning is also not allowed if the program mainly addresses children.[23] Furthermore, a person or character that has a prominent role in a program that mainly addresses children may not be in a commercial if broadcasted on TV.[24] Advertisements that contravene the Radio and TV Act are deemed unfair under the Marketing Practice Act.

It has been controversial whether or not the Radio and TV Act has been far-reaching in regards to the regulations on advertisement to children compared to Directive 2005/29/EC concerning unfair business-to-consumer commercial practices. Therefore, this needed to be investigated, and the Swedish Government found and stated in the preparatory work of the Marketing Practice Act that the regulation does not contravene the Directive.[25]

The Alcohol Act states that the marketing of alcohol may not be directed or presented to persons under 25 years of age.[26] It is also prohibited to address children and young people in the promotion of tobacco in accordance with the preparatory work of the Tobacco Act.[27]

According to Swedish case law, direct mail advertising in any type of medium is not allowed towards persons under 16 years of age.[28]

The Swedish self-regulating body, the Market Ethical Council[29], now replaced by the Swedish Advertising Ombudsman (Sw. *Reklamombudsmannen*), supervised the compliance of all marketing in Sweden with the ICC's rules. They stated that if the marketing affects a lot of children, even if it is meant for adults, it must comply with the rules of advertising to children.[30]

22 Chapter 8, Sections 3 and 7 of the Radio and TV Act (2010:696).

23 Chapter 6, Section 2 of the Radio and TV Act (2010:696).

24 Chapter 8, Section 8 of the Radio and TV Act (2010:696).

25 Prop. 2007/08:115 p 133 f.

26 Chapter 7, Section1 of the Alcohol Act (2010:1622).

27 Prop. 2004/05.118 p. 38.

28 MD 2012:14.

29 Sw. *MarknadsEtiska Rådet.*

30 MarknadsEtiska Rådet 16/2005 – Dnr 29/2004.

II. Misleading Advertising

1. What are the national rules on misleading advertising with respect to foodstuffs?

Sweden has a National Food Administration[31] that implements EC directives into its regulations and publishes them in the National Food Administration's Code of Statues (LIVSFS). Article 2 (1) of Directive 2000/13 on labeling, presentation and advertising of foodstuffs is implemented into Swedish law in paragraph 5 of the LIVSFS 2004:27.

The general rule is that labeling must not be misleading. Labeling must be clear and concise and explain what a claim means. It is not sufficient that a claim is factually correct and substantiated. It must be presented in such a way that the consumers' impression and interpretation is not skewed, for instance by exaggerations, graphic depictions, claims in large print and explanations or attempts to explain in small print, etc. A food product must not be attributed properties it does not have. The advertiser always has to be prepared to substantiate the claims made. Nor is it permissible to claim a property that is common for all, or most, products on the market and in doing so give the consumer the impression that the product is unique in this regard.

In determining whether or not a claim is misleading, an overall assessment is to be made taking into consideration not only what is claimed on the pack, but also in other in-store media, such as the shelves.

It is permissible to include advertising claims, pictures, etc. that go beyond the obligatory information, provided these elements are not misleading. Examples of this are illustrations, pictures, décor and the like which might mislead the consumer as to the content of the product. For instance, pictures of fruit on products which do not contain the fruit in question or where the picture misleads as to the amount of fruit included in the products. Another example is pictures or claims misleading the consumer about the level of preparation.

SE

31 Sw. *Livsmedelsverket.*

In Sweden, the Marketing Practice Act ("MPA") also regulates misleading advertising. It implements Directive 2005/29/EC on unfair business practices. *Lex specialis* for food advertising is, of course, the Food Act and the specific regulations for labeling, nutrition and health claims etc. as well as the prohibitions in those regulations against misleading labeling and advertising. Advertising in violation of these regulations is also considered to be in violation of the MPA. The principle is that advertising or marketing in violation of other laws and regulations also violates the MPA.

However, the MPA is broader in its scope. The MPA is applicable regardless of product, medium or intended target group. The MPA is intended to protect both consumers and businesses and is thus applicable to both business-to-consumer advertising as well as business-to-business advertising. It also regulates practices which are not directly covered by the food legislation but which might still occur in food advertising, such as misleading packaging size, passing-off – that is where a company imitates, for instance, a product or its package design in a misleading way comparative advertising, price claims and comparisons, denigration or ridiculing of competitors and/or their products also where the denigration is not misleading.

The assessment of a marketing measure according to the MPA could also differ from the assessment made according to the food legislation. One reason is that different courts handle cases according to the MPA and the food legislation. Another reason is that the MPA requires not only an assessment of whether or not the advertising is misleading but also if the advertisement is likely to materially distort the economic behavior of the average consumer.

Having said this, what is misleading food advertising under the food legislation is also, in general, misleading under the MPA.

The possibility of applying the MPA to cases like this gives the operator another prosecutorial avenue in relation to a competitor's misleading advertising measures with different sanctions, including interim sanctions and also with the possibility of demanding compensation for damages.

2. What are the national landmark cases regarding misleading advertising for foodstuffs?

a. Cases from the Administrative Courts pursuant to the food legislation

Findus v. the National Food Agency[32]

Findus made the following claims on packaging: Without unnecessary additives, without preservatives, without trans-fatty acids, only natural colors, without flavor enhancers. The National Food Agency rendered a decision in which it ordered Findus to cease and desist from using these claims on the pack "as soon as possible" (in Swedish "*snarast*"). It also issued an injunction against Findus prohibiting it from placing products on the market that include these claims with a transitional period of six months after the decision. Findus appealed the decision, asking the Administrative Court in Uppsala Court to overturn the decision in its entirety.

SE

The Court found that the claim "without unnecessary additives" was misleading because the label did not state which relevant additives the product did not contain or why the additives were considered unnecessary. Therefore, the claim could substantially mislead the consumer about the product and its properties.

The Court considered the claim, "Without preservatives", misleading for the following reasons. The products in question were frozen products. Since freezing is a form of preservation, practically no such products on the market contained preservatives. The claim was therefore irrelevant and gave the consumer the impression that the products had properties that others did not.

The claim "Without trans-fatty acids" similarly gave the consumer the impression that trans-fatty acids were common in the product category concerned. The claim was considered to violate Regulation 1924/2006/EC

32 Administrative Court in Uppsala case no 3453-10 and 3454-10 Findus Sverige AB v. The National Food Agency.

because claims of trans-fatty acids do not appear in the appendix of permissible nutrition claims.

The claim "Only natural colors" had not been used in the labeling or presentation of the products. It only appeared in a general description of Findus' ambitions. The labeling regulations were not applicable, and the Court overturned the decision concerning this claim.

The Court considered the claim "Without flavor enhancer" to be relevant information whereas Findus had changed its recipe for its product Indian Tikka Masala. In such cases, it can be justified to make such a claim during a limited period following the change. The Court granted Findus a transitional period of six months following the Court's decision.

b. Cases from the Market Court pursuant to the Marketing Practices Act

Sveriges Spannmålsodlare (SpmO) AB v. Kooperativa Förbundet (KF), ekonomisk förening – misleading denigration

The so-called Änglamark-case[33] concerned environmental claims for a range of products sold under the trademark Änglamark, a name which first appeared in the lyrics of a song and in Sweden is strongly associated with preservation of nature and the environment. A TV commercial for the products showed a restaurant scene with a couple that had just been served their food. A man with a pesticide sprayer on his back approaches the table and starts spraying the food on the plates. When asked by the customer what he is spraying on their food, he simply answers "poison" and that there is no scientific research showing that it is dangerous: "Everybody else is eating it". The commercial ended with "Änglamark – guaranteed unsprayed". The Court found the commercial to be misleading. First of all, it suggested that ecologically produced products were not sprayed with pesticides, which is not correct. They are not sprayed with chemicals. Secondly, the commercial gave the impression that other food contained poison. Even if it had been

33 Market Court's decision 2002:8 *Sveriges Spannmålsodlare (SpmO) AB v. Kooperativa Förbundet (KF), ekonomisk förening.*

shown that some food products contained residues from pesticides the claim was too categorical and oversimplified. Also, the commercial discredited food producers who used pesticides in their production.

Svensk Mjölk v. Valio – misleading denomination[34]

Marketing of margarine with the claim "Soft butter using canola oil" was found to be in violation of the food legislation (Regulation (EC) 1234/2007). Butter is a protected denomination and cannot be used for a product consisting of 67 % milk fat and 33 % canola oil.[35]

Danske Slagterier, SA Bruxelles v. Scan Foods AB – misleading claim[36]

The leading Swedish meat producer made the following claims: "Choose imported pork so you can get medicine in the bargain. That we cannot offer, because our meat is free of antibiotics" and "Christmas ham from the best pork in the world". The first claim was considered misleading because the advertiser could not prove that foreign produced meat contained antibiotics while meat produced in Sweden did not. The second claim was also considered misleading as a general and unconditional quality assertion which should be understood as a claim that the pork produced by the advertiser is truly superior to all other pork. The Court questioned if such a claim could ever be substantiated.

SF

Bayer AB v. Bringwell Sverige AB and Bringwell AB – misleading advertising violation of good marketing practice[37]

This is the first case applying Regulation 1924/2006 on nutritional claims and health claims for food – this case concerned marketing of food supplements. Bringwell marketed a food supplement called Mivitotal. Bayer

34 Market Court's decision 2010:15 *Svensk Mjölk AB v. Valio Sverige AB.*

35 Market Court's decision 2010:15 *Svensk Mjölk AB ./. Valio Sverige AB.*

36 Market Court's decision 2005:8 *Danske Slagterier, SA Bruxelles v. Scan Foods AB.*

37 Market Court's decision 2013:13 *Bayer AB v. Bringwell Sverige AB and Bringwell AB.*

brought the case before the Market Court, and the Market Court rendered a prohibitive injunction against no less than 74 claims used by Bringwell. The defendant was also subject to a fine for each of the claims for the product in question in the amount of SEK 1,000,000 in the event of non-compliance with the injunction. The case is an exercise in the Regulation's articles on nutritional claims and health claims as well as in the application of the Medical Products Act on claims made for food products. Bayer's suit concerned general health claims, specific health claims and medical claims. All of the claims that were prohibited were also considered misleading according to the Marketing Practices Act. Below follows a few examples of the claims that were prohibited.

The following are examples of general nutrition claims that were also held to be misleading: "contains more than 100 vitamins and minerals" and "contains more than 100 minerals, vitamins and nutrients". Bringwell could not substantiate these claims which were therefore deemed misleading.

Examples of Article 10.3 claims which were prohibited include the following: "stamina and energy of the body can be extended," "muscle fatigue prevention, oxygen uptake increases, energy metabolism maintaining and increasing stress tolerance," ""It is vital that you get in a wide spectrum of vitamins and minerals", and "A lack of a single vitamin or mineral can be harmful to the whole body and also often to other substance uptake is impaired".

The following are examples of medicinal claims which were prohibited: "A lack of among other things calcium can result in osteoporosis," "People today are exposed to much more information than ever before in history with the result that we have significantly increased levels of free radicals in the body that can be a contributing factor to the emergence of a wide range of diseases", and "Vitamins can serve as medicines but are not classified as drugs."

The case is yet an example of where a company sues a competitor using the Marketing Practices Act with reference to the food legislation and the Medical Products Act. In such cases the defendant company not only has to pay the claimant's costs, but it will also be issued an injunction which, if violated, will result in an order to pay a fine of SEK 1,000,000. Furthermore, it is possible for the claimant to ask for damages since the claims have been found misleading (see below section 5.1).

Institut National des Appelations d´Origine (INAO) et al. v. Arla Foods AB – misleading geographical origin[38]

In 1999, Arla Foods launched two yogurt products called Yoggi Champagne and Yoggi Original Champagne. The marketing for these products also made reference to Champagne. A press release contained the following text: "Champagne producers have busy days. Millennium approaches and hysteria increases. What to do? Go to a party, stay home, pretend like it's raining? While the darkness of winter settles over Sweden. What is needed is something that cheers you up. Something that adds flavor to life – Yoggi Champagne." In other advertisements, the products were presented as yogurt with a champagne flavor. The advertising made reference to champagne with pictures of bubbles, people at parties with glasses of Champagne, etc.

The Market Court found that Arla exploited the goodwill of Champagne in violation of the Marketing Practices Act. The Court also considered the design and color scheme of yogurt packaging and posters where glasses of champagne and champagne bottles were replaced with Arla yogurt packaging. In light of the foregoing this was, in the Market Court's view, a clear case of a conscious passing off.

SE

The Court also found the marketing to be misleading. First, it found that the use of the claim "champagne taste" in connection with the appearance of the packaging was likely to give consumers the impression that the yogurt had been flavored with Champagne or tasted like Champagne. The list of ingredients on the pack was considered insufficient to neutralize this impression. As for the taste of Champagne it was apparent from the evidence that the ingredients could not give this flavor. Arla was not able to show that the yogurt actually tasted of Champagne. Thus, Arla had misled consumers.

However, the Court did not find the claim "champagne flavor" to mislead the consumer concerning the product's commercial or geographical origin. The reason the Court gave was that yogurt and Champagne are totally separate products.

38 Market Court's decision 2002:20 Institut National des Appelations d´Origine (INAO) et al. v. Arla Foods AB

III. Mandatory Labelling: Name the Product

Are there any national definitions for the following products?

a. Energy drinks and sport drinks

There are no specific Swedish definitions of energy drinks and sport drinks. However, the use of the terms must comply with (EC) No 1924/2006 on nutrition and health claims made on foods.

b. Yogurt

The Swedish Food Regulator's regulations regarding milk and cheese[39] state that yogurt must consist of active bacterial culture.[40] There is no additional definition of yogurt in the Swedish national legislation.

c. Cheese

The definition of cheese is regulated in the Swedish Food Regulator's regulations regarding milk and cheese (Sw. *Livsmedelsverkets föreskrifter om mjölk och ost* (LIVSFS 2003:39)). The regulation states that cheese must be a product of milk or milk product and the relation of whey protein and casein may not exceed the corresponding relation in milk. In addition, cheese must be produced by coagulation in whole or in part of the protein in milk or a milk product by means of rennet or other coagulating substance and in part separated from the whey produced. It can also be produced by another process of manufacture that includes coagulation of the protein in milk or milk product, and which supplies an end product with physical, chemical and organoleptic characteristics resembling the characteristics of a product created using the coagulation process mentioned.[41] The regulation does not

39 Sw. *Livsmedelsverkets föreskrifter om mjölk och ost* (LIVSFS 2003:39).

40 Section 6 of LIVSFS 2003:39.

41 Section 8 of LIVSFS 2003:39.

apply to products produced or sold in other EU countries or countries that are members of the EEA.

d. Other relevant definition not defined under EU law: Cider

Sweden has, in the Swedish Food Regulator's regulations regarding Cider[42], a definition of Cider that only applies to products that are sold in Sweden. Cider must be made of fermented fruit juice from apple or pear. Cider may be made of permitted food additives and natural and natural identical aromas as well as non-fermented fruit juice of apple and/or pear, water and sugar. The product must contain at least 15 % volume fruit juice. The cider may be carbonated.[43] The regulation does not apply to products produced in other EU countries, countries that are members of the EEA or Turkey. That means that if, for example, France has another definition of Cider, their Cider products may be distributed in Sweden if they are produced in France.

SE

IV. Voluntary Labelling

1. "Clean labels" – Are there any national definitions or requirements for the use of claims such as 'natural', 'pure', 'home-made', 'additive-free'?

a. "Natural"

In Sweden, a foodstuff may be defined as natural or as a natural product if it subsists in its existing condition in nature or has undergone only minimal treatment, according to the guidance of the Swedish Food Regulator's regulation of marking and presentation of foodstuffs. A compound foodstuff can

42 Sw. *Livsmedelsverkets föreskrifter om cider* (LIVSFS 2005:11).

43 Sections 1 and 2 of LIVSFS 2005:11.

never be a natural product. To be allowed to use the expression "consists of natural ingredients" all ingredients in the product must be natural.[44]

b. "Pure"

In accordance with the guidance, the use of the expression "pure" is regarded as misleading if it is used on a product that has a protected term. For example, you may not promote honey as pure honey because honey is not to be promoted as honey if it is not pure.[45]

c. "Home-made"/"grandmother recipe"

There is no regulation in Sweden regarding the expressions "home-made" and "grandmother recipe". Nevertheless, there has been public opinion stating that it may be misleading to say that something is made from grandmother's original recipe if it contains additives. However, this issue has not yet been litigated before a court.

d. Other similar claims related to "clean labels" (e.g. "additive-free")

i. Fresh produce

Expressions such as "fresh" generally have no clear meaning and should be used restrictively. The term should be explained, specifying in what sense the product is fresh also vis-à-vis the current date. There are foods where fresh is part of the name, such as new potatoes which can be translated as "fresh potatoes" ("färskpotatis") or cottage cheese – which can be translated as "fresh

44 The guidance of the Swedish Food Regulator's regulation of marking and presentation of foodstuffs (*sw.* Vägledning till Livsmedelsverkets föreskrifter (LIVSFS 2004:27) om märkning och presentation av livsmedel), p. 22.

45 The guidance of the Swedish Food Regulator's regulation of marking and presentation of foodstuffs (*sw.* Vägledning till Livsmedelsverkets föreskrifter (LIVSFS 2004:27) om märkning och presentation av livsmedel), p. 22.

cheese" ("färskost"). This is generally accepted provided it is not misleading. The expression "fresh produce" should thus be used restrictively according to the guidance. It should only be used if the producer can justify why the label is used. Regarding fresh meat, fish or shellfish it may only have been conserved by refrigeration or deep-freezing, including vacuum-packed or packed in a controlled atmosphere. For ready-cooked meals the expression may be used if the food has not been frozen or preserved.[46]

2. Nutrition & health claims

a. Substances that are prohibited or considered as a medicinal substance

The Marketing Practice Act has issued a substance guide in which companies can check the substances in its products and determine if the product contains a substance that may lead to classification as a medicinal product. Examples of substances that have medical use and are present as active substances in pharmaceuticals are glucosamine, melatonin and sildenafil. These are not permitted in food supplements.[47]

SE

b. Recommendations or endorsements by national associations et al. according to Article 11.

There are no such laws or regulations in Sweden permitting food business operators to make reference to recommendations or endorsements by national associations, medical, nutrition or dietetic professionals or health related charities.

46 The guidance of the Swedish Food Regulator's regulation of marking and presentation of foodstuffs (*sw.* Vägledning till Livsmedelsverkets föreskrifter (LIVSFS 2004:27) om märkning och presentation av livsmedel), p. 22f.

47 http://www.lakemedelsverket.se/upload/allmanhet/Olagliga%20l%c3 %a4kemedel/Amnesguiden2013_05.pdf.

c. National laws or regulations regulating the use of nutrition or health claims on non-prepackaged food

With regard to non-prepackaged food Sweden applies article 1.2 of the Regulation[48] in that it is not required to have a nutritional chart. However, there is legislation by which warnings must be given for certain substances, for instance products containing glycyrrhizin acid (liquorice). The warning should be given on the pack or in relation to non-prepacked foods using a warning sign adjacent to the product.[49]

d. Notification procedures required prior to/for marketing foodstuffs bearing nutritional or health claims

There are no notification procedures prior to the marketing of foodstuffs with nutritional or health claims. The same goes for food supplements and enriched or fortified food. Obviously the companies must register their businesses with the Swedish National Food Agency or the food authority in the municipality in which the business premises is located. Also, it should be noted that the Swedish customs may impound products which, for instance, contain substances not permitted in food or food supplements. However, there is no requirement for prior notification or authorization for the products *per se*.

V. Enforcement of Food Law and Self Regulating Bodies

1. Which actions may one risk in case of non-compliance with the labelling or advertising requirements?

It should be noted that the administration of misleading food marketing in Sweden is divided between two government agencies based on the medium used. The National Food Agency is the central administrative authority in

48 Regulation1924/2006 on nutritional claims and health claims for food.

49 LIVSFS 2002:47.

matters concerning food. The Agency is an autonomous government agency reporting to the Ministry of Rural Affairs, Food and Fisheries, which is the central administrative authority for matters concerning food. Sweden is divided into counties (21) and municipalities (290). Food control at the local level is the responsibility of the relevant municipal committee(s), usually the Environment and Health Protection Committee. The County Administrations are responsible for food control at farms and for co-ordinating food control within each county.

These authorities (primarily the municipal committees) handle food control including misleading labeling and in-store marketing measures in direct vicinity of the products.

Other advertising measures, magazine advertisements, TV, outdoor, Internet, etc. are administered by the Swedish Consumer Agency.

According to the national Food Agency's guideline with regard to sanctions, the chosen sanction should be proportionate. The negative consequences that the decision might have must not outweigh the public interest. The Agency should also refrain from issuing more severe sanctions than is necessary to achieve the intended result.

In relation to misleading labeling and marketing, which fall under the jurisdiction of the Food Agency and the municipal committees, the sanction chosen depends on the nature of the transgression. If the misleading labeling endangers the public, the authorities can require a recall. In less severe cases it can demand correction in the form of an order subject to a fine, i.e. if the company does not comply with the order, payment of the fine can be imposed in varying amounts. The fine is supposed to function as a deterrent, and the amount in each individual case is set accordingly, taking into consideration the nature of the transgression, the size of the company, number of repeated offences, etc. In these cases, the authorities may also allow a transitional period of three to six months. In certain severe cases, or where the company has persisted or repeated the transgression, a company may also be prosecuted and sentenced to pay a fine. These cases are very rare.

According to the Marketing Practice Act a trader whose marketing practices are unfair may be enjoined from continuing the practice or from adopting any other similar practice.[50] The order or injunction is under penalty of a fine, which can be quite substantial and is intended to serve as a deterrent. In cases of minor importance, the Consumer Ombudsman may issue these orders also under penalty of a fine. When the trader accepts the order it applies as if it was the final judgment of the court.[51] Should the company violate the order or injunction and repeat the practice, or launch a similar practice, a court of law can order the company to pay the fine. The normal practice is that the company is ordered to pay the fine in its entirety although it can be reduced if the company can show mitigating circumstances. However, these cases are exceptions to the rule.

If a trader, in the course of marketing, fails to provide material information to the general public, he can be ordered to provide such information.[52] A party who intentionally or negligently violates an order shall compensate the consumer or trader for any damage suffered thereby.[53]

When a TV commercial aims to gain the attention of children under twelve years of age or a character that has a prominent role in a program that mainly addresses children are in a commercial broadcasted on TV, a trader may be ordered to pay a special fine (fine for disruptive marketing practices).[54] It is the Consumer Ombudsman that supervises and enforces these rules.[55] It is very seldom that a fine for disruptive marketing practices is imposed. A special fine may be imposed if product placement is made in programs that mainly address children or if a TV commercial aims to gain the attention of children or a commercial is broadcasted on TV before, during or after a television broadcast that mainly addresses children.[56] Both fines are fixed at not less than SEK 5,000 and not more than SEK 5 million, and it may

50 Section 23 of the Marketing Practice Act (2008: 486).

51 Section 28 of the Marketing Practice Act (2008: 486).

52 Section 24 of the Marketing Practice Act (2008: 486).

53 Section 37 of the Marketing Practice Act (2008: 486).

54 Section 29 of the Marketing Practice Act (2008: 486).

55 Chapter 16, Section 4 of the Radio and TV Act (2010:696).

56 Chapter 17, Section 5 of the Radio and TV Act (2010:696).

not exceed 10 percent of the trader's annual turnover. [57] The Stockholm District Court is the tribunal of first instance if the Consumer Ombudsman does not handle the case. The Swedish Market Court is the court of appeal and has the ultimate authority.

Proceedings for an injunction or order shall be brought in the Market Court and are subject to a fine of approximately one million SEK. However, proceedings for an injunction or order shall be brought in the Stockholm District Court where the same plaintiff, or another plaintiff in consultation with such plaintiff, concurrently commences proceedings for the imposition of a fine for disruptive marketing practices or for damages on the basis of the marketing practice.[58]

As mentioned above, all advertising must be moderate. It must not be intrusive, proactive or encourage the use of alcohol. This applies to all marketing of alcoholic beverages. Marketing of alcoholic beverages must not be directed to consumers under the age of 25 or showing persons under that age. A breach hereof shall be deemed unfair in accordance with section 6 of the MPA. This results in the mandatory use of the above-mentioned actions of the MPA when this section of the Alcohol Act is not complied with.

Proceedings in respect of an order or injunction may be commenced by the Consumer Ombudsman, the trader affected by the marketing practices or an organization of consumers, traders or employees.[59] A consumer may report a trader for unfair marketing practices to the Consumer Ombudsman who can handle the complaint in court.

It should be noted that anyone, traders or other companies including advertising agencies and media as well as employees, CEOs, marketing directors, board members, etc. who have contributed to the marketing activity are liable according to the Marketing Practices Act.

57 Section 31 of the Marketing Practice Act (2008: 486) and Chapter 17, Section 6 of the Radio and TV Act (2010:696).

58 Section 47 of the Marketing Practice Act (2008: 486).

59 Section 47 of the Marketing Practice Act (2008: 486).

2. Are there any national self-regulating bodies with respect to advertising for foodstuffs?

As mentioned above, the Consolidated ICC Code of Advertising and Marketing Communication Practice is of importance for guidance as to what are generally accepted marketing practices.

Prior to 2009, the Market Ethical Council supervised the compliance of all marketing in Sweden with the ICC's rules. Their statements serve as guidance of what is consistent with generally accepted marketing practices. After 2009, this is the responsibility of the Swedish Advertising Ombudsman[60]. The Advertising Ombudsman examines whether advertisements follow the rules of the ICC. The decision cannot impose any penalties or fines, but most traders remove advertisements that the Ombudsman finds inconsistent with the ICC rules.

The Swedish Consumer Agency[61] monitors that traders' advertise in accordance with the law and produces guidelines for advertisements. They also make agreements with different industries to ensure that their marketing complies with the rules. The director-general of the Consumer Agency is the Consumer Ombudsman. The Agency shall primarily seek voluntary compliance from the traders, e.g. accepting the Agency's position with regard to certain activities and to accept to cease or make changes in future activities. Many issues are resolved in this way without sanctions being imposed and do not have any further implications for the trader provided it upholds its end of "the bargain". The Agency has two options if it wishes to secure the adherence of the trader. The obvious option is to file a lawsuit, but there is also a "softer" option without having to bring the matter before a court of law. The Consumer Ombudsman may issue orders conditioned on a fine which becomes binding provided the trader accepts the Consumer Ombudsman's assessment and signs the order. In this case, the order functions as a prohibitive injunction issued by a Court. In case of a transgression of the injunction the Consumer Ombudsman may ask a court to order the trader to pay the fine. If the trader does not accept the Agency's and/or the

60 Sw. *Reklamombudsmannen.*

61 Sw. *Konsumentverket.*

Ombudsman's position, it may commence proceedings against the trader in the consumer's interests.

The Ethical Council of Direct Marketing[62] has founded by the industry to determine what are the acceptable marketing ethics for direct marketing. The Council makes statements and gives information with regards to direct and interactive marketing. There are no legal consequences of the council's decision, but the decision is published on its webpage.

SF

62 Sw. *Etiska nämnden för direktmarknadsflring.*

CHAPTER 17
Switzerland

Karola Krell

I. Possible Bans on Food Advertising

1. Is there any general national legislation or code of conduct regulating the promotion of foodstuffs?

Beside the rules aiming to prevent the consumer from being misled (see section II.1.), Switzerland has not adopted specific legislation regulating the promotion of foodstuffs.

2. Is the promotion of certain foodstuffs restricted or prohibited by any national mandatory and/or soft laws (e.g., code of practice, case law)?

CH

a. Alcoholic beverages

The Swiss alcohol policy is based on a number of legal provisions. First and foremost, they regulate product safety, production and trade. In addition, there are different requirements for the protection of health and, in particular, the protection of minors. These involve rules relating to tax restrictions, deception, taxation, advertising, road safety and job security. Alcoholic beverages fall under the Federal Act on Foodstuffs and Utility Articles (FSA).[1] The age limit for the sale of alcoholic beverages and the prohibition of misleading advertisement are defined in the corresponding

1 The FSA (SR 817.0) can be found in English at http://www.admin.ch/opc/en/classified-compilation/19920257/index.html. English is not an official language of the Swiss Confederation. Theses translations are provided for information purposes only and have no legal force. All other legal texts can be found in German, French and Italian under the respective number of the systematic law collection (SR).

ordinances. Furthermore, the ordinances stipulate the requirements for alcoholic beverages, the labelling obligations and the restrictions for advertising.[2]

According to article 11 of the Ordinance on Foodstuffs and Utility Articles, alcoholic beverages may not be sold or given away to children and adolescents under 16 years. Further restrictions are regulated in the Ordinance on alcoholic beverages.

Furthermore, alcoholic beverages must be offered for sale in such a way that they are clearly distinguishable from non-alcoholic beverages. A clearly visible sign must be installed at the point of sale indicating that the sale of alcoholic beverages to children and adolescents is prohibited as well as the minimum age applicable.

Any advertising that is especially directed to adolescents under 18 years is prohibited. Prohibited in particular is advertising a) at places and cultural, sports or other events that are mostly visited by adolescents, b) in media that mostly address adolescents, c) on items that are mostly used by adolescents, d) on items that are given away for free to adolescents, f) on school material, and g) on toys.

Article 3 of the Ordinance on alcoholic beverages[3] requires producers to include the following information on sweet alcoholic beverages of any composition that can be organoleptically confused with non-alcoholic soft drinks such as sodas, table drinks, nectars, fruit juices or iced tea (so-called "alcopops"): that it is a. "alcoholic soft drink" and b. "contains x % alcohol".

The Federal Act on the distilled spirits (Alcohol Law) and the corresponding regulation govern the manufacture and trade of distilled spirits.[4] Further provisions include the fiscal burdens for spirits, the conditions for sale and provisions for advertising. Commercial business selling distilled spirits to children under 18 years old is forbidden. The Alcohol Law also forbids

2 Ordinance on Foodstuffs and Utility Articles (SR 817.02); Ordinance on alcoholic beverages (SR 817.022.110).

3 SR 817.022.110.

4 SR 680.0; Ordinance on Alcohol, SR 680.11.

"Happy Hour" sales of spirits (article 41, para. 1 and article 42b, para. 2) or any other action making the consumption of distilled spirits more attractive. Such advertising in word, picture or tone may only contain facts that are directly linked to the product and its characteristics. Comparisons in price or the promise of further price cuts or gifts are prohibited. Advertising for distilled spirits is not allowed in the radio and television, in public buildings or areas, in public transport, at sports places and events, at events that are mostly visited by children and adolescents, in companies that mainly sell drugs or that are active in this business. Competitions for which distilled spirits are the advertising object or the price, or for which the consumption of such products are the condition for participation, are forbidden.

b. Energy drinks

Up to now "energy drinks" have been regulated as "special drinks containing caffeine" by article 23 of the Ordinance on Special Foods.[5] Since January 1, 2014 they are included in the Ordinance on non-alcoholic beverages[6] and fall under the category of "instant drinks containing caffeine" (article 34).

The label of such energy drinks needs to indicate the caffeine content "contains caffeine" (up to 150 mg/l caffeine) or "increased caffeine content (more than 150 mg/l caffeine), not recommended for children, pregnant or nursing women". Furthermore, such caffeine-containing instant drinks have to be labelled with: 1. an indication that the drink should be consumed in limited quantities due to the increased caffeine content; 2. a nutrition declaration; 3. the content of taurine and glucuronolactone in mg per 100 ml or their percentage; and 4. the recommended daily dose. The former mandatory warning, "Do not mix with alcohol", has been deleted.

5 SR 817.022.104.

6 SR 817.022.111.

c. Steviol glycosides (E 960)

Up to now the use of the sweetener steviol glycosides needed to be either authorized or notified to the Federal Office of Public Health (FOPH[7]). Since January 1, 2014, Switzerland has transferred the conditions of use for steviol glycosides according to Regulation (EU) No 1131/2011 into its Ordinance on Food Additives.[8] In October 2010 the FOPH published an information letter on guidance concerning the labeling and advertising for food with steviol glycosides. According to the letter the label may claim "suitable for diabetics", "with steviol glycosides", with "steviol glycosides from Stevia" or "with the sweetener steviol glycosides from Stevia", as these statements reflect accepted facts. However, claims like "with sweetener from Stevia", "used since centuries by the indigenous people in Brazil" or "wonder of nature" are prohibited because they are not true or remain unproven.

3. Is the promotion of (certain) foodstuffs towards a specific section of the population restricted or prohibited by any national mandatory and/or soft laws?

The Swiss Ordinance on special foods[9] contains lots of advertising restrictions on infant formula food supplements concerning the advertisement of these products for use during the first six months of life in order to prevent any interference with breast feeding. The requirements are in line with the WHO Code, however, the Swiss Industry for Infant Nutrition has developed some particular marketing codes and regulates its practices within a self-governing body.

Article 11 of the Ordinance on foodstuffs and utility articles[10] regulates the sale and advertisement of alcoholic beverages to minors. Alcoholic bever-

7 Please note that the FOPH has merged with the Federal Office for Veterinary Affairs and is named Federal Office for Food Safety and Veterinary Affairs since January 1, 2014 (www.blv.admin.ch).

8 SR 817.022.31.

9 SR 817.022.104.

10 SR 817.02.

ages shall not be directed to children and adolescents under the age of 16 years. Alcoholic beverages must be offered for sale in a way that is clearly distinguishable from soft drinks. A visible sign in legible text noting that the provision of alcoholic beverages to children and adolescents is prohibited and a reference to the legal age minimum according to the relevant alcohol legislation must be placed at the point of sale. Any praise of alcoholic beverages that specifically focuses on young people under 18 years is prohibited. In particular, advertising is prohibited in the following: a. places and events that are mostly visited by young people; b. in publications that primarily target young people; c. on objects mainly used by young people; and d. on objects which are given free of charge to young people. Alcoholic beverage labels may not show information or images that are specifically aimed at young people under the age of 18.

Advertising restrictions on advertising to children has been a topic during the latest legislative discussions for the revision of the FSA. The newly proposed article 14, para. 2bis, that restricting the advertising of unhealthy foods specifically focusing on children, has been dropped.

II. Misleading Advertising

1. What are the national rules on misleading advertising with respect to foodstuffs?

The Swiss FSA aims at the protection of consumers from misleading advertising relating to foodstuffs (article 1). Designations, data, illustrations, packaging, labels, the type of presentation and the advertising must correspond to the facts and/or may not mislead namely on nature, origin, production, type of production, composition, contents and storage life of the food concerned (article 10, para. 1 Ordinance on Foodstuffs and Utility Articles[11]).

Not allowed are in particular (article 10, para. 2 Ordinance on Foodstuffs and Utility Articles):

11 SR 817.02.

1) Indications on effects or characteristics of foodstuffs, which are scientifically insufficiently proven;
2) Self-evident references, like "without stabilizers", if such additives are not allowed for this food category;
3) Any kind of reference attributing to the food characteristics of prevention, treatment or healing of a human illness or slimness effects or leading to the impression that such characteristics exist;
4) Presentations of any kind, which give foods the appearance of a medicinal product.

The following are permitted:

1) References to regulations applicable to a certain category of foodstuffs (e.g. concerning ecological production, appropriate animal care or food safety);
2) References to characteristics, which foodstuffs belonging to a certain category of foodstuffs possess, e.g. "milk products", "cacao in chocolate products";
3) References to the effect of essential or nutritionally useful food additives for reasons of public health;
4) References to the special purpose and special nutritional effects of special foods[12], like foods for diabetics, foods for a weight-controlling nutrition, food supplements or special beverages containing caffeine.

Further advertising requirements, including the conditions for nutrition and health related allegations, are regulated in the Ordinance on Food Labelling[13] as well as in the specific Food Ordinances (positive principle in Swiss Food Law).

Additionally, the Federal Act against Unfair Commercial Practices[14] aims to ensure fair and unaltered commercial practices and thus prohibits false and misleading advertising and sales-methods. This Act complements the

12 Ordinance on Special Foods, SR 817.022.104.

13 SR 817.022.21.

14 SR 241.

Food Law regulations, since most of the advertising restrictions in the Swiss Food Law resolve from the general principles on fair commercial practices.

2. What are the national landmark cases regarding misleading advertising for foodstuffs?

The dispatch to the Federal Food Act stated that the risk of deception can be avoided to a large extent by an understandable name, under which the product is sold, and a clear indication of the composition of the food. It can be expected from the consumer that he notices the labelled information and is able to take his decision accordingly.[15] According to the federal jurisdiction a designation is deceptive in the sense of the FSA, if it is suitable to cause confusion in the average public. The Federal Court assumed that the average public sets the benchmark for the question of a deception.[16] In several cases concerning misleading origin labeling for wine the Swiss Courts confirmed that the determination of the existence of fraud does not constitute a question of fact, but rather a matter of experience of life and may as such be freely reviewed by the courts.[17] It must be determined if a risk of misleading exists with respect to the average consumer, provided that the wine producer himself cannot be deceived by such a name and therefore did not need the protection of the law. Subsequent decisions were based on the European concept of a well-informed, attentive and circumspect consumer stating that the Swiss Food Law has been harmonised with the European Food Law to an important extent (see also article 38 Federal Food Act).[18]

However, while the former Swiss laws[19] allowed the addition of sugar to orange juice for sweetening or tasting effects, whereas the addition of sugar

CH

15 Dispatch to the Federal Food Act of 30 January 1989, BBl 1989 I 932.

16 See Federal Court Decision of 10 June 1998, ATF 124 II 398 *"Coron"*.

17 ATF 104 IV 21, 45, 193 considered 2a, with references, ATF 107 IV 200/203.

18 Administrative Court Basel-Landschaft, Judgment of 14 June 2000 (No. 132), 4(d).

19 The requirements for the addition of sugar to fruit juices were adapted to the European Directive 2001/112/EC in 2007.

to apple juice was not allowed, the Federal Court[20] agreed with the labelling of *"Orange juice, no added sugar"* with respect to the necessary information provided to consumers. It argued that "the average consumer does not know the food law regulations and is not necessarily capable to draw a correct conclusion on the addition of sugar from the name, under which the product is sold, and from the mandatory labelling of the composition of an orange juice." In 2006 the Federal Court[21] held that the marking of an apple juice with the reference *"100 % naturally pure, no added sugar"* is not self-evident and thus not misleading. Despite the fact that the addition of sugar to apple juice is prohibited and thus such advertising rather increases the risk of deception in this case, the Court found that the legitimate need for information of the average consumer is decisive: "He does not know the detailed regulations on apple juice. In particular he does not and must not know, that orange juice may exceptionally contain added sugar, which is not the case for apple juice. Thus the labelling "no added sugar" defines for the consumer the demarcation between a fruit juice without added sugar and all other fruit juices and fruit beverages, for which the addition of sugar is permissible."

The Administrative Court of Zurich[22] then returned to its former conception. It had to decide on the misleading character of illustrations of strawberries on syrup *"Strawberry Syrup – pure sugar with flavours"*. The Court held that the impartial average consumer may read the exact composition of the product (especially the addition of flavours) in the case of further interest. Illustrations of fruits on flavoured syrup are not deceiving if the consumer can reach a conclusion about the addition of flavours from the reference "Strawberry Syrup – pure sugar with flavours", and if the exact composition of the ingredients is labelled.

20 Federal Court Decision of 15 January 2004, BGE 180 II 83 *"Ramseier Premium Orangensaft"/"Sunair Orangensaft"*.

21 Federal Court Decision of 7 December 2006, 2A.307/2006 *"Ramseier naturreiner Süessmost"*.

22 Administrative Court of Zurich, 14 January 2010, VB.2009.00564 *"Strawberry Syrup – pure sugar with flavours"*.

III. Mandatory Labelling: Name of the Product

1. Are there any national definitions for the following products?

a. Energy drinks

Since January 1, 2014 energy drinks have been regulated as "instant drink with caffeine" under article 33b of the Ordinance on non-alcoholic beverages. Instant drinks containing caffeine with or without the addition of taurine, glucuronolacton or inositol provide 190 kJ or 45 kcal per 100 ml and contain 25 mg/100 ml caffeine up to 160 mg/day. These beverages may be sold under the name "caffeine-containing instant drink" or, alternatively, "caffeine-containing soft drink", " energy drink" (for energy drinks) or "energy shot" (for energy shots).

b. Sport drinks

CH

Sport drinks are regulated in article 20 of the Ordinance on Special foods as foods[23] for persons with increased energy and nutrient requirements. The requirements for products that provide energy are stipulated in Annex 11 of the Ordinance. Products with vitamins, minerals (volume or trace elements) or other materials that are relevant with increased energy and nutrient requirements for persons must take account of the typical loss of nutrients in these individuals. Electrolyte beverages must contain the essential minerals present in sweat such as sodium, potassium, calcium or magnesium. The admissibility of the other added nutrients and their maximum and minimum amounts are based on Annexes 12, 13 and 14.

23 SR 817.022.104.

c. Yogurt

The requirements for yogurt are stipulated in article 56 of the Ordinance on food from animal origin.[24] According to article 56 yogurt is produced by fermentation of milk with *lactobacillus delbrueckii ssp bulgaricus* and *streptococcus thermophilus*. Yogurt with other bacterial strains is produced by the fermentation of milk with *streptococcus thermophilus* and harmless species of *lactobacillus*. The final product must contain a total of at least 10 million colony forming units of microorganisms. Yogurt can contain other suitable microorganisms.

With regard to the milk fat content the ordinance requires the following: a. skimmed yogurt: maximum of 5 g/kg; b. partly skimmed yogurt: more than 5 g but less than 35 g/kg; c. yogurt or whole milk yogurt: at least 35 g/kg; d. yogurt produced from milk and cream: at least 50 g/kg.

d. Cheese

Cheese is regulated in articles 36 – 42 of the Ordinance on food from animal origin.[25] According to article 40 of the Ordinance cheese may bear in the place of a denomination a cheese description, like an appellation of geographical origin or a geographical indication. Cheese with a fancy name or a non-protected cheese label must bear the specific denomination "cheese". In addition to the general information corresponding to the Ordinance on Food Labelling[26], the label has to indicate a. the flavoring of spices, herbs, treatment with smoke, spirits or other ingredients; b. the use of buttermilk; c. in ripened cheese, the strength level (hard, semi-hard, etc.) in accordance with article 38, para. 2 of the Ordinance, the term "produced with raw milk", provided that a part of the milk used for the production comes from raw and that the manufacturing process does not include any heat treatment or physical or chemical treatment.

24 SR 817.022.108.

25 SR 817.022.108.

26 SR 817.022.21.

e. Bread

Bread is defined in article 14 of the Ordinance on cereals, grains, etc.[27] as baked dough that has been made exclusively from normal flour, water, salt and yeast or sourdough. Special bread is a. normal bread with ingredients such as milk, fat, fruit or dietary fibres or b. the baked dough made of special flour with or without ingredients such as milk, fat, fruit or fibres. Since a "white", "half-white" or "whole wheat bread" may only be called normal bread. Special bread must be designated accordingly (e.g. as rye, spelt, graham, five-grain, milk, butter twist, toast or fruit bread). If special bread is named after a cereal, its percentage must be in the total amount of grain, and the following requirements apply: 1. in wheat, spelt and rye flour, more than 50 percent, and 2. in maize, rice, barley, oats, sorghum, millet and triticale, more than 25 percent.

f. Other relevant definitions not defined under EU law?

Swiss law does not have other relevant definitions of foodstuffs that are not defined under EU law.

CH

2. Are there any national legal rules requiring the mention of the country or place where the foodstuffs were manufactured?

Article 15 of the Ordinance on Food Labelling[28] requires the indication of the country of origin of the food product. In exceptionally confusing cases, even the origin of main ingredients must be given according to 16 of the Ordinance.

The Federal Court[29] ruled that the label of a wine bottle "*Vin de Romandie, Goron, Cépage nobles, Saint Clovis, Mis en bouteille par Caves A. Ruedin*

27 SR 817.022.109.

28 SR 817.022.21.

29 Federal Court Decision of 10 June 1998, BGE 124 II 398.

SA, Cressier", which does not contain wine from the Valais (canton in Switzerland), where *"Goron"* wine is protected by a cantonal designation of origin, is deceptive. Even though the indications "Romandie" (covers also parts of the Valais) and "Cressier" (outside of the Valais) point to places outside of the Valais, the indication of *"Goron"* creates the false impression that the fruits used for the production of the beverage originated from the Valais.

The designation *"Original Alpen Müsli"*, breakfast flakes produced in England and imported to Switzerland, was found to be not misleading.[30] For products that are not specifically Swiss or Alpine products and/or do not directly reference the Alps[31], the term "Alpen" is too broad to be considered as a landmark of Switzerland and does not mislead the average consumer on the place of origin of the product, which has to be indicated on the product packaging anyway (see article 15 Ordinance on Food Labelling).

IV. Voluntary Labelling

1. "Clean labels" – Are there any national definitions or requirements for the use of specific claims?

The Swiss Ordinances stipulate the conditions for the use of the reference *"natural"* for added flavours, cooking oils and mineral water. The Federal Office for Public Health (FOPH) considers other foods as natural if they do not contain any additives or any added vitamins or minerals and if they have not been refined, re-diluted or have not undergone any heating or any hormonal treatment. For fruit jam, which contains more than 10 mg/kg sulphur dioxide transferred from fruits or from previous production, the reference *"contains sulphite"* is mandatory. The advertising of such a jam as *"100 % natural"* would be considered as deceptive.

Swiss Law has not laid down specific requirements with respect to the indications of the terms "pure" or "home-made / Grand-Mother recipe". This

30 Administrative Court Basel-Landschaft, Judgment of 14 June 2000 (No. 132).

31 Cf. Decision of the Federal Court of 5 February 1985, PMMBL 1985, p. 54.

will thus follow the principles imposed on the operators to provide the consumer with clear accurate information.

With respect to other similar claims related to "clean labels" (e.g. 'additive-free'), "clean labels" contain correct information that can mislead the consumer if it is a matter of self-evidence. This leads to the principle that the advertising "*without glutamate*" can only remain if this characteristic is not self-evident for the respective foodstuff. To that extent the emphasis is possible as an exception to the rule. A reference "*without artificial flavours*" to an ice cream that tastes like vanilla presupposes the use of a natural vanilla flavour. For foods that may contain colorants the reference "*without artificial colorants*" is permissible because it concerns a special characteristic of this food in comparison to other foods of the same category. The comparison has to be examined and proven.

Whether the description "new" represents a deception is generally judged from the rule for medicinal product advertising, which provides that the novelty of a product is void if the product is on the Swiss market for more than one year. Blatant exaggerations of value judgements, whose content cannot be examined in any way, are permitted if consumers can recognize them as exaggerations. Thus, expressions like "*the best*", "*unsurpassable*", etc. are permissible. The more humorous and impertinent, the higher the tolerance threshold; however, if information is given, which is objectively revisable, it has to be correct.[32]

2. Nutrition & health claims

a. What are the laws and regulations, including case law, regulating the use of nutrition or health claims regarding foodstuffs?

Since April 1, 2008 section 11a as well as Appendices 7 and 8 of the Ordinance on Food Labelling regulate "nutrition and health related allegations" on foods.

32 Federal Court Decision BGE 87/1961 II 116 = GRUR Int. 1961 544.

Appendix 7 specifies the conditions for permissible nutritional allegations according to the European Regulation (EC) No 1924/2006. Exceptionally Switzerland provides legal conditions for the references *"poor in cholesterol"* (max. 20 mg/100 g or 10 mg/100 ml) and *"cholesterol free"* (max. 5 mg/100 or 5 mg/100 ml).

The allowed health-related allegations for vitamins, minerals, and other substances or ingredients are listed in Appendix 8. The list contains the authorised health claims of the EU (among others from Regulation (EU) No 432/2012) with some exceptions. According to the Swiss Food Control the listed claims must be used literally; it is not allowed to circumscribe their meaning or to use extracts of them. However, one may choose the most suitable from several possible claims or combine several authorized claims for one substance in one claim. Since January 1, 2014 the list comprises the authorised claims from Regulation (EU) No 1048/2012 and (EU) No 536/2013. Not included are the claims concerning DHA/EPA. However, Switzerland will permit "caffeine" claims that are still on hold in the EU, but may thus be used after December 31, 2013 on the Swiss market. Products with a caffeine content of at least 75 mg caffeine/portion may claim *"Caffeine contributes to the improvement of concentration, performance, alertness and attention"* or *"Caffeine serves short-term physical performance"*. The warning, *"Contains caffeine. Not recommended for children and pregnant women"*, must be added.

Further or other nutrition or health related claims require the authorisation of the Federal Office for Public Health (FOPH).

b. Within the list of health claims authorised pursuant to Regulation 1924/2006, are there any related substances which are prohibited or considered as a medicinal substance within your jurisdiction?

Yes, the health claims for activated carbon, lactulose, melatonin and Monascus purpureus have not been included in Annexe 8 of the Ordinance of Food Labelling because these substances are considered to have pharmacological effects and are covered by the law on therapeutic products pursuant to article 2, para. 4 lit. b FSA.

c. Are there any national laws and regulations permitting food business operators to make reference to recommendations or endorsements by national associations, medical, nutrition or dietetic professionals, and health related charities?

No, the allowance of such references follows the general principle that they may not mislead the consumer. Since advertisements, which give food the appearance of a medicinal product, are generally inadmissible, it is not allowed to use references to medicinal effects (terms like "*healing, therapy, cure, treatment, active pharmaceutical ingredients*", etc.) as well as organ-specific references ("*coughing drops, kidney tea, for a healthy heart, for the stomach*", etc.). Furthermore, references which leave the impression that the abdication of a product affects the general health, like "*recommended by Dr. med. X*", "*Indispensable for the health of your children*" or "How *do you get enough calcium?*" are prohibited.

d. Are there any national laws or regulations regulating the use of nutrition or health claims on non-prepackaged food?

CH

No.

e. Is there a notification procedure required prior to/ for marketing foodstuffs bearing nutritional or health claims?

No.

Apart from infant nutrition products and foods for special medical purposes, neither food supplements nor fortified foods or other food products need to be notified to the Swiss Authorities.

V. Enforcement of Food Law and Self-Regulating Bodies

1. Which actions may one risk in case of non-compliance with the labelling or advertising requirements?

a. Public authorities

In the case of a violation of the Food Law the food control authorities can issue orders, which may contain sales bans, prohibitions of names or advertisements and brochures. He who deliberately or negligently delivers wrong or deceiving information on foods or omits or incorrectly indicates mandatory labelling information concerning food, commits a criminal offence punishable with imprisonment or penalties up to +/- 50,000.00 Euros (article 48 FSA). In most of the (minor) cases the authorities issue a caution without a charge (article 48 (3) FSA). A criminal complaint will be reported in the case of grave misleading or recurrence. In the area of advertising, a criminal procedure is also possible against media, publishing houses or outsourced advertising agencies for aiding and abetting (article 48 (2) FSA).

b. Competitors

Article 23 Federal Act against Unfair Commercial Practices punishes offences against fair competition, especially in the case of false and misleading advertising and sales-methods, with imprisonment up to three years or with fines up to 125,000.00 Euros. These fines need to be paid to the State. Furthermore, civil actions from competitors can lead to the payment of punitive damages; however, such cases are rather rare in Switzerland.

c. Consumers / (consumer) associations

Complaints to the Swiss Fair Trading Commmission (see here under V.2).

2. Are there any national self-regulating bodies with respect to advertising for foodstuffs?

The Swiss Fair Trading Commission ("Lauterkeitskommission" www.lauterkeit.ch) is a self-regulating body that monitors advertising in Switzerland. Consumers, media and advertisers are equally entitled to file a complaint with the Commission against an unfair advertising. If the complaint concerns a competitor's advertising the plaintiff needs to pay an administrative fee of EUR 6,250.00; complaints from individuals cost EUR 62.00. The Commission, organised as a foundation, evaluates the fairness of commercial communication through a two-chamber processs and issues principles in order to convert the general unfair competition regulations into practical instructions.

Among others the Commission regulates according to the following principles with respect to food advertising:

> Principle No 2.1 – "The use of the term "Swiss product" or any other term with the same meaning is unfair with the exception for 1. Indigenous products or 2. Products, that have been manufactured to 100 % in Switzerland, or, as far as they are transformed in Switzerland into new products with by the majority other distinctive features and with a completely different usage, or, as far as any other processing in Switzerland causes in terms of value at least 50 % of the total production costs (raw materials, semi-finished products, accessories, wages, manufacturing overheads)."
>
> Principle No 2.4 – "In the advertising of products, devices and methods that are not subject to state control, but that are associated with health benefits, it is not permitted to refer to medical care professionals or to medical-technical staff in order to let the advertised product appear as a drug or a remedy similar product."

CH

The Commission principles contain further rules on comparative advertising (No 3.5), self-evident advertising (No 3.6) and advertising for tobacco products and alcoholic beverages.

The Commission may impose any of the following as sanctions: a. The publication of the decision with the name of the abusing party; b. the recommendation for expulsion from professional associations; c. inviting the advertising companies to exclude the unfair advertising from further distribution, and d. The application for revocation of the recognition as consultants. The case decisions can be found at www.faire-werbung.ch/faelle.htm.

CHAPTER 18
United Kingdom

Hilary Ross, Dominic Watkins and Anne Marie Taylor

I. Possible Bans on Food Advertising

1. Is there any general national legislation or code of conduct regulating the promotion of foodstuffs?

Currently, the promotion of foodstuffs is subject to the Food Labelling Regulations 1996 and Food Safety Act 1990 which implement EU requirements. Offences are provided where advertising and labelling is false or misleading as to nature, substance or quality. The Food Labelling Regulations 1996 will be repealed in December 2014 and replaced by the Food Information Regulations 2013.[1]

The UK implementation of the Unfair Commercial Practice Directive is in The Consumer Protection from Unfair Trading Regulations 2008.

UK

The UK Government has sought to agree 'Public Health Responsibility deals' with individual food manufacturing, catering and retail businesses covering action on portion sizes, fat, salt and sugar content and promotion of products to children.

The UK has a sophisticated self-regulatory system applying to all aspects of advertising. Advertising codes (known as the CAP Code and BCAP Code)[2] fall under the responsibility of the Advertising Standards Authority and cover both broadcast and non-broadcast media. An industry group, The Portman Group, also has a Code for alcohol. TV and radio advertising is subject to a pre-approval system.

1 Food Labelling Regulations 1996/1499; Food Safety Act 1990; Draft Food Information 2013

2 UK Code of Non-Broadcast Advertising, Sales Promotion and Direct Marketing (CAP Code); UK Code of Broadcast Advertising (BCAP Code).

The advertising codes require all advertising to be legal, decent, honest and truthful and that all claims must be supported by evidence. They also specifically cover such things as scheduling of advertising, promotion of high, fat, salt and sugar foods to children and nutrition and health claims.

2. Is there any specific national restriction or prohibition (mandatory legislation and code of conduct)?

a. Restrictions relating to certain products in particular

i. Alcohol

It is illegal to sell alcohol to those under the age of 18 and liqueur chocolates to those under 16. Alcohol is defined as being above 0.5 % ABV.

Alcohol can only be sold from licensed premises. A licence is obtained from the local government in which the premises are located and local premises licensing requirements can result in various restrictions including restricting the age of individuals entering licensed premises and the opening hours that can apply.

There are often restrictions on short term price discounts that encourage excessive consumption and in Scotland these types of discounts, e.g. 'happy hours', are prohibited by statute under the Licensing (Scotland) Act 2005.

The imposition of minimum pricing per unit of alcohol is being actively considered in Scotland and Northern Ireland.

The Department of Health in the UK has agreed 'Public Health Responsibility' deals with a number of retailers, importers and packers including individual commitments on the promotion of alcohol, for example, requiring that alcohol is not located at the checkouts in a supermarket. This is a voluntary pledge and failure to comply carries no sanction.[3]

3 https://responsibilitydeal.dh.gov.uk/public-health-responsibility-deal-collective-pledges/

ii. Drinks with added sugar, salt or artificial sweeteners/ manufactured food products

There are no specific requirements over and above the EU rules in respect of declarations of added sugar, salt or artificial sweeteners. There are, however, restrictions on when TV advertising for food high in fat, sugar or salt can be shown. This prevents the advert from being shown at times indexing highly with children.

Where sweeteners are present EU rules require the product name to include the statement 'with sweeteners' or 'with sugar and sweeteners' and a specific declaration of the presence of polyols – 'excessive consumption may induce laxative effects' and for aspartame – 'contains a source of phenylalanine'.

iii. Energy drinks

Energy drinks usually contain high levels of caffeine, amongst other ingredients, such as glucuronolactone, taurine and herbal substances. Currently, in line with EU rules, drinks containing more than 150 mg per litre of caffeine must be labelled with the declaration 'high caffeine content' in the same field of vision as the name of the drink followed by a reference in brackets to the caffeine content expressed per 100 ml of the product. These labelling requirements do not apply to tea or coffee.

UK

The EU Food Information for Consumers Regulations 1169/2011 (FIC), implemented by the Food Information Regulations 2013, will introduce additional labelling requirements from 13 December 2014. The new declaration required is *'High caffeine content. Not recommended for children or pregnant or breast-feeding women'*. This must appear in the same field of vision as the name of the drink followed by the caffeine content in mg per 100 ml. This labelling will also be required for high caffeine drinks and foods where caffeine is added for a physiological effect.

'Energy Drink' is regarded in the UK as a general health claim. Health claims relating to caffeine are currently on hold and the Department of Health has advised that until such time that a final decision is taken on the status of caffeine related claims, such claims can continue to be made on drinks labels in the UK assuming that the relevant conditions under the Regulation on Nutrition and Health Claims 1924/2006 are met.

While not relevant to energy drinks specifically, as a general note, making any claim that a food product can cure or treat a human disease or condition or a claim that a product has 'Tonic properties' is prohibited in the UK.[4]

Under UK Food Labelling Regulations, Schedule 6, the name "Indian tonic water" or "quinine tonic water" shall not be applied to any drink unless the drink contains not less than 57 mg of quinine (calculated as quinine sulphate B.P.) per litre of the drink.

b. Restrictions relating to a specific section of the population

i. Alcohol

Alcohol may not be sold to those aged under 18 or those who are intoxicated. Liqueur chocolates may not be sold to those under 16.

ii. Drinks with added sugar, salt or artificial sweeteners/ manufactured food products

UK Food Labelling Regulations require that the descriptions "dietary" or "dietetic" cannot be applied to any food unless it is a food for a particular nutritional use (excluding such foods formulated for infants and young children in good health) which –

(a) has been specially made for a class of persons whose digestive process or metabolism is disturbed or who, by reason of their special physiological condition, obtain special benefit from a controlled consumption of certain substances; and

(b) is suitable for fulfilling the particular nutritional requirements of that class of persons.

Section 32 of the BCAP Code prohibits the advertising of high fat, salt and sugar foods to children during scheduled children's programming or programmes indexing highly with children.

4 http://www.legislation.gov.uk/uksi/1996/1499/schedule/6/made

Food or drink products that are assessed as being those that are high in fat, salt or sugar (HFSS) based on a nutrient profiling scheme were published by the UK Food Standards Agency (FSA) on 6 December 2005.[5]

The British Code of Advertising Practice for non-broadcast media also contains detailed rules on advertising and promotion of food to children.[6]

UK pressure groups regularly complain about websites and advertising allegedly breaking these rules.

iii. Drinks and foodstuffs

Local planning laws are sometimes used to prevent the location of fast-food takeaway premises near schools.

Self-regulatory rules enforced by the Advertising Standards Authority (ASA) prevent broadcast advertising of high fat, sugar or salt foods aimed at children during children's programming.

iv. Energy drinks

UK

The UK British Soft Drinks Association has issued a Code of Practice for its members on the marketing of high caffeine content soft drinks (greater than 150 mg/l caffeine as defined by Commission Directive 2002/67/EC).

This Code recommends additional advice on product labels to that currently required under the Food Labelling Regulations 1996, that is the wording should include:

"Not suitable for children, pregnant women and persons sensitive to caffeine". This will need to be reviewed in light of the new wording required under FIC, which includes "breast-feeding women".

5 http://collections.europarchive.org/tna/20100927130941/http://food.gov.uk/healthiereating/advertisingtochildren/nutlab/nutprofmod

6 http://www.cap.org.uk/Advertising-Codes/Non-broadcast-HTML/Section-5-Children.aspx

In addition, the code requires that there should be no advertising of such products in any media with more than 35 % participation by under-16s and that due responsibility should be exercised if high caffeine containing soft drinks are linked with the consumption of alcohol.[7] The link between energy drinks and alcohol has had significant negative press coverage in the UK, so the rules set out in the BCAP and CAP Codes for the advertising of alcohol should be carefully considered.

II. Misleading Advertising

1. What are the national rules on misleading advertising with respect to foodstuffs?

UK law
The EU requirements (as laid down by Art. 2(1) of Directive 2000/13) are implemented in the UK by the Food Labelling Regulations 1996 until the Food Information to Consumers Regulation comes into force in December 2014. In addition, the provisions of the Food Safety Act 1990 prohibit false or misleading information. The Act also requires food to be of the nature, substance and quality demanded by the purchaser. The Consumer Protection from Unfair Trading Regulations 2008, implementing the Unfair Commercial Practices Directive, which prohibit false and misleading trading practices also apply to food in the UK.

2. What are the national landmark cases regarding misleading advertising for foodstuffs?

Prosecutions for misleading advertising are not common in the UK. The leading case is Lewin v Purity Soft Foods Ltd 2004, in which the prosecution stated that the defendant's fruit-based drinks included a false description in that they indicated on the label that the drinks were 100 % juice because

7 http://www.britishsoftdrinks.com/PDF/130924 %20high%20caffeine%20soft%20drinks.pdf

they contained the name of the fruit with the word 'juice' after the word 'burst'. Additionally, the local trading standards authority contended that contrary to the Trade Descriptions Act 1968, the labels contained a false description and that the ingredients list could not amount to an effective disclaimer. The Court dismissed the case, on the basis that they found that the word 'burst' was part of the trade description and qualified the word 'juice' such that the drink was not necessarily 100 % juice and that a reasonable consumer would read the label as a whole, including the ingredients list. Upon appeal by the prosecution, the appeal was dismissed.

It is more common for misleading advertising to be considered by the ASA. Some relevant ASA adjudications include:

- *ASA Adjudication on Unilever UK Ltd, 3 October 2012*
  A complaint was made by a children's food campaign group, the basis of which was that the text and images in the advertisements gave a misleading impression of the nutritional value of Twister, Solero, Calippo, Cornetto and Frusi Pot ice creams because they implied a high level of fruit content which the products did not warrant. The ASA concluded that the imagery and text of adverts on Wall's ice cream's website were appropriate to the products and did not overemphasise the fruit content of the ice creams, therefore resulting in the adjudication that the adverts were not misleading.

- *ASA Adjudication on Leaf Italia SRL, 14 March 2012*
  A complaint was made by a children's food campaign group, the basis of which was whether the game on the Chewit website gave a misleading impression of the nutritional or health benefits of Chewit sweets because it suggested to children that eating the product was equivalent to eating fruit. The ASA considered that it was not clear from the game on the Chewit website that the fruit symbols along the bottom of the screen were intended to promote the consumption of fruit as part of a healthy lifestyle. The ASA concluded that children and adults would assume that the fruit and other food symbols (including ice cream and cola) were intended to represent the various flavours of Chewit that were to be found in each of the landmarks. Therefore it concluded that the Chewit website was unlikely to give a misleading impression of the nutritional and health benefits of the product.

– *ASA Adjudication on Coca-Cola Great Britain, 27 April 2011*
  A complaint was made by three competitors, the basis of which was whether the claim that the product was "nutritious" was misleading. The ASA upheld the complaint that Vitamin Water's claim that it was "nutritious" was misleading as the product contained four of five teaspoons of added sugar.

Country of origin labelling

Declaration of country of origin (for those products not already covered by EU rules e.g. meat, produce) is required under UK law where consumers might otherwise be misled by the omission of such an indication.

The UK Government Department for Food, Environment and Rural Affairs has published detailed voluntary guidelines for the declaration of country of origin.[8]

The rules would be likely to be a point of reference if proceedings were instituted in respect of alleged misleading business practice under the UK Consumer Protection from Unfair Commercial Practices Regulations 2008 or UK Food Safety Act 1990.

The Scottish Government has launched a public campaign to encourage clarity in the origin marking of foods sold in Scotland and has been actively encouraging local sourcing.

The Trade Descriptions Act 1968 provides that goods/food shall be deemed to have been manufactured or produced in the country in which they last underwent a treatment or process resulting in a substantial change.

8 http://www.fdf.org.uk/publicgeneral/principles_on_country_of_origin_information.pdf

III. Mandatory Labelling: Name of the Product

1. Are there any national definitions of a foodstuff that could hamper the marketing of an imported food product?

a) Energy drinks

There is no legal definition in the UK, but the Food Standards Agency describe them as *"generally drinks with high caffeine levels that are claimed by the manufacturers to give the consumer more 'energy' than a typical soft drink".*

b) Sport drinks

No UK definition over and above Parnuts.

c) Yogurt

Codex Standard 243-2003 defines yogurt as Fermented Milks which are characterized by specific starter cultures (Symbiotic cultures of *Streptococcus thermophilus* and *Lactobacillus delbrueckii* subsp. *Bulgaricus or* any *Lactobacillus species*) used for fermentation.

d) Cheese

Maximum percentage water contents are applied by UK Food Labelling Regulations for traditionally recognised UK cheese varieties as follows: Cheddar 39 %, Blue Stilton 42 %, Derby 42 %, Leicester 42 %, Cheshire 44 %, Gloucester 44 %, Double Gloucester 44 %, Caerphilly 46 %, Wensleydale 46 %, White Stilton 46 %, Lancashire 48 %.[9]

9 http://www.legislation.gov.uk/uksi/1996/1499/schedule/8/made.

e) Cream

Compositional requirements are set by UK Food Labelling Regulations for use of the following terms:

- Clotted cream – the cream is clotted and contains not less than 55 % milk fat.
- Double cream – the cream contains not less than 48 % milk fat.
- Whipping cream – the cream contains not less than 35 % milk fat.
- Whipped cream – the cream contains not less than 35 % milk fat and has been whipped.
- Sterilised cream – the cream is sterilised cream and contains not less than 23 % milk fat.
- Cream or single cream – the cream is not sterilised cream and contains not less than 18 % milk fat.
- Sterilised half cream – the cream is sterilised cream and contains not less than 12 % milk fat.
- Half cream -the cream is not sterilised cream and contains not less than 12 % milk[10]

f) Bread

Use of the terms 'wholemeal' and 'wheat germ' is restricted by UK Regulations as follows:

- 'wholemeal' – all the flour used as an ingredient in the preparation of the bread must be wholemeal;
- 'wheat germ' – bread has an added processed wheat germ content of not less than 10 % calculated on the dry matter of the bread.[11]

10 http://www.legislation.gov.uk/uksi/1996/1499/schedule/8/made

11 http://www.legislation.gov.uk/uksi/1998/141/regulation/6/made

g) Other relevant definition not defined under EU law?

- Meat products:

  UK National Regulations set minimum meat contents for use of the following terms: burger, hamburger, chopped x [e.g. chopped pork], corned x [e.g. corned beef], luncheon meat, meat pie, meat pudding, Melton Mowbray pie, game pie, Scottish pie, Scotch pie, sausage roll, sausage.

  Where a meat product has the appearance of a cut slice or joint of meat, the presence of additional meat and non-meat ingredients is required to be declared in the product name. Where a product contains added water in excess of 5 % for non-cured products or 10 % for cured products this is required to be declared in the product name e.g. Cooked roast beef with not more than 15 % added water'.

  It has been proposed that these national requirements be removed on UK implementation of the Food Information Regulation.[12]

- Fish products:

  An industry code of practice agreed with the Food Standards Agency sets out conditions for the use of various descriptions including scampi, whole tail scampi, formed pieces scampi, fish cakes and use of terms for fish fingers and similar products derived from frozen fish blocks produced to various standards.[13]

12 http://www.legislation.gov.uk/uksi/2003/2075/schedule/2/made

13 http://www.seafish.org/media/Publications/Fish_Content_CoP.pdf

IV. Voluntary Labelling

1. "Clean labels" – Are there any national definitions or requirements with respect to claims such as 'natural', 'pure', 'home-made', 'additive-free'?

The UK Food Standards Agency developed detailed guidance around use of a wide range of terms including the following: Fresh, Pure, Natural, Traditional, Original, Authentic, Real, Genuine, Farmhouse, Farmhouse pâté, Farmhouse pie, Homemade, Hand Made, Premium, Finest, Quality, Best.

This guidance has also been adopted by our regional administrations in Scotland, Wales and Northern Ireland and Government Department for Environment Food and Rural Affairs.

The guidance is 'voluntary' but does form the basis of advice provided to business operators by the Local Authority Food Authorities and is often referred to in court.[14]

Furthermore, the UK Food Standards Agency has issued the guidance on the use of the term 'additive free' and on claims made with regard to the presence of Allergenic material[15]:

The UK Government has also issued guidance on the use of Environmental/Green claims[16]:

The UK Department of Health and Food Standards Agency has developed and promoted the adoption of a voluntary Nutritional Signposting system based on traffic light colours red, amber and green which reflect on the content of fat, saturates, salt and sugar that products contain[17]:

14 http://www.food.gov.uk/multimedia/pdfs/markcritguidance.pdf

15 http://www.food.gov.uk/multimedia/pdfs/publication/allergenlabelguidance09.pdf

16 https://www.gov.uk/government/publications/green-claims-guidance

17 http://www.food.gov.uk/scotland/scotnut/signposting/#.UxO2xK_iv6U

2. Nutrition & health claims

a. Within the list of health claims authorised pursuant to Regulation 1924/2006, are there any related substances which are prohibited or considered as a medicinal substance within your jurisdiction?

This is not typically the case in the UK, however, if a claim suggests curative properties, e.g. that a product can treat or cure illness, the product could be considered to be medicinal and be subject to medicinal controls. The UK applies the EU definition for medical devices and medicines. The Medicines and Healthcare Products Regulatory Agency (MHRA) regulate medicines and medical devices in the UK. The MHRA has a team called the Borderline Section who determine the status of products that fall in the grey area between foods, medicines and medical devices. The MHRA's Borderline Section offer advice on the status of a product after considering the claims being made, the product ingredients, and the way it is presented to consumers via labelling, packaging and advertisements.

Certain ingredients, such as herbal ingredients, are more likely to be borderline where they are commonly used in cosmetics, medicines and foods. Use of these ingredients may create a higher risk, particularly where used in combination with a claim that does not closely follow the authorised claim wording.

b. Are there any national laws and regulations permitting food business operators to make reference to recommendations or endorsements by national associations, medical, nutrition or dietetic professionals, and health-related charities?

The ban on such endorsements included in the EU Nutrition and Health Claims Regulation applies in the UK.

c. Is the use of nutrition or health claims on non-prepackaged food further regulated at the national level?

Where nutrition claims are made for loose products (that is products that are not pre-packed), these are required to be accompanied by a nutritional declaration for energy and for the nutrient concerned per 100 g/100 ml.

Public Health Responsibility deals agreed between the UK Department of Health and retail food service chain operators have required calorie information per portion to be displayed at point of sale and included on menus.

d. Is there a notification procedure required prior to / for marketing foodstuffs bearing nutritional or health claims?

In general, pre-notification of marketing of foods, including supplements and fortified food, bearing nutrition and health claims is not required in the UK.

That said, all broadcast advertising (e.g. TV and radio adverts) must be pre-cleared by Clearcast and the Radio Advertising Clearance Centre (RACC) regardless of the nature of products being marketed, whether food or non-food products.

V. Enforcement of Food Law and Self-regulating Bodies

1. Which actions may one risk in case of non-compliance with the labelling or advertising requirements?

Non-compliance with advertising or labelling requirements	**Criminal prosecution** Food Safety Act 1990 Food Labelling Regulations 1996 Consumer Protection from Unfair Trading Regulations 2008 Food Information Regulation	Maximum fine in the lower Magistrates courts for selling food not of the nature, substance or quantity demanded is £20k and/or imprisonment for a term not exceeding six months. For more serious cases, the fine in the higher Crown court is unlimited and/or imprisonment for a term not exceeding two years. It is also an offence to obstruct or provide false information to a local authority officer, which is liable to a fine currently not exceeding £5,000 and/or to imprisonment for a term not exceeding three months Food labelling offences in the lower courts are subject to a fine currently not exceeding £5k per item. Numbers of prosecutions have been falling in the UK in recent years by around 200 instances per year. Local Authorities have a legal duty to investigate consumer complaints, but not necessarily to take enforcement action as a result. Almost all food law in the UK is subject to an 'all reasonable steps' due diligence defence.
Non-compliance with advertising or labelling requirements	**Self-regulatory advertising control system**	Investigations of complaints regarding food are published weekly – the number of adjudications varies dramatically with up to 35 adjudications per week. If complaints are upheld, the advertiser will be told not to run the same advertising and to amend the advertising for future promotions or to cancel the advertising campaign. If the advertiser refuses, the ASA can ask the media concerned not to publish the advertising or seek an injunction to prevent its continued use.

UK

Non-compliance with advertising or labelling requirements	**Civil Action taken by trade competitors**	Such civil actions are unusual in the UK and usually based on trade mark infringement, or less commonly, other intellectual property infringements, such as passing off. In these cases, cease and desist actions and injunctions would also be possible.
Non-compliance with advertising or labelling requirements	**Civil action by consumers and pressure groups** **British Heart Foundation, Action on Salt and Sugar on Health, Sustain, WHICH, Children's Food Campaign coalition**	Pressure groups will conduct surveys and name and shame individual businesses based primarily of high fat, salt or sugar content of foods. Their reports can often attract extensive media coverage.
Non-compliance with public health responsibility deals and government guidance	**Food Standards Agency** **Department of Health**	May carry out surveys and monitor performance against 'Public Health Responsibility deals – no apparent sanction other than to name and shame.

2. Are there any national self-regulating bodies with respect to advertising for a.o. foodstuffs?

The UK Advertising Standards Authority has provided a self-regulatory mechanism for dealing with advertising complaints in the UK for at least fifty years.

The ASA administers detailed British Codes of Advertising Practice covering both print (including brand owner's websites) and broadcast media.

The ASA undertakes some self-generated survey activity to gauge compliance but its main focus is on the investigation of complaints.

The ASA will investigate complaints whether they are made by individual members of the public, campaign organisations or trade competitors. Where a complaint is received from a trade competitor, the ASA has recently required that attempts to resolve the complaint have taken place at senior level between the businesses concerned.

Whilst the ASA has no formal powers to request information from advertisers, it is normal in the UK for commercial operations to cooperate.

The ASA will uphold complaints against organisations that fail to respond to its requests for information.

The results of investigations are reported to its committee on advertising practice. A list of typically 20 (but sometimes as many as 35) rulings are published each week of investigations where complaints have been found to be either Upheld or not Upheld.

Case reports include a summary of the complaint and response of the advertiser together with the reasons for the decision of the ASA. A number of complaints are also resolved informally and sometimes these are published with minimal detail of either the complaint or the investigation that has taken place or conclusions reached.

Rulings for the ASA, certainly in respect of major UK retailers, food manufacturers, campaign groups and public bodies, regularly receive medium or high profile media attention – normally in the national printed press.

It is unusual for ASA rulings to be challenged in the courts and in almost all cases to date advertisers take note of the rulings issued and amend future advertising.

The ASA has the ultimate sanction of being able to ask media organisations not to carry advertising from businesses that have found to be in breach of the Codes of Advertising practice.

ASA Code of Advertising practice – Non-broadcast
http://www.cap.org.uk/Advertising-Codes/Non-broadcast-HTML.aspx

ASA Code of practice – Broadcast
http://www.cap.org.uk/Advertising-Codes/~/media/Files/CAP/Codes%20BCAP%20pdf/BCAP%20Code%200712.ashx

The ASA is also able to make complaints to the UK Office of Fair Trading recommending investigation under the Control of Misleading Advertising Regulations.

Investigation processes by the ASA vary in length varying from a few months up to eighteen months.

In respect of alcoholic products there is a business led group, the Portman group, funded by the major producer alcohol brands, which operates a detailed code of practice.

A large number of retailers also subscribe to meeting the code as part of their responsible alcohol retailing strategies.

There is a mix of advertising and product label survey and follow up to complaints.

In addition to publishing details of complaints and rulings following investigation, the Portman group will also issue 'instructions' to retailers not to stock products against which rulings have been issued.

The industry appears to accept Portman group rulings – even the UK supermarkets in respect of their private label products.[18]

18 http://www.portmangroup.org.uk/codes/alcohol-marketing/code-of-practice/code-of-practice
http://www.portmangroup.org.uk/codes/alcohol-marketing/alcohol-labelling

Contributors

Remco Bäcker

Loyens & Loeff N.V., Rotterdam

Remco J.G. Bäcker (1976), attorney at law, is a member of the Competition & Regulatory practice group. He specialises in environmental and spatial planning law (the law of the physical environment), general administrative procedure law, construction law, and the overlapping area between public/private law and rental law. He advises project developers, investors, contractors, various government authorities and housing corporations. Remco also assists companies in the food industry, pharmaceutical companies, and companies in other regulated markets. He is a member of the Food and Beverage Team and the Pharmaceuticals & Life Sciences Team.
Remco is a member of the Association for Construction Law, the Association of Real Estate Law Lawyers, and the Association for Administrative Law. He is a member of the German Desk and also teaches internal and external courses. Furthermore he is a teacher at the Law Firm School.

Margarida Brito da Cruz

SRS Advogados, Lisbon

Margarida is a Trainee Lawyer of SRS Advogados, working in the Life Sciences Department since 2011. Margarida provides legal assistance to the pharmaceutical industry and to the biotechnology industry. She also assists on pharmaceutical regulatory procedures, review of documentation regarding promotion and marketing of medicinal products and data protection law, including health data bases. Margarida holds a Degree in Law from the Catholic University of Portugal and an LL.M. (Master of Laws) in European Law from Maastricht University's Faculty of Law. Margarida successfully completed post-graduate studies in Pharmaceutical Law, at the Centre for Biomedical Law of Coimbra University, in 2014.

Javier Carreras

Uría Menendez, Barcelona

After graduating with a law degree from Salamanca University, Javier obtained an LL.M. in European Intellectual Property Law at Stockholm University (Sweden). He focuses his practice on advising national and multinational companies on matters relating to intellectual property, information technology, life sciences and food law. Javier regularly represents clients before regulatory bodies and Spanish courts, both in civil and administrative law proceedings. From September 2012 to March 2013, he was seconded to a law firm in Sweden as a visiting IP attorney.

Martin Draebye Gantzhorn

Horten, Copenhagen

As Sector Head of Horten's top tier Life Sciences & Healthcare Practice Group, Martin and his team of dedicated regulatory lawyers advise international and national businesses on all aspects of relevance to the Life Sciences & Healthcare Sectors. Combining legal skills and industry knowledge, he and the Practice Group provide a full service offering the broadest range of commercial, corporate, IP and regulatory services to some of the leading companies in the Life Sciences & Healthcare Sectors. Martin assists with his legal and commercial expertise at every step of the life cycle of a product. He is specialized within IP Litigation (primarily patents and utility models) and Regulatory Life Science & Healthcare. For a decade he has advised on complex and technically complicated Danish and international IP litigation and regulatory proceedings. Knowing the Life Sciences & Healthcare Sectors from within, Martin assists on various regulatory matters relating to among other (Nordic) market access, marketing authorisations, pharmacovigilance, reimbursement/ pricing, clinical trials, promotional compliance, SOPs/audits and product liability. He advises on the conclusion of all forms of regulatory and commercial contracts.

Leonie Evans (Née Kirchner)

Meisterernst Rechtsanwälte, Munich

Leonie Evans is a qualified lawyer admitted to the bar in Germany. She is an Associate at the law firm Meisterernst Rechtsanwälte in Munich where she works with both domestic and international clients. Leonie specialises in food and feed law, intellectual property and competition law. She serves on the Editorial Staff of the European Food and Feed Law Review (EFFL). Leonie studied law at the University of Passau in Germany and obtained a Diploma in Legal Studies with distinction at King's College London. She completed her legal training in Munich and Sydney specialising in European and international civil law. Leonie Evans has gained work experience in international law firms in Germany, Switzerland, Australia and the UK.

Magnus Friberg

Setterwalls Advokatbyrå, Malmö

Magnus Friberg works mainly with issues regarding a company's advertising and other market-communicative operations in a wider context. His areas include consumer protection, unfair commercial practices in business to consumer and business to business relations as well as agreements in the advertising business, media specific legislation, protection of integrity, intellectual property rights and competition law. His expertise also includes purely product regulatory legislation including life sciences, for example food and pharmaceuticals. Lund University (L.L.M) 1990, University of Copenhagen, EC Law. Practicing lawyer since 1990.

Véronique Hoffeld

Loyens & Loeff, Luxembourg

Véronique Hoffeld, attorney-at-law, is a member of the Executive Committee of Loyens & Loeff Luxembourg and heads the Luxembourg Commercial and Litigation department. She can be considered as a generalist lawyer, whose activities cover matters in the areas of commercial law (negotiation of contracts), litigation and arbitration, bankruptcy & restructuring, IP law, real estate law, environment law, E-commerce and new technologies. Véronique is also occasionally involved in maritime and administrative law matters. She is a member of the Corporate Investigations Team.

Eva-Maria Kostenzer

Schönherr Attorneys at Law, Vienna

After graduating with a law degree and a degree in international economic and business studies from University of Innsbruck, Eva Maria obtained an LL.M. in European and International Business and Tax Law at Management Center Innsbruck and Frankfurt School of Finance and Management. From 2008 to 2012, she gathered experience as university assistant at the Department of European Law and Public International Law at University of Innsbruck. Eva Maria focuses her practice on European and Austrian food law, product law and litigation. She regularly acts for clients in civil and administrative law proceedings.

Karola Krell

Markwalder Emmenegger, Berne

Karola Krell has specialized in Swiss and European Food and Commodities Law and Product Safety Law. She advises companies of these economic sectors on issues regarding market access (marketability of products, marketing methods and distribution practices – contract management), administrative problems with control authorities and the implementation of self-control and crisis management systems as well as in connection with liability cases. Karola is furthermore Country correspondent for the journal "European Food and Feed Law Review (EFFL)" and Consultante juridique à l'Association Face à Face, Geneve (www.face-a-face.info). She holds a Dr. iur. (PhD) from the University of Bayreuth's Research Centre for German and European Food Law.

Claudia Lenertz

Loyens & Loeff, Luxembourg

Claudia Lenertz joined the Commercial & Litigation department of Loyens & Loeff Luxembourg in September 2011. She specializes in dispute resolution, and advises on commercial and civil law. Her areas of expertise also include employment law, food law and real estate law.

Nina Charlotte Lindbach

Haavind AS, Oslo

After graduating with a law degree from the University of Bergen's Faculty of Law in 2013, Nina became an associate at the law firm Haavind. Nina works in the business area Technology, media and IPR, and she primarily assists clients within the intellectual property sector.

Kim Lucassen

Loyens & Loeff N.V., Rotterdam

Kim Lucassen (1979), attorney at law, is a member of the litigation and risk management group and of the Benelux Food and Beverages Team. She specialises in regulatory law, such as pharmaceutical law, data protection law, food law, telecommunications law, general administrative law as well as (international) contracts. Kim is a member of the Association for Administrative Law and the Privacy Law Association. She has graduated from Grotius Academie (domestic and international contract law in 2010 and administrative law in 2007) and Radboud University (Law in 2003).

Aude Mahy

Loyens & Loeff, Brussels

Aude Mahy, attorney at law, is a member of the litigation and risk management group, specialised in (international) Commercial Law and European and Belgian Food Law. Aude presides the Loyens & Loeff Food & Beverages Team. In this capacity, she advises and assists food business operators on various matters such as Nutrition & Health Claims, labelling issues, market practices & advertising, food safety, placement on the market, importation in the European Union, etc. This involves close collaboration with the relevant authorities and also includes dispute resolution before the Courts. Aude is an active member of the European Food Law Association (EFLA) and of the Food Lawyers Network (FLN). She cooperates with the European Journal of Food and Feed Law (EFFL – Lexxion The Legal Publisher) as a correspondent for Belgium and is a regular speaker at seminars and conferences on Food Law topics. Aude has been admitted to the Brussels bar since 2004. She graduated from the Law Faculty of the Université libre de Bruxelles and completed a certificate in EU Food Law at the University of Michigan.

Andreas Meisterernst

Meisterernst Rechtsanwälte, Munich

Andreas Meisterernst is lawyer and specialist in administrative law, born in 1966. He studied law at Ludwig-Maximilians-University in Munich. Trainee lawyer at a US law firm specializing in German-American legal transactions. Being lawyer in Munich since 1995, he spent 5 years working in a national law firm oriented towards business and business administration law, focusing on IT law. In early 2000 he founded the law firm meyer meisterernst, in 2003 the scientific consulting company m//m science GmbH (now RDA GmbH), January 2012 the law firm Meisterernst Rechtsanwalte. Andreas Meisterernst primarily advises enterprises in the food, pharmaceuticals and related industries. Issues concern product development, sales including contractual drafting and finalization, and product advertising while taking into account questions of competition law and European law. He represents his clients before German courts and the ECJ, and in hearings, negotiations and application proceedings before German, foreign and European authorities. He lectures in food law at the TU Munich and is a member of the legal committee of BLL and the BLL working group on food supplements; he is council member of the European Food Law Association (EFLA), founder and managing editor of the European Food and Feed Law Review (EFFL), co-editor of the Zeitschrift für Stoffrecht (both Lexxion Publisher), co-editor of the legal commentary "Health & Nutrition Claims", of the manual "Nahrungserganzungsmittel und erganzende bilanzierte Diaten" and of "Recht der Apothekenpraxis". He is also the author of a large number of expert articles on food law and the law governing pharmaceuticals. Andreas Meisterernst regularly conducts German and international events, delivering speeches in German and English.

Ana Menéres
SRS Advogados, Lisbon

Ana is a Managing Associate of SRS Advogados, leading the Life Sciences Department since 2011. She is a specialist in Pharmaceutical law, Biotechnology, Cosmetics and Food law and other Life Sciences legal practices. Her experience also encompasses transactional, commercial and corporate legal matters, mergers, acquisitions, real estate and contractual work. Ana has advised many international pharmaceutical, medical devices and other Life Sciences companies on regulatory and transactional matters.

Ana was a Partner at Cuatrecasas, Gonçalves Pereira & Associados RL leading the Pharmaceutical Law Department, since 2005 until 2011. From 1989 to 2005, Ana was an associate lawyer at Gonçalves Pereira, Castelo Branco & Associados, at the Corporate Law Department and a trainee lawyer at Gonçalves Pereira, Vinhas e Associados, at the Corporate Law Department, between 1987 and1989.

Ana has an undergraduate degree in Law, Universidade Lusíada, Lisbon in 1987 and the Pharmaceutical Law and Practice Self-Study Course of the Informa Professional Academy degree. Ana is registered at the Portuguese Bar Association and the International Bar Association.

Christian Marquard Svane
Horten, Copenhagen

Christian Marquard Svane is an assistant attorney at Horten and advises public and private clients on EU-law, including regulatory requirements and public procurement law. He joined Horten's Life Sciences & Healthcare team in 2011, and has since specialized in the areas of food law, medical device law and pharmaceutical law. He holds a Master of Laws from the University of Copenhagen.

Andreas Natterer
Schönherr Attorneys at Law, Vienna

Andreas Natterer is a partner of Schönherr since 2008, where he specialises in litigation, food and pharmaceutical law. He is one of Austria's leading experts in food law and has 15 years of experience in several areas of litigation with a focus on claims arising out of product liability, compensation for damages and distribution agreements, representing Austrian and international corporates out of and before court. Andreas Natterer is advising many major companies of the food and pharmaceutical industry. He is lecturer on Food Law at the University of Natural Resources and Applied Life Sciences, Vienna and at the University of Applied Science, FH Campus Vienna/Austria.

Lovisa Nelson
Setterwalls Advokatbyrå, Malmö

Lovisa Nelson works mainly with matters concerning intellectual property rights and marketing law. Within this field Lovisa primarily represents clients in matters relating to life sciences and food law. Lund University (LL.M) 2011, University of Edinburgh, School of Law, 2009. Hässleholm District Court 2011–2013.

Christophe Nusbaumer
Bird & Bird, Paris

Christophe is an associate in Bird&Bird's EU & Competition practice based in Paris. His experience encompasses cartels, abuse of dominance, merger control and vertical relations. He also advises clients on all major aspects of distribution law. Christophe worked also for Vogel & Vogel for three years and trained with major firms including Freshfields and White & Case. Christophe holds an LL.M. degree in Competition Law (King's College London) and a double degree in English and French law (King's College London/University Paris I Sorbonne).

Sylwia Paszek
Wardyński & Partners, Warsaw

Sylwia Paszek is a legal adviser and a member of the Life Science and Regulatory Team at Wardyński & Partners. She advises in civil and administrative law. She specializes in regulatory matters within Life Science and FMCG sector: pharmaceuticals, foodstuffs, medical devices, cosmetics, biocides and other consumer goods. Sylwia's practice includes issues of compliance within manufacturing, labelling, introduction into trade, selling, distributing and advertising. She represents the clients in all the types of administrative proceedings within the above-mentioned area, including inspections. Another area of Sylwia's expertise is organization of sales networks, retailers' compliance and sales structures. She also advises on consumer laws regulations and data protection. In 2005-2008, Sylwia Paszek worked for Polpharma S.A., the largest Polish drugs manufacturer. She assisted business development department in product portfolio extension (licensing contracts, R&D works contracts, toll manufacturing contracts). She also advised on regulatory issues related to launch of new products onto the market. Sylwia Paszek is a graduate in law at Gdańsk University (2000). She was admitted to the bar of legal advisers in 2007. In 2010 she completed the postgraduate course in Medical Law, Bioethics and Sociology of Medicine at Warsaw University. She is an author of number of publications and lectures at the workshops and conferences.

Filip Pauwels
Loyens & Loeff, Brussels

Filip Pauwels is a member of the Loyens & Loeff Litigation & Risk Management Practice Group in Belgium. He is also a member of the Benelux Food & Beverages team and the Automotive team. He specialises in (international) commercial law, distribution law (including franchising law) and market practices (including advertising, labelling and packaging). He both advises clients in these fields and represents them in related court and arbitration proceedings.

Núria Porxas
Uría Menendez, Barcelona

Núria is a lawyer in the Barcelona office of the Spanish law firm Uría Menéndez, where she specialises in intellectual property, life sciences and food law. She joined the firm in 1997 and was made counsel in January 2009. Núria regularly advises innovative national and multinational companies in business sectors such as pharmaceutical, food and beverages, software and home-care products. She has particular expertise in dealing with trademark matters, unfair business-to-consumer and business-to-business commercial practices and, above all, advertising issues. She is regularly involved in promotional, communication and consumer protection matters, and has extensive experience in representing clients within the framework of self-control proceedings relating to advertising, including food functional communication.

Hilary Ross
DWF, London

Qualified in both English and Scottish Law, Hilary advises in all aspects of EU and UK regulatory issues. She has particular expertise in food law. Chambers Guide to the Legal Profession consistently ranks Hilary as a star performer in the field of food law and praises her as being "undoubtedly a dominant force in the marketplace". Chambers also ranks Hilary as a leader in the field of advertising and marketing stating she is "applauded for her direct way of attacking problems and giving advice". Over the last five years, Hilary has guided clients through the uncertainty caused by the impact of legislation governing health and nutrition claims and food labelling and helped develop workable strategies and policies; highlighting unforeseen problems to regulators to achieve workable solutions. Hilary works closely with clients to help them understand the potential impact on their products of any new law or government initiatives.

Giorgio Rusconi

Mondini Rusconi Studio Legale, Milano

Holder of a Diplôme Superieur en Droit Comparé at the International Faculty of Comparative Law in Strasbourg and a Law Degree at the Universitá degli Studi di Milano, Giorgio Rusconi is since 2003 partner of the law firm Mondini Rusconi in Milan, dealing, amongst others, with food law in product liability, labeling, advertising, regulatory matters and litigation. He is also founder and permanent board member of FLN – Food Lawyers' Network Worldwide, and has been visiting expert on European Food Law at Harvard University (January 2013).

David Stros

Štros & Kusák, Prague/Bratislava

After graduating with a law degree from the Charles University in Prague, David focuses his practice on advising multinational and national companies on matters relating to intellectual property, focusing on trademarks, patents, designs and copyright litigations, and unfair competition, life sciences and food law and antitrust with special focus on retail business. David regularly represents clients before courts, including highly specialized litigation before the Supreme and Constitutional Courts, and other administrative bodies, both in civil and administrative law proceedings.

Anne Marie Taylor

DWF, London

Anne Marie Taylor is a solicitor in DWF's London regulatory team, who specialises in all aspects of food law. She advises across a wide range of both contentious and non-contentious issues impacting the food sector from safety and hygiene to compositional standards of food, including food labelling and the claims that can be made on labelling and in advertising. Anne Marie has an array of experience of advising the food sector on a range of issues relating to the sale and marketing of food products, particularly in relation to nutrition and health claims, as well as having significant experience of advising on PARNUTS products. Anne Marie regularly interacts with UK enforcement authorities on behalf of clients in order to ensure that they secure the best possible outcome from any challenges brought against them.

Marie Vaale-Hallberg

Haavind AS, Oslo

Marie Vaale-Hallberg works as an attorney at law in Haavind law firm situated in Oslo, Norway. The firm offers a wide range of law services and is one of a few Norwegian firms working dedicated with food law. Vaale-Hallberg joined the firm in 2011, but she has worked with the food industry since she graduated from the University of Oslo in 2003. Vaale-Hallberg works mainly with the food industry, but she also give advice to other industries, many advertisers and marketing agencies concerning marketing and intellectual property. Vaale-Hallberg`s particular interest for the food industry awoke when working as in-house counsel in TINE SA, the biggest dairy company in Norway owned by the Norwegian farmers. In this period Vaale-Hallberg worked i.e. with R&D, intellectual property and marketing, but she also gained valuable commercial insight while working as company secretary and staff for top management from 2009. Marie Vaale-Hallberg is a member of Food Lawyers Network and she also is a country correspondent for EFFL (European Food and Feed Law Review).

Victor van Ahee

Loyens & Loeff N.V., Rotterdam

Victor van Ahee graduated from the Erasmus University in Rotterdam in Corporate Law as well as in Financial Law. He works in the Competition and Regulatory practice group in the Rotterdam-office of Loyens & Loeff where he focuses on regulatory aspects such as environmental law, zoning/real estate law and food- and beverages in administrative and private law. He practices both in an advising role and as attorney before administrative bodies and (high) courts.

Joseph Vogel

Vogel & Vogel, Paris

A member of the Union of European Lawyers (UEL), of the Collège de droit économique and of the French Association for Competition Studies (AFEC), Joseph Vogel is founding partner of the Paris law firm Vogel & Vogel. He holds a Degree from the Institute from Political Studies in Paris, from the HEC Business School, and a Master's Degree in Business Law from the University Paris II-Panthéon Assas. In 1990 he was admitted to the New York Bar of Lawyers. He has published extensively on competition and distribution law.

Dominik Watkins

DWF, London

Dominic Watkins leads the Food Group at DWF and is a Partner in the regulatory team based in London. Dominic has spent his career advising household name food manufacturers, food retailers and hospitality clients. Dominic also has the unique experience of having been seconded to many of the UK's best known food businesses including Danone, Marks and Spencer, Sainsbury's and Tesco during his career. This experience means that Dominic understands the importance of practical advice which allows the client to achieve its commercial objectives. Dominic has vast experience of all areas of food law and compliance from launching countless products to judicially reviewing the Department of Health's decision that our client's food cannot be marketed.

Joanne Zaaijer

Loyens & Loeff N.V., Rotterdam

Joanne Zaaijer graduated cum laude from Leiden University in Corporate Law and Intellectual Property Law. Currently, she works in the Litigation and Risk Management practice group in the Rotterdam-office of Loyens & Loeff, where she focusses on matters relating to privacy law, pharmaceutical law, telecommunications law and food law. This involves close collaboration with the relevant authorities and also includes dispute resolution before the Courts.